ARBITRATION IN CHINA

In the context of harmonisation of arbitration law and practice worldwide, to what extent do local legal traditions still influence local arbitration practices, especially at a time when non-Western countries are playing an increasingly important role in international commercial and financial markets? How are the new economic powers reacting to the trend towards harmonisation? China provides a good case study, with its historic tradition of non-confrontational means of dispute resolution now confronting current trends in transnational arbitration. Is China showing signs of adapting to the current trend of transnational arbitration? On the other hand, will the Chinese legal culture influence the practice of arbitration in the rest of the world?

To address these challenging questions it is necessary to examine the development of arbitration in the context of China's changing cultural and legal structures. Written for international business people, lawyers, academics and students, this book gives the reader a unique insight into real arbitration practice in China, based on a combination of theoretical analysis and practical insights. It explains contemporary arbitration in China from an interdisciplinary perspective and with a comparative approach, setting Chinese arbitration in its wider social context to aid understanding of its history, contemporary practice, the legal obstacles to modern arbitration, and possible future trends.

In 2011 the thesis on which this book was based was named 'Best Thesis in International Studies' by the Swiss Network for International Studies.

Volume 5 in the China and International Economic Law Series

CHINA AND INTERNATIONAL ECONOMIC LAW SERIES

General Editors: Wenhua Shan, Qing Zhang & Xin Zhang

Volume 1: The Legal Framework of EU–China Investment Relations: A Critical Appraisal *Wenhua Shan*
Volume 2: International Trade Regulation in China: Law and Policy *Xin Zhang*
Volume 3: The European Union and China, 1949–2008: Basic Documents and Commentary *Edited by Francis Snyder*
Volume 4: The EU, the WTO and China: Legal Pluralism and International Trade Regulation *Francis Snyder*

Arbitration in China

A Legal and Cultural Analysis

Kun Fan

OXFORD AND PORTLAND, OREGON
2013

Published in the United Kingdom by Hart Publishing Ltd
16C Worcester Place, Oxford, OX1 2JW
Telephone: +44 (0)1865 517530Fax: +44 (0)1865 510710
E-mail: mail@hartpub.co.uk
Website: http://www.hartpub.co.uk

Published in North America (US and Canada) by
Hart Publishing
c/o International Specialized Book Services
920 NE 58th Avenue, Suite 300
Portland, OR 97213-3786
USA
Tel: +1 503 287 3093 or toll-free: (1) 800 944 6190
Fax: +1 503 280 8832
E-mail: orders@isbs.com
Website: http://www.isbs.com

© Kun Fan 2013

Fan Kun has asserted her right, under the Copyright, Designs and Patents Act 1988,
to be identified as the author of this work.

All rights reserved. No part of this publication may be reproduced, stored in a retrieval system, or
transmitted, in any form or by any means, without the prior permission of Hart Publishing,
or as expressly permitted by law or under the terms agreed with the appropriate reprographic
rights organisation. Enquiries concerning reproduction which may not be covered
by the above should be addressed to Hart Publishing Ltd at the address above.

British Library Cataloguing in Publication Data
Data Available

ISBN: 978-1-84946-377-5

Typeset by Hope Services (Abingdon) Ltd
Printed and bound in Great Britain by
TJ International Ltd, Padstow, Cornwall

Foreword

China has now become a major player in the world economy. China's interactions with globalisation have aroused great academic and practical interest. This book, which was first presented as a PhD thesis at Geneva University, is timely as it takes up this important topic and examines contemporary Chinese arbitration law and practice, in a historical background and in a dynamic modern context. What distinguishes this work from other books on international arbitration is its interdisciplinary perspective and comparative approach. It examines the development of arbitration in China in the context of the global harmonisation of arbitration law and practice, and takes into account China's specific legal, cultural, sociological, political and economic conditions.

After an overview of the Chinese legal framework and arbitration system, the book compares the law and practice of arbitration in China with generally accepted standards (which I call transnational standards) in terms of the arbitration agreement, the arbitral tribunal, recognition and enforcement of arbitral awards, the practice of arbitration institutions, as well as the combination of mediation with arbitration. Each topic is reviewed in depth with an analysis of the theory underpinning it and case law. The legal characteristics of arbitration in China, especially those that differ from transnational standards, are presented in a clear and convincing manner.

The theoretical analysis is greatly assisted by the author's first-hand experience of arbitration and her empirical studies. The empirical research was conducted while the author worked with me at the University of Geneva for a research project on arbitration in China, funded by the Swiss National Research Fund, during which we travelled together to Hong Kong and mainland China and conducted a series of interviews with arbitration specialists, including academics, arbitrators, arbitration commission officials, judges and legislators. This allowed us to see how arbitration operates in practice in China and brought to light certain differences compared to transnational standards, beyond the institutional reports and descriptions found in literature.

More importantly, the book goes well beyond the law to explain such differences. The author examines the cultural, philosophical and historical aspects of dispute resolution in Chinese society. The result of this analysis most helpfully highlights the reasons behind the characteristics of Chinese arbitration law and practice. In that sense, this work serves as a welcome contribution to our thinking about commercial dispute resolution and the relationship between law and society in general. Arguing largely from a universal perspective, the author is at the same time mindful of cultural differences. This places her study on a balanced ground and makes her arguments appealing to scholars of various disciplines.

The book not only benefits from the author's empirical studies, it also gains from her academic and practical experience in international commercial arbitration, in China and on a comparative basis. Her experience as counsel at the ICC Court of Arbitration contributed to her understanding of the workings of arbitration. During recent years she has also been exposed to a wide number of countries and different legal cultures, including China, United States, France, Switzerland, and Hong Kong, which provided her with a good basis to engage in comparative studies.

In sum, this book makes a remarkable contribution to the understanding of arbitration in China and transnational arbitration in general. Academics, scholars and students of international arbitration, comparative studies and globalisation may all find this book stimulating. It also provides useful guidance for practitioners involved or interested in arbitration in China.

Gabrielle Kaufmann-Kohler

Preface

In the context of globalisation, there is a strong movement towards harmonisation of the law and practice of modern arbitration. To what extent are Western and Chinese legal traditions still influential on their modern arbitration practice? Contrary to the Western legal tradition which is significantly based on private law such as *jus civile* in ancient Roman law and *lex mercatoria* in medieval Europe, the Chinese approach to dispute resolution is predicated, to a great extent, upon Confucian philosophy that emphasises harmony and conflict avoidance. Now that China's legal system has evolved, to what extent is this non-confrontational culture still influential on the law and practice of arbitration in contemporary China?

Furthermore, in the new era of globalisation, non-Western countries are playing an increasingly important role in international commercial and financial markets. An important question to ask in the study of transnational arbitration is how the new economic players will react to this movement of harmonisation. Will they follow and adapt to the movement? Or will they attempt to shape transnational arbitration, to suit their economic requirements and legal background? China, again, serves as a good example in this regard, as one of the main new economic players which increasingly interacts with global commerce. Is China showing signs of adaptation to the current trend of transnational arbitration? On the other hand, will Chinese legal culture influence the practice of arbitration in the rest of the world?

This book gives readers a unique insight into real arbitration practice in China, based on a combination of theoretical analysis and practical considerations. Where there is society, there is law. Where there is law, there is society (*ubi societas ibi jus, ubi jus ibi societas*). This book examines the development of arbitration in China in the context of the changing economic, social and legal structure of Chinese society.

First, to understand the interactions between global norms and local traditions, it is important to study arbitration in China in the context of globalisation and to compare Chinese practice with transnational standards. 'Transnational standards' refers to principles and practices that are widely accepted by national laws, an accumulation of national standards. Comparisons are made in terms of legislation and court practice, the practice at arbitration institutions and the role of arbitrators in facilitating settlement. These comparisons may shed light on the uniqueness of the Chinese arbitration system, and may also illustrate the role of China, as a new economic player, in the development of transnational arbitration.

Furthermore, given the wide gap between statutes and practice in China, empirical study is needed to confront paper law with real practice. Based on the legal analysis of the current arbitration regime in China, the book examines a number of judicial decisions and arbitral awards so as to understand the actual practice at the courts and arbitration institutions. This empirical approach is in part achieved by referring to a series of interviews conducted with Professor Kaufmann-Kohler during a research trip to China (which included Hong Kong, Beijing and Wuhan) between March and April 2007. This first-hand information reliably tells us how arbitration operates in China and what the problems in the current regime are.

Finally, this book addresses an important theoretical question on the interactions between globalisation of law and local culture and legal traditions. Through the lens of the transplantation of arbitration in China, the book demonstrates that tradition and culture do play a very significant role in accepting and reshaping a borrowed legal institution, despite the general trend that modernisation of law is inevitable. I argue that the development of transnational arbitration is a process of 'glocalisation', which reflects combined impacts of globalisation of law and local culture and traditions. It predicts its prospect as the coexistence of the historical and the contemporary, the coexistence of China and the West, all in harmony. Analysing the current legal system from a cultural and historical perspective will help readers to understand traditional influences on contemporary practice, to assess where the legal obstacles to modern arbitration arise, and to predict what future trends might be.

I hope that this book proves to be a useful and informative contribution to the study of transnational arbitration in China and elsewhere. It may be of interest for practitioners in arbitration, scholars of international commercial and comparative law, specialists in dispute resolution and students on arbitration/mediation courses. The interdisciplinary approach may arouse greater readership in the broader context of legal transplantation, law and society, and globalisation of law.

Kun Fan
September 2012
Hong Kong

Acknowledgements

There have been numerous people and institutions that have greatly assisted me in completing this book.

To begin with, I owe the greatest debt of gratitude to my supervisor Professor Gabrielle Kaufmann-Kohler from the University of Geneva. She has inspired me to carry out legal research and comparative studies on transnational arbitration. I am also very lucky to have had the opportunity to work with her on a research project on International Arbitration in China at the University of Geneva. Many ideas in this book were formed during this research project. My special thanks must also go to my co-supervisor, Professor Lu Song from the China Foreign Affairs University, who led me into the world of international arbitration and inspired me to conduct further research on arbitration in China. Sincere thanks are due to Professor Jacque de Werra and Professor Gian Paolo Romano from the University of Geneva, and Professor Yu Xingzhong from Cornell University, who provided extremely useful comments on an earlier draft of the manuscript when they acted as examiners of my PhD thesis. I should also thank an anonymous reviewer of my book proposal for his or her very helpful comments.

In addition, my thanks are also due to the arbitration experts who gave interviews and spent precious time sharing their practical experiences and insightful knowledge. These experts include Mr Bao Guanqian, Professor Che Peizhao, Ms Teresa Cheng SC, Professor Jerome Cohen, Professor Dong Shizhong, Mr Fei Zongyi, Mr Daniel Fung, Judge Gao Xiaoli, Mr Simon Greenberg, Professor Huang Jin, Mr Andrew Jeffries, Mr Jia Dongming, Professor Jiang Ping, Mr Li Denghua, Ms Lu Fei, Professor Song Lianbin, Judge Song Jianli, Mr Gary Soo, Ms Sun Huawei, Professor Tang Houzhi, Mr Tao Jingzhou, Professor Wang Guiguo, Ms Wang Hongsong, Dr Wang Wenying, Judge Wang Yun, Mr Wei Yaorong, Professor Xiao Yongping, and Mr Xiong Shizhong.

I must not forget to mention the Geneva University School of Law and the Swiss National Research Foundation, which provided me with a scholarship to conduct the research. I wish to record my gratitude to the ICC International Court of Arbitration, where I worked as a Deputy Counsel at the Secretariat in Paris. The experience gave me much insight into the practices at the leading arbitration institution, during which my arguments were further enriched. Many thanks also go to Mr David Branson, Mr Mark McLawhorn and Mr Fred Rocafort for their kind assistance in proofreading the manuscript and all the people I worked with at Hart Publishing.

Finally, I am deeply indebted to my parents and my husband, whose endless care and support have, in fact, made the writing of this book possible. This book is dedicated to them.

Once again, thanks to all those mentioned above, and to anyone who may have been accidentally omitted, for their support. Any lingering errors and omissions are solely my own.

Kun Fan
September 2012
Hong Kong

Summary of Contents

Foreword	v
Gabrielle Kaufmann-Kohler	
Preface	vii
Acknowledgements	ix
Table of Contents	xiii
List of Abbreviations	xxiii
Table of Cases	xxv
Table of Legislation and Legislative Instruments	xxxiii
Introduction	1
1 Overview of the Chinese Legal Framework and Arbitration System	9
2 Arbitration Agreement	29
3 Arbitral Tribunal	53
4 Recognition and Enforcement of Arbitral Awards	71
5 The Practice of Arbitration Institutions	114
6 The Combination of Mediation with Arbitration	137
7 Chinese Characteristics in Arbitration Law and Practice	170
8 Traditional Legal Culture and its Influence on Contemporary Arbitration Practice	181
9 The Modernisation of Law and Cultural Influences on the Arbitration Practice	213
10 Conclusion	232
Bibliography	247
Appendix 1: Arbitration Law of the People's Republic of China (1995)	273
Appendix 2: Interpretation of the SPC on Certain Issues Relating to Application of the Arbitration Law of the People's Republic of China (2006)	287
Appendix 3: Relevant Provisions of the Civil Procedure Law (2012 Amendment)	293
Index	295

Table of Contents

Foreword   v
    Gabrielle Kaufmann-Kohler
Preface   vii
Acknowledgements   ix
List of Abbreviations   xxiii
Table of Cases   xxv
Table of Legislation   xxxiii

Introduction   1

1   Overview of the Chinese Legal Framework and Arbitration System   9
    1.1   Chinese Judicial Organisation   10
    1.2   Legal Framework   12
        1.2.1   Public Sources   12
            A. National Sources   12
            B. International Sources   14
                a. International Conventions   14
                b. Bilateral Investment Treaties (BITs)   15
        1.2.2   Private Sources   16
    1.3   Historical Development of Arbitration Legislation in China   17
        1.3.1   Prior to the Enactment of the Arbitration Law   17
            A. Domestic Arbitration   17
            B. Foreign-related Arbitration   18
        1.3.2   After the Implementation of the Arbitration Law   20
    1.4   Types of Arbitration in China   21
        1.4.1   Classification of Arbitration in the Arbitration Law and Civil Procedure Law   21
        1.4.2   Lack of Recognition of the Concept of Legal Seat   23
        1.4.3   Dual System in the Current Legal Regime   25
            A. Domestic Arbitration may not be Seated Outside China   26
            B. Chinese Substantive Law Applies in Domestic Arbitration   26
            C. Domestic Arbitration is Subject to Substantive Review by the Courts   26

xiv *Table of Contents*

		D. Report System Applies Only to Foreign-related Arbitration	27
2	Arbitration Agreement		29
	2.1	The Principle of Severability of the Arbitration Agreement	29
		2.1.1 Transnational Standards	30
		2.1.2 Law and Practice in China	31
		A. Application of the Autonomy of the Arbitration Agreement with a Limited Scope	31
		B. Misapplication of the Principle of Severability	33
	2.2	The Substantive Requirements for the Validity of the Arbitration Agreement	34
		2.2.1 Transnational Standards	35
		2.2.2 Law and Practice in China	37
		A. Strict Interpretation of Defective Arbitration Clauses	38
		B. Exclusion of Ad Hoc Arbitration	40
		a. Enforcement of Foreign Ad Hoc Awards in China	42
		b. Legal Obstacles to the Recognition of Ad Hoc Arbitration in China	44
		C. Unclear Status of Foreign Arbitration Institutions	44
		a. Practical Difficulties	45
		(i) *Whether a Clause Selecting the ICC Rules without Specifying the ICC Court as the Arbitral Institution is Valid*	45
		(ii) *Whether the Designation of the ICC Court as the Arbitration Institution Satisfies the Requirement of Article 16 of the Arbitration Law*	46
		b. Inconsistent Court Decisions	47
		c. Legal Obstacles	50
		(i) *Lack of Recognition of the Concept of Seat*	50
		(ii) *Policy Consideration*	51
3	Arbitral Tribunal		53
	3.1	Arbitral Jurisdiction	53
		3.1.1 Transnational Standards	54
		A. The Principle of Competence-competence	54
		B. The Court's Review of the Arbitral Tribunal's Jurisdictional Decision	54

		3.1.2	Chinese Practice	56
			A. Arbitration Institution v Arbitral Tribunal	57
			B. Court v Arbitration Institution	59
	3.2	Constitution of the Arbitral Tribunal		61
		3.2.1	Transnational Standards	61
			A. The Appointment Mechanism	62
			B. Independence, Impartiality and Availability of Arbitrators	62
		3.2.2	Chinese Practice	64
			A. The Appointment Mechanism	64
			a. Strict Statutory Qualification of Arbitrators	64
			b. Compulsory Panel System	65
			B. Independence and Impartiality of Arbitrators	67
4	Recognition and Enforcement of Arbitral Awards			71
	4.1	Transnational Standards		72
		4.1.1	Recognition and Enforcement of Arbitral Awards	72
			A. Grounds which Must be Raised by the Party Resisting Recognition or Enforcement	74
			a. Incapacity or Invalid Arbitration Agreement (Article V(1)(a) of the New York Convention)	74
			b. No Proper Notice of Appointment of Arbitrator or of the Proceedings; Lack of Due Process (Article V(1)(b) of the New York Convention)	74
			c. Ultra Vires (Article V(1)(c) of the New York Convention)	74
			d. Composition of Tribunal or Procedure not in Accordance with Arbitration Agreement or the Relevant Law (Article V(1)(d) of the New York Convention)	75
			e. Award not Binding, Suspended, or Set Aside (Article V(1)(e) of the New York Convention)	76
			(i) *Award not Binding*	76
			(ii) *Award is Set Aside*	77
			(iii) *Award is Suspended*	78
			B. Grounds which can be Raised by the Courts on their Own Motion	79
			a. Arbitrability (Article V(2)(a) of the New York Convention)	79

			b. Public Policy (Article V(2)(b) of the New York Convention)	80
	4.1.2	Setting Aside of Arbitral Awards		81
4.2	Chinese Practice			82
	4.2.1	The Legal Regime		83

A. Legal Framework — 83
    a. Setting Aside of Arbitral Awards — 83
        (i) Domestic Awards — 83
        (ii) Foreign-related Awards — 84
    b. Recognition and Enforcement of Arbitral Awards — 84
        (i) Domestic Awards — 84
        (ii) Foreign-related Awards — 85
        (iii) Foreign Awards — 85

B. Unique Features of the Legislation — 87
    a. Substantive Review for Domestic Awards — 87
    b. No Discretion for the Court to Decide upon Enforcement — 88
    c. Report System for Foreign-related and Foreign Awards — 88
    d. Dual Supervision Mechanism — 90

4.2.2 Statistical Assessment of the Enforcement Record — 91
4.2.3 Case Analysis — 95

A. Setting Aside/Recognition and Enforcement of Foreign-related Awards — 95
    a. Lack of a Valid Arbitration Agreement (Article 274(1)(1) of the Civil Procedure Law) — 95
    b. Violation of Due Process (Article 274(1)(2) of the Civil Procedure Law) — 96
    c. Irregularities in the Composition of the Arbitral Tribunal or in the Arbitral Procedure Pursuant to the Rules of Arbitration (Article 274(1)(3) of the Civil Procedure Law) — 97
    d. The Matters Decided in the Award Exceed the Scope of the Arbitration Agreement or the Authority of the Arbitration Institution (Article 274(1)(4) of the Civil Procedure Law) — 99
    e. Social and Public Interest (Article 274(2) of the Civil Procedure Law) — 100

B. Recognition and Enforcement of Foreign Awards — 101

Table of Contents xvii

	a. Incapacity or Invalid Arbitration Agreement (Article V(1)(a) of the New York Convention)	101
	b. No Proper Notice of Appointment of Arbitrator or of the Proceedings; Lack of Due Process (Article V(1)(b) of the New York Convention)	105
	c. Ultra Vires (Article V(1)(c) of the New York Convention)	106
	d. Composition of Tribunal or Procedure not in Accordance with Arbitration Agreement or the Relevant Law (Article V(1)(d) of the New York Convention)	107
	e. Award not Binding, Suspended, or Set Aside (Article V(1)(e) of the New York Convention)	109
	f. Arbitrability (Article V(2)(a) of the New York Convention)	110
	g. Public Policy (Article V(2)(b) of the New York Convention)	110

C. Further Observations Arising From the Case Analysis — 112

    a. Inconsistent Decisions — 112
    b. Local Protectionism — 113
    c. Problems of Delays — 113

5   The Practice of Arbitration Institutions — 114

  5.1 Legislative Background of the Establishment of Arbitration Institutions in China — 114
  5.2 Comparison between the CIETAC and the ICC Court — 117

     5.2.1 Establishment, Nature, and Development — 118

        A. The ICC Court — 118
        B. The CIETAC — 119

          a. Founding Period (1956–1966) — 121
          b. Adjustment Period (1967–1979) — 121
          c. Growth Period (1980–1988) — 121
          d. Acceleration Period (1989–1994) — 122
          e. Expansion Period (1995–present) — 122

     5.2.2 Structure and Personnel Management — 123

        A. The ICC Court — 123
        B. The CIETAC — 124

     5.2.3 Financial Management — 125

        A. The ICC Court — 125
        B. The CIETAC — 125

xviii Table of Contents

	5.2.4	Relationship between the Arbitration Institution and Arbitrators	127
		A. Institution's General Role in Case Management	127
		a. The ICC Court	127
		b. The CIETAC	128
		B. Allocation of Fees	129
		a. The ICC Court	129
		b. The CIETAC	130
		C. Scrutiny of Arbitral Awards	131
		a. The ICC Court	131
		b. The CIETAC	132
5.3		Status of Local Arbitration Institutions in China	133
	5.3.1	The Establishment: Government Support	134
	5.3.2	The Government's Interference Continues After the Establishment	134

6 The Combination of Mediation with Arbitration   137

6.1		The Theoretical Debates on the Arbitrators' Role in Settlement Facilitation	138
	6.1.1	Supporters of Arb-Med	139
		A. Mission of Arbitrators to Resolve the Dispute in the Most Efficient Way	139
		B. Free Will and Voluntariness of the Parties	140
		C. Efficiency of Dispute Resolution	141
	6.1.2	Opponents of Arb-Med	142
		A. Mission of Arbitrators to Render a Binding Decision	143
		B. Due Process and Natural Justice	143
		C. Impartiality of Arbitrators	143
6.2		Comparative Study of the Law and Practice of Arb-Med	144
	6.2.1	National Laws	144
		A. Civil Law Jurisdictions	144
		B. Common Law Jurisdictions	146
	6.2.2	Institutional Rules	148
	6.2.3	Actual Arbitration Practice: Some Empirical Studies	151
		A. Two Surveys of Arbitration and Mediation Practitioners (1994, 2004)	151
		B. Corporate Attitudes and Practices about International Arbitration (2008)	152

			C. A Survey of Arbitration and Settlement in International Commercial Disputes in Asia (2006–2007)	153
			D. Summary of the Empirical Findings	154
	6.3	The Chinese Experience of Combining Mediation with Arbitration		155
		6.3.1	Mediation in General	155
			A. Historical Development	155
			B. Contemporary Practice	159
			a. People's Mediation	159
			b. Administrative Mediation	160
			c. Institutional Mediation	161
			d. Mediation within Litigation Proceedings	162
		6.3.2	Mediation within Arbitration Proceedings	163
			A. Historical Development	163
			B. Contemporary Practice	164
			a. Who Raises the Idea of Mediation during the Arbitration Proceedings, the Parties or the Arbitral Tribunal?	165
			b. When do Arbitrators make the Mediation Proposal?	166
			c. How do Arbitrators Facilitate Settlement?	166
			(i) Facilitative or Evaluative	166
			(ii) Meeting the Parties Separately or Caucusing	166
			(iii) Giving Opinions on the Merits	167
			(iv) Proposing a Settlement Formula	167
			d. Chinese Approaches to the Concerns of Arb-Med	168
7	Chinese Characteristics in Arbitration Law and Practice			170
	7.1	Deficiencies in the Legislation		171
	7.2	Inconsistencies in the Implementation of the Law		173
	7.3	Administrative Intervention		173
	7.4	Conceptual Differences		174
		7.4.1	The Western Concept of Consensual Arbitration – Bottom-up	175
		7.4.2	The Chinese Notion of Arbitration – Top-down	179
	7.5	The Emphasis on Amicable Resolution of Disputes		180
8	Traditional Legal Culture and Its Influence on Contemporary Arbitration Practice			181

xx   *Table of Contents*

8.1	The Emphasis on Rituals	185
	8.1.1 *Li* v *Fa*	186
	8.1.2 Codification Centered on Criminal Offences and Rigidity of Written Law	189
	8.1.3 Implementation of Law: *Qing* mixed with *Fa*	190
8.2	The Emphasis on Relational Network	192
8.3	The Emphasis on Harmony and Conflict Avoidance	194
	8.3.1 Philosophical Influence	194
	8.3.2 Practice to Suppress Litigation	196
	A. Suppression of Litigation by Local Magistrates	196
	B. Limitation on Individual's Right to Sue within Local Groups	199
8.4	Commercial History and Dispute Resolution	200
	8.4.1 Agrarian Economy and Lack of Commercial Laws	201
	8.4.2 Resolution of Commercial Disputes	203
	A. Government-organised Marketplaces	203
	B. Guilds (*hanghui*) and *Landsmannschaften* (*huiguan*)	204
	C. Transplantation of Arbitration in China	207
8.5	Analysis of Historical Links to Modern Practice	208
	8.5.1 Flexibility in Implementation of the Law and the Emphasis on Equity – The Historical Emphasis on Rituals	209
	8.5.2 The Conceptual Differences in Arbitration – The Historical Emphasis on Relational Network	210
	8.5.3 The Emphasis on Amicable Resolution – The Historical Legal Culture of Avoidance of Litigation	211

9   The Modernisation of Law and Cultural Influences on Arbitration Practice   213

9.1	The Role of Law in Modern China	216
	9.1.1 The Instrumental Notion of Law	217
	9.1.2 The Remarkable Burst of Legislative Efforts and the Lack of an Integrated Legal System	218
	9.1.3 The Implementation of Law: *heqing, heli, hefa*	220
9.2	The Role of the Individual in Modern China	220
9.3	The Cultural Aversion to Formal Dispute Resolution	221
	9.3.1 The Impact of Communist Ideology	221
	9.3.2 The Relational Mode of Association	222
9.4	The Development of Commercial Law in the Economic Transition	223

		9.4.1	Centralised Planned Economy and Internal Resolution	223
		9.4.2	Development of Commercial Law in the Transition to the Market Economy	224
			A. Legislative Efforts to Establish Recognition and Authorisation of 'Private Rights' Legally	224
			B. Continued State Control and the Struggle for Authority among Central, Provincial and Local Government	225
	9.5	Explanation of Contemporary Arbitral Practice From Cultural and Historical Perspectives		226
		9.5.1	Tolerance of Uncertainty and the Notion of *Biantong* – The Sustained Tolerance of Uncertainty	227
		9.5.2	The Lack of Party Autonomy and Administrative Features of Arbitration – The Collectivist Society	228
		9.5.3	The Wide Use of Mediation – The Cultural Preference for Amicable Resolution	229
10	Conclusion			232
	10.1	Adaptations of Chinese Law and Practice Towards Transnational Standards		233
		10.1.1 Legislative Reforms		234
		10.1.2 Institutional Reforms		235
			A. Reforms of the Financial System	235
			B. Reforms of the Management System	236
			a. Management of Arbitrators	236
			(i) *Hiring of Arbitrators*	236
			(ii) *Independence of Arbitrators*	237
			(iii) *Training and Assessment of Arbitrators*	237
			(iv) *Arbitrators' Remuneration*	237
			b. Management of its Personnel	237
			c. Information Network Management System	238
			C. Innovations in Arbitration Service	238
			a. Partial Settlement	238
			b. Confirmation Arbitration	238
		10.1.3 Chinese Adaptations to Arb-Med		239
	10.2	The Influence of Chinese Legal Culture on the Practice of Arbitration Worldwide		241

Bibliography 247
    Books 247
    Theses 252
    Articles 253
    Conference Papers 270
    Official and Historical Documents 271

Appendix 1: Arbitration Law of the People's Republic of China (1995) 273
Appendix 2: Interpretation of the SPC on Certain Issues Relating to Application of the Arbitration Law of the People's Republic of China (2006) 287
Appendix 3: Relevant Provisions of the Civil Procedure Law (2012 Amendment) 293

Index 295

List of Abbreviations

AAA	American Arbitration Association
ADR	Alternative Dispute Resolution
app	appendix
Arbitration Law	The Arbitration Law of the People's Republic of China of 1995
Arb-med	The combination of mediation with arbitration
ARI	The Arbitration Research Institute of the China Chamber of International Commerce
ASA Bulletin	Bulletin de l'Association Suisse d'Arbitrage
BAC	Beijing Arbitration Commission
BIT	Bilateral Investment Treaty
BPC	Basic People's Court (PRC)
CCOIC	China Chamber of International Commerce
CCP	Chinese Communist Party
CCPIT	China Council for the Promotion of International Trade
CEDR	Centre for Effective Dispute Resolution
CEDR Commission	Commission on Settlement in International Arbitration
CIETAC	China International Economic and Trade Commission
CMAC	China Maritime Arbitration Commission
DIS	Deutsche Institution für Schiedsgerichtsbarkeit (German Institution of Arbitration)
ed	Editor or edition
eds	Editors
English Arbitration Act	English Arbitration Act of 1996
FIEs	Foreign Invested Enterprises
fn/fns	footnote/footnotes (reference to a footnote outside the chapter/book)
French Code of Civil Procedure	The French Code of Civil Procedure modified by the Decree of 13 January 2011
FTAC	Foreign Trade Arbitration Commission
HKIAC	Hong Kong International Arbitration Centre
HPC	Higher People's Court (PRC)
IBA	International Bar Association
IBA	International Bar Association
ICC	International Chamber of Commerce

xxiv List of Abbreviations

ICC Bulletin	ICC International Court of Arbitration Bulletin
ICCA	International Council of Commercial Arbitration
ICSID	International Centre for Settlement of Investment Disputes
IPC	Intermediate People's Court (PRC)
JCAA	Japan Commercial Arbitration Association
JV	Joint Venture
KCAB	Korea Commercial Arbitration Board
LCIA	London Court of International Arbitration
LGDJ	Librairie Générale de Droit et de Jurisprudence
MFN clauses	Most Favoured Nation clauses
Model Law	UNCITRAL Model Law on International Commercial Arbitration of 1985 (as amended in 2006)
New York Convention	The Convention on the Recognition and Enforcement of Foreign Arbitration Awards of 10 June 1958
NPC	National People's Congress
n/nn	footnote/footnotes (reference to a footnote within the chapter/book)
Ordinance	Hong Kong Arbitration Ordinance (Chapter 609)
PRC	People's Republic of China
PUF	Presses Universitaires de France
QMUL	The School of International Arbitration, Queen Mary, University of London
SCC	Stockholm Chamber of Commerce
SETLF	Shenzhen Economic and Trade Law Firm
SOE	State Owned Enterprises
SPC	Supreme People's Court
SPC Interpretation 2006	Interpretation of Supreme People's Court on Several Issues Regarding the Application of the Arbitration Law, effective from 8 September 2006
Swiss PIL 1987	The Swiss Private International Law Act of 18 December 1987
UNCTAD	United Nations Conference on Trade and Development
USSR	Union of Soviet Socialist Republics
Washington Convention	The Convention on the Settlement of Investment Disputes
WIPO	World Intellectual Property Organization
WTO	World Trade Organization

Table of Cases

Canada

Rio Algom Ltd v Sammi Steel Corp Ltd, Ontario Court of Justice, 1 March 1991, XYIII Yearbook Commercial Arbitration 16 (1993).	56

China

China National Technical v Swiss Industrial Resources Company Incorporated, reproduced in *Selected Cases of the SPC* (1989), vol 1, 26–27.	31, 32
Chinese company v Hong Kong company, [1991] Hui Zhong Fa Jing Shen No 22 (Huizhou IPC, 23 August 1991), cited in Guo, 'The Validity and Performance of Arbitration Agreements in China' (1994) 11 *Journal of International Arbitration* 1, 52.	32
Chinese company v Hong Kong company, [1991] Yue Fa Jing Shang Zi No 222 (Huizhou HPC, 9 December 1991), cited in Guo, 'The Validity and Performance of Arbitration Agreements in China', 52.	32
Guangzhou Ocean Shipping Co Ltd v Marships of Connecticut (Guanzhou Maritime Court, 1992), reported in Selected Cases of the SPC (1992) vol 1, 163–67.	43
Norbok Cargo Transport Services Co, Ltd (Hong Kong) v China Navigation Technology Consultation & Services Company (China) (Beijing IPC, 26 August 1992), reproduced in Selected Cases of the SPC (consolidated 1992–1996), vol 1, 2179.	103, 113

xxvi *Table of Cases*

Dongfeng Garments Factory of Kai Feng City and Tai Chun International Trade (HK) Co, Ltd v Henan Garments Import and Export Group Company (Zhenzhou IPC), cited in Dejun Cheng, Michael Moser and Shengchang Wang, *International Arbitration in the People's Republic of China: Commentary, Cases and Materials* (Singapore, Butterworths Asia, 1995) 131.	100
Fujian Production Material Co v Jingge Hangyun Co Ltd [1995] Fa Han No 135 (SPC, 1995), cited in 宋连斌, 《国际商事仲裁管辖权研究》(北京, 法律出版社, 2000), 96 (Lianbin, Song, *Research on the Jurisdiction of International Commercial Arbitration* Beijing, Legal Press, 2000, 96).	43
Chinese party v Swiss party (Haikou IPC, 1995), unreported, cited in Shengchang Wang, 'The Practical Application of Multilateral Conventions Experience with Bilateral Treaties Enforcement of Foreign Arbitral Awards in the People's Republic of China' in Albert Jan van den Berg (ed), *ICCA Congress Series no 9* (The Hague, Kluwer Law International, 1999) 483–84.	47
Revpower Ltd (Hong Kong) v Shanghai Far East Aerial Technology Import and Export Corporation (SFAIC) (Shanghai No 2 IPC, 1 March 1996), unreported, cited in Xianchu Zhang, 'The Agreement between Mainland China and the Hong Kong SAR on Mutual Enforcement of Arbitral Awards: Problems and Prospects' (1999) 29 *Hong Kong Law Journal* 463, 468.	102, 103, 113
Züblin International GmbH v Wuxi Woco-Tongyong Rubber Engineering Co Ltd, [2003] Xi Min San Zhong Zi No 1 (Wuxi IPC ruling, 19 July 2006), cited in Friven Yeoh and Fu Yu, 'The People's Courts and Arbitration—A Snapshot of Recent Judicial Attitudes on Arbitrability and Enforcement' (2007) 24 *Journal of International Arbitration* 6, 648; Nadia Darwazeh and Friven Yeoh, 'Recognition and Enforcement of Awards under the New York Convention—China and Hong Kong Perspectives' (2008) 25 *Journal of International Arbitration* 6, 841–42.	48, 104
China Leasing Company Limited v Shenzhen Zhongji Industry & Development Center, (Shenzhen IPC, 30 October 1996), unreported, cited in Wang, 'The Practical Application of Multilateral Conventions Experience with Bilateral Treaties Enforcement of Foreign Arbitral Awards in the People's Republic of China', 486–87.	97
Taiwan Fuyuan Enterprise Company v Xiamen Weiguo Wood Manufacturing Company (Xiamen IPC, 1997), reproduced in *Selected Cases of the SPC* (1997) vol 2.	48

Table of Cases xxvii

Nautilus Transport and Trading Co, Ltd (Hong Kong) v China Jilin Province International Economic and Trade Development Corporation (China) (Dalian Maritime Court, 25 April 1997), unreported, cited in Wang, 'The Practical Application of Multilateral Conventions Experience with Bilateral Treaties Enforcement of Foreign Arbitral Awards in the People's Republic of China', 499–501.	103
Jiangsu Materials Group Light Industry and Weaving Co v (HK) Top-Capital Holdings Ltd & (Canada) Prince Development Ltd, Jiangsu IPC (1998), reproduced in *Selected Cases of the SPC* (1998) vol 3, 109–10.	32
Hong Kong Longhai Company v Wuhan Zhongyuan Scientific Company, [1998] Wuhan IPC No 0277; [1999] E Fa Shen Jian Jing Zai Zi (Hubei HPC 1999).	33, 34
China International Construction and Consultant Corporation (CICCC) v Beijing Lido Hotel Company (Lido), Beijing IPC, unreported, cited in Wang, 'The Practical Application of Multilateral Conventions Experience with Bilateral Treaties Enforcement of Foreign Arbitral Awards in the People's Republic of China', 489.	99
Hong Kong Wah Hing Development Company v Xiamen Dongfeng Rubber Manufacturing Company, Xiamen IPC, unreported, cited in Wang, 'The Practical Application of Multilateral Conventions Experience with Bilateral Treaties Enforcement of Foreign Arbitral Awards in the People's Republic of China', 487–88.	88
Pan Asia Trading Co, Ltd (China) v Newport Trading Co (HK), (Jiangmen IPC), unreported, cited in Wang, 'The Practical Application of Multilateral Conventions Experience with Bilateral Treaties Enforcement of Foreign Arbitral Awards in the People's Republic of China', 486–87.	97
Xi'an New Materials & Machinery Research Institute (China) v New Makasu Co Ltd (Japan) (Xiamen IPC), unreported, cited in Wang, 'The Practical Application of Multilateral Conventions Experience with Bilateral Treaties Enforcement of Foreign Arbitral Awards in the People's Republic of China', 487.	97
Beijing Libang International Transportation Ltd v Hong Kong Wenbang International Ltd, Beijing No 2 IPC (2001), unreported, cited in Kong Yuan, 'Recent Cases Relating to Arbitration in China' (2006) 2 Asian International Arbitration Journal 2, 183–84.	33
Mitsui & Co (Japan) v Hainan Province Textile Industry Corporation, [2001] Min Si Ta Zi No 12 (SPC, 13 July 2005), reproduced in Exiang Wan (ed), *Guide on Foreign-related Commercial and Maritime Trials*, People's Court Press, vol 11 (2005), 109–12.	110

xxviii *Table of Cases*

Jiajun Development Co, Ltd v Beijing Jinyu Group Co, Ltd, [2001] Er Zhong Min Te Zi No 1679 (Beijing No 2 IPC, 29 November 2001), cited in Jingzhan Tao, *Arbitration Law and Practice in China*, 2nd edn (The Hague, Kluwer Law International, 2008) 183–84.	98
Dalian Dongda Clothing Co, Ltd v Dalian Liangshi Clothing Co Ltd, [2002] Er Zhong Min Te Zi No 01312 (Beijing No 2 IPC, 15 April 2002), cited in Tao, *Arbitration Law and Practice in China*, 182–83.	98
Bao Yangbo v Chongqing Shangqiao Industrials Co et al, [2002] Min Si Ta Zi No 39 (SPC, 27 May 2003), reproduced in Exiang Wan (ed), *Guide on Foreign-related Commercial and Maritime Trials*, vol 5 (2003), 30–42.	96
Beijing Yayun Garden Real-Estate Development Co Ltd v Lin Dunye (a Hong Kong citizen), [2002] Er Zhong Min Te Zi No 05139 (Beijing IPC, 20 June 2002), unreported, cited in Tao, *Arbitration Law and Practice in China*, 180.	98
Guangdong Guanghope Power Co Ltd v The People's Insurance Company of China, Guangdong Branch, [2002] Min Si Zhong Zi No 29 (SPC, 31 October 2002), cited in Paul Donovan Reynolds and Song Yue, The PRC Supreme People's Court on the Validity of an Arbitration Clause, 70 Arbitration 2 (2004), 142–50.	43
ED&F Man (HK) Co, Ltd v China National Sugar & Wines Group Corp, [2003] Min Si Ta Zi; No 3 (SPC, 1 July 2003), reproduced in Exiang Wan (ed), *Guide on Foreign-related Commercial and Maritime Trials*, vol 7 (2004), 12–17.	110
Gerald Metals Inc (US) v Wuhu Smeltery (China), [2003] Min Zi Ta Si No 12 (SPC, 12 November 2003), reproduced in Exiang Wan (ed), *Guide on Foreign-related Commercial and Maritime Trials*, People's Court Press, vol 7 (2004), 30–35.	106
Shanxi Tianli Shiye Co, Ltd v Wei Mao International (Hong Kong) Co, Ltd [2004] Min Si Ta Zi No 6 (SPC, 5 July 2004), reproduced in Exiang Wan (ed), Author *Guide on Foreign-related Commercial and Maritime Trials*, vol 9 (2004), 50–60.	23
Züblin International GmbH v Wuxi Woco-Tongyong Rubber Engineering Co Ltd, [2003] Min Si Ta Zi No 23 (SPC, 8 July 2004), reproduced in Exiang Wan (ed), *Guide on Foreign-related Commercial and Maritime Trials*, vol 9 (2004), 36–40.	48, 104
China Xiamen Xiangyu Co, Ltd v Swiss Mechel Trading AG, [2004] Xia Min Ren Zi 81 (Xiamen IPC, 2004), unreported case summary available in Chinese at www.hznet.gov.cn/hzac/alfx/aL8.htm.	48
TS Haimalu Co Ltd v Daqing PoPeyes Food Co Ltd, [2005] Min Zi Ta Si No 46 (SPC, 3 March 2006), reproduced in Exiang Wan (ed), *Guide on Foreign-related Commercial and Maritime Trials*, vol 12 (2006), 51–57.	105

Table of Cases   xxix

Cosmos Marine Management SA v Tianjin Kaiqiang Trade Co Ltd, [2006] Min Si Ta Zi No 34 (SPC, 10 January 2007), reproduced in Exiang Wan (ed), *Guide on Foreign-related Commercial and Maritime Trials*, vol 14 (2007), 83–86.	106
Boertong Corp (Group) v Beijing Liantaichang Trade Co Ltd, [2006] Min Si Ta Zi No 36 (SPC, 14 December 2006), reproduced in Exiang Wan (ed), *Guide on Foreign-related Commercial and Maritime Trials*, vol 14 (2007), 94–96.	105
First Investment Corp of Marshal Island v seller, [2007] Min Si Ta Zi No 35 (SPC, 27 February 2008); [Fujian Mawei Shipbuilding Ltd and and Fujian Shipbuilding Industry Group Corp (collectively 'The Fujian respondents').	108
Duferco SA v Ningbo Arts and Crafts Imp and Exp Co, [2008] Yong Zhong Jian Zi No 4 (Ningbo IPC, 22 April 2009).	49, 51
PepsiCo Inc v Sichuan Pepsi-Cola Beverage Co Ltd, [2008] Cheng Min Chu Zi No 912 (Chendu IPC, 30 April 2008); *PepsiCo Investment (China) Ltd v Sichuan Province Yun Lu Industrial Co Ltd*, [2008] Cheng Min Chu Zi No 36 (Chengdu IPC, 30 April 2008), both cited in 邹晓乔，"浅析四川百事合作经营合同案中的几个法律问题"，《北京仲裁》第56辑，第69–76页 (Xiaoqiao, Zou, A Brief Analysis of Legal Issues in the *Pepsi Co Case*, 56 *Beijing Arbitration*, 69–76).	107, 108, 113
Hemofarm DD et al v Jinan Yongning Pharmaceutical Co, [2008] Min Si Ta Zi No 11 (SPC, 2 June 2008), reproduced in Exiang Wan (ed), *Guide on Foreign-related Commercial and Maritime Trial*, People's Court Press, vol 1 (2009), 124–134.	111, 112
Xiaxin Electronics Co, Ltd v Société de Production Belge AG, [2009] Min Min Di Zi No 7 (SPC, 2009).	49
North American Foreign Trading Corporation v Shenzhen Laiyingda Co, Ltd, Shenzhen Laiyingda Technology Co, Ltd, Shenzhen Cangping Import & Export Co, Ltd, Shenzhen Light Industry Import & Export Co, Ltd, [2009] Min Si Ta Zi No. 30, (2 September 2009): reproduced in Exiang Wan (ed), *Guide on Foreign-related Commercial and Maritime Trial*, People's Court Press, vol 2 (2009), 87–92.	109
Aidwoladuo (Mongolia) Co, Ltd v Zhejiang Zhancheng Construction Group Co, Ltd, [2009] Min Si Ta Zi No. 46 (SPC, 8 December 2009), reproduced in Exiang Wan (ed), *Guide on Foreign-related Commercial and Maritime Trial*, People's Court Press, Vol 1, (2010), 87–93.	101, 105

England

Naviera Amazonica Peruana SA v Compañía Internacional de Seguros del Peru, (1988) 1 Lloyd's Rep 116.	24
Harbour Assurance Co (UK) Ltd v Kansa General International Insurance Co Ltd, (1992) 1 Lloyd's Rep 81.	31

xxx Table of Cases

France

Cour de cassation, 1 civil chamber, 7 May 1963, Gosset: Jurisclasseur périodique (La semaine juridique) 1963 II 13405, and Bertold Goldman's note; Journal du droit international (Clunet) (1964) 82, and Jean-Denis Bredin's note; Revue critique de droit international privé (1963) 615, and Henry Motulsky's note; Recueil Dalloz (1963) 545, and Jean Robert's note.	30
Strasbourg Tribunal of First Instance, 9 October 1970, Animalfeeds International Corp v SAA Becker & Cie, II Yearbook Commercial Arbitration (1977), 244 (France No 2).	76
Cour de cassation, 1 civil chamber, 18 May 1971, Impex (first decision): Journal du droit international (Clunet) (1972) 62, and Bruno Oppetit's note; Revue de l'arbitrage (1972) 2, and Philippe Kahn's note.	30
Paris Court of Appeal, 9 March 1972, Lefrère René v Les Pétroles Pursan, Revue trimestrielle de droit commercial (1972) 344.	56
Cour de cassation, 1 civil chamber, 4 July 1972, Hecht: Journal du droit international (Clunet) (1972), 843, and Bruno Oppetit's note; Revue critique de droit international privé (1974), 82, and Patrice Level's note; Revue de l'arbitrage (1974), 89.	30
Cour de cassation, 1 civil chamber, 14 December 1983, Epoux Convert v Droga: Revue de l'arbitrage (1984), 483, and Marie-Claire Rondeau-Rivier's note.	30
Cour de cassation, 1 civil chamber, 9 October 1984, Norsolor: Revue de l'arbitrage (1985) 431, and Berthold Goldman's note; Journal du droit international (Clunet) (1985) 679, and Philippe Kahn's note; Recueil Dalloz (1985) 101, and Jean Robert's note. See also Berthold Goldman, 'Une bataille judiciaire autour de la lex mercatoria: l'affaire Norsolor', Revue de l'arbitrage (1983) 379.	77
Paris Tribunal of First Instance, 31 January 1986, Fillold CM v Jacksor Enterprise, Revue de l'arbitrage (1987) 179.	37
Paris Court of Appeal, 5 May 1989, Dutco, Revue de l'arbitrage (1989) 723.	37
Paris Court of Appeal, 22 March 1991, Mavian v Mavian, Revue de l'arbitrage (1992) 652.	37
Cour de cassation, 1 civil chamber, 10 March 1993, Polish Ocean Line, Revue de l'arbitrage (1993) 255 (second decision), and Dominique Hascher's note; Journal du droit international (Clunet) (1993) 360 (first decision), and Philippe Kahn's note.	77
Cour de cassation, 1 civil chamber, 23 March 1994, Hilmarton, Revue de l'arbitrage (1997) 376, and Philippe Fouchard's note; Journal du droit international (Clunet) (1997) 1033, and Emmanuel Gaillard's note.	77, 78

Table of Cases xxxi

Paris Court of Appeal, 7 December 1994, *V2000 v Renault*, *Revue de l'arbitrage* (1996) 245, and Charles Jarrosson's note; *Revue trimestrielle de droit commercial* (1995) 401, and Jean-Claude Dubarry and Eric Loquin's note.	56
Cour de cassation, 1 civil chamber, 21 May 1997, *V2000 v Renault*: *Revue de l'arbitrage* (1997) 537, and Emmanuel Gaillard's note.	56
Cour de cassation, 1 civil chamber, 29 June 2007, *Putrabali*, *Bulletin de la Cour de cassation I*, no 251; XXXII *Yearbook Commercial Arbitration* 299–302 (France, no 42); partial English translation extracted in Philippe Pinsolle, 'The Status of Vacated Awards in France: The Cour de cassation Decision in *Putrabali*', (2008) 24 *Arbitration International* 2, 294; *Revue de l'arbitrage* (2007) 507, and Jean-Pierre Ancel's report and Emmanuel Gaillard's note; *Journal du droit international (Clunet)* (2007) 1236, and Thomas Clay's note; *Revue trimestrielle de droit commercial* (2007) 682, and Eric Loquin's note.	77, 78

Hong Kong

Pacific International Lines (pte) Ltd v Tsinlien Metals and Minerals Co Ltd (Hong Kong Supreme Court, 30 July 1993) XVIII *Yearbook Commercial Arbitration* 180 (1993).	56
Klöckner Pentaplast GmbH & Co KG v Advance Technology (HK) Co Ltd (CFI, 6 July 2011), [2011] 4 HKLRD 262.	49
Gao Haiyan v Keeneye Holdings Ltd (12 April 2011, CFI), [2011] HKEC 514.	169

Switzerland

Léopold Lazarus Ltd v Chrome Resources SA (Court of Justice of the Canton of Geneva, 17 September 1976), IV *Yearbook Commercial Arbitration* 311 (1979).	81
Fondation M v Banque X (Swiss Federal Tribunal, 29 April 1996), *ASA Bulletin* 527 (1996).	56
Bundesgericht, I Zivilabteilung, TAG v H Company (Swiss Supreme Court, 24 March 1997), 15 *ASA Bulletin* 2 (1997).	24

United States

Moses H Cone Mem'l Hosp v Mercury Constr Corp, 460 US 1 (1983).	79
Chromalloy Aeroservices Inc v Arab Republic of Egypt, 939 F Supp 907 (DDC 1996).	77, 78
Baker Marine Ltd (Nig) v Chevron Ltd (Nig), 191 F3d 194 (2nd Cir 1999).	78
Spier v Tecnica, 71 F Supp 2d 279 (SDNY 1999).	78
Termorio SA ESP v Electranta SP, 421 F Supp 2d 87 (DDC 2006).	78
Termorio SA ESP v Electranta SP, 487 F 3d 928 (DC Cir 2007).	78

ICC Awards

ICC Award No 1434 (1975), Multinational group A v State B, 103 JDI 978 (1976).	37
ICC Award No 3380 (1980), Italian enterprise v Syrian enterprise, 108 JDI 917 (1981).	37
ICC Award No 3460 (1980), French company v Ministry of an Arab country, 108 JDI 939 (1981).	37

ICSID Awards

Amco Asia Corp v Republic of Indonesia, ICSID Case No ARB/81/1, 25 September 1983, 1 ICSID Report 389 (1993).	37
Holiday Inns SA v Government of Morocco, ICSID Case No ARB/72/1, in Pierre Lalive, The First World Bank Arbitration (Holiday Inns v Morocco) Some Legal Problems, 1 ICSID Reports 645 (1993).	37

Table of Legislation and Legislative Instruments

The items without page numbers but marked * include legislation and rules not directly cited in the text but highly relevant to the subject matter of the book and are provided by way of general reference for the reader.

Statutes

I. International Conventions

UNCITRAL Model Law on International Commercial Arbitration of 1985 (with Amendments in 2006).	6, 23, 24, 30, 31, 35, 41, 54, 56, 61, 81, 82, 87, 90
The Convention on the Recognition and Enforcement of Foreign Arbitration Awards, done in New York, 10 June 1958.	3, 6, 14, 22, 23, 35, 36, 41, 43, 49, 50, 51, 55, 56, 72–81, 86, 87, 88, 98, 101, 103–07, 109–10, 142, 218, 239
The Convention on the Settlement of Investment Disputes between States and Nationals of Other States, 14 October 1966.	14

II. National Legislation

China

Abolished Law and Regulations

Tianjin Municipality Interim Rules of Organisation for Mediation and Arbitration Commission 《天津市调解仲裁委员会暂行组织条例》	Issued by Tianjin Municipal Government in 1949.	*

xxxiv *Table of Legislation and Legislative Instruments*

Working Rules for the State-Owned Industrial Enterprises (Draft) 《国营工业企业工作条例（草案）》	Issued by the Central Committee of the CPC in September 1961.	17
Notice Concerning the Strict Implementation of Basic Construction Procedure and the Strict Implementation of Economic Contracts 《关于严格执行基本建设程序、严格执行经济合同的通知》	Issued by the Central Committee of the CPC and the State Council on 10 December 1962.	17
Economic Contract Law 《中华人民共和国经济合同法》	Promulgated by the Standing Committee of the NPC on 13 December 1981 and effective from 1 July 1982, and subsequently revised on 2 September 1993. Abolished on 1 October 1999.	17, 19, 20
Civil Procedure Law of the People's Republic of China (for Trial Implementation) 《中华人民共和国民事诉讼法（试行）》	Promulgated by the Standing Committee of the NPC on 8 March 1982 and implemented on a trial basis from 1 October 1982. Abolished on 9 April 1991.	20, 92, 162, 219
Regulations on the Economic Contract Arbitration of the People's Republic of China 《中华人民共和国经济合同仲裁条例》	Issued by the State Council on and effective from 22 August 1983. Abolished on 6 October 2001.	17, 18
Organisational Rules of Economic Contract Arbitration Commission (for Trial Implementation) 《经济合同仲裁委员会组织规则（试行）》	Issued by the State Administration of Industry and Commerce on and effective from 23 December 1983. Abolished on 3 December 1998.	*
Opinion Concerning Some Questions Regarding the Enforcement of the Civil Procedure Law (for Trial Implementation) 《最高人民法院关于贯彻执行<民事诉讼法（试行）>若干问题的意见》	Issued by the SPC on and effective from 30 August 1984. Abolished on 14 July 1992.	*
Foreign Economic Contract Law 《中华人民共和国涉外经济合同法》	Promulgated by the Standing Committee of the NPC on 21 March 1985 and effective from 1 July 1985. Abolished on 1 October 1999.	19, 20

Table of Legislation and Legislative Instruments xxxv

Rules for the Handling of Cases by Economic Contract Arbitration Commissions 《经济合同仲裁委员会办案规则》	Issued by the State Administration of Industry and Commerce on and effective from 10 August 1985. Abolished on 3 December 1998.	*
Technology Contract Law 《中华人民共和国技术合同法》	Promulgated by the Standing Committee of the NPC on 23 June 1987 and effective from 1 November 1987. Abolished on 1 October 1999.	*
Provisional Regulations for the Resolution of Labor Disputes in State Enterprises 《国营企业劳动争议处理暂行规定》	Issued by the State Council on 31 July 1987 and effective from 15 August 1987. Abolished on 1 August 1993.	*
Reply of the SPC to Several Questions Concerning the Application of the Foreign-related Economic Contract Law 《关于适用<涉外经济合同法>若干问题的解答》 ('SPC Reply on Substantive Law')	Issued by the SPC on and effective from 19 October 1987. Abolished on 25 July 2000.	*
Certain Provisions on Judicial Interpretations 《最高人民法院关于司法解释工作的若干规定》	Issued by the SPC on 23 June 1997 and effective from 1 July 1976. Abolished on 1 April 2007.	*
Provisional Organic Rules of People's Mediation Committees 1954 《人民调解委员会暂行组织通则》	Issued by the Government Administration Council of the Central People's Government on and effective from 22 March 1954. Abolished on 17 June 1989.	159

Effective Law and Regulations

Constitution of the PRC 《中华人民共和国宪法》	Promulgated by the NPC on and effective from 4 December 1982, and subsequently revised on 12 April 1988, 29 March 1993, 15 March 1999, and 14 March 2004.	10, 12, 159
Resolution of the Standing Committee of the National People's Congress Providing an Improved Interpretation of the Law 《全国人大常委会关于加强法律解释工作的决议》	Promulgated by the Standing Committee of the NPC on 10 June 1981.	12

xxxvi *Table of Legislation and Legislative Instruments*

Law of the PRC on the Laws Applicable to Foreign-related Civil Relations 《全国人民代表大会常务委员会关于我国加入〈承认及执行外国仲裁裁决公约〉的决定》	Adopted at the Standing Committee of the NPC on and effective from 2 December 1986.	14, 50, 86
General Principles of the Civil Law of the People's Republic of China 《中华人民共和国民法通则》	Promulgated by the NPC on 12 April 1986 and effective from 1 January 1987.	218
Decision to Ratify the Convention on the Settlement of Investment Disputes Between States and Nationals of Other States 《全国人民代表大会常务委员会关于批准〈关于解决国家和他国国民之间投资争端公约〉的决定》	Execution by representative of China on 9 February 1990; passed by decision of the Standing Committee of the NPC issued on 1 July 1992; ratified on 7 January 1993; entered into effect in China on 6 February 1993.	14
Arbitration Law of the PRC 《中华人民共和国仲裁法》	Adopted by the Standing Committee of the NPC on 31 August 1994, effective from 1 September 1995.	12, 17, 19, 20–22, 24, 27, 31–34, 37–41, 44–51, 57, 59, 64, 65, 83–85, 87–88, 90, 91, 99, 110, 113, 115–17, 122, 133, 134, 146, 163–65, 170, 171, 173, 174, 179, 209, 210, 219, 229, 234
Contract Law of the PRC 《中华人民共和国合同法》	Promulgated by the NPC on 15 March 1999 and effective from 1 October 1999.	12, 26, 38
Sino-foreign Co-operative Joint Venture Law 《中华人民共和国中外合作经营企业法》	Promulgated by the NPC on and effective from 13 April 1988, and subsequently revised on 31 October 2000.	*

Table of Legislation and Legislative Instruments xxxvii

Sino-foreign Equity Joint Venture Law of the PRC《中华人民共和国中外合资经营企业法》	Promulgated by the Standing Committee of the NPC on and effective from 8 July 1979, and subsequently revised on 4 April 1990 and 15 March 2001.	19, 32
Civil Procedure Law 2012《中华人民共和国民事诉讼法》	Promulgated by the NPC on and effective from 9 April 1991. The first revision was on 28 October 2007. The second revision was made on 31 August 2012, which will come into force on 1 January 2013.	12, 22, 24, 25, 50, 51, 83, 84, 85, 88, 95–97, 99–100, 106, 146, 219, 290, 292, 293–94
The People's Mediation Law of the PRC《中华人民共和国人民调解法》	Adopted by the Standing Committee of the NPC on 28 August 2010, effective from 1 January 2011.	160, 219
Law of the People's Republic of China on the Laws Applicable to Foreign-related Civil Relation《中华人民共和国涉外民事关系法律适用法》	Adopted by the Standing Committee of the NPC on 29 October 2010, effective from 1 April 2011.	25
SPC's Notice on the Implementation of China's Accession to the Convention on the Recognition and Enforcement of Foreign Arbitral Awards《最高人民法院关于执行我国加入的<承认及执行外国仲裁裁决公约>的通知》 ('Convention Implementation Notice')	Issued by the SPC on 10 April 1987.	13
Opinions of the SPC for Certain Issues Concerning the Implementation of the Civil Procedure Law《最高人民法院关于适用<中华人民共和国民事诉讼法>若干问题的意见》	Issued by the SPC on and effective from 14 July 1992.	*
Notice of the SPC on Several Issues Regarding the Handling by the People's Courts of Certain Issues Pertaining to Foreign-related Arbitration and Foreign Arbitration《最高人民法院关于人民法院处理与涉外仲裁及外国仲裁事项有关问题的通知》	Issued by the SPC on and effective from 28 August 1995.	13, 27

Reply of the SPC to Questions Concerning the Validity of an Arbitration Clause in which Two Arbitration Institutions are Simultaneously Selected 《最高人民法院关于同时选择两个仲裁机构的仲裁条款效力问题的函》	Issued by the SPC on and effective from 12 December 1996.	13
SPC Reply on the Manner of Determining Jurisdiction in a Sino-Mongolian Contract that Fails to Provide for Arbitration. 《最高人民法院关于涉蒙经济合同未直接约定仲裁条款如何认定案件管辖权的复函》	Issued by the SPC on and effective from 14 December 1996.	*
SPC Reply on the Validity of an Arbitration Clause with Selected Arbitration Venue but No Arbitration Institution 《最高人民法院关于仅选择仲裁地点而对仲裁机构没有约定的仲裁条款效力问题的函》	Issued by the SPC on and effective from 19 March 1997.	*
Notice on Several Issues Concerning Implementation of the Arbitration Law of the People's Republic of China 《最高人民法院关于实施<中华人民共和国仲裁法>几个问题的通知》	Issued by the SPC on and effective from 26 March 1997.	13
Reply of the SPC regarding a Case in which the Validity of the Arbitration Clause Remained Unaffected by the Omission of Words from the Name of the Arbitration Institution Therein 《最高人民法院对仲裁条款中所选仲裁机构的名称漏字，但不影响仲裁条款效力的一个案例的批复意见》	Issued by the SPC on and effective from 2 April 1998.	*

Interpretations of the Application of Laws in Regard to the Refusal of Cases for the Enforcement of Judgments and Rulings 《最高人民法院关于审理不执行判决、裁定案件具体应用法律若干问题的解释》	Issued by the SPC on and effective from 17 April 1998.	*
Notice of the SPC Regarding Matters Relating to People's Courts Setting Aside Foreign-related Arbitral Awards 《最高人民法院关于人民法院撤销涉外仲裁裁决有关事项的通知》	Issued by the SPC on and effective from 23 April 1998.	28
SPC's Provisions on the People's Courts' Recognition of Civil Judgments Made by Courts in Taiwan Region 《最高人民法院关于人民法院认可台湾地区有关法院民事判决的裁定》	Issued by the SPC on 22 May 1998 and effective from 26 May 1998.	13, 87
Regulations of the SPC for Certain Issues Concerning Enforcement by the People's Court (for Trial Implementation) 《最高人民法院关于人民法院执行工作若干问题的规定（试行）》	Issued by the SPC on and effective from 8 July 1998.	*
SPC Reply to Several Questions Regarding the Hearing of Party's Application for the Setting-aside of an Arbitration Award 《最高人民法院关于审理当事人申请撤销仲裁裁决案件几个具体问题的批复》	Issued by the SPC on 21 July 1998 and effective from 28 July 1998.	13

xl *Table of Legislation and Legislative Instruments*

Reply of SPC Regarding the Determination by the People's Court of Enforcement Applications where an Original Arbitrator is No Longer Appointed《最高人民法院关于未被续聘在仲裁员的原参加审理的案件裁决书上签名人民法院应当执行该仲裁裁决的批复》	Issued by the SPC on 13 July 1998 and effective from 5 September 1998.	*
SPC Reply Regarding Several Issues Relating to the Validity of Arbitration Agreements《最高人民法院关于确认仲裁协议效力几个问题的批复》	Issued by the SPC on 26 October 1998 and effective from 5 November 1998.	13, 60
Regulation of the SPC Regarding the Problems of Collecting Fees and Time Limits for Review of Recognition and Enforcement of Foreign Arbitral Awards《最高人民法院关于承认和执行外国仲裁裁决收费及审查期限问题的规定》	Issued by the SPC on 14 November 1998 and effective from 21 November 1998.	13
Reply of the SPC to the Question Whether a People's Court Should Accept a Retrial Request by a Party Who is Not Satisfied with the People's Court Ruling to Set Aside an Arbitral Award《最高人民法院关于当事人对人民法院撤销仲裁裁决的裁定不服申请再审人民法院是否受理问题的批复》	Issued by the SPC on 11 February 1999 and effective from 16 February 1999.	13
SPC Reply to Questions Concerning the Partial Setting Aside of Arbitration Awards Rendered by Chinese Arbitration Institutions《最高人民法院关于我国仲裁机构作出的仲裁裁决能否部分撤销问题的批复》	Issued by the SPC on 25 August 1999 and effective from 31 August 1999.	13

Table of Legislation and Legislative Instruments xli

Summary of the National Conference on the Quality of the Trial of Civil Cases 《全国民事案件审判质量工作座谈会纪要》	Issued by the SPC on 11 November 1999.	*
Regulation of the SPC Concerning Several Issues Related to the Unified Administration of Enforcement Work by the High People's Courts 《最高人民法院关于高级人民法院统一管理执行工作若干问题的规定》	Issued by the SPC on and effective from 14 January 2000.	*
Arrangement Concerning Mutual Enforcement of Arbitral Awards between the Mainland and the Hong Kong Special Administrative Region 《最高人民法院关于内地与香港特别行政区相互执行仲裁裁决的安排》	Issued by the SPC on 24 January 2000 and effective from 1 February 2000.	22, 86
Certain Regulations for Strengthening and Improving Entrustment Enforcement Work 《最高人民法院关于加强和改进委托执行工作的若干规定》	Issued by the SPC on 8 March 2000 and effective from 11 March 2000.	*
Notice on Several Questions in Adjudication and Enforcement concerning Civil and Commercial Cases with Foreign Elements 《最高人民法院关于审理和执行涉外民商事案件应当注意的几个问题的通知》	Issued by the SPC on and effective from 17 April 2000.	13
Provisions of the SPC on some Issues Concerning the Jurisdiction of Civil and Commercial Cases Involving Foreign Elements 《最高人民法院关于涉外民商事案件诉讼管辖若干问题的规定》	Issued by the SPC on 25 February 2002 and effective from 1 March 2002.	*

xlii Table of Legislation and Legislative Instruments

Some Regulations of the SPC Concerning Evidence in Civil Litigation 《最高人民法院关于民事诉讼证据的若干规定》	Issued by the SPC on 21 December 2001 and effective from 1 April 2002.	*
Some Opinions Regarding the Strengthening of the Construction of the Professionalisation of Judges 《最高人民法院关于加强法官队伍职业化建设的若干意见》	Issued by the SPC on and effective from 18 July 2002.	*
Measures for the Payment of Court Fees for Various Types of Cases 《最高人民法院关于本院各类案件诉讼费收交办法》	Issued by the SPC on 27 August 2003 and effective from 1 September 2003.	*
Certain Provisions Regarding the Handling by the People's Courts of Cases Involving Foreign-related Arbitration and Foreign Arbitrations (Draft for Comment) 《最高人民法院关于人民法院处理涉外仲裁及外国仲裁案件的若干规定（征求意见稿）》	Draft issued by the SPC on 31 December 2003.	*
Notice on the Withdrawal of Judges in their Active Duty from their Duty as Arbitrators 《最高人民法院关于本院现职法官不得担任仲裁员的通知》	Issued by the SPC on and effective from 13 July 2004.	*
Letter of Reply on the Jurisdictional Issue in the Insurance Subrogation Dispute between PICC Xiamen Branch and the Chinese-Polish Joint Stock Shipping Company 《最高人民法院关于中国人民保险公司厦门市分公司与中波轮船股份公司保险代位求偿纠纷管辖权问题的复函》	Issued by the SPC on and effective from 2 December 2004.	*

Table of Legislation and Legislative Instruments xliii

SPC's Reply on Jurisdiction of Party's Challenge to the Validity of Arbitration Agreement 《最高人民法院最高人民法院关于确认仲裁协议效力请示的复函》	Issued by the SPC on and effective from 1 December 2005.	*
SPC's Reply on Jurisdiction of Party's Challenge to the Validity of Arbitration Agreement 《最高人民法院最高人民法院关于确认仲裁协议效力请示的复函》	Issued by the SPC on and effective from 9 March 2006.	*
SPC's Interpretations of Certain Issues Concerning the Application of the Arbitration Law of the People's Republic of China 《最高人民法院关于适用<中华人民共和国仲裁法>若干问题的解释》 ('SPC Interpretations 2006')	Issued by the SPC on 23 August 2006 and effective from 8 September 2006.	14, 26, 33, 34, 39, 46, 49, 60, 91, 234
Provisions of the SPC on Some Time Limits for Handling Enforcement Cases by the People's Courts 《最高人民法院关于人民法院办理执行案件若干期限的规定》	Issued by the SPC on 23 December 2006 and effective from 1 January 2007.	*
Several Opinions on the Establishment and Improvement of the Multiple Dispute Resolution System Connecting Litigation and Non-litigation Methods 《最高人民法院关于建立健全诉讼与非诉讼相衔接的矛盾纠纷解决机制的若干意见》	Issued by the SPC on and effective from 24 July 2009.	*

xliv *Table of Legislation and Legislative Instruments*

Beijing HPC's Opinion on Several Issues on the Determination of the Validity of Arbitration Agreements or the Application for Setting Aside Arbitral Awards 《北京市高级人民法院关于审理请求裁定仲裁协议效力、申请撤销仲裁裁决案件的暂行规定》 ('Beijing HPC Opinion 1999')	Issued by Beijing HPC on and effective from 3 December 1999.	32, 33, 39, 40, 234
Circular of the Beijing HPC on the Alteration of Court Jurisdiction over the Enforcement of Domestic Arbitration Awards 《北京市高级人民法院关于变更国内仲裁裁决执行案件级别管辖的通知》	Issued by the Beijing HPC on and effective from 10 March 2000.	*
Shanghai HPC's Opinions on the Implementation of the Arbitration Law of the People's Republic China 《上海市高级人民法院执行<中华人民共和国仲裁法>若干问题的处理意见》 ('Shanghai HPC Opinion 2001')	Issued by the Shanghai HPC on 31 January 2001 and effective from 1 February 2001.	40, 234
Decision of the Government Administration Council of the Central People's Government concerning the Establishment of a Foreign Trade Arbitration Commission within the China Council for the Promotion of International Trade 《中央人民政府政务院关于在中国国际贸易促进委员会内设立对外贸易仲裁委员会的决定》	Issued by the Government Administration Council on and effective from 6 May 1954.	18, 120

Table of Legislation and Legislative Instruments xlv

Decision of the State Council concerning the Establishment of a Maritime Arbitration Commission within the China Council for the Promotion of International Trade 《中华人民共和国国务院关于在中国国际贸易促进委员会内设立海事仲裁委员会的决定》	Issued by the State Council on and effective from 21 November 1958.	*
Notice Concerning the Conversion of the Foreign Trade Arbitration Commission into the Foreign Economic and Trade Arbitration Commission 《国务院关于将对外贸易仲裁委员会改称为对外经济贸易仲裁委员会的通知》	Issued by the State Council on and effective from 26 February 1980.	121
Official Reply Concerning the Renaming of the Maritime Arbitration Commission as the China Maritime Arbitration Commission and the Amendment of its Arbitration Rules 《国务院关于将海事仲裁委员会改名为中国海事仲裁委员会和修订仲裁规则的批复》	Issued by the State Council on and effective from 21 June 1988.	*
Regulations on the Organisation of the People's Mediation Committees 1989 国务院颁布《人民调解委员会组织条例》	Issued by the State Council on and effective from 17 June 1989.	159
Cooperative Joint Venture Implementing Rules 《中华人民共和国中外合作经营企业法实施细则》	Issued by Ministry of Commerce on and effective from 4 September 1995.	*
Circular No 44 Concerning the Method of Collecting Arbitration Fees by Arbitration Institutions 国务院办公厅关于印发《仲裁委员会仲裁收费办法》的通知，国办发[1995]44号。	Issued by the General Office of State Council in 1995.	126

Circular No 44 Concerning the Reorganisation of Domestic Arbitration Institutions 国务院办公厅国关于印发《重新组建仲裁机构方案》的通知，国办发[1995] 44号。	Issued by the General Office of State Council in 1995	126
Measures for Charging Fees by Arbitration Commissions 《仲裁委员会仲裁收费办法》	Issued by the State Council on 28 July 1995 and effective from 1 September 1995.	*
Model Provisional Rules for Arbitration Commissions 《仲裁委员会仲裁暂行规则示范文本》	Issued by the General Office of the State Council on and effective from 28 July 1995.	*
Model Articles of Association of Arbitration Commissions 《仲裁委员会章程示范文本》	Issued by the General Office of the State Council on and effective from 28 July 1995.	*
Provisional Measures for the Registration of Arbitration Commissions 《仲裁委员会登记暂行办法》	Issued by the General Office of the State Council on 28 July 1995 and effective from 1 September 1995.	*
Notice of General Office of the State Council on Some Notable Issues Concerning Execution of the PRC Arbitration Law 《国务院办公厅关于贯彻实施<中华人民共和国仲裁法>需要明确的几个问题的通知》	Issued by the State Council on and effective from 8 June 1996.	*
Measures of Using Administrative Mediation to Resolve Contract Disputes 《合同争议行政调解办法》	Issued by the State Administration for Industry and Commerce on and effective from 3 November 1997.	161

Table of Legislation and Legislative Instruments xlvii

Regulations Concerning the Commission Service Fees 六个中央政府部委关于印发《中介服务收费管理办法》的通知，国家发展计划委员会、国家经济贸易委员会、财政部、监察部、审计署、国务院纠风办文件 计价格[1999] 2255号。	Issued by six central government departments in 1999.	126
Implementation Regulations for the Sino-foreign Equity Joint Venture Law of the PRC 《中华人民共和国中外合资经营企业法实施条例》	Issued by the State Council on 20 September 1983, and subsequently revised on 15 January 1985, 21 December 1987, and 22 July 2001.	19
Regulations on the Administration of the Operation of Offices of Foreign Law Firms in China 《外国律师事务所驻华代表机构管理条例》	Issued by the State Council on 22 December 2001 and effective from 1 January 2002.	*
Implementation Rules of the Ministry of Justice for the Regulations on the Administration of Representative Offices of Foreign Law Firms Operating in China 《司法部关于执行<外国律师事务所驻华代表机构管理条例>的规定》	Issued by the Ministry of Justice on 4 July 2002, and effective from 1 September 2002.	*
Some Provisions of the SPC on Trying Civil Cases Involving the People's Mediation Agreements 《最高人民法院关于审理涉及人民调解协议的民事案件的若干规定》	Issued by the SPC on 16 September 2002, and effective from 1 November 2002.	*
Several Provisions on the Work of the People's Mediation 《人民调解工作若干规定》	Issued by the Ministry of Justice on 26 September 2002, and effective from 11 November 2002.	159, 160

xlviii *Table of Legislation and Legislative Instruments*

Circular No 29 Concerning the Amendment of the Arbitration Fee for 'the Separation of Distribution and Income' Financial System 国家四部委将仲裁收费变更确定为'收支两条线'管理制度的财综[2003] 29号《通知》。	Issued by four departments of State Council in 2003.	125, 126
Confirmation of the Administrative Office of Ministry of Justice Issued Clarification that Representative Offices of Foreign Law Firms and their Representatives Can Serve as Legal Agents in International Arbitration in China 《司法部办公厅明确认为外国律师事务所驻华代表处及其代表可以代理人身份参与在华国际仲裁活动》	Issued by the Administrative Office of Ministry of Justice on and effective from 6 January 2003.	*

France

The French Code of Civil Procedure, Book IV 'Arbitration', enacted by the decree of 12 May 1981, modified by decree no 2011–48 of 13 January 2011 concerning arbitration reform, which became effective on 1 May 2011.	6, 37, 54, 61, 145
French Civil Code	37

Germany

German Code of Civil Procedure (ZPO).	144, 145
German Civil Code	37

Hong Kong

The Hong Kong Arbitration Ordinance (Chapter 609), effective from 1 June 2011.	147

Singapore

| International Arbitration Act of Singapore (Chapter 143A), as amended and revised on 31 December 2002. | 147 |

Switzerland

| Swiss Private International Law Act, ch 12: International Arbitration, effective from 18 December 1987. | 7, 30, 54, 61, 82 |
| Swiss Code of Civil Procedure, effective from 1 January 2011. | 145 |

The Netherlands

| Dutch Arbitration Law 1986, effective from 1 December 1986. | 146 |

United Kingdom

| The English Arbitration Act 1996, effective from 17 June 1996. | 7, 24, 31, 54, 56, 61, 106, 109 |

III. Arbitration Rules

| Provisional Rules of Arbitral Procedure of the Foreign Trade Arbitration Commission of the China Council for the Promotion of International Trade 《中国国际贸易促进委员会对外贸易仲裁委员会仲裁程序暂行规则》 | Revised and effective from 1 January 1989. | * |

Table of Legislation and Legislative Instruments

The CIETAC Ethical Rules for Arbitrators 《贸仲仲裁员守则》	Revised and effective from 6 May 1994.	*
The CIETAC Stipulations for the Appointment of Arbitrators 《贸仲仲裁员聘任规定》	Effective from 1 March 2005.	*
The CIETAC Arbitration Rules 2005 《中国国际经济贸易仲裁委员会仲裁规则》(2005年版)	Effective from 1 May 2005.	16, 26, 59, 66, 69, 98
The CIETAC Arbitration Rules 2012 《中国国际经济贸易仲裁委员会仲裁规则》(2012年版) ('CIETAC Rules 2012')	Effective from 1 May 2012	16, 25, 58, 59, 66, 67, 69, 98, 130, 132, 148, 164, 240
The BAC Arbitration Rules 2008 《北京仲裁委员会仲裁规则》(2008年版) ('BAC Rules 2008')	Effective from 1 April 2008.	16, 148, 149, 239
The BAC Ethical Rules for Arbitrators 《北京仲裁委员会仲裁员守则》	Effective from 1 September 2006.	237
The BAC Stipulations for the Appointment of Arbitrators 《北京仲裁委员会仲裁员聘用管理办法》	Effective from 1 September 2006.	*
BAC Mediation Rules 2008 《北京仲裁委员会调解规则》	Effective from 1 April 2008.	240
ICC Rules 1998	Effective from 1 January 1998.	45, 46–49
ICC ADR Rules 2001	Effective from 1 July 2001.	150
DIS Rules 1998	Effective from 1 July 1998.	148
KCAB Rules 2004	Amended and effective from 13 December 2004.	149
JCAA Rules 2008	Amended and effective from 1 January 2008.	149

LCIA Rules 1998	Effective from 1 January 1998.	148
WIPO Arbitration Rules 2002	Effective from 1 October 2002.	149
WIPO Mediation Rules 2002	Effective from 1 October 2002.	149

Introduction

ARBITRATION IS PROBABLY the oldest means of peaceful dispute resolution in human history.[1] It is said to have existed 'long before law was established, or courts were organized, or judges had formulated law'.[2] Martin Domke found the first recorded arbitration as early as 2550 BC, and stated that 'all through early history, whenever and wherever commerce reached a high degree of development, arbitration was resorted to for the settlement between buyers and sellers'.[3] At its core, international commercial arbitration remains much as it always was; a 'primitive' method of resolving disputes. Bruno Oppetit considers that competition has contributed to the development of an informal sector for dispute resolution. Accordingly, 'private justice has developed its own legitimacy independent from state recognition'.[4]

---

[1] For a discussion on the history of arbitration, see François de Menthon, *Le rôle de l'arbitrage dans l'évolution judiciaire*, Thèse Paris (1926); René David, 'Arbitrage et droit comparé' *RIDC* (1959) 5; René David, 'Arbitrage du XIXe et arbitrage du XXe siècle' in *Mélanges offerts à René Savatier* (1965) 219–32; Anghelos C Foustoucos, *L'arbitrage-interne et international en droit privé hellénique*, Litec (1978) 3; Ottoarndt Glossner, 'Arbitration – A Glance into History' in *Hommage à Frédéric Eisemann* (1978) 19–22; Jean-Jacques Clère, 'L'arbitrage révolutionnaire' *Rev arb* (1981) 3; Charles Jarrosson, *La notion d'arbitrage*, préface de Bruno Oppetit (Paris, LGDJ, 1987) 1–25; Jean-François Poudret, 'Deux aspects de l'arbitrage dans les pays romands au Moyen Âge: l'arbitrabilité et le juge-arbitre' *Revue de l'arbitrage* (1999) 3; Yves Jeanclos, 'La pratique de l'arbitrage du XIIe au XVe siècle. Eléments d'analyse' *Revue de l'arbitrage* (1999) 417; Serge Dauchy, 'Le recours contre les sentences arbitrales en perspective historique. Aux origines des arts 1481–1491 NCPC' *Revue de l'arbitrage* (1999) 763; Derek Roebuck, 'Best to Reconcile: Mediation and Arbitration in the Ancient Greek World' 66 *Journal of Institute of Arbitrators* 4 (2000) 275; Julie Velissaropoulos-Karakostas, 'L'arbitrage dans la Grèce antique. Epoques archaïque et classique' *Revue de l'arbitrage* (2000) 9; Sophie Lafont, 'L'arbitrage en Mésopotamie' *Revue de l'arbitrage* (2000) 557; Jean Hilaire, 'L'arbitrage dans la période moderne (XVIe-XVIIIe siècle)', *Revue de l'arbitrage* (2000) 187; Fabrizio Marrella, 'L'arbitrage à Venise (XIIe–XVIe siècles)' *Revue de l'arbitrage* (2002) 263; Thomas Clay, *L'arbitre*, préface de Philippe Fouchard (Paris, Dalloz, 2001) 1–10; Derek Roebuck, *Ancient Greek Arbitration* (Oxford, Holo Books, 2001) 3; Derek Roebuck, *The Charitable Arbitrator: How to Mediate and Arbitrate in Louis XIV's France* (Oxford, Holo Books, 2002); Derek Roebuck, *Early English Arbitration* (Oxford, Holo Books, 2008); Derek Roebuck, *Disputes and Differences: Comparisons in Law, Language and History* (Oxford, Holo Books, 2010); Derek Roebuck and Bruno de Loynes de Fumichon, *Roman Arbitration* (Oxford, Holo Books, 2004).

[2] Francis Keller, *American Arbitration: Its History, Functions and Achievements* (New York, Harper & Brothers, 1948).

[3] Martin Domke, *Domke on Commercial Arbitration*, vol 3 (Callaghan, 2003).

[4] Bruno Oppetit, *Théorie de l'arbitrage* (Paris, PUF, 1998) 21. In the original text, Oppetit argues that 'la logique du marché joue néanmoins en faveur du développement d'un secteur informel de résolution des conflits. Dès lors, les formes de justice privée acquièrent par elles-mêmes une légitimité indépendante de toute reconnaissance étatique'.

2 Introduction

The extra-judicial nature of arbitration and the concept of 'private justice' can be traced back to the eras of ancient Greece and Rome. The Greek arbitral concept of finality and free will and the principle of Roman arbitration as a formless transaction based on parties' consent have been carried on in modern day arbitration, with generational modifications enhancing arbitration's utility and effectiveness.[5] In medieval Europe, merchants began to transact beyond the political, cultural and geographical barriers; they transported the most favourable local trade practices to the foreign markets. As the transnationality of trade expanded, the bonds of localised systems were broken to develop an international system of commercial law. This new system of law governing commercial transactions and administered by private judges drawn from commercial rank became known, even in its day, as the *lex mercatoria* or the Law Merchant.[6] In the meantime, disputes over transactions at the merchant fairs required a resolution mechanism that suited the needs of the merchant class. This paved the way for the development of arbitration. Disputes were resolved by arbitrators out of the merchant class itself. Arbitration, like the *lex mercatoria*, was outside the judicial system of any nation, and amounted to self-regulation by the merchant class.[7] In some aspects,

> it is in this tradition of *lex mercatoria* that international commercial arbitration has evolved into an alternative means of resolving disputes to national courts of law. It is also in this tradition that modern international commercial arbitration has purported to ground itself in expeditious, low cost, informal and speedy mercantile justice.[8]

The arbitral linkage progressively extended from the Greeks to the Romans to the Law Merchants. As Mr Gemmell describes, 'the emphasis on good faith, equity and practicality as the essential attributes of the Greek, Roman and Law Merchant arbitral worlds represent archetypal characteristics sought after in the practice of modern day arbitration'.[9] An 'arbitral chain' could be found that linked the eras of the West's arbitral past with its arbitral present.[10] In this context, it is argued that arbitration is 'universal' and has 'no boundaries of time

---

[5] See George Mousarakis, *The Historical and Institutional Context of Roman Law* (Surrey, Ashgate Publishing, 2003); Roebuck, *Ancient Greek Arbitration*; Roebuck and Fumichon, *Roman Arbitration*; Derek Roebuck, 'Best to Reconcile: Mediation and Arbitration in the Ancient Greek World' (2000) 6 *Arbitration* 4; Peter Stein, *Roman Law in European History* (Cambridge, Cambridge University Press, 2002).

[6] For a discussion of the history of Law Merchant, see Francis Burdick, 'What is the Law Merchant?' (1902) 2 *Columbia Law Review* 470; Avner Greif, *Institutions and the Path to the Modern Economy: Lessons from Medieval Trade* (Cambridge, Cambridge University Press, 2006); Avner Greif, Paul Milgrom and Barry Weingast, 'Coordination, Commitment, and Enforcement: The Case of the Merchant Guild' (1994) 102 *Journal of Political Economy* 4; Paul Milgrom, Douglass North and Barry R Weingast, 'The Role of Institutions in the Revival of Trade: The Law Merchant, Private Judges, and the Champagne Fairs' (1990) 2 *Economics and Politics* 1.

[7] Burdick, 'What is the Law Merchant?' 472–75.

[8] Leon Trackman, 'Legal Traditions and International Commercial Arbitration' (2006) 17 *American Review of International Arbitration* 1.

[9] Arthur Gemmell, *Western and Chinese Arbitration: The Arbitral Chain* (Lanham, University Press of America, 2008) 79.

[10] ibid.

and space', given that human nature in all countries and at all times embraces 'the desire for justice'.[11]

Nevertheless, when the universality of arbitration was claimed, little consideration was given to arbitral history in Asia. If we continue our historical journey to the East, can we find a similar tradition and continuity of arbitration? In ancient China, for instance, one of the oldest civilisations of the world, the notion of private law (a reflection of market exchanges among equal persons) was absent. The Chinese approach to dispute resolution was influenced, to a great extent, by Confucian philosophy that emphasises harmony and conflict avoidance. Under the Confucian tradition, the rule of law, and a formal dispute resolution system did not reach a high level of development in ancient China. An old Chinese proverb – 'it is better to die of starvation than to become a thief; it is better to be vexed to death than to bring a lawsuit' – vividly illustrates the fear of lawsuits among the general public. China's legal system has now evolved, and Chinese business people are more experienced with commercial disputes as a result of the development of international trade and the increasing awareness of legal rights. However, the consensual spirit that has for such a long time marked dispute resolution in China remains prevalent in modern society. How does this non-confrontational culture influence the law and practice of arbitration in modern China? To put it in broader terms, what is the role of native legal traditions in the process of modernisation of law?

The developments in communications and technology have ushered the world into an era of globalisation. In the trend of globalisation, arbitration has developed significantly in recent years as the preferred method of dispute resolution for international commerce. It is perceived, rightly or wrongly, as being cheaper and less time-consuming than court proceedings and, in many states, the process is more confidential. The award is generally easier to enforce in a foreign country than a court judgment, thanks to the New York Convention on the Recognition and Enforcement of Foreign Arbitration Awards of 1958 (New York Convention). More importantly, arbitration is now acknowledged to be a neutral method of settling commercial disputes between parties from different nations, allowing each of the parties to avoid the 'home' courts of its co-contractor. Finally, arbitration gives the parties substantial liberty to design their own dispute resolution mechanism, largely free of the constraints of national law.[12] Modern arbitration is building on its own dynamics. On the one hand, it develops away from the grip of the states and, on the other hand, it leads the law and practice of arbitration towards an ever-increasing global harmonisation, a constant development towards clearly identifiable points of

---

[11] Thomas Clay, *L'arbitre* (Paris, Dalloz, Nouvelle Bibliothèque de thèse, 2001) 9, n 1. In the original text, Clay states that 'l'universalité de l'arbitrage n'étonne guère, compte tenu de sa dimension profondément humaine. Il correspond en effet à l'une des aspirations les plus naturelles de chacun et qui se retrouve à travers les siècles et les pays: le souci de justice'.

[12] Emmanuel Gaillard and John Savage (eds), *Fouchard Gaillard Goldman on International Commercial Arbitration* (The Hague, Kluwer Law International, 1999) 1.

convergence.[13] This movement towards international arbitration as a transnational institution reflects the needs and expectations of the 'consumers' of international arbitration, as international business itself becomes increasingly global and less country-specific. In this context, 'a uniform, transnational mechanism for resolving disputes is clearly the way forward'.[14] This trend has been commonly referred to as the development of 'transnational arbitration'.[15]

In the past, globalisation was controlled mainly by European and Western economic players. Today, however, the new era of globalisation has significantly changed the traditional global markets, with the non-Western countries playing an increasingly important role in the international commercial and financial markets. An important question to ask in the study of transnational arbitration is how the new economic players will react to this movement of harmonisation. Will they follow and adapt to the movement? Or will they influence transnational arbitration, and adapt it to their economic requirements and legal and cultural background? China serves as a good example in this regard because it is one of the main new economic players, and it is increasingly interacting in global commerce. Since its reforms and opening-up in 1978, the economic regime in China has gone through dramatic changes. China has been moving away from a planned economy towards a more liberal market economy. The growth in terms of cross-border commercial exchanges and foreign investments has also resulted in a dynamic development of dispute resolution mechanisms. Is China showing signs of adaptation to the current trend of transnational arbitration? Or, on the other hand, will Chinese legal culture and practice influence the practice of arbitration in the rest of the world?

To address these perplexing questions concerning transnational arbitration, legal tradition and legal harmonisation, it is necessary to conduct a thorough study of current arbitration law and practice in China in the global context, and to look beyond the discipline of law to examine the development of arbitration in the context of the changing economic, social and legal structure of Chinese society. This book explains contemporary arbitration in China from an interdisciplinary perspective and with a comparative approach. Putting the Chinese arbitration system into the social context will help readers to understand historical links to contemporary practice, to assess where the legal obstacles to modern arbitration arise, and to predict what the future trends might be.

Since 1978, China has been a legislative laboratory. A vast array of laws and rules has been promulgated to establish institutions that did not exist before the start of economic reforms. Given the wide gap between statutes and practice, in

---

[13] For discussions on the points of convergence, see Gabrielle Kaufmann-Kohler, 'Globalization of Arbitral Procedures' (2003) 36 *Vanderbilt Journal of Transnational Law* 1313, 1313–33.
[14] Gaillard and Savage, *Fouchard Gaillard Goldman on International Commercial Arbitration* 3.
[15] See generally, ibid; Piero Bernardini, Emmanuel Gaillard, International Chamber of Commerce et al, *Transnational Rules in International Commercial Arbitration*, ICC Publication No 480/4 (1993); Marc Blessing, 'Globalization (and Harmonization?) of Arbitration' (1992) 9 *Journal of International Arbitration* 1.

particular in the Chinese context, an empirical approach was needed to examine judicial decisions and arbitral awards, in order to compare 'paper law' to real practice. Case analysis is a difficult task due to the scarcity of reported cases in China. Although the Supreme People's Court (SPC) publishes opinions on typical cases selected for guidance for lower courts and general prospective interpretations of laws in the *Selected Cases of the SPC*, it contains only a fraction of rulings and interpretations of national legislation. Systematically assembled collections of cases and administrative interpretations of existing laws and rules generally remain unpublished. Thanks to the centralised report and review system (Report System) established by the SPC,[16] some negative rulings by local courts have become accessible. Since September 2001, the Fourth Division of Civil Trials of the SPC started to publish its replies to its subordinate courts' reports on whether to refuse applications for enforcement of foreign-related and foreign arbitral awards in a series of books named Guide on Foreign-related Commercial and Maritime Trials (from 2004 onwards) or Guide and Study on China's Foreign-related Commercial and Maritime Trials (from 2001–2003).[17] The Beijing Arbitration Commission (BAC) also publishes selected court decisions in the BAC Arbitrators Manual. These reported cases form the main resource for the case analysis in this book. Reference is also made to arbitral awards published by arbitration institutions, cases cited in books, journal articles or conference papers, and first-hand information obtained through direct contacts. The book will be focused on the cases concerning the courts' determination on the validity of the arbitration agreement and on the recognition and enforcement of arbitral awards, in order to demonstrate the Chinese judicial attitude towards arbitration. This empirical approach is in part achieved by the interviews conducted during research trips in China (including Hong Kong, Beijing and Wuhan) between March and April 2007. In the research trips the author, together with Professor Gabrielle Kaufmann-Kohler, visited a number of universities and law firms, as well as the China International Economic and Trade Arbitration Commission (CIETAC), the BAC, the Wuhan Arbitration Commission (WAC), the SPC, and the Commission of Legislative Affairs, Standing Committee of the National People's Congress (NPC). A series of interviews was conducted with Chinese arbitration specialists, including academics, lawyers acting as counsel, arbitrators, SPC judges and heads and staff of government service in charge of preparing legal reforms, and heads and staff

---

[16] For an explanation of the Report System, see ch 1, s1.4.3-D below.
[17] 万鄂湘(主编),《中国涉外商事海事审判指导与研究》人民法院出版社, 总1-6辑 (Exiang Wan (ed), *Guide and Study on China's Foreign-related Commercial and Maritime Trials*). 万鄂湘(主编),《涉外商事海事审判指导》, 人民法院出版社, 总7-18辑 (Exiang Wan (ed), *Guide on Foreign-Related Commercial and Maritime Trials*). Judge Gao Xiaoli of the Fourth Division of Civil Trials mentioned that nearly all cases reported to the SPC, except for those raising substantial issues, have been published in the *Guide on Foreign-related Commercial and Maritime Trial* since 2001. Gao Xiaoli's speech at the Annual Conference of International Economic Law, organised by the Northwest University of Politics and Law at Xi'an, Shanxi, China, in November 2006.

of arbitration institutions.[18] The duration of each interview was approximately one hour. This first-hand information reliably tells us how arbitration operates in China. Interviewees revealed the existing problems in the current regime.

To understand the interaction between global norms and local traditions, it is important to study arbitration in China in the context of globalisation and to compare Chinese practice with transnational standards. 'Transnational standards' refer to principles and practices that are widely accepted by national laws – accumulation of national standards. Using 'standards', the comparison is not limited to international and national laws, but also includes internationally accepted principles and practices reflected in soft laws and practices at arbitration institutions. In terms of arbitration laws, reference was made to the United Nations Commission on International Trade Law (UNCITRAL) Model Law on International Commercial Arbitration of 1985 with Amendments as Adopted in 2006 (Model Law),[19] and the New York Convention. The twin pillars are said to be the foundation of the success of modern international commercial arbitration. The former facilitates and safeguards the enforcement of arbitration agreements and arbitral awards worldwide. The latter forms the basis for states without an arbitration law to adopt one ready-made or to substitute it for one that is out of date. Although the Model Law does not take the form of a treaty, legislators who have decided to review their arbitration legislation have all 'given due consideration' to the Model Law as recommended by the United Nations General Assembly.[20] All this has contributed greatly to achieving the harmonisation of international arbitration law. Comparison also includes some important national sources: (i) French law: reference will be made to the French Code of Civil Procedure, Book IV, Arbitration enacted by the decree of 12 May 1981, and modified by Decree no 2011-48 of 13 January 2011 (Decree 2011)[21] and its well-

---

[18] This research trip was conducted while the author worked at Geneva University Law School on a research project on international arbitration in China. The research project was directed by Gabrielle Kaufmann-Kohler, and funded by the Swiss National Science Foundation. Apart from a general acknowledgement, the names and opinions of the interviewees have been kept anonymous, unless specifically authorised otherwise by the interviewee.

[19] The Model Law was adopted by the UNCITRAL on 21 June 1985, at the end of the 18th Session of the Commission. It was amended by the UNCITRAL on 7 July 2006, at the 39th Session of the Commission. For a list of jurisdictions whose legislation is based on the Model Law, see www.uncitral.org/uncitral/en/uncitral_texts/arbitration/1985Model_arbitration_status.html.

[20] The General Assembly, in its resolution 40/72 of 11 December 1985, recommended 'that all States *give due consideration* (emphasis added) to the Model Law on International Commercial Arbitration, in view of the desirability of uniformity of the law of arbitral procedures and the specific needs of international commercial arbitration practice'. Subsequently, the General Assembly, in its resolution 61/33 of 4 December 2006, recommended 'that all States give favourable consideration to the enactment of the revised arts of the UNCITRAL Model Law on International Commercial Arbitration, or the revised UNCITRAL Model Law on International Commercial Arbitration, when they enact or revise their laws . . .' See Gaillard and Savage, *Fouchard Gaillard Goldman on International Commercial Arbitration* 109.

[21] Décret no 2011-48 of 13 January 2011 'portant réforme de l'arbitrage', which became effective on 1 May 2011: *Journal Officiel de la République Française* no 0011, 14 January 2011, 777, text 9, with the report to the Prime Minister by Bertrand and Yves Derains, 773, text 8. For commentaries see Thomas Clay (ed), *Le nouveau droit français de l'arbitrage* (Paris, Lextenso, 2011); *Recueil*

established case law, which is considered by many to be, if not a model, then at least an essential point of reference in terms of international arbitration;[22] (ii) Swiss law: the Swiss Private International Law Act, effective from 18 December 1987 (Swiss PIL 1987) will be used as a main reference, which represents a significant step towards liberalisation of arbitration;[23] and (iii) English law: England has been long been considered a centre for international commercial arbitration due to its pivotal position as the centre for shipping, insurance, commodity and financing businesses. The comparison will include the English Arbitration Act, effective from 17 June 1996 (English Arbitration Act 1996), which is considered of profound international importance.[24] These jurisdictions are chosen as they are seen as jurisdictions with developed arbitration laws. The laws which are more adapted to the needs of commercial parties may be maintained and spread over other jurisdictions. In fact, Switzerland, France and the UK have the most popular seats of arbitration. According to the ICC statistics in 2010, Paris (124 cases), London (70 cases), Geneva (48 cases) and Zurich (30 cases) are the places most frequently selected as the seat of arbitration in ICC arbitration proceedings.[25] Commercial parties who select these jurisdictions as the seat of arbitration will comply with their arbitration laws. In this sense, the laws in the above three jurisdictions are representative in the study of transnational standards. In terms of institutional practice, the research compared the practice of Chinese arbitration institutions with those of leading Western arbitration institutions. Benefiting from the author's practical insights while working as a Deputy Counsel at the ICC International Court of Arbitration (ICC Court), an in-depth comparative study was conducted between the way arbitration is conducted at the ICC Court and at the CIETAC.

Dalloz (2011) 175, by Emmanuel Gaillard and Pierre de Lapasse; *Revue de l'arbitrage* (2011) 5, by Charles Jarrosson and Jacques Pellerin; *Droit & patrimoine* 203 (2011) 30, by Pierre Mayer.

[22] For a discussion of French arbitration law, see generally Jean-Louis Delvolvé, Jean Rouche and Gerald H Pointon (eds), *French Arbitration Law and Practice* (The Hague, Kluwer Law International, 2003); Yves Derains and Rosabel Goodman-Everard, 'French National Report' in Jan Paulsson (ed), *International Handbook on Commercial Arbitration* (The Hague, Kluwer Law International, 1998); Gaillard and Savage, *Fouchard Gaillard Goldman on International Commercial Arbitration*.

[23] For a discussion of Swiss arbitration law, see Pierre Lalive and Emmanuel Gaillard, *Le nouveau droit de l'arbitrage international en Suisse*, 116 *Journal du droit international (Clunet)* (1989) 905; Claude Reymond, 'La nouvelle loi suisse et le droit de l'arbitrage international – Réflexions de droit comparé' *Revue de l'arbitrage* (1989) 385; Robert Briner, 'Switzerland' in Jan Paulsson (ed), *International Handbook on Commercial Arbitration* (The Hague, Kluwer Law International, 1998); Gabrielle Kaufmann-Kohler and Blaise Stucki (eds), *International Arbitration in Switzerland: A Handbook for Practitioners* (The Hague, Kluwer Law International, 2004).

[24] For a discussion of English arbitration law, see Michael Mustill, 'La nouvelle loi anglaise sur l'arbitrage de 1996: philosophie, inspiration, aspiration' *Revue de l'arbitrage* (1997) 29; Roy Goode, 'The Adaptation of English Law to International Commercial Arbitration' (1992) 8 *Arbitration International* 1, 1–16; Johan Steyn, 'Towards a New English Arbitration Act' (1991) 7 *Arbitrational International* 17, 17–26; VV Veeder, 'English National Report' in Jan Paulsson (ed), *International Handbook on Commercial Arbitration* (The Hague, Kluwer Law International, 1997).

[25] '2010 Statistical Report' 22 *ICC Bulletin* 1 (2011).

8 *Introduction*

The book starts to examine the contemporary law and practice of the arbitration system in China measured by transnational standards, in terms of Chinese arbitration laws and court practice (chapters two to four), practices at Chinese arbitration institutions[26] (chapter five), and the role of mediation in the modern arbitration system in China (chapter six). Based on the above analysis, it highlights the unique features and the legal obstacles to arbitration in contemporary China (chapter seven). Further, the book analyses cultural influences on these 'Chinese characteristics' of arbitral practice, looking for explanations from traditional Chinese legal culture (chapter eight) and legal reception and legal modernisation in China (chapter nine). Finally, the author attempts to foresee how China will react to the movement of transnational arbitration and, in the other direction, what impact China may have on arbitration law and practice elsewhere (chapter ten).

---

[26] Often referred to as 'arbitration commission' (仲裁委员会) by Chinese legislation. The book will adopt the term 'arbitration institution' as is generally used in international arbitration.

1

Overview of the Chinese Legal Framework and Arbitration System

'Measure what is measurable, and make measurable what is not so'.

Galileo

CHINA HAS MADE considerable efforts since its accession to the World Trade Organization (WTO) to provide a stable framework for foreign investment and economic growth. An important part of this reform is the development of international arbitration practice, which has developed as a preferred dispute resolution method for cross-border transactions. The current Chinese arbitration regime has adopted most of the essential principles of contemporary arbitration practice. Nevertheless, a degree of divergence still exists in China's arbitration law and practice. This is due to the presence of what are known as 'Chinese characteristics'. One commentator has compared arbitration in China to Chinese chess, and stated that '[Chinese arbitration] shares a common ancestry with international arbitration standards, but also has differences that make it unique'.[1] The first task of this study is to identify the unique characteristics of contemporary Chinese arbitration law and court practice as compared to transnational standards (chapters two, three, and four), the functions of arbitration institutions in China (chapter five), and the role of mediation in the modern arbitration system in China (chapter six).

Before examining the unique features of arbitration law and practice in contemporary China, we will first give a general overview of the Chinese judicial organisation, the legal framework, the historical development of arbitration legislation and the current arbitration regime. It is commonly accepted by the People's Republic of China (PRC) judicial and arbitral authorities that Hong Kong, Macao and Taiwan are deemed to be 'foreign' in terms of civil procedure and arbitration.[2] When the term 'China' or 'PRC' is used in this book, it normally refers to mainland China and does not, in the absence of any special statement, include Hong Kong, Macao or Taiwan.

---

[1] Peter Chow, cited in Julius Melnitzer, 'Reforms Make Arbitration in China a Safer Bet: Regs Still Not Up to US Standards' *Inside Counsel*, July 2005.
[2] Under the Stipulations on Certain Issues regarding Judicial Jurisdiction over Foreign-related Civil and Commercial Cases issued by the SPC, 1 March 2003, jurisdiction over civil and commercial cases involving parties from Hong Kong, Macao or Taiwan is dealt with in accordance with the Stipulations.

1.1 CHINESE JUDICIAL ORGANISATION

According to the Constitution of the PRC and the Organic Law of the People's Courts (as amended in 2006),[3] the people's courts are the judicial organs of the state. The judicial system in China is characterised by 'four levels and two instances of trials'. Under the system of two instances of trials, a party may bring an appeal only once to the people's court at the next level, and the people's procurator may lodge a protest against a court decision or order to the people's court at the next level; judgments and orders of first instance at various levels become legally effective if, within the prescribed period for appeal, no party makes an appeal; and judgments and orders of the court of second instance are final.

Judicial authority is exercised by the following people's courts: (i) local people's courts at various levels, (ii) military courts and other special people's courts, and (iii) the Supreme People's Court (SPC). The local people's courts are further divided into: (i) the basic people's courts (BPC), (ii) the intermediate people's courts (IPC), and (iii) the high people's courts (HPC).

Chart 1: The Structure of the People's Courts

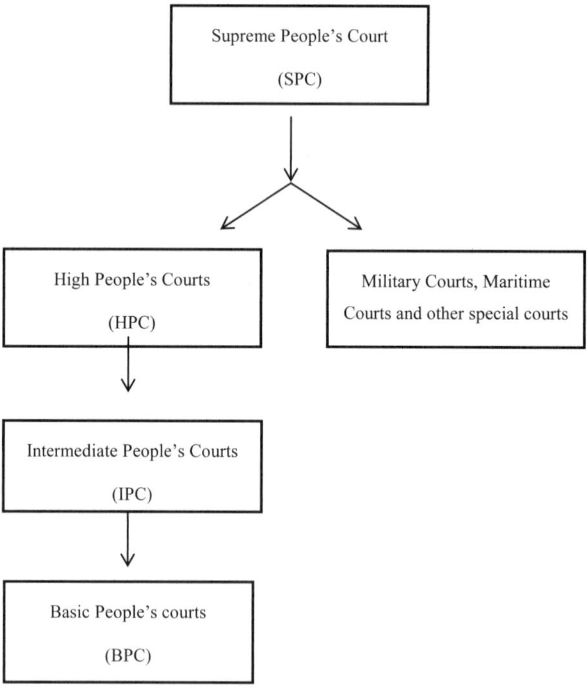

```
                    ┌─────────────────────────┐
                    │ Supreme People's Court  │
                    │         (SPC)           │
                    └─────────────────────────┘
                        ↙             ↘
    ┌──────────────────────┐    ┌─────────────────────────────┐
    │ High People's Courts │    │ Military Courts, Maritime   │
    │        (HPC)         │    │ Courts and other special    │
    │                      │    │ courts                      │
    └──────────────────────┘    └─────────────────────────────┘
              ↓
    ┌──────────────────────────────┐
    │ Intermediate People's Courts │
    │            (IPC)             │
    └──────────────────────────────┘
              ↓
    ┌──────────────────────────────┐
    │   Basic People's courts      │
    │            (BPC)             │
    └──────────────────────────────┘
```

---

[3] Adopted at the Second Session of the Fifth NPC on 1 July 1979. Revised for the third time according to the Decision of the Standing Committee of the NPC on Amending the Organic Law of the People's Courts of the PRC as adopted at the 24th Session of the Standing Committee of the 10th NPC on 31 October 2006.

The BPCs, at the lowest level, are established in counties, municipalities, autonomous counties, and municipal districts.[4] A BPC may establish people's tribunals in towns or townships according to the conditions of the locality, population and cases. A people's tribunal is a component of the BPC, and its judgments and orders are accorded the same legal effect as the judgments and orders of the BPC.[5] Additionally, BPC adjudicates criminal and civil cases of first instance except where otherwise provided by law or decree.[6]

The IPCs are established in prefectures of a province or autonomous region, municipalities directly under the Central Government, municipalities directly under the jurisdiction of a province or autonomous region, or autonomous prefectures.[7] Their jurisdiction covers cases of first instance assigned by laws and decrees, cases of first instance transferred from the BPCs, appeals and protests lodged against judgments and orders of the BPCs, and protests lodged by the people's procuratorate in accordance with the procedures of judicial supervision.[8]

The HPCs are courts of provinces, autonomous regions and municipalities directly under the Central Government.[9] Their jurisdiction covers cases of first instance assigned by laws and decrees to their jurisdiction, cases of first instance transferred from people's courts at lower levels, appeals and protests lodged against judgments and orders of people's courts at lower levels, and protests lodged by the people's procuratorate in accordance with the procedures of judicial supervision.[10]

The SPC is the highest judicial organ of the state. It supervises the administration of justice by the local people's courts at various levels and by the special people's courts.[11] The SPC handles cases of first instance assigned by laws and decrees to its jurisdiction and which it considers it should try itself, appeals and protests lodged against judgments and orders of higher people's courts and special people's courts, and protests lodged by the Supreme People's Procuratorate in accordance with the procedures of judicial supervision.[12] Moreover, the SPC interprets questions concerning the specific application of laws and decrees in judicial proceedings.[13]

---

[4] Art 18 of the Organic Law of the People's Courts.
[5] Art 20 of the Organic Law of the People's Courts.
[6] Art 21 of the Organic Law of the People's Courts.
[7] Art 23 of the Organic Law of the People's Courts.
[8] Art 25 of the Organic Law of the People's Courts.
[9] Art 26 of the Organic Law of the People's Courts.
[10] Art 28 of the Organic Law of the People's Courts.
[11] Art 30 of the Organic Law of the People's Courts.
[12] Art 32 of the Organic Law of the People's Courts.
[13] Art 33 of the Organic Law of the People's Courts.

12 *Chinese Legal Framework*

1.2 LEGAL FRAMEWORK

1.2.1 Public Sources

A. National Sources

According to the Constitution of the PRC, the NPC and its Standing Committee are vested with the legislative power to enact and amend laws.[14] The two national laws directly applicable to international arbitration in China today are the Arbitration Law of 1995 (Arbitration Law)[15] and the Civil Procedure Law (adopted in 1991, revised in 2007 and 2012).[16] Also of significant importance is the Contract Law of the PRC of 1999 (Contract Law). These laws were enacted following the dramatic changes brought about by China's opening-up policy in the late 1970s.[17] The massive and still increasing interests in foreign trade and investment have led to a large number of disputes to be resolved, and prompted the promulgation of several laws related to foreign investment.[18]

The power to interpret laws is vested in several organs in the PRC. First, the NPC and its Standing Committee interprets legislation. Secondly, the SPC and the Supreme People's Procuratorate provide judicial interpretations of the laws of the PRC. Finally, the State Council, which is the administrative arm of the PRC, interprets administrative rules.[19] Since the Arbitration Law came into force, the SPC has issued a number of judicial interpretations concerning the application of relevant laws and treaties by Chinese courts. In practice, the SPC's judicial interpretations provide important guidance for lower courts on the application of the Arbitration Law, and also fill interpretative gaps not addressed by the Arbitration Law. The following are some important SPC interpretations relevant to arbitration issued in recent years:

---

[14] Art 68 of the Constitution of the PRC, adopted at the Fifth Session of the Fifth NPC on 4 December 1982, and the latest amendment was adopted at the First Session of the Eighth NPC on 14 March 2004.

[15] The Arbitration Law of the PRC, adopted at the Ninth Session of the Standing Committee of the Eighth NPC on 31 August 1994, and effective as of 1 September 1995.

[16] Civil Procedure Law of the PRC, adopted on 9 April 1991 at the Fourth Session of the Seventh NPC. The first revision was made according to the Decision of the Standing Committee of the NPC on Amending the Civil Procedure Law of the PRC as adopted at the 30th Session of the Standing Committee of the 10th NPC on 28 October 2007. The second revision was made according to the Decision of the Standing Committee of the NPC on Amending the Civil Procedure Law of the PRC as adopted at the 28th Session of the Standing Committee of the 11th NPC on 31 August 2012, which will come into force on 1 January 2013.

[17] For a brief chronology and overview, see Jianli Zhu, 'Alternative Dispute Resolution in the Context of Chinese Commercial Law' (1999) 2 *International Arbitration Law Review* 5, 181–85.

[18] Notable examples include the Law of Chinese-Foreign Equity Joint Venture (2001), the Law of Chinese-Foreign Contractual Joint Venture Law (2000), available at www.lawinfochina.com.

[19] Resolution of the Standing Committee of the NPC Providing an Improved Interpretation of the Law, adopted at the 19th Session of the Standing Committee of the Fifth NPC on 10 June 1981.

- 'SPC's Notice on the Implementation of China's Accession to the Convention on the Recognition and Enforcement of Foreign Arbitral Awards', promulgated on 10 April 1987;
- 'Notice of the SPC on Several Issues Regarding the Handling by the People's Courts of Certain Issues Pertaining to Foreign-Related Arbitration and Foreign Arbitration', on and effective from 28 August 1995;
- 'SPC Response to Questions Concerning the Validity of an Arbitration Clause in Which Two Arbitration Institutions Are Simultaneously Selected', on and effective from 12 December 1996;
- 'Notice on Several Issues Concerning Implementation of the Arbitration Law', on and effective from 26 March 1997;
- 'Notice of the SPC on Relevant Issues Relating to the Annulation by the People's Court of Foreign-Related Arbitral Awards', on and effective from 23 April 1998[20];
- 'SPC's Provisions on the People's Courts' Recognition of Civil Judgments Made by Courts in Taiwan Region', promulgated on 22 May 1998 and effective from 26 May 1998;
- 'SPC Reply to Several Questions Regarding the Hearing of Party's Application for the Setting-Aside of an Arbitral Award', promulgated on 21 July 1998 and effective from 28 July 1998;
- 'SPC Reply Regarding Several Issues Relating to the Validity of Arbitration Agreements', promulgated on 26 October 1998 and effective from 5 November 1998;
- 'SPC Reply to Several Questions concerning Confirmation of the Effectiveness of an Arbitration Agreement', promulgated on 26 October 1998 and effective from 5 November 1998;
- 'Regulation of the SPC Regarding the Problems of Collecting Fees and Time Limits for Review of Recognition and Enforcement of Foreign Arbitral Awards', promulgated on 14 November 1998 and effective from 21 November 1998;
- 'Reply of the SPC to the Question whether a People's Court Should Accept a Retrial Request by a Party Who is Not Satisfied with the People's Court Ruling to Set Aside an Arbitral Award', promulgated on 11 February 1999 and effective from 16 February 1999;
- 'SPC Reply to Questions concerning the Partial Setting Aside of Arbitration Awards Rendered by Chinese Arbitration Institutions', promulgated on 25 August 1999 and effective from 31 August 1999;
- 'Notice on Several Questions in Adjudication and Enforcement concerning Civil and Commercial Cases with Foreign Elements', promulgated on and effective from 17 April 2000;

---

[20] Art 1 of the Reply was amended by the art 58 of Decision of the Supreme People's Court on Adjusting the Sequential Number of the Articles of the Civil Procedure Law of the People's Republic of China Cited in Judicial Interpretations and Other Documents.

14 *Chinese Legal Framework*

- 'Interpretation of SPC on Several Issues Regarding the Application of the Arbitration Law' (SPC Interpretation 2006), *fa shi* No 7/2006, promulgated on 26 December 2005, effective from 8 September 2006. This interpretation is generally pro-arbitration, and addresses a number of important issues relating to the interpretation and validity of the arbitration agreement, as well as the setting-aside and enforcement of arbitral awards.[21]

Furthermore, although not authorised by the Constitution, local Chinese HPCs also issue guidelines on issues which the SPC has not interpreted. Such guidelines, usually issued in the form of 'opinions' or 'provisions', have some practical guidance for lower courts within their jurisdiction, insofar as they do not contradict interpretations of the SPC. In some instances, the 'opinions' of the HPCs provide the basis for the later judicial interpretations by the SPC.

B. International Sources

a. International Conventions

On 2 December 1986, the Standing Committee of the NPC issued a decision on China's accession to the New York Convention, which became effective in China on 22 April 1987.[22] The adoption of the New York Convention in China is intended to encourage foreign investors to submit their disputes to arbitration, as arbitral awards rendered in other contracting states will be more easily recognised and enforced in China. In acceding to the New York Convention, China adopted both the reciprocity reservation and the commercial reservation. The former provides that China will recognise and enforce only those arbitral awards made in other states that are signatories to the Convention. The commercial reservation limits the scope of recognition and enforcement only to arbitral awards that have been rendered in commercial cases.

China is also a member of the Convention on the Settlement of Investment Disputes between States and Nationals of Other States (ICSID Convention).[23] However, when ratifying the ICSID Convention, China made a reservation under Article 25(4) of the ICSID Convention that 'the Chinese government will only consider submitting to the jurisdiction of the ICSID disputes over compensation resulting from expropriation and nationalisation'.

---

[21] For a commentary, see John Choong and Peter Yuen, 'The Supreme People's Court's Draft Interpretation to Several Issues Regarding Application of PRC Arbitration Law' (2006) 7 *Mealey's International Arbitration Quarterly Law Review* 3, 79–105.

[22] The Standing Committee of the NPC issued a decision on China's access to the New York Convention on 2 December 1986, and the ratification became effective as of 22 April 1987.

[23] The Standing Committee of the NPC issued a decision to ratify the Washington Convention on 1 July 1992, which became effective as of 6 February 1993.

b. Bilateral Investment Treaties (BITs)

China has entered into BITs with nearly all of its most important trading partners (with the exception of the United States and Russia), such as most EU countries, Japan, Korea, Singapore, Malaysia, Australia and Thailand. China has concluded a total of 130 BITs,[24] and is still very active in entering into new treaties as well as renegotiating existing ones. A BIT determines the substantial rights of a foreign investor and contains dispute settlement provisions. Typically, a BIT addresses the following four substantive issues: (1) definition of investment; (2) conditions for the admission of foreign investors to the host state; (3) standards of treatment of foreign investors (ie, fair and equitable treatment, national treatment, most-favoured-nation clause); and (4) protection against expropriation.[25] Over time, Chinese investment treaties have evolved significantly. In terms of their content, Chinese investment treaties can be divided into three phases.[26]

The first generation of BITs concluded from 1982 to 1998[27] was generally limited in scope of protection and dispute resolution. Many of these early China BITs did not include any investor-state arbitration clause, or contained an investor-state arbitration clause which only covered disputes relating to the amount of compensation payable following an expropriation.

Beginning in 1998, China started to develop a more liberal approach on investment protection in line with its economic transformation from a country receiving foreign direct investment (FDI) to a country with outbound investment. This development has not only influenced the number of Chinese BITs, but also their content. This second generation of BITs[28] departed from the first generation BITs in that they incorporated broad dispute resolution clauses, providing for arbitration of all investor-state disputes under the treaty without any restrictions as to the subject matter of the dispute.

---

[24] Information provided by United Nation Conference on Trade and Development (UNCTAD), up to 1 June 2011, www.unctad.org/sections/dite_pcbb/docs/bits_china.pdf.

[25] For more detailed discussions, see Andreas F Lowenfeld, *International Economic Law* (Oxford, Oxford University Press, 2003) 474–84.

[26] For a discussion of the development of Chinese investment treaties, see generally Elodie Dulac, 'The Emerging Third Generation of Chinese Investment Treaties' (2010) 7 *Transnational Dispute Management* 4; Nils Eliasson, 'Investor-State Arbitration and Chinese Investors: Recent Developments in Light of the Decision on Jurisdiction in the Case Mr Tza Yap Shun v The Republic of Peru' (2009) 2 *Contemporary Asia Arbitration Journal* 2; Kong Gingjiang, 'Bilateral Investment Treaties: The Chinese Approach and Practice' (2003) 8 *Asian Yearbook of International Law* 105; Monika CE Heymann, 'International Law and the Settlement of Investment Disputes Relating To China' (2008) 11 *Journal of International Economic Law* 507; Kim M Rooney, 'ICSID and BIT Arbitrations and China' (2007) 24 *Journal of International Arbitration* 6; Stephan W Schill, 'Tearing Down the Great Wall: The New Generation Investment Treaties of the People's Republic of China' (2007) *Cardozo Journal of International and Comparative Law*.

[27] See, for instance, China–Sweden BIT (1982), China–France BIT (1984), China–Singapore BIT (1985), China–Kuwait BIT (1985), China–Sri Lanka BIT (1986) and China–New Zealand BIT (1988).

[28] See, for instance, China–Botswana BIT (2000), China–Netherlands BIT (2001), China–Germany BIT (2003), China–Finland BIT (2004), and China–Latvia BIT (2006).

16 *Chinese Legal Framework*

Since 2008 a third generation of Chinese BITs[29] has been emerging, which is characterised by provisions that are more balanced (in the sense that they are less geared towards outbound investment) and more detailed. Under the third generation regime, broad dispute resolution clauses are still favoured, but are subject to restrictive language in a number of respects ranging from the definition of 'investment' to substantive protections.

1.2.2 Private Sources

Arbitration institutions play a fundamental role in the Chinese context, more so than in other parts of the world. Ad hoc arbitration is not yet statutorily recognised in China.[30] Although the arbitration rules do not carry the force of law, they play an important part in guiding the practice of the respective arbitration institution.

The CIETAC is by far the most significant arbitral institution in China with a long and distinguished history starting in the early 1950s. The CIETAC was created under the auspices of the China Council for the Promotion of International Trade (CCPIT).[31] The CIETAC's arbitration rules were first adopted in 1956 under its formal name – Foreign Trade Arbitration Commission (FTAC). Since then, the CIETAC is constantly reviewing and revising its arbitration rules, in order to meet the increased competition for international arbitration from local arbitration institutions and to address some of the criticisms voiced by foreign practitioners. Various revisions were made in 1994, 1995, 1998, 2000, and 2005. The latest version of the CIETAC arbitration rules was revised and adopted by the China Council for the Promotion of International Trade/China Chamber of International Commerce on 3 February 2012, and became effective as of 1 May 2012 (CIETAC Rules 2012).

The CIETAC is facing increasing competition from local arbitration institutions. More than 200 different arbitration institutions have been registered in China[32] and each maintains its own institutional rules. The BAC, which was established in 1995 upon registration with the Beijing Judicial Department, is a major competitor of the CIETAC. The Arbitration Rules of the BAC were first adopted in 1995 and were revised in 1996, 1997, 1999, 2001, and 2004. The latest version of the BAC rules came into force in April 2008 (BAC Rules 2008) and seeks to reflect the trend of modern international arbitration practice.

---

[29] See, for instance, China–Mexico BIT (2008), China–Colombia BIT (2008), China–Mali BIT (2009), China–Malta BIT (2009), and China–Switzerland BIT (2009, renegotiated).

[30] The status of ad hoc arbitration in China will be further discussed in ch 2, s 2.2.2-B.a below.

[31] The history of the CIETAC will be discussed in ch 5, s 5.2.1-B below.

[32] The latest official statistics on the number of arbitration institutions were released during the National Arbitration Forum of 2010, held in Beijing from 21–22 April 2010. It was reported that there were 202 arbitration institutions all over China up to 2009.

1.3 HISTORICAL DEVELOPMENT OF ARBITRATION LEGISLATION IN CHINA

1.3.1 Prior to the Enactment of the Arbitration Law

Prior to the enactment of the Arbitration Law of 1995, domestic and foreign-related arbitration systems were entirely separate and distinct. Domestic arbitrations were administered by domestic arbitration bodies, which were affiliated with governmental administrative authorities. Foreign-related arbitrations, on the other hand, were dominated by the only two international arbitration commissions: the CIETAC and the China Maritime Arbitration institution (CMAC).

A. Domestic Arbitration

The domestic arbitration system has its origins in the early 1950s, when the government actively promoted arbitration and mediation as the preferred means for resolving domestic economic disputes. In the early 1960s, various regulations were promulgated that provided for mandatory arbitration of economic contract disputes.[33] The Economic Contract Law of the PRC of 1982 (Economic Contract Law)[34] provided the statutory foundation for the pre-1995 domestic arbitration regime. According to the Economic Contract Law, parties to a dispute arising from economic contracts should resolve it through consultation. If consultation was not successful, either party had the option to apply to the contract administration authorities specified by the state for mediation or arbitration or to file a suit in the people's court.[35] In the case of a decision made after arbitration, the contract administration authorities specified by the state would issue a written arbitration decision. If either party did not agree with the arbitration decision, either party was permitted to file a suit in the people's court within fifteen days from the date of receiving the written arbitration decision. If no suit was filed within that period, the arbitration decision would become legally effective.[36] In 1983, the State Council promulgated the Regulations on Economic Contract Arbitration of the PRC pursuant to the Economic Contract Law. These regulations provided that economic contract arbitration should be

---

[33] See, for instance, Working Rules for the State-Owned Industrial Enterprises (Draft), issued by the State Council in September 1961; the Opinions of the State Economic Commission Concerning the Arbitration of Disputes Arising from Defaulting on Loan Payments Among the State-Owned Industrial Enterprises by the Economic Commissions at Various Levels (Draft), adopted by the State Economic Commission on 13 August 1952; The Notice Concerning the Strict Implementation of Basic Construction Procedure and the Strict Implementation of Economic Contract, issued by the State Council on 10 December 1962.

[34] Adopted at the Fourth Session of the Fifth NPC and promulgated by Order No 12 of the Chairman of the Standing Committee of the NPC on 31 December 1981, and effective as of 1 July 1982.

[35] Art 48 of the Economic Contract Law.

[36] Art 49 of the Economic Contract of the PRC.

handled by dedicated economic contract arbitration institutions established by the State Administration of Industry and Commerce at both the state and local levels.[37]

Following the economic contract arbitration model, as new commercial transactions were defined by legislation in the early 1980s, similar rules and regulations were promulgated to resolve various disputes. The sources of those laws varied from the State Council, State Planning Commission, and State Economic Commission to highly specialised agencies such as those responsible for fishing, harbours, labour, and inspection of medical products. A number of different types of arbitration organisation existed, each affiliated with a government authority at various levels, and each specialising in the arbitration of disputes arising in a particular field.

The main features of China's domestic arbitration system prior to the promulgation of the Arbitration Law may be summarised as follows:

- **Lack of independence**: the domestic arbitral institutions were attached to the administrative organs of the government;
- **Lack of party autonomy**: domestic arbitration institutions accepted arbitration applications based on administrative law and regulations rather than the parties' voluntary arbitration agreement;
- **Arbitral award without binding force**: the arbitral awards were not final and could be appealed to the people's courts.[38]

B. Foreign-related Arbitration

The foreign-related arbitration regime has its roots in the Protocol for General Conditions of Delivery of Goods signed between China and the Soviet Union in April 1950, which provides that any dispute arising from a contract should be settled through arbitration. It further provides that where the respondent is a Soviet enterprise or organisation, arbitration would be conducted in the Soviet Union. On the other hand, if the respondent was a Chinese enterprise or organisation, arbitration would be undertaken in China. In order to implement such an undertaking, it was necessary to establish a dedicated arbitral body to deal with the international disputes, separate and distinct from those established domestic arbitral bodies which were administrative in nature.[39]

Against this background, on 6 May 1954, the PRC Government Administration Council (now the State Council) issued a decision[40] to establish the FTAC (now the CIETAC). The purpose of the FTAC was to facilitate arbitration of disputes

---

[37] Art 2 of the Regulations on Economic Contract Arbitration of the PRC.

[38] See Jingzhou Tao, *Arbitration Law and Practice in China*, 2nd edn (The Hague, Kluwer Law International, 2008) 4.

[39] See ibid.

[40] Decision of the Government Administration Council of the Central People's Government Concerning the Establishment of the Foreign Trade Arbitration Commission within CCPIT, issued on 6 May 1954.

that arose from contracts and transactions in foreign trade, particularly disputes between foreign firms, companies, or other economic organisations. The Decision clearly laid down the basic principles for foreign-related arbitration in China, including: (i) arbitration shall be based on the arbitration agreement between the parties; (ii) the parties have the freedom to choose the arbitrators; and (iii) the award rendered by the arbitration institution is final and the people's court shall enforce it at the request of the concerned party. Before the promulgation of the Arbitration Law, this Decision served as the first de facto arbitration regulation in China, and enabled China's international commercial arbitration practice to start harmonising with international practice during the beginning of the 1950s.

The real impetus for the development of foreign-related arbitration was the movement of reform and opening up in the late 1970s. In July 1979, the Sino-Foreign Equity Joint Venture Law was promulgated to provide foreign investors with a degree of certainty in the undertaking of commercial transactions in China.[41] This law provided for the resolution of disputes between parties to a joint venture (JV) through mediation or arbitration if consultation by the board failed.[42] Subsequently, the State Council promulgated the Regulation on the Implementation of the Sino-Foreign Equity Joint Venture Law in 1983,[43] which contains more detailed provisions with respect to dispute settlement. The Regulation provided that

> disputes arising over the interpretation or execution of the agreement, contract or articles of association between the parties to the JV shall, if possible, be settled through friendly consultation or mediation. Disputes that cannot be settled through these means may be settled through arbitration or courts.[44]

It further stipulated that

> parties to a JV shall apply for arbitration in accordance with the relevant written agreement. They may submit the dispute to the Foreign Economic and Trade Arbitration Commission of the CCPIT in accordance with its arbitration rules. With mutual consent of the parties concerned, arbitration can also be conducted before an arbitration institution in the country where the respondent party is located or through one in a third country in accordance with the arbitration institutions' rules.[45]

Similar provisions for the arbitration of disputes involving foreign elements were adopted in subsequent laws and regulations. For instance, the Foreign-related Economic Contract Law of the PRC of 1985 provided that parties may

---

[41] Adopted by the Second Session of the Standing Committee of the Fifth NPC on and effective as of 8 July 1979. It was subsequently revised on and effective from 15 March 2001.
[42] Art 14 of the Sino-Foreign Joint Venture Law.
[43] Issued by the State Council and became effective on 20 September 1983. It was revised on and effective from 22 July 2001.
[44] Art 109 of the Regulation on the Implementation of the Sino-Foreign Equity Joint Venture Law.
[45] Art 110 of the Regulation on the Implementation of the Sino-Foreign Equity Joint Venture Law.

20   *Chinese Legal Framework*

submit their dispute to a Chinese arbitration institution or any other arbitration institution for arbitration in accordance with the arbitration clause provided in the contract or a written arbitration agreement reached by the parties afterwards.[46]

In March 1982, the Civil Procedure Law (for Trial Implementation) was adopted by the Standing Committee of the NPC, which included a chapter specifically dealing with foreign-related arbitration. The Civil Procedure Law was finally adopted in April 1991, by the NPC, to replace the Civil Procedure Law (for Trial Implementation). Chapter 28 of the Civil Procedure Law 1991 contains dedicated provisions pertaining to foreign-related arbitration. It clarifies that the existence of an arbitration agreement excludes the jurisdiction of the courts. Article 257 of the Civil Procedure Law 1991 provides that

> in the case of a dispute arising from the foreign economic, trade, transport or maritime activities of China, if the parties have had an arbitration clause in the contract concerned or have subsequently reached a written arbitration agreement stipulating the submission of the dispute for arbitration to foreign-related arbitration institution, or to any other arbitral body, they may not bring an action in a People's Court. If the parties have not had an arbitration clause in the contract concerned or have not subsequently reached a written arbitration agreement, they may bring an action in a People's Court.

1.3.2 After the Implementation of the Arbitration Law

The Arbitration Law was adopted at the 9th Session of the Standing Committee of the eighth NPC of the PRC on 31 August 1994 and came into force on 1 September 1995. The Arbitration Law represents a historical milestone in the development of arbitration in China. The driving force behind the birth of the Arbitration Law was the desire to diminish administrative interference in the domestic arbitration system, and the attempt to create a new nationwide arbitration system in China.[47]

The Arbitration Law sets the basic principles for the development of arbitration. These principles lay the foundations for the development of arbitration in China in conformity with transnational standards:

- **Party autonomy** (*dang shi ren yi si zi zhi*): the parties' submission to arbitration shall be made 'on the basis of both parties' free will and an arbitration agreement reached between them';[48] the parties are free to agree to arbitration, to choose the arbitration institution,[49] and to appoint arbitrators;[50]

---

[46] Art 37 of the Foreign-related Economic Contract Law.
[47] See Daniel R Fung and Shengchang Wang (eds), *Arbitration in China: A Practical Guide*, vol 1 (Hong Kong, Sweet & Maxwell Asia, 2004) 14.
[48] Art 4 of the Arbitration Law.
[49] Art 6 of the Arbitration Law.
[50] Art 31 of the Arbitration Law.

- **Courts have no jurisdiction when there is a valid arbitration agreement** (*huo cai huo shen*): the people's court shall not accept the case if there is an arbitration agreement between the parties, unless the arbitration agreement is null and void.[51] Under this principle, where the parties have reached an arbitration agreement before or after the disputes arise, they are bound to submit the dispute to arbitration, and not to the people's court;
- **Independence of arbitration** (*du li zhong cai*): this principle refers to the independence of arbitration institutions, namely, arbitration institutions shall be independent from administrative organs; there shall be no subordinate relationships between the arbitration institutions and the administrative organs, or between the different arbitration institutions; and[52]
- **Arbitral awards are final** (*yi cai zhong ju*): the court or other arbitration institutions shall not accept a case where the arbitral award has been rendered.[53] This is in contrast with the old system of '*yi cai liang shen*', which allowed parties the right to appeal after the arbitral award was made.

As a significant step forward, the Arbitration Law also requires the reorganisation of former domestic arbitration bodies under administrative organs, and the establishment of a significant number of new arbitration institutions all over the country. These new arbitration institutions are to be 'independent of administrative bodies having no subordinate relationship with administrative authorities'.[54] The Notice of the General Office of the State Council of 1996 empowered domestic arbitration institutions to handle domestic arbitrations as well as foreign-related arbitrations that the parties submit to them by agreement.[55] On the other hand, in response to the competition from domestic arbitration institutions, the CIETAC Arbitration Rules of 2000 extended the CIETAC's jurisdiction to purely domestic disputes that parties submit to by agreement. In fact, domestic cases have become a substantial part of CIETAC's caseload. Therefore, it makes little sense today for arbitral institutions to be classified into domestic arbitration institutions or foreign-related arbitration institutions, as every Chinese arbitration institution can accept both domestic and foreign-related arbitration cases, subject only to the parties' agreement.

1.4 TYPES OF ARBITRATION IN CHINA

1.4.1 Classification of Arbitration in the Arbitration Law and Civil Procedure Law

Generally, there are three types of arbitration in China: 'domestic arbitration', 'foreign-related arbitration' and 'foreign arbitration'. Chapter VII of the

---
[51] Art 5 of the Arbitration Law.
[52] Art 14 of the Arbitration Law.
[53] Art 9 of the Arbitration Law.
[54] Art 14 of the Arbitration Law.
[55] Notice of State Council No 22, as of 6 June 1996.

22 Chinese Legal Framework

Arbitration Law specifically deals with foreign-related arbitration, with respect to the forms of organisations, the qualifications of arbitrators, the rules of arbitration, the courts involved to support or supervise, and the grounds for setting aside or refusing to enforce an arbitral award, which are distinct from the provisions pertaining to domestic arbitration. However, the distinction between the three types of arbitration is not unequivocally defined in the legislation.

There is no dispute that an arbitration taking place in China with all the elements within China is a 'domestic arbitration'.

An arbitration taking place in China with 'foreign element(s)' is generally considered a 'foreign-related arbitration'. A dispute involves a 'foreign element' if:

(i) either one or both of the parties is a person with a foreign nationality or a stateless person, or a company or organisation domiciled in a foreign country;
(ii) the legal facts that establish, change, or terminate the civil legal relationship between the parties take place in a foreign country; or
(iii) the subject matter of the dispute is situated in a foreign country.[56]

Nevertheless, the term used in Article 260 of the Civil Procedure Law 1991 is 'arbitral awards made by a foreign-related arbitration institution of the PRC', which is applicable for the setting aside and recognition and enforcement of 'foreign-related arbitration' by application of Articles 70 and 71 of the Arbitration Law. The revised Civil Procedure Law 2007[57] and Civil Procedure Law 2012[58] adopted the same terminology, although such distinction in terms of the authority of arbitration institutions has disappeared. The Arbitration Law did not attempt to reconcile the inconsistencies in the definition.

In respect of 'foreign arbitration', Chinese academics agree that it refers arbitration where the seat of arbitration is located in a foreign country.[59] However, the term used in the Civil Procedure Law is an award made by 'a foreign arbitration institution'.[60] Such inconsistent provisions have caused some confusion in judicial practice. The SPC has in the past characterised a 'foreign arbitration' as an arbitration administered by a foreign arbitration institution. In a Reply of the Fourth Civil Trial Division of the SPC on 5 July 2004, when examining whether the New York Convention or Arrangement of the SPC Concerning Reciprocal Enforcement of Arbitral Awards between the Mainland and Hong Kong Special Administrative Region (Arrangement),[61] was applicable to the rec-

---

[56] Art 304 of the SPC Opinions Concerning Implementation of the Civil Procedure Law of the PRC, *Fa Shi* (92) No 22, adopted by the Judicial Committee of the SPC on 14 July 1992.
[57] Art 258 of Civil Procedure Law 2007.
[58] Art 274 of Civil Procedure Law 2012.
[59] See Song Lu, 'National Report for China' in Jan Paulsson (ed), *International Handbook on Commercial Arbitration* (The Hague, Kluwer Law International, 2009) 7.
[60] Art 283 of the Civil Procedure Law 2012.
[61] Arrangement of the SPC Concerning Reciprocal Enforcement of Arbitral Awards between the Mainland and Hong Kong Special Administrative Region, issued by the SPC on 24 January 2000 and came into effect on 1 February 2000.

ognition and enforcement of an ICC award[62] where Hong Kong was the place of arbitration, the SPC held that:

> [s]ince the ICC Court is an arbitration institution established in France, both China and France are member states of [the New York Convention], we shall apply the provisions of this Convention for reviewing the recognition and enforcement of the award to this case. The Arrangement is not applicable . . .[63]

1.4.2 Lack of Recognition of the Concept of Legal Seat

The core issue in the ambiguous classification of different types of arbitration in China is the lack of recognition of the concept of the seat of arbitration in the legislation and judicial practice. The seat of arbitration or the place of arbitration is generally understood to be a legal connection, rather than a physical or geographical location.[64] The seat of arbitration bears the following legal consequences: (i) it may influence which law governs the arbitration; (ii) it has a bearing on the issue of which courts can exercise supervisory and supportive powers in relation to the arbitration; and (iii) it determines the nationality of the award which is relevant for the ultimate enforcement of the award.[65] Pursuant to Article 20(1) of the Model Law, the parties are free to select the seat of arbitration. The choice of the place or seat of arbitration is one of the key issues in drafting an arbitration agreement.

The New York Convention refers to the concept of 'the law of the country where the arbitration took place'[66] and, synonymously, to 'the law of the country where the award is made'.[67] Thus, the New York Convention makes a clear territorial link between the seat of arbitration and the law governing that arbitration, the *lex arbitri*.

The Model Law also attaches legal consequences to the seat of arbitration, which determines (i) the applicability of the Model Law,[68] and (ii) the place of origin of the award for enforcement purposes.[69] Article 31(3) of the Model Law provides that '[t]he award shall state its date and the place of arbitration as determined in accordance with article 20(1). The award shall be deemed to have

---

[62] Final Award No 10334/AMW/BWD/TE.
[63] *Shanxi Tianli Shiye Co, Ltd v Wei Mao International (Hong Kong) Co, Ltd*, [2004] Min Si Ta Zi No 6 (SPC, 5 July 2004), reproduced in Exiang Wan (ed), *Guide on Foreign-related Commercial and Maritime Trials*, People's Court Press, vol 9 (2004) 50–60.
[64] See generally Gabrielle Kaufmann-Kohler, 'Identifying and Applying the Law Governing the Arbitral Procedure – the Role of the Place of Arbitration' in Albert Jan van den Berg (ed), *ICCA Congress Series no 9* (The Hague, Kluwer Law International, 1999) 356–65.
[65] See Julian Lew, Loukas Mistelis and Stefan Kröll, *Comparative International Commercial Arbitration* (The Hague, Kluwer Law International, 2003) paras 8–24.
[66] Art V(1)(d) of the New York Convention.
[67] Art V(1)(a) and (e) of the New York Convention.
[68] Art 1(2) of the Model Law.
[69] Art 31(3) of the Model Law provides that the award shall state the place of arbitration and shall be deemed to have been made at that place.

been made at that place'. The effect of this provision is to emphasise that the final making of the award constitutes a legal act. In other words, the arbitral proceedings need not be carried out at the place designated as the legal seat of arbitration, and the making of the award may be completed through deliberations held at various places, by telephone or correspondence. In addition, the award does not have to be signed by the arbitrators physically gathering at the same place.[70]

In England, in *Peruana*,[71] Lord Justice Kerr of the Court of Appeal emphasises the distinction between the legal localisation of an arbitration on the one hand and the appropriate or convenient geographical locality for arbitration hearings on the other hand. The *Peruana* decision further states that the legal seat of arbitration remains the same even if the physical place changes from time to time, unless the parties agree to change it. Section 3 of the English Arbitration Act 1996 expressly states that the seat in the meaning of the Act is a legal, juridical connection.

The Swiss Supreme Court has also stressed the legal nature of the place or seat and its distinction from the physical hearing of arbitration:

> By choosing a Swiss legal domicile for the arbitral tribunal, the parties manifestly intended to submit their dispute to Swiss arbitration law, not to provide for an exclusive location for meetings among arbitrators at the place of arbitration . . . [T]he determination of a given place of arbitration is of significance to the extent that the award is deemed to be rendered at such place. It is irrelevant that a hearing was effectively held or that the award was effectively issued there.[72]

The legal nature of the seat of arbitration is also recognised in most major arbitration rules. These rules confirm the parties' freedom to choose the place of arbitration and the possibility of holding meetings and hearings elsewhere.[73]

In China, however, the concept of the seat of arbitration is neither defined in the Arbitration Law nor the Civil Procedure Law. Instead of referring to the 'seat of arbitration' when classifying the different categories of awards, the Civil Procedure Law distinguishes the different regimes for enforcement of awards based on the nature of arbitration institutions. These different regimes include, 'an arbitration institution established according to the (Chinese) law';[74] an award made by 'the foreign-related arbitration institution of the PRC';[75] and an

---

[70] Explanatory Note by the UNCITRAL Secretariat on the 1985 Model Law on International Commercial Arbitration as amended in 2006, para 40.

[71] *Naviera Amazonica Peruana SA v Compañia Internacional de Seguros del Peru* (1988) 1 Lloyd's Rep 116.

[72] *Bundesgericht, I Zivilabteilung, T AG v H Company* (Swiss Supreme Court, 24 March 1997), 15 ASA Bulletin 2 (1997) 329–30.

[73] For instance, Art 18 of the ICC Rules (2012); Art 16 of the London Court of International Arbitration Rules; Art 13 of the International Dispute Resolution Procedures Rules of the AAA (2009); Art 18 of the Singapore Arbitration Rules; Art 1(3) of the Rules of Arbitration and Conciliation of the International Arbitral Centre of the Federal Economic Chamber Vienna; Art 22 of the Rules of the Netherlands Arbitration Institute.

[74] Art 237 of the Civil Procedure Law 2012.

[75] Art 274 of the Civil Procedure Law 2012.

award made by 'a foreign arbitration institution'.[76] The lack of recognition of the concept of seat, and the ambiguous classification of awards in China, has caused much confusion in judicial practice. For instance, Chinese courts have encountered great difficulty in the recognition and enforcement of arbitral awards rendered by foreign arbitration institutions with the seat in China.[77]

The Law of the People's Republic of China on the Laws Applicable to Foreign-related Civil Relation (Conflict of Laws 2011)[78] makes reference to 'the seat of arbitration'. Unfortunately, it connects the law applicable to the arbitration agreement with either 'the place where the arbitration institution is located' or 'the seat of arbitration' in the absence of the parties' choice, which has caused further confusion.[79] One positive step is the definition of the seat of arbitration under the CIETAC Rules 2012, which distinguishes the concept of the seat of arbitration with the place of oral hearing[80] and provides that the arbitral award shall be deemed as being made at the place of arbitration.[81] It also recognises the parties' freedom to choose the place of arbitration.[82] Where the parties have not agreed on the seat of arbitration, the previous CIETAC Rules deem it to be the city where the CIETAC (or any of its sub-commissions) is located, namely a place inside mainland China. The 2012 Rules now allow CIETAC to decide that the seat shall be a city other than the location of the CIETAC, which could be a city outside mainland China.[83] However, this institutional rule, being contractual in nature, has not yet caused the legislation or attitude of the judiciary to change on this issue. In judicial practice, the location of the arbitration institution, rather than the seat of arbitration, is still considered to be relevant in determining the nationality of the arbitral award.[84]

1.4.3 Dual System in the Current Legal Regime

Despite the elimination of the historical classification of domestic and foreign-related arbitration based on the authority of arbitration institutions, a dual system is maintained for arbitration conducted in China based on the nature of the dispute. Foreign-related arbitration is less strictly controlled than domestic arbitration. The distinction between the two systems has

---

[76] Art 283 of the Civil Procedure Law 2012.
[77] See ch 2, s 2.2.2-C below.
[78] Adopted at the 17th Session of the Standing Committee of the 11th NPC on 28 October 2010, and effective from 1 April 2011.
[79] Art 18 provides that: 'the parties may by agreement choose the law applicable to their arbitration agreement. Absent any choice by the parties, the law of the place where the arbitration institution locates or the law of the seat of arbitration shall be applied'.
[80] Arts 7 and 34 of the CIETAC Rules 2012.
[81] Art 7(3) of the CIETAC Rules 2012.
[82] Art 7(1) of the CIETAC Rules 2012.
[83] Art 7(2) of the CIETAC Rules 2012.
[84] Exiang Wan, vice president of the SPC, speech at the 50th anniversary of the New York Convention in Beijing, 2008.

significant legal consequences, namely, (A) domestic arbitration may not be seated outside China; (B) Chinese substantive law applies in domestic arbitration; (C) domestic arbitration is subject to substantive review by the court; and (D) a report system applies only to foreign-related arbitration.[85]

A. Domestic Arbitration may not be Seated Outside China

Article 128 of the Contract Law explicitly allows the parties to a foreign-related contract to submit their dispute to Chinese arbitration institutions or to other (ie, non-Chinese) arbitration institutions. It is often interpreted as implying that a dispute of a domestic nature may only be submitted before a Chinese arbitration institution.

This provision creates doubts as to whether domestic arbitrations can be seated outside China. Although the CIETAC has opened the way for such arbitrations to be conducted outside China in its 2005 Arbitration Rules,[86] the SPC has indicated some restrictions in this respect in its Draft Provision Regarding the Handling By the People's Court of Cases Involving Foreign-related Arbitrations and Foreign Arbitrations dated 31 December 2004, in which it states that an arbitration agreement providing for domestic parties to conduct arbitration in a foreign country in relation to a dispute that does not contain a foreign element is unenforceable. It is therefore unlikely that a domestic dispute may be subject to arbitration abroad, even if the arbitration is administered by a Chinese arbitration institution such as the CIETAC. The SPC Interpretation 2006 has not provided any further clarification concerning the enforceability of domestic arbitrations conducted outside mainland China.

B. Chinese Substantive Law Applies in Domestic Arbitration

Article 126 of the Contract Law provides that parties to a foreign-related contract may choose the law to be applied to the settlement of the disputes arising from the contract, unless otherwise provided by mandatory Chinese law. This is commonly understood to mean that non-foreign-related arbitrations are always governed by Chinese law.

C. Domestic Arbitration is Subject to Substantive Review by the Courts

With respect to the judicial review of the awards, the people's courts' review of foreign-related awards is limited to procedural issues and public policy, whereas the review of domestic awards also encompasses substantive issues.[87] The courts

---

[85] See Clarisse von Wunschheim and Kun Fan, 'Arbitrating in China: The Rules of the Game. Practical Recommendations Concerning Arbitration in China' (2008) 26 *ASA Bulletin* 1, 39–41.
[86] Art 31(1) of the CIETAC Rules 2005 provides that 'where the parties have agreed on the place of arbitration in writing, the parties' agreement shall prevail'.
[87] See ch 4, s 4.2.1-A.a(i) and b(i) below.

may refuse to enforce a domestic award on the grounds that there is a definite error in the application of the law or there is insufficiency of evidence for ascertaining the facts.[88] Similarly, the courts may set aside a domestic award on the grounds that the award was based on forged evidence, or the other party withheld evidence sufficient to affect the impartiality of the arbitration.[89] These grounds do not apply to foreign-related arbitrations.

D. Report System Applies Only to Foreign-related Arbitration

The Report System demonstrates the SPC's effort to combat local protectionism and to boost the confidence of foreign investors. In 1992, Justice Ren Jianxin, the President of the SPC, advocated the formula of what he called 'five prohibitions' to battle against local protectionism.[90] These are as follows:

1. prohibiting local party cadres from interfering with judicial process in an attempt to protect local interests;
2. prohibiting government officials and other parties from making threats or launching campaigns against judicial personnel carrying out the execution of court orders;
3. prohibiting judicial organs from practising favouritism towards local parties by making unfair rulings or avoiding their proper responsibilities;
4. prohibiting officials of the public security and procuratorial organs from interfering with the adjudication of economic cases by treating contract and debt disputes as offences; and
5. prohibiting any organ or individual from obstructing the execution orders of the people's courts in any other way.

Justice Ren's 'five prohibitions' formula opposed local protectionism in all its manifestations. However, it is only a political declaration. To further improve the enforcement legal regime, in August 1995, the SPC issued a document entitled Notice of the Supreme Court Regarding the Handling by the People's Court of Certain Issues Relating to Foreign-related Arbitration and Foreign Arbitration,[91] which established a Report System. Under the Report System, where an IPC considers that a foreign-related award or a foreign award ought to be denied enforcement, it must report its finding to the HPC before issuing a decision. In turn, should the HPC concur with an IPC, it must submit an

---

[88] Art 63 of the Arbitration Law, and Art 217 of the Civil Procedural Law.
[89] Art 58 of the Arbitration Law.
[90] Ren Jianxin, a speech delivered at the National Conference on Politics and Law held in December 1999. Cited in Shengchang Wang, 'The Practical Application of Multilateral Conventions – Experience with Bilateral Treaties – Enforcement of Foreign Arbitral Awards in the People's Republic of China' in Albert Jan van den Berg (ed), *ICCA Congress Series no 9* (The Hague, Kluwer Law International, 1999) 474–75.
[91] Notice of the SPC on Several Issues Regarding the Handling by the People's Courts of Certain Issues Pertaining to Foreign-related Arbitration and Foreign Arbitration, issued by the SPC on and effective from 28 August 1995.

approval advice to the SPC. The lower courts may not refuse enforcement until the SPC issues a determination. The Report System also applies where the IPC considers that the arbitration agreement is invalid or incapable of being enforced. In other words, for foreign-related arbitrations, a lower court cannot deny the validity of an arbitration agreement without the prior examination and confirmation of the SPC. Subsequently, in April 1998, the SPC issued another notice establishing a Reporting System specifically applicable to any decision by lower courts to set aside a foreign-related award.[92] The Report System attempts to reduce the risk of decisions being invalidated because of local protectionism and lower court corruption. However, it only applies to foreign-related and foreign awards, and does not apply to domestic arbitrations. Foreign investors should be aware that Foreign Invested Enterprises (FIEs), including joint ventures and wholly foreign-owned enterprises, are considered to be Chinese entities established under Chinese law. Therefore, arbitration between Chinese subsidiaries of a French company and of a US company would be considered domestic, unless any other foreign elements are present. As a result, they cannot enjoy the more favourable treatment of foreign-related arbitration meant to protect foreign investors.

---

[92] Notice of the SPC on Relevant Issues Relating to the Setting Aside of International Awards by the People's Courts, issued by the SPC on and effective from 23 April 1998.

2

Arbitration Agreement

'The whole duty of government is to prevent crime and to preserve contracts'.

William Lamb, Lord Melbourne

TO EXAMINE THE laws of arbitration and court practice in China, we will follow the chronology of a typical arbitration. Thus, we will compare Chinese law and practice with transnational standards in terms of the arbitration agreement (chapter two), the arbitral tribunal (chapter three), and the enforcement of arbitral awards (chapter four).[1]

The arbitration agreement is the foundation of arbitration. There can be no arbitration between parties which have not agreed to arbitrate their disputes. The contractual nature of arbitration requires the consent of each party for an arbitration to happen. State courts derive their jurisdiction either from statutory provisions or from a jurisdiction agreement. In contrast, the arbitral tribunal's jurisdiction is based solely on an agreement between two or more parties to submit their existing or future disputes to arbitration.[2]

What are the transnational standards with respect to an arbitration agreement? What is the legal framework and practice in China? Is it consistent with transnational standards? The unique features of arbitration in China with respect to an arbitration agreement will be demonstrated in the following aspects: the principle of severability of the arbitration agreement (section 2.1); and the requirements for the validity of the arbitration agreement (section 2.2).

2.1 THE PRINCIPLE OF SEVERABILITY OF THE ARBITRATION AGREEMENT

One of the fundamental principles of international arbitration is the autonomy of an arbitration agreement.[3] According to this principle, the validity of the

---

[1] For the purpose of this study, the analysis is limited to selected issues, in light of the divergence between different jurisdictions, particularly where Chinese arbitration law maintains its own characteristics.

[2] See Lew, Mistelis and Kröll, *Comparative International Commercial Arbitration*, para 6-1.

[3] On the autonomy of the arbitration agreement, see Pierre Mayer, 'L'autonomie de l'arbitre international dans l'appréciation de sa propre compétence', *Collected Courses of the Hague*

arbitration agreement is independent from the validity of the main contract. This principle is generally referred to as the 'separability',[4] 'severability',[5] or 'autonomy'[6] of the arbitration agreement.

2.1.1 Transnational Standards

The principle of severability has now been widely recognised in national legal systems and is also expressly provided for under the Model Law.

In France, this principle has long been established. In the 1963 *Gosset* decision, the Cour de cassation held that:

> in international arbitration, the arbitration agreement, whether concluded separately or included in the contract to which it relates, shall, save in exceptional circumstances . . ., have full legal autonomy and shall not be affected by the fact that the aforementioned contract may be invalid.[7]

Subsequently, the principle has been consistently reaffirmed by the French courts,[8] but the courts have abandoned the reservation regarding 'exceptional circumstances', which had never been applied in practice.

In Switzerland, the severability of the arbitration agreement is also expressly set out in the Swiss PIL 1987, which provides that 'the validity of an arbitration agreement cannot be contested on the ground that the main contract may not be valid'.[9]

The most significant development in the principle of severability of the arbitration agreement came in 1985, with the adoption of the Model Law. Article 16(1) of the Model Law provides that

> an arbitration clause which forms part of a contract shall be treated as an agreement independent of the other terms of the contract. A decision by arbitral tribunal that the

---

Academy of International Law (1989), vol 217, part V; Gaillard and Savage, *Fouchard Gaillard Goldman on International Commercial Arbitration*, 198–214; Pierre Mayer, 'The Limits of Severability of the Arbitration Clause' in Albert Jan van den Berg (ed), *ICCA Congress Series no 9* (The Hague, Kluwer Law International, 1999) 261–67.

  [4] See Nigel Blackaby et al, *Redfern and Hunter on International Arbitration*, 5th edn (Oxford, Oxford University Press, 2009) 117–21.
  [5] Mayer, 'The Limits of Severability of the Arbitration Clause', 261–67.
  [6] See Gaillard and Savage, *Fouchard Gaillard Goldman on International Commercial Arbitration*, 198–217.
  [7] Cour de cassation, 1 civil chamber, 7 May 1963, *Gosset: Juris-Classeur périodique (La semaine juridique)* 1963 II 13405, and Bertold Goldman's note; *Journal du droit international (Clunet)* (1964) 82, and Jean-Denis Bredin's note; *Revue critique de droit international privé* (1963) 615, and Henry Motulsky's note; *Recueil Dalloz* (1963) 545, and Jean Robert's note.
  [8] See Cour de cassation, 1 civil chamber, 18 May 1971, *Impex* (first decision): *Journal du droit international (Clunet)* (1972) 62, and Bruno Oppetit's note; *Revue de l'arbitrage* (1972) 2, and Philippe Kahn's note; Cour de cassation, 1 civil chamber, 4 July 1972, *Hecht: Journal du droit international (Clunet)* (1972) 843, and Bruno Oppetit's note; *Revue critique de droit international privé* (1974) 89, and Patrice Level's note; *Revue de l'arbitrage* (1974) 89; Cour de cassation, 1 civil chamber, 14 December 1983, *Epoux Convert v Droga: Revue de l'arbitrage* (1984) 483, and Marie-Claire Rondeau-Rivier's note.
  [9] Art 178(3) of the Swiss PIL 1987.

contract is null and void shall not entail ipso jure the invalidity of the arbitration clause.

The wording was maintained in the amendments adopted in 2006. A number of jurisdictions have implemented arbitration legislation based on the Model Law. As a result, the principle of severability has become widely accepted.

In line with this trend, this principle was also acknowledged in England, despite its longstanding hostility to the rule. In *Harbour v Kansa*, the severability of an arbitration agreement was fully recognised.[10] Subsequently, this case law was codified in the English Arbitration Act 1996, which has expressly set forth the principle of severability:

> Unless otherwise agreed by the parties, an arbitration agreement which forms or was intended to form part of another agreement (whether or not in writing) shall not be regarded as invalid, non-existent or ineffective because that other agreement is invalid, or did not come into existence or has become ineffective, and it shall for that purpose be treated as a distinct agreement.[11]

Given the transnational recognition of the principle of severability, it can now be considered as 'a true transnational rule of international commercial arbitration'.[12]

2.1.2 Law and Practice in China

In China, the Arbitration Law recognises the principle of severability of the arbitration agreement. In practice, however, the core of the principle has not always been fully appreciated by the courts at all levels in different regions in China. Some courts interpreted the principle of severability with a limited scope (A). Some courts wrongly applied the principle as requiring the proof of a separate acceptance of the arbitration agreement in case of assignment of the main contract, and had wrongly denied the binding effect of the arbitration clause on the transferee (B).

A. Application of the Autonomy of the Arbitration Agreement with a Limited Scope

Prior to the promulgation of the Arbitration Law 1988, the Shanghai HPC held in *China National Technical v Swiss Industrial*[13] that as the contract was found to be void ab initio due to fraud, the arbitration clause was also void.

---

[10] *Harbour Assurance Co (UK) Ltd v Kansa General International Insurance Co Ltd* (1992), 1 *Lloyd's Rep* 81.
[11] Section 7 of the English Arbitration Act 1996.
[12] See Blessing, 'Globalization (and Harmonization?) of Arbitration', 83–84; Gaillard and Savage, *Fouchard Gaillard Goldman on International Commercial Arbitration* 12.
[13] *China National Technical v Swiss Industrial Resources Company Incorporated,* reproduced *in Selected Cases of the SPC* (1989) No 1, 26–27.

The Arbitration Law acknowledges the principle of severability by providing that '[t]he Arbitration Agreement shall exist independently [from the main contract]. The amendment, rescission, termination or invalidity of a contract shall not affect the validity of the arbitration agreement'.[14] However, the Arbitration Law does not expressly provide for the severability of the arbitration agreement in cases in which the contract has not taken effect or has not been concluded.

In practice, different courts took a different approach and some local courts applied the principle of severability with a limited scope. In an unreported case in 1991,[15] a Chinese company and a Hong Kong company executed an equity joint venture contract, which included an arbitration clause. According to the Sino-Foreign Equity Joint Venture Law of 1979, the contract required the approval of the relevant authorities to become valid. A dispute occurred between the two parties, however, before the contract had been submitted for government approval. The Chinese party submitted the dispute to the Huizhou IPC, and the Hong Kong company challenged the court's jurisdiction on the grounds of the existence of an arbitration clause in the contract. The Huizhou IPC ruled that the arbitration clause was invalid because the contract was not approved and had not yet come into force. This decision was overturned by the Guandong HPC, which ruled that notwithstanding the invalidity of the main contract, a written arbitration agreement existed and that the latter was not subject to the approval of an administrative authority. Thus, the court ruled that it had no jurisdiction over a dispute falling within the scope of the arbitration agreement.[16]

Conflicting judicial practices on the issue of severability were finally addressed by the SPC in *Jiangsu Light v Top-Capital & Prince Development*[17] in 1998. In that case, the Jiangsu HPC made reference to the earlier decision rendered by the Shanghai HPC in *China National Technical v Swiss Industrial*,[18] and denied the validity of an arbitration clause on the ground that the contract was invalid due to fraud. This decision was overturned by the SPC, which revoked the court's jurisdiction over the case on the basis of the separate and independent existence of a valid arbitration agreement. The SPC thus affirmed the severability of the arbitration clause from the main contract, even when the main contract did not take effect due to fraud.

Following the SPC's decision in *Jiangsu Light v Top-Capital & Prince Development*, the Beijing HPC issued the Opinion on Some Issues Regarding the Determination of an Application for Ascertaining the Validity of an Arbitration

---

[14] Art 19 of the Arbitration Law.

[15] *Chinese company v Hong Kong company*, [1991] Hui Zhong Fa Jing Shen No 22 (Huizhou IPC, 23 August 1991), cited in Xiaowen Guo, 'The Validity and Performance of Arbitration Agreements in China' (1994) 11 *Journal of International Arbitration* 1, 52.

[16] *Chinese company v Hong Kong company*, [1991] Yue Fa Jing Shang Zi No 222 (Huizhou HPC, 9 December 1991), cited in ibid.

[17] *Jiangsu Materials Group Light Industry and Weaving Co v (HK) Top-Capital Holdings Ltd & (Canada) Prince Development Ltd*, Jiangsu IPC (1998), reproduced in *Selected Cases of the SPC* (1998) vol 3, 109–10.

[18] See n 13 above.

Agreement and Motions to Revoke an Arbitration Award in 1999. According to this opinion, the validity of an arbitration clause would be confirmed even if it was contained in a contract executed under duress. The court emphasised the independence and severability of the arbitration agreement, and held that in the absence of evidence showing that the arbitration agreement *itself* was executed under duress, the arbitration agreement would be considered an authentic record of the parties' intention to arbitrate their disputes, and that the invalidity of an underlying principal contract would have no bearing on the validity of the arbitration agreement.[19] Subsequently, in *Beijing Lihang v Hong Kong Wenhang*,[20] the Beijing IPC affirmed the principle that the illegality of the main contract was not sufficient to invalidate the arbitration clause, in light of the severability principle.

The complete recognition of the severability of the arbitration agreement was reaffirmed in the SPC Interpretation 2006 as follows:

> Where a concluded contract *has not taken effect* or has been revoked, the provisions in the first paragraph of article 19 of the Arbitration Law shall apply in the determination of the arbitration agreement's validity. Where the parties reach an arbitration agreement at the time when they agree to contract, the validity of the arbitration agreement shall not be affected *by the contract that has not yet been concluded* (emphasis added).[21]

B. Misapplication of the Principle of Severability

The severability of an arbitration agreement is a legal concept, not a factual determination. Thus, it does not imply that the acceptance of an arbitration agreement must be separate from that of the main contract. The signature of a contract containing an arbitration clause constitutes acceptance of both the main contract and the arbitration agreement. However, it does not mean that the arbitration agreement cannot follow the main contract where the latter is assigned to a third party. The acceptance of the assignment of a contract containing an arbitration clause must lead to the conclusion, in the absence of a clear indication to the contrary, that the assignee has accepted the contract as a whole, including the dispute resolution provisions.[22]

Judges sometimes misunderstood this latter principle. In *Hong Kong Longhai v Wuhan Zhongyuan*,[23] the original JV contract was signed between Hong Kong Longhai and Wuhan Donghu Import and Export Company (Donghu). The original JV contract's arbitration clause provided for CIETAC arbitration.

---

[19] Issued by the Beijing HPC on and effective from 3 December 1999.
[20] *Beijing Lihang International Transportation Ltd v Hong Kong Wenhang International Ltd*, Beijing No 2 IPC (2001), unreported, cited in Kong Yuan, 'Recent Cases Relating to Arbitration in China' (2006) 2 *Asian International Arbitration Journal* 2, 183–84.
[21] Art 10 of the SPC Interpretation 2006.
[22] Gaillard and Savage, *Fouchard Gaillard Goldman on International Commercial Arbitration*, 427–29.
[23] *Hong Kong Longhai Company v Wuhan Zhongyuan Scientific Company*, Wuhan IPC (1998) No 0277.

Donghu assigned all its equities to Zhongyuan. Subsequently, Hong Kong Longhai and Wuhan Zhongyuan signed a new JV contract, in which Wuhan Zhongyuan agreed to take over all the rights and obligations of Donghu in the original JV contract. When a dispute arose out of the investment, Hong Kong Longhai applied to the CIETAC for arbitration in Beijing, while Wuhan Zhongyuan challenged the arbitral jurisdiction before the Wuhan IPC. The Wuhan IPC ruled that the arbitration clause was not binding upon Wuhan Zhongyuan on the basis that '[t]he arbitration clause has independent character so that the clause in the original contract has no legal force upon the new assignee'. Upon reporting to the higher court, the Hubei HPC replied that the arbitration agreement should survive the contract assignment and CIETAC jurisdiction was affirmed.[24] In this case, the Wuhan IPC wrongfully applied the principle of severability which led to the denial of arbitral jurisdiction. The principal of the severability of the arbitration agreement does not require proof that the parties had two distinct intentions, one regarding the main contract, and another regarding the arbitration agreement. Any other interpretation would create new obstacles to the validity of the arbitration agreement, despite the fact that the principle of severability was precisely intended to promote that validity. The above decision by the Wuhan IPC raises concerns with respect to the understanding of modern arbitration norms by lower courts, despite the general recognition of the principle under the Arbitration Law. Again, this case highlights the difference between the law as it is provided on 'paper' and its actual implementation in practice in China.

In light of the above confusion, the SPC clarified the issue in its SPC Interpretation 2006, which has provided useful guidance for courts at all levels in the application of the principle of severability:

> An arbitration agreement shall bind a transferee of any creditor rights and debts transferred whether in whole or in part, unless the parties agreed otherwise, or where the transferee clearly objected or was unaware of the existence of a separate arbitration agreement at the time of the transfer.[25]

2.2 THE SUBSTANTIVE REQUIREMENTS FOR THE VALIDITY OF THE ARBITRATION AGREEMENT

Despite its procedural effects, the arbitration agreement is primarily a substantive contract under which the parties agree to refer their disputes to arbitration instead of the state courts. This implies that for the agreement to come into existence, the requirements for the conclusion of a contract must be fulfilled. The parties must have agreed the extent of the referral to arbitration and there should be no factors present which might vitiate their consent under general

---

[24] *Hong Kong Longhai Company v Wuhan Zhongyuan Scientific Company*, [1999] E Fa Shen Jian Jing Zai Zi (Hubei HPC, 1999).
[25] Art 9 of the SPC Interpretation 2006.

contract law. Furthermore, the parties must have had the capacity to enter into an arbitration agreement. In this respect, the arbitration agreement is a contract like any other contract.[26] Apart from the ordinary requirements for the conclusion of a contract, are there any specific terms that have to be contained in the arbitration agreement to make it valid? What is the transnational standard on the validity of an arbitration agreement? Is the Chinese approach different from transnational standards?

2.2.1 Transnational Standards

The New York Convention is the starting point for determining the transnational requirements regarding the validity of an arbitration agreement. One objective of the New York Convention is to 'provide common legislative standards for the recognition of arbitration agreements'.[27] Article II(1) of the New York Convention lays down the positive requirements of a valid arbitration agreement. All Contracting States undertake to recognise and give effect to an arbitration agreement when the following requirements are fulfilled:

(i) the agreement is in writing;
(ii) it deals with existing or future disputes;
(iii) these disputes arise in respect of a defined legal relationship, whether contractual or not; and
(iv) they concern a subject matter capable of settlement by arbitration.

A similar approach is adopted in the Model Law. According to the Model Law definition, 'an arbitration agreement is an agreement by the parties to submit to arbitration all or certain disputes which have arisen or which may arise between them in respect of a defined legal relationship, whether contractual or not'.[28] This provision envisages the first three positive requirements of a valid arbitration agreement provided in the New York Convention. The fourth requirement is contained in Article 34(2)(b) and Article 36(2)(b)(i) of the Model Law.

As to the writing requirement, Article II(2) of the New York Convention states that 'the term "agreement in writing" shall include an arbitral clause in a contract or an arbitration agreement signed by the parties or contained in an exchange of letters or telegrams'. In light of the widening use of electronic communications and enactments of domestic legislation as well as case law, which are more favourable than the New York Convention in respect of the form requirement, the UNCITRAL adopted a Recommendation on 7 July 2006 which encourages states to apply Article II(2) of the New York Convention

---

[26] Lew, Mistelis and Kröll, *Comparative International Commercial Arbitration*, para 7-3.
[27] See Objectives of the New York Convention, available at www.uncitral.org/uncitral/en/uncitral_texts/arbitration/NYConvention.html.
[28] Art 7 of the Model Law.

36   *Arbitration Agreement*

'recognizing that the circumstances described therein are not exhaustive'.[29] In accordance with the pro-enforcement approach and the current international practices where contracts are executed through different means, 'there is a widespread trend to apply the "in writing" requirement under the Convention liberally'[30]. Courts generally follow a guiding principle that an arbitration agreement is valid where it can reasonably be asserted that the offer to arbitrate was accepted (*consensus ad idem*). There is no need for separate signature of the arbitration clause. Furthermore, an arbitration agreement contained in an exchange of letters, telegrams or similar communications is generally considered to meet the writing requirement. There is no requirement that the letters and telegrams are signed.[31]

Apart from the form of the writing requirement, there are no substantive requirements relating to the validity of an arbitration agreement under the New York Convention or the Model Law. According to the UNCITRAL Working Group Report in 1982:

> There was general agreement that the Model Law should not set forth grounds for the invalidity of an arbitration agreement, including grounds specially directed to arbitration agreements. It was noted that the formulation of an exhaustive list of clearly defined grounds was extremely difficult. Consequently, the question of validity should be left to the applicable law.[32]

On comparative law, national legislation rarely stipulates specific requirements that have to be contained in an arbitration agreement to be valid. In light of the principle of party autonomy, as far as the parties' consent for arbitration is established, where the disputes are capable of being submitted to arbitration, the arbitration agreement is generally held to be valid. Ambiguities in the arbitration agreement will not lead per se to the invalidity of the arbitration agreement. The validity of the arbitration agreement will be denied only if, based on the interpretation of the arbitration agreement, no consent to arbitration can be ascertained. To interpret the parties' consent to arbitration, the most widely accepted principles are (i) the principle of interpretation in good faith; and (ii) the principle of effective interpretation.

The principle of interpretation in good faith is aimed at detecting the true intention of the parties, based on an interpretation of their statements and attitude as they would reasonably have been understood by any third party. In other words, one should interpret the arbitration agreement by looking for the

---

[29] 2006 – Recommendation regarding the Interpretation of Art II(2) and Art VII(1) of the Convention on the Recognition and Enforcement of Foreign Arbitral Awards (New York, 1958), available at www.uncitral.org/uncitral/uncitral_texts/arbitration/2006recommendation.html.

[30] ICCA, *ICCA's Guide to the Interpretation of the 1958 New York Convention: A Handbook for Judges* (The Hague, International Council for Commercial Arbitration, 2011) 68.

[31] ibid.

[32] Report of the Working Group on International Contract Practices on the Work of its Third Session, UN Doc A/CN.9/216, para 25.

parties' common intention, rather than simply restricting oneself to examining the literal meaning of the terms used.[33]

The principle of effective interpretation means that, if in doubt, one should prefer the interpretation which gives meaning to the words. This principle is widely accepted by the courts and arbitrators to be a universally recognised rule of interpretation.[34] In most cases, the arbitrators or the courts, relying on the principle of effective interpretation, would prefer to salvage an arbitration clause by construing it as best they can to restore the true intent of the parties, rather than prevent the parties from having recourse to arbitration.[35]

2.2.2 Law and Practice in China

Chinese law sets out substantive requirements relating to the validity of an arbitration agreement which are different from transnational standards. Article 16 of the Arbitration Law provides as follows:

> An arbitration agreement shall include arbitration clauses stipulated in the contract and agreements of submission to arbitration that are concluded in other written forms before or after disputes arise. An arbitration agreement shall contain the following particulars:
>
> (i) the expression of the parties' intention to arbitrate;
> (ii) the matters to be submitted to arbitration; and
> (iii) a designated arbitration institution.

---

[33] See eg, Art 1134-3 of the French Civil Code and Art 133 of the German Civil Code. The principle of interpretation in good faith was applied by arbitrators, for instance in *Amco Asia Corp v Republic of Indonesia*, ICSID Case No ARB/81/1, 25 September 1983, 1 ICSID Report 389 (1993) which provides that 'any convention, including conventions to arbitrate, should be construed in good faith, that it to say by taking into account the consequences of their commitments to the parties may be considered as having reasonably and legitimately envisaged'. For a commentary on the principle of interpretation in good faith applicable to arbitration agreements, see eg, Gaillard and Savage, *Fouchard Gaillard Goldman on International Commercial Arbitration*, para 477; Pierre Mayer, 'Le principe de bonne foi devant les arbitres du commerce international' in *Etudes de droit international en l'honneur de Pierre Lalive* (Basel, Helbing & Lichtenhahn, 1993) 543–56.

[34] Gaillard and Savage, *Fouchard Gaillard Goldman on International Commercial Arbitration*, para 478, citing numerous arbitral awards and court decisions applying the principle of effective interpretation among them, eg, ICC Award No 1434 (1975), *Mutinational group A v State B*: 103 *Journal du droit international (Clunet)* 978, 979–90 (1976); ICC Award No 3380 (1980), *Italian enterprise v Syrian enterprise*: 108 *Journal du droit international (Clunet)* (1981) 917; ICC Award No 3460 (1980), *French company v Ministry of an Arab country*: 108 *Journal du droit international (Clunet)* (1981) 939; ICSID Case No ARB/72/1, *Holiday Inns SA v Government of Morocco* in Pierre Lalive, *The First World Bank Arbitration (Holiday Inns v Morocco) – Some Legal Problems*, 1 ICSID Reports 645 (1993); Paris Tribunal of First Instance, 31 January 1986, *Fillold CM v Jackson Enterprise*: Revue de l'arbitrage (1987) 179; Paris Court of Appeal, 22 March 1991, *Mavian v Mavian*: Revue de l'arbitrage (1992) 652; Paris Court of Appeal, 5 May 1989, *Dutco*: Revue de l'arbitrage (1989) 723.

[35] ibid. See also Zina Abdulla, 'The Arbitration Agreement' in Gabrielle Kaufmann-Kohler and Blaise Stucki (eds), *International Arbitration in Switzerland: A Handbook for Practitioners* (The Hague, Kluwer Law International, 2004) 18.

38 *Arbitration Agreement*

Article 18 of the Arbitration Law further provides that if the parties fail to designate an arbitration institution in the arbitration agreement, or if such designation is unclear, then the arbitration agreement will be considered invalid, unless the parties reach a supplementary agreement.

Reading Articles 16 and 18 of the Arbitration Law together, the designation of an arbitration institution constitutes a compulsory requirement for an arbitration agreement to be valid. This peculiar requirement under Chinese law leads to the following practical consequences: (A) the Chinese courts tend to adopt a strict interpretation of defective arbitration clauses; (B) such requirement excludes ad hoc arbitration in China; and (C) the legislation creates doubts as to the enforceability of awards rendered in China under the auspices of foreign arbitration institutions.

A. *Strict Interpretation of Defective Arbitration Clauses*

Pursuant to Articles 16 and 18 of the Arbitration Law, failure to designate an arbitration institution in the arbitration agreement, or if such designation is unclear, the arbitration agreement will be held invalid, unless the parties reach a supplementary agreement. What if the parties have designated an arbitration institution but wrongly spelt its name, or designated a non-existent arbitration institution, or designated two or more arbitration institutions? How should these defective clauses be interpreted?

While the principle of interpretation in good faith and the principle of effective interpretation are widely adopted by arbitrators and judges to interpret the validity of arbitration agreements,[36] these principles are not frequently invoked by the Chinese courts when interpreting the validity of arbitration agreements. The Contract Law does recognise the principle of good faith[37] and the principle of interpretation *contra stipulatorem* concerning standard clauses.[38] However, in arbitral practice, the Chinese courts rarely apply contract interpretation principles to interpret defective arbitration clauses. A strict interpretation of Articles 16 and 18 of the Arbitration Law means that an ambiguity in the arbitration agreement will usually lead to its invalidity, unless the parties remedy such ambiguity by a supplementary agreement. This attitude is in sharp contrast with international practice, where the courts and arbitral tribunals seek to restore the parties' true intent to arbitration despite ambiguities and poor drafting.

Furthermore, there are no general guidelines as to how to interpret arbitration agreements in China. When local or intermediate courts are requested to rule on the validity of the arbitration agreement, each court will often address the issue in its own way, which leads to different and sometimes contradictory decisions across the country. In order to deal with the issue of inconsistent inter-

---

[36] See s 2.2.1 above.
[37] Art 125 of the Contract Law.
[38] Art 41 of the Contract Law.

pretations, the SPC and a few HPCs[39] have recently issued a number of guidelines on the interpretation of Articles 16 and 18 of the Arbitration Law.

For instance, the SPC Interpretation 2006 contains the following rules which deal with the interpretation of the arbitration agreement when there are some defects in the designation of an arbitration institution, specifically:

> Where the name of the arbitration institution agreed in the arbitration agreement is not accurate, but the specific arbitration institution can nevertheless be determined, that arbitration institution shall be deemed designated;[40]
>
> Where the arbitration agreement only agrees upon the applicable arbitration rules, it shall be deemed that no arbitration institution has been agreed upon, except where the parties concerned have reached a supplementary agreement, or where the arbitration institution can be determined according to the arbitration rules that have been agreed on;[41]
>
> Where more than two arbitration institutions have been agreed upon in the arbitration agreement, the parties may choose by agreement to apply to one of the specified arbitration institutions for arbitration; if the parties fail to reach an agreement on the arbitration institution, the arbitration agreement shall be deemed invalid;[42]
>
> Where the arbitration agreement specifies that the arbitration shall be handled by the arbitration institution at a certain place, and there is only one arbitration institution at that place, that arbitration institution shall be deemed designated. Where there are two or more arbitration institutions at that place, the parties may choose by agreement one of these arbitration institutions; and where they fail to reach an agreement on the arbitration institution, the arbitration agreement shall be deemed invalid;[43]
>
> Where the parties agree that they may submit their dispute to an arbitration institution or to the People's Court to resolve their disputes, the arbitration agreement shall be deemed invalid, except where one party applies for arbitration at the arbitration institution and the other party fails to raise any objection within the period specified in article 20(2) of the Arbitration Law.[44]

The Beijing HPC's Opinion on Several Issues on the Determination of the Validity of Arbitration Agreements or the Application for Setting Aside Arbitral Awards issued in 1999 (Beijing HPC Opinion 1999)[45] deals with, inter alia, the interpretation of arbitration agreements where the parties designate two or more arbitration institutions:

---

[39] Although there is no clear legal basis for HPCs to issue guidelines on the application of law, these guidelines have a certain authority over lower courts within their jurisdiction insofar as they do not contradict the laws and judicial interpretations of the SPC. This is because decentralisation in the course of economic reforms has fuelled local judicial efforts to develop their own practice in implementing the national rules according to their own needs.

[40] Art 3 of the SPC Interpretation 2006.
[41] Art 4 of the SPC Interpretation 2006.
[42] Art 5 of the SPC Interpretation 2006.
[43] Art 6 of the SPC Interpretation 2006.
[44] Art 7 of the SPC Interpretation 2006.
[45] Beijing HPC's Opinion on Several Issues on the Determination of the Validity of Arbitration Agreements or the Application for Setting Aside Arbitral Awards, promulgated on and effective from 3 December 1999, available at www.chinalawinfo.com.

40 *Arbitration Agreement*

Where parties have expressly and clearly designated two or more arbitration institutions, such an arbitration agreement is enforceable and the parties may choose one of these arbitration institutions.[46]

The Shanghai HPC's Opinion on the Implementation of the Arbitration Law issued in 2001 (Shanghai HPC Opinion 2001) provides some general guidance on the interpretation of the validity of arbitration agreements:

> Courts should not deny the validity of the arbitration agreement simply because the arbitration institution is not clearly designated. If the expression does not lead to logistical or logical confusion and the arbitration institution can be ascertained linguistically and logically, the courts should confirm the validity of the arbitration agreement.[47]

The Shanghai HPC Opinion 2001 further provides a list of expressions in which the arbitration institution can be ascertained: expressions such as 'arbitration commission in Shanghai', 'arbitration commission within the Shanghai government', and 'arbitration with relevant departments under the Shanghai municipality' shall be interpreted as designating the Shanghai Arbitration Commission; expressions such as 'Shanghai Branch of the China International Economic and Trade Arbitration Commission', 'Shanghai International Economic and Trade Arbitration Commission', and 'Shanghai Foreign-Related Economic Arbitration Commission' shall be interpreted as designating the Shanghai sub-branch of the CIETAC.[48]

The above judicial guidelines demonstrate a positive development in the interpretation of arbitration agreements in China. Nevertheless, they only cover a couple of specific circumstances when the ambiguities in the arbitration agreement can be bridged by interpretation. Some general principles on the interpretation of arbitration agreements need to be recognised, so that the parties' intention to arbitrate will not be easily denied due to poor drafting.

B. Exclusion of Ad Hoc Arbitration

Ad hoc arbitration is a form of arbitration which is conducted pursuant to rules agreed by the parties or laid down by the arbitral tribunal. Where parties have not selected an arbitration institution, the arbitration will be ad hoc.[49] Arbitration has been conducted on an ad hoc basis around the world for centuries.[50] Today, it is still an important alternative to institutional arbitration which offers the parties the maximum degree of flexibility to agree and specify the arbitration procedure as they wish. However, ad hoc arbitration cannot derogate from mandatory law

---

[46] Art 8 of the Beijing HPC's Opinion 1999.
[47] Shanghai HPC's Opinion on the Implementation of Arbitration Law of PRC, promulgated and effective from 1 February 2001, available at www.chinalawinfo.com.
[48] Art 2 of the Shanghai HPC Opinion 2001.
[49] Martin Hunter et al, *Redfern and Hunter on International Arbitration* (Oxford, Oxford University Press, 2009) 52–53.
[50] Lew, Mistelis and Kröll, *Comparative International Commercial Arbitration*, 18.

in the seat of arbitration. Such mandatory law includes, inter alia, how the arbitrators are to be appointed, how many arbitrators there should be, the procedure to be followed, the arrangements for the presentation of evidence and how the arbitration should be pleaded.[51] Both the Model Law and the New York Convention recognise ad hoc arbitration as one form of arbitration. Article 2 of the Model Law defines arbitration as 'any arbitration whether or not administered by a permanent arbitral institution'. Similarly, pursuant to Article I(2) of the New York Convention, arbitral awards shall include not only institutional awards but also ad hoc awards. Most jurisdictions recognise ad hoc arbitration and do not require the designation of an arbitral institution in an arbitration agreement. There is no reliable data on the total number of ad hoc arbitrations that take place around the world every year. We know, at least, that many of the well-known arbitrations under the oil concession agreements were conducted ad hoc.[52]

In China, however, arbitration is conducted predominately by arbitration institutions. Ad hoc arbitration is not recognised under Chinese law. Pursuant to Articles 16 and 18 of the Arbitration Law, failure to designate an arbitration institution causes the arbitration agreement to be invalid. Although these provisions do not expressly prohibit ad hoc arbitration, they are generally construed as a legislative rebuttal to any assumptions regarding the legality of ad hoc arbitration in China.[53]

Despite the absence of a legal basis, ad hoc arbitration is actually practised in China. If the parties perform the award voluntarily, the matter will not become public. Therefore, most of these practices are not reported.[54] A three-member tribunal in Shenzhen reportedly conducted the first ad hoc arbitration in China in December 1985. This arbitration matter dealt with an agreement in which Party B was required to secure the application of a licence for the export of silk for Party A with a certain commission fee. The parties agreed to appoint the Shenzhen Economic and Trade Law Firm (SETLF) to 'supervise' the performance of the contract and to 'arbitrate' in the case of any disputes arising concerning the performance of the contract. Both parties contributed a certain amount of deposit to the account of the SETLF as performance guarantee. In 1985, disputes arose as to the performance of the contract and the parties requested arbitration in accordance with their agreement. The tribunal was constituted of three lawyers from the SETLF, with Xu Jian as the presiding arbitrator and two other lawyers as co-arbitrators. On 25 December 1985, after a hearing of two hours, and a deliberation of half an hour, the three-member tribunal decided that Party A had breached the contract and should pay Party B damages of 400,000 yuan and interest. The decision was announced orally to

---

[51] ibid.
[52] See Hunter et al, *Redfern and Hunter on International Arbitration*, 53.
[53] Tao, *Arbitration Law and Practice in China*, 69.
[54] During the interviews conducted in the research trip in 2007, some arbitration experts confirmed to the author the existence of ad hoc arbitration in practice according to their personal knowledge.

the parties by the presiding arbitrator. The tribunal's decision was immediately enforced, as the performance deposit had already been paid into the SETLF's account. The parties to the dispute did not challenge the decision. However, a related third party subsequently attempted to set aside the decision before the Shenzhen IPC, which refused to accept the case. The third party then filed a complaint with the Shenzhen Ministry of Justice, accusing the SETLF of 'setting up [a] private courtroom' or 'setting up [an] *ad hoc* arbitral tribunal'. In 1988, the Bureau of Justice in Guangdong Province in its investigation report instructed the law firm not to arbitrate economic disputes in the future.[55]

The most cited ad hoc arbitration was conducted by Hu Zhengliang, a professor at Dalian Maritime University. In this case, the parties had entered into a charter agreement which contained an arbitration clause providing that 'all disputes arising out of the contract shall be arbitrated in Beijing'. The arbitration clause did not specify an arbitration institution. When a dispute arose, both parties agreed for the dispute to be arbitrated by Hu Zhengliang. Within two months of knowing of this appointment, Hu Zhengliang drafted a decision based on the parties' submissions and an expert report provided by an expert specialising in navigation technology. Due to the absence of a legal basis for ad hoc arbitration in China, Hu Zhengliang delivered to the parties his decision by way of a document entitled 'An Opinion on Mediation'. Despite the use of the term 'mediation', it is clear from the parties' intention, the way the proceeding was conducted, and the manner in which the decision was rendered that it was an ad hoc arbitration, rather than a mediation. The parties voluntarily complied with the arbitral decision. However, failing voluntary compliance, there is a risk that an ad hoc award rendered in China may be unenforceable in the Chinese courts.[56]

a. Enforcement of Foreign Ad Hoc Awards in China

Will an ad hoc award rendered outside China be enforced by the Chinese courts? Being a member state to the New York Convention, Chinese courts are under an obligation to recognise and enforce ad hoc awards rendered in other states. Xiao Yang, former Chief Justice of the SPC, has addressed this issue as follows:

> The current arbitration law only provided for administered arbitration and did not provide for *ad hoc* arbitrations or special arbitrations. . . . However, for the purpose of fully respecting the intention of the parties and encouraging the development of arbitration system[s] to create a good environment for investment, China's courts would also recognise the validity of arbitration agreements involving foreign parties which

---

[55] Reported in 张国栋, 我是'中国民间第 一 裁'但他们说我'私设公堂',《南方都市报》2008年6月15日 (Guodong Zhang, 'I Made the First Ad Hoc Decision in China, But They Accused Me of Setting Up Private Courtrooms', *Southern Metropolitan Journal*, 15 June 2008).

[56] See, for instance, 康明,《商事仲裁服务研究》, 法律出版社2005年版, 第213页 (Ming Kang, *Research on Commercial Arbitration Service* (Beijing, Legal Press, 2005) 213); 沈四宝 (主编),《国际商法论丛》第5 卷, 法律出版社 2003 年版, 第508 页 (Sibao Shen (ed), *Series on International Commercial Law*, vol 5 (Beijing, Legal Press, 2003) 508).

provide for *ad hoc* arbitration on a case by case basis *in the event that the laws of the country where the ad hoc arbitration was conducted recognised ad hoc arbitration* (emphasis added).[57]

In judicial practice, Chinese courts generally recognise the validity of an ad hoc arbitration clause if the seat of arbitration is in a foreign country, consistent with their commitment under the New York Convention. For instance, in *Fujian Production v Jingge Hangyun*,[58] the SPC confirmed the validity of an arbitration clause providing for ad hoc arbitration in a foreign country. In *Guangzhou Ocean v Marships of Connecticut*,[59] the Guangzhou Maritime Court enforced an ad hoc award rendered in London.

Another issue often raised is whether ad hoc awards rendered in Hong Kong, Macao or Taiwan will be enforced in mainland China. In Hong Kong, for instance, ad hoc arbitration is permitted, and indeed widely practised. Therefore, in accordance with the Arrangement,[60] ad hoc awards rendered in Hong Kong would be enforced in mainland China in the same manner as under the New York Convention. Not surprisingly, parties wishing to select ad hoc arbitration are often advised to designate the seat of arbitration outside mainland China (ie, in Hong Kong). However, this designation must be specific: in the context of 'One Country, Two Systems', a choice of law or choice of forum clause referring to China is generally interpreted to refer to mainland China only, and does not include Hong Kong. In *Guanghope Power v Guangdong Insurer*,[61] the arbitration clause provided for ad hoc arbitration in the PRC, governed by the laws of the PRC. The Guangdong Insurer challenged the validity of the ad hoc arbitration clause on the grounds that the reference to the PRC included Hong Kong where ad hoc arbitration was recognised. The SPC rejected this argument, and ruled:

> When the term PRC is used to indicate the legal forum or choice of law, it is normally understood to mean mainland China and does not, in the absence of any special stipulation, include laws of Hong Kong, Macao, or Taiwan.
>
> In analyzing the applicable law to determine the validity of the arbitration clause, the SPC ruled that it was the common intent of the parties that the law applicable to the substantive contract was the law of PRC, and that the arbitration be conducted in the PRC.

---

[57] 高菲，"中国法院对仲裁的支持和监督 – 访最高人民法院院长肖扬"，《仲裁与法律》, 2001年合订本 (Fei Gao, *The Chinese Courts' Support and Supervision to Arbitration – An Interview with the President of SPC Xiao Yang*, Arbitration and Law, 2001 collected).

[58] *Fujian Production Material Co v Jingge Hangyun Co Ltd*, [1995] Fa Han No 135 (SPC 1995), cited *in* 宋连斌：《国际商事仲裁管辖权研究》，法律出版社2000年版，第96页 (Lianbin Song, *Research on the Jurisdiction of International Commercial Arbitration* (Beijing, Legal Press, 2002) 96).

[59] *Guangzhou Ocean Shipping Co Ltd v Marships of Connecticut* (Guangzhou Maritime Court, 1992), reported in *Selected Cases of the SPC* (1992) vol 1, 163–67.

[60] See, ch 1, s1.4.1, n 61 above.

[61] *Guangdong Guanghope Power Co Ltd v The People's Insurance Company of China, Guangdong Branch*, [2002] Min Si Zhong Zi No 29 (SPC, 31 October 2002), cited in Paul Donovan Reynolds and Song Yue, The PRC Supreme People's Court on the Validity of an Arbitration Clause, 70 *Arbitration* 2 (2004) 142–50.

Applying Chinese law, the SPC denied the validity of this ad hoc arbitration clause for failure to designate an arbitration institution.[62]

This decision reaffirmed that an agreement for arbitration in the mainland must designate an arbitration institution, and there is no room for allowing ad hoc arbitration in mainland China under the current legal regime.

b. Legal Obstacles to the Recognition of Ad Hoc Arbitration in China

Apart from the legal constraints, the real difficulty in recognising ad hoc arbitration in China lies in the collective mindset, rooted from the Chinese people's trust in institutions instead of individuals. According to some legal experts that the author interviewed during the above-mentioned research trip in China,[63] the legislative reluctance to recognise ad hoc arbitration in China is due to the concern that if arbitration is allowed to be conducted without the supervision of any established administrative bodies, it would be difficult to control the behaviour of arbitrators and to ensure the quality of arbitration. Moreover, the government would have no access to information regarding most ad hoc arbitrations unless a party initiated court proceedings. In some circumstances, the arbitration institution may even play a role in protecting the safety of arbitrators (one interviewee referred to instances where the parties threatened the arbitrators). Accordingly, they believe that introducing ad hoc arbitration is still premature at this stage, when a system of 'trust' is not yet fully developed in China. This reflects the legislative spirit that arbitration institutions have semi-judicial power. People trust institutions, and are doubtful about individual power.

Given these concerns, it may take quite a while before ad hoc arbitration is introduced in China. The absence of ad hoc arbitration severely restricts party autonomy because parties are subjected to institutional administration or control. Further, the unitary institutional arbitration system in China may make the arbitration institutions excessively bureaucratic and insufficiently transparent.[64]

C. Unclear Status of Foreign Arbitration Institutions[65]

Articles 16 and 18 of the Arbitration Law also create an unclear status for foreign arbitration institutions. Some commentators suggest that Articles 16 and 18 of the Arbitration Law amount to a de facto 'Great Wall' preventing foreign arbitration institutions from operating in China because of the protectionist and restrictive way these provisions are interpreted and handled by different

---

[62] ibid.
[63] Introduction, fn 18.
[64] See ch 5 below.
[65] A discussion on the unclear status of foreign arbitration institutions administrating arbitration in China was originally published in Kun Fan, 'Prospects of Foreign Arbitration Institutions Administering Arbitration in China' (2011) 28 *Journal of International Arbitration* 4, 343–53.

people's courts.[66] Although nothing in the law indicates that such an arbitration institution may not be foreign, under the current legal regime, there are practical difficulties and legal obstacles in the recognition and enforcement of an award rendered in an arbitration having its seat in China but handled under the auspices of a foreign arbitration institution. The people's courts' inconsistent decisions on this matter have created further uncertainties.

a. Practical Difficulties

The strict requirement of designation of an arbitration institution under the Arbitration Law may give rise to two potential issues with respect to the foreign arbitration institutions (eg, the ICC Court) conducting arbitration in China.

(i) Whether a Clause Selecting the ICC Rules without Specifying the ICC Court as the Arbitral Institution is Valid

The first issue relates to the wording of arbitration clauses, specifically whether a clause which selects the ICC Arbitration Rules (ICC Rules), without actually specifying that the ICC Court will administer the case, is valid. The standard arbitration clause recommended by the ICC to all parties wishing to obtain recourse to ICC arbitration is as follows: 'all disputes arising out of or in connection with the present contract shall be finally settled under the Rules of Arbitration of the International Chamber of Commerce by one or more arbitrators appointed in accordance with the said Rules'. This clause, as is the case for many of the model clauses of international arbitral institutions, does not contain a specific reference to the arbitral institution, and therefore, may risk not meeting the requirement of Article 16 of the Arbitration Law. Such clause may be declared null and void by Chinese courts.

To avert this risk, in January 2005, the ICC made the following specific suggestions with respect to ICC arbitration in China:

> It would be prudent for parties wishing to have an ICC arbitration in mainland China to include in their arbitration clause an explicit reference to the ICC Court of Arbitration, so as to avoid the risk of having the standard ICC clause declared null and void for lack of a sufficiently explicit reference to the arbitration institution of their choice.[67]

To this end, the Chinese version of the ICC Model Clause was amended as follows:

> All disputes arising out of or in connection with the present contract *shall be submitted to the International Court of Arbitration of the International Chamber of Commerce* and shall be finally settled under the Rules of Arbitration of the International Chamber

---

[66] Jingzhou Tao and Clarisse von Wunschheim, 'Articles 16 and 18 of the PRC Arbitration Law: The Great Wall of China for Foreign Arbitration Institutions' (2007) 23 *Arbitration International* 2, 309.

[67] See ICC website at www.iccwbo.org/court/arbitration/id4090/index.html.

of Commerce by one or more arbitrators appointed in accordance with the said Rules (emphasis added).

This issue was later clarified in the SPC Interpretation 2006 which provides that the lack of an express stipulation of an arbitration institution does not automatically invalidate an arbitration clause if the arbitration institution can be *ascertained* pursuant to the rules.[68] In this regard, the ICC Rules contains ample references to the administration of arbitrations by the ICC Court. The Preface of the ICC Rules 1998 clearly sets out that '[t]he rules contained in this booklet are for use *only* in proceedings administered by the ICC International Court of Arbitration. No other institution can administer an arbitration under the ICC Rules (emphasis added)'. The new ICC Rules, which came into effect on 1 January 2012, also provide that 'the [ICC] Court is *the only body authorized* to administer arbitrations under the Rules, including the scrutiny and approval of awards rendered in accordance with the Rules (emphasis added)'. Accordingly, by selecting ICC Rules, it is sufficient to ascertain that the ICC Court is chosen by the parties as the arbitration institution. This difficulty is thus moot now in light of the SPC clarifications.

(ii) Whether the Designation of the ICC Court as the Arbitration Institution Satisfies the Requirement of Article 16 of the Arbitration Law

A more problematic issue is whether a foreign arbitration institution such as the ICC qualifies as a 'designated arbitration institution' within the meaning of Article 16 of the Arbitration Law. With respect to arbitration institutions, Article 10 of the Arbitration Law provides:

> Arbitration institutions may be established in municipalities directly under the central government and in municipalities that are the seats of the People's Governments of provinces and autonomous regions. They may also be established in other municipalities with districts, according to need. Arbitration institutions shall not be established at each level of the administrative divisions. . . . The establishment of an arbitration institution shall be registered with the administrative department of justice of the relevant province, autonomous region or municipality directly under the central government.

A restrictive interpretation is to read Article 16 together with Article 10 of the Arbitration Law. In this sense, foreign arbitration institutions would not appear to qualify as 'arbitration institutions' within the definition of Article 10 of the Arbitration Law.[69] Accordingly, some consider that Article 16 should be interpreted as requiring the designation of a Chinese arbitration institution.

A more liberal view is that Article 10 of the Arbitration Law does not purport to set out the definition of the term 'arbitration institution' as it is used in Article 16 and other provisions of the Arbitration Law. It has been stated the

---

[68] Art 4 of the SPC Interpretation 2006.
[69] See Friven Yeoh and Fu Yu, 'The People's Courts and Arbitration – A Snapshot of Recent Judicial Attitudes on Arbitrability and Enforcement' (2007) 24 *Journal of International Arbitration* 6, 647.

requirement in Article 16 of the Arbitration Law for the specification of an 'arbitration institution' is only meant to prohibit ad hoc arbitrations, but not arbitrations administered by foreign arbitration institutions. In this context, a few PRC officials have made remarks regarding foreign-administered arbitrations in China. In November 2003, Judge Zhang Fuqi of the SPC indicated that China's accession to the WTO had opened the arbitration services industry to Contracting States; thus, he concluded that foreign arbitration institutions were no longer restricted by Chinese law from conducting arbitrations in the PRC.[70] In May 2004, at the International Council of Commercial Arbitration (ICCA) conference in Beijing, Dr Wang Shengchang, former Secretary General of the CIETAC, also addressed the question of whether foreign arbitration institutions may fix China as the seat of arbitration, and concluded that the terminology 'arbitration institution' in Article 16 of the Arbitration Law should be 'interpreted broadly to include any arbitration institution'.[71] It certainly appears to be a more sensible interpretation that a 'designated arbitration institution' should include any permanent arbitration institution, whether Chinese or foreign. However, the SPC has not given any express clarifications on this matter. The controversies in the interpretations of the above provisions have caused great concerns in practice when a foreign arbitration institution is chosen with the seat of arbitration in mainland China.

b. Inconsistent Court Decisions

In the absence of any guidance from the SPC, awards rendered by arbitral tribunals constituted in accordance with the ICC Rules with the seat of arbitration in China may run the risk of non-enforcement in China. A study of case law illustrates that Chinese courts have taken divergent views on this matter.

In a case between a Chinese party and a Swiss party in 1995,[72] the arbitration clause provided that 'any disputes arising from or in connection with the present contract shall be finally settled in accordance with the ICC Rules of Conciliation and Arbitration. The seat of arbitration should be London'. The Haikou IPC held that the arbitration clause was invalid under Chinese law because, firstly, the parties had failed to nominate an arbitration body to administer the arbitration and, secondly, the ICC Rules were not necessarily solely utilised by the ICC International Court of Arbitration. Consequently, the arbitration clause was considered 'ambiguous' and pursuant to Article 18 of the Arbitration Law, an ambiguous arbitration clause is deemed invalid.

---

[70] Cited in David Livdahl and Xiaodan Qin, *ICC Arbitration Administered in China*, Asian Dispute Resolution (2006) 50.

[71] Shengchang Wang, speech held at the 17th ICCA Conference, Beijing (May 2004), cited in David Wagoner, *A Breath of Fresh Air in Chinese Dispute Resolution*, 24 *ASA Bulletin* 1 (2006) 29.

[72] *Chinese party v Swiss party* (Haikou IPC, 1995), unreported, cited in Shengchang Wang, 'The Practical Application of Multilateral Conventions Experience with Bilateral Treaties Enforcement of Foreign Arbitral Awards in the People's Republic of China' in Albert Jan van den Berg (ed), *ICCA Congress Series no 9* (The Hague, Kluwer Law International, 1999) 483–84.

On the contrary, in *Taiwan Fuyuan v Xiamen Weiguo Wood*,[73] the Xiamen IPC held that an arbitration clause which provided that 'dispute: amicably settled through negotiation or as per arbitration by the International Chamber of Commerce' was valid. In its reasoning, the Court held that since the ICC Court was the sole arbitration body to implement the ICC Rules, the parties had, through their arbitration clause, expressed their intention to have an arbitration administered by the ICC Court under the ICC Rules.

The most 'famous' case is the SPC's ruling in *Züblin*.[74] In this case, the SPC addressed the issue regarding the validity of an arbitration clause which provided that 'arbitration: ICC Rules, Shanghai shall apply'. On 8 July 2004, the SPC held the clause to be invalid on the grounds that it failed to designate an arbitration institution in accordance with Article 16 of the Arbitration Law.[75] The SPC's above ruling casts further doubt on the admissibility of ICC and other foreign arbitration institutions administering arbitration in China. The SPC based its ruling on the grounds that the clause, as a matter of interpretation, did not properly specify an arbitral institution in accordance with the Arbitration Law. Nevertheless, the SPC did not expressly hold that a foreign arbitration institution could not administer cases with the seat of arbitration in China.

The *Züblin* decision was distinguished in *Xiamen Xiangyu v Swiss Mechel*[76] in late 2004. The Xiamen IPC ruled that an arbitration clause providing that '[a]ll disputes would be finally settled under the Rules of Arbitration of the ICC by one or more arbitrators to be appointed in accordance with the said rules (...). Seat of arbitration shall be Beijing, China' was valid under Chinese law. In reaching this conclusion, the Xiamen IPC reasoned:

1. It could be inferred from the arbitration clause, without further input or explanation by the parties, that the only arbitration institution to have jurisdiction over the case is the ICC;
2. According to widely accepted international arbitration theory and to the prevailing theory in China, if the parties agree that the rules of a certain arbitration institution shall govern a proceeding, and if the parties do not name another institution, then the institution whose rules govern should have jurisdiction over the case; and
3. The intention of the parties was to submit the dispute to the ICC International Court of Arbitration.[77]

---

[73] *Taiwan Fuyuan Enterprise Company v Xiamen Weiguo Wood Manufacturing Company* (Xiamen IPC, 1997), reproduced in *Selected Cases of the SPC* (1997) vol 2.

[74] *Züblin International GmbH v Wuxi Woco-Tongyong Rubber Engineering Co Ltd* [2003] Min Si Ta Zi No 23 (SPC, 8 July 2004), reproduced in Exiang Wan (ed), *Guide on Foreign-related Commercial and Maritime Trials*, People's Court Press, vol 9 (2004) 36–40.

[75] For discussions on the enforcement of an arbitral award based on such arbitration clause, see ch 4, s 4.2.3-B.a below.

[76] *China Xiamen Xiangyu Co, Ltd v Swiss Mechel Trading AG* [2004] Xia Min Ren Zi 81 (Xiamen IPC, 2004), unreported; case summary is available in Chinese at www.hznet.gov.cn/hzac/alfx/al8.htm.

[77] ibid.

In 2009, in the case of *Xiaxin Electronics*,[78] the SPC denied the validity of an arbitration clause which selected ICC Rules with the seat of arbitration alternating between Xiamen and Brussels. The SPC reasoned as follows:

> In the present case, although the arbitration clause has stipulated that the arbitration shall be under the Rules of International Chamber of Commerce, the arbitration commission is still not expressly stipulated. The International Chamber of Commerce recommends that in cases where the arbitration place agreed upon by the parties is mainland China, all parties wishing to make reference to ICC arbitration shall use and cite the clause of the ICC International Court of Arbitration in their contracts. However, the parties in the present case did not use such standard clause. Since the arbitration institution cannot be determined according to the Rules of the International Chamber of Commerce and the parties did not reach a supplementary agreement to specify the arbitration institution, therefore, according to Article 4 of [the SPC Interpretation 2006] the arbitration institution is not expressly designated by the parties in the arbitration clause in the present case. According to Article 18 of the Arbitration Law, the arbitration clause in the present case is invalid.[79]

In contrast to the SPC's above decision, the Ningbo IPC recognised and enforced an ICC award seated in Beijing in the decision of *Duferco* rendered in 2009.[80] In that case, the arbitration clause provided that

> [a]ll disputes in connection with this Contract or the execution thereof shall be settled by friendly negotiation. If no settlement can be reached, the case in dispute shall then be submitted to the Arbitration of the International Chamber of Commerce in China, in accordance with the United Nations Convention on the International Sales of Goods . . .

In the ruling of 22 April 2009, the Ningbo IPC dismissed the challenge to the validity of the arbitration agreement on the ground that it was not made in a timely manner according to Article 13 of the SPC Interpretation 2006.[81] On the issue of enforcement, the Court ruled that the ICC award made in China should be considered as a 'non-domestic award' under Article I of the New York Convention. Accordingly, the Ningbo IPC decided to recognise and enforce the award because no grounds for refusing to enforce an award set forth in the New York Convention existed. Such a decision reflects a positive trend in opening up the market of arbitration in China to foreign arbitration institutions. However,

---

[78] *Xiaxin Electronics Co, Ltd v Société de Production Belge AG*, [2009] Min Min Di Zi No 7 (SPC, 2009). The decision of the SPC was expressly referred to by the Hong Kong Court of First Instance *in Klöckner Pentaplast GmbH & Co KG v Advance Technology (HK) Co Ltd*, [2011] 4 HKLRD 262. It was held in that case that PRC law invalidates arbitration agreements that fail to designate an arbitration institution to administer the arbitration.

[79] ibid.

[80] *Duferco SA v Ningbo Arts and Crafts Imp and Exp Co*, [2008] Yong Zhong Jian Zi No 4 (Ningbo IPC, 22 April 2009).

[81] Art 13 of the SPC Interpretation 2006 provides that where a party has not objected to the validity of an arbitration agreement before the first hearings, but the party subsequently applies to the people's court to determine the invalidity of the arbitration agreement, the people's court shall not accept the application.

50 *Arbitration Agreement*

this ruling only reflects the view of that particular court, and it is not clear at this stage whether other IPCs will take the same view in enforcing ICC awards rendered in China.[82]

c. Legal Obstacles

A closer look reveals the legal obstacles to the administration of arbitration in China by foreign arbitration institution including: (i) the lack of recognition of the concept of 'seat of arbitration' in the legislation and judicial practice; and (ii) the Chinese government's policy decision to protect local arbitration institutions.

(i) Lack of Recognition of the Concept of Seat

The lack of understanding about the seat of arbitration raises difficulties for the enforcement of an award rendered by a foreign arbitration institution in China. As discussed earlier, under the Arbitration Law, awards rendered in China are either domestic awards or foreign-related awards, depending on whether or not there is a foreign element present.[83] The fact that the award is rendered by a foreign arbitration institution is not a foreign element. Following the classification of the Arbitration Law, an ICC award rendered in China seems to fall into the category of domestic arbitration, unless (i) one or both of the parties is a foreign national or a stateless person, or a company or organisation domiciled in a foreign country; (ii) the legal facts establishing, changing or terminating the civil law relationship between the parties occur in a foreign country; or (iii) the subject of the dispute is situated in a foreign country.

This is, however, inconsistent with the provisions of the Civil Procedure Law. Awards rendered by foreign arbitration institutions fall into the third category defined in Article 283 of the Civil Procedure Law 2012, regardless of the seat of arbitration. Thus, an ICC award rendered in China is subject to provisions concerning the recognition and enforcement of 'awards rendered by foreign arbitration institutions' under the Civil Procedure Law, which provides:

> If an award made by a foreign arbitration institution needs the recognition and enforcement of a people's court of the PRC, the party shall directly apply to the intermediate people's court located in the place where the party subject to the enforcement has its domicile or where its property is located. The people's court shall deal with the matter according to *the relevant provisions of the international treaties concluded or acceded to by the PRC* or *on the principle of reciprocity* (emphasis added).

On 2 December 1986, China acceded to the New York Convention, which governs: (i) arbitral awards made in the territory of a state other than the state where the recognition and enforcement of such awards are sought; and (ii) arbitral

---

[82] According to the Report System, a lower court's decision to enforce a foreign award is not required to report this to the SPC.
[83] See ch 1, s 1.3.1 above.

awards not considered domestic in the state where their recognition and enforcement are sought. China's accession to the New York Convention is subject to the 'reciprocity' reservation, which means that the Convention will only be applicable to those awards which are made 'within the territory of another contracting state'. Accordingly, for the enforcement of an ICC award rendered in China, the New York Convention is not applicable. Due to the lack of consistencies in the classification of the awards, the Ningbo IPC in the *Duferco* case considered the ICC award rendered in China as a 'non-domestic award' and applied the New York Convention to enforce it.[84] However, the court has not attempted to reconcile such definition with China's reciprocity reservation.

(ii) Policy Consideration

Apart from the legal obstacles in the defects of legislation, a deeper reason is the Chinese government's policy dilemma between protecting Chinese arbitration institutions on the one hand, and attracting foreign investment on the other. Opening the door to foreign arbitration institutions will certainly increase competition for local arbitration institutions, but the nature of competition will be a strong incentive for Chinese arbitration to become more efficient.

In practice, while ICC arbitration is taking place all over the world, the place of arbitration was designated in mainland China in ICC proceedings only 16 times from 1992 to 2010. During these proceedings, the parties chose the seat of arbitration by agreement.[85] In light of the uncertainties regarding the enforcement of an ICC award rendered in mainland China before Chinese courts, the ICC Court is reluctant to fix the seat of arbitration in mainland China in the absence of the parties' express agreement. As Robert Briner, former Chairman of the ICC Court, pointed out, 'a narrow and restrictive interpretation of relevant provisions of the Arbitration Law would essentially run contrary to China's own interest'.[86] For parties wishing to choose ICC-administered arbitration, they would presently have no other safe choice than to fix the seat of arbitration outside mainland China, which will cause unnecessary inconvenience and increase the costs of arbitration. This clearly cannot be in the interest of the development of arbitration in China.

There is a growing need for the ICC Court and other foreign arbitration institutions to administer arbitration in China. When the Arbitration Law and the Civil Procedure Law were drafted in the 1990s, arbitrations were conducted predominately by Chinese arbitration institutions and the drafters of the law had not predicted the possibility of foreign arbitration institutions administering arbitration in China. Unfortunately, the Civil Procedure Law revised in 2007

---

[84] See n 80 above.
[85] See ICC Statistical Reports from 1992 to 2010, published in the *ICC Bulletin*.
[86] Robert Briner, speech held at the 17th ICCA Conference, Beijing, May 2004. See Robert Briner, 'Arbitration in China seen from the Viewpoint of the International Court of Arbitration of the International Chamber of Commerce' in Albert Jan van den Berg (ed), *ICCA Congress Series no 12* (The Hague, Kluwer Law International, 2005) 25.

and 2012 failed to take into account the recent developments. As the legal regime currently stands, whether arbitral awards rendered in China administered by the ICC Court or other foreign arbitration institutions can be enforced in China remains unclear. The lack of clarification in the legislation has caused inconsistencies in judicial decisions. Further clarifications in the law and judicial interpretations regarding the status of foreign arbitration institutions in China are urged, in order to remove the remaining doubts and to promote China as an attractive seat of arbitration in the international community.

3

Arbitral Tribunal

'Arbitration is as good as arbitrators'.[1]
Proverb in the arbitration community

'THE ARBITRATOR IS the *sine qua non* of the arbitral process. The process cannot rise above the quality of the arbitrator'.[2] The arbitrator plays a key role in every arbitration. In this chapter, we will discuss the role of arbitrators in arbitration proceedings from two aspects: first, the source of arbitrators' power – arbitral jurisdiction (section 3.1), and second, how arbitrators are selected – the constitution of the arbitral tribunal (section 3.2).

3.1 ARBITRAL JURISDICTION

The jurisdiction of the tribunal is fundamental to the authority and decision making power of the arbitrators. Awards rendered without jurisdiction have no legitimacy. Given the contractual nature of arbitration, '[t]he granting of jurisdictional power is carried out by mere private parties: the actual contractors'.[3] The arbitration agreement – a contract in which the parties submit their existing or future disputes to arbitrators and not to the courts – provides the basis for the jurisdiction of the arbitral tribunal.[4] The effect of conferring jurisdiction on the arbitral tribunal to hear all disputes covered by the arbitration agreement is sometimes referred to as a 'positive effect of [an] arbitration agreement'.[5] The question often encountered in practice is, when a party challenges the jurisdiction of the arbitral tribunal by arguing that it is not bound by the arbitration agreement, who should determine such a challenge. Is the issue of arbitral jurisdiction to be determined

---

[1] This phrase has been so widely cited that it has become a proverb in the arbitration community. For a list of references, see Clay, *L'arbitre*, 11, fn 3.
[2] Arthur von Mehren, 'Concluding Remarks' (1995) Special Supp, The Status of the Arbitrator, ICC Bulletin 126, 129.
[3] Henri Motulsky, *Ecrits, Etudes et notes sur l'arbitrage*, vol II (Paris, Dalloz, 1974) 239.
[4] Ch 2 above.
[5] Another positive effect of the arbitration agreement, as argued by Fouchard Gaillard Goldman, is to oblige the parties to honour their contractual commitment to submit disputes covered by an arbitration agreement to arbitration. See Gaillard and Savage, *Fouchard Gaillard Goldman on International Commercial Arbitration*, 393–401.

by the arbitrators themselves, by an arbitral institution, or by a court of competent jurisdiction? We will examine transnational standards (section 3.1.1) and Chinese practice (section 3.1.2) regarding this issue.

3.1.1 Transnational Standards

A. The Principle of Competence-competence

It is generally accepted that an arbitral tribunal has the power to rule on its own jurisdiction, which is known as 'the principle of competence-competence'.[6] This enables the arbitral tribunal to continue with the proceedings even where the existence or validity of the arbitration agreement is challenged. This principle is expressly recognised in Article 16 of the Model Law, which provides that 'the arbitral tribunal may rule on its own jurisdiction, including any objections with respect to the existence or validity of the arbitration agreement'. Article 1465 of the French Code of Civil Procedure provides that 'the arbitral tribunal is exclusively competent to rule on the challenges concerning its jurisdiction'.[7] Similarly, Article 186 of the Swiss PIL 1987, Article 8(1) of the Swiss Concordat, and Section 30 of the English Arbitration Act 1996 all recognise the principle of competence-competence. The principle of competence-competence is now recognised by the main international conventions on arbitration, by all modern arbitration laws, and by the majority of institutional arbitration rules. As a result, 'challenging the existence or validity of the arbitration agreement will not prevent the arbitral tribunal from proceeding with the arbitration, ruling on its own jurisdiction and, if it retains jurisdiction, making an award on the substance of the dispute'.[8]

B. The Court's Review of the Arbitral Tribunal's Jurisdictional Decision

While allowing the arbitrators to rule on their own jurisdiction by virtue of the competence-competence principle, most national laws recognise that arbitrators are not the sole judges of their jurisdiction: any decision given by an arbitral tribunal as to its jurisdiction is subject to review by the courts. Comparative law differs as to when that court review should take place. Courts may be asked at both the pre-award and post-award stages to deal with questions relating to the jurisdiction of the arbitration tribunal. In some jurisdictions, court review of the arbitral tribunal's jurisdiction is postponed until *after* the award is made

---

[6] See ibid. Hunter et al, *Redfern and Hunter on International Arbitration*, 347–49. Lew, Mistelis and Kröll, *Comparative International Commercial Arbitration*, para 14-12.

[7] Translation by the author. Art 1465 of the French Code of Civil Procedure provides that 'Le tribunal arbitral est seul compétent pour statuer sur les contestations relatives à son pouvoir juridictionnel'.

[8] Gaillard and Savage, *Fouchard Gaillard Goldman on International Commercial Arbitration*, 406.

– known as the 'negative effect of competence-competence';[9] in other jurisdictions, a reluctant respondent can challenge the arbitral tribunal's jurisdiction in the court *before* any award has been issued – known as 'concurrent control', under which a national court is involved in the question of jurisdiction before the tribunal has issued a final award on the merits.[10]

As a valid arbitration agreement is the basis for the arbitrators' jurisdiction, the contentious issue of the negative effect of the competence-competence principle is related to the court's review of the existence and validity of the arbitration agreement.[11] The court may be asked to examine the validity of an arbitration agreement either at the stage of upholding the arbitration agreement under Article II(3) of the New York Convention, or at the stage of enforcing the award or setting aside the award. Article II(3) of the New York Convention provides:

> [t]he court of a contracting State, when seized of an action in a matter in respect of which the parties have made an agreement within the meaning of this article shall, at the request of one of the parties, refer the parties to arbitration, unless it finds that the said agreement is null, void, inoperative or incapable of being performed.

A court applying Article II(3) of the New York Convention may determine, in order to refer the parties to arbitration, whether the arbitration agreement is 'null and void, inoperative or incapable of being performed'. However, no indication is provided as to the standard that should be applied for such determination.

One way to interpret Article II(3) of the New York Convention is to limit the court's review to a prima facie determination that the agreement is not 'null and void, inoperative or incapable of being performed' and give the priority to the arbitrators. This approach is a direct application of the 'negative effect of competence-competence', which means

> the arbitrators must be the first (as opposed to the sole) judges of their own jurisdiction and that the courts' control is postponed to the stage of any action to enforce or to set aside the arbitral award rendered on the basis of the arbitration agreement.[12]

Following this approach, a court that is confronted with the question of whether an arbitration agreement is valid 'must refrain from hearing substantive arguments as to the arbitrators' jurisdiction until such time as the arbitrators themselves have had an opportunity to do so'.[13] Jurisdictions that have recognised the

---

[9] See Emmanuel Gaillard and Yas Banifatemi, 'Negative Effect of Competence-Competence: The Rule of Priority in Favor of the Arbitrators' in Emmanuel Gaillard and Domenico Di Pietro (eds), *Enforcement of Arbitration Agreements and International Arbitral Awards: The New York Convention in Practice* (London, Cameron May, 2009).
[10] Hunter et al, *Redfern and Hunter on International Arbitration*, para 5.113.
[11] Strictly speaking, there is a distinction between the issue of arbitration jurisdiction and the validity of arbitration agreement. A valid arbitration agreement is a necessary but not sufficient condition for the establishment of arbitral jurisdiction.
[12] Gaillard and Banifatemi, 'Negative Effect of Competence-Competence: The Rule of Priority in Favor of the Arbitrators', 259.
[13] ibid.

negative effects of competence-competence include France,[14] Switzerland,[15] Hong Kong,[16] and Canada.[17]

While the position described above appears desirable in light of the object and purpose of the New York Convention, no explicit provision within the Convention prevents courts from making a full review of the arbitration agreement and issuing a final and binding judgment on its validity at an early stage of the dispute.[18] Another approach is to allow a court which has been asked to rule on the merits of the case to review the existence and validity of such agreement fully without waiting for a decision from the arbitrators on those issues.[19] This approach was followed in England prior to 1996. The English Arbitration Act 1996 substantially narrowed this particular option for challenging jurisdiction. Under that Act, the courts may only rule on the issue of jurisdiction with the permission of the other party (or parties) and the arbitral tribunal. In the latter case, the court must also find that (i) its decision is liable to save substantial cost, (ii) the application was made promptly, and (iii) there is a valid reason for the claim to be heard by a court.[20]

Despite the differences in terms of the timing of court reviews, the fact that the tribunal's decision on its jurisdiction may be overruled subsequently by a competent court does not prevent the tribunal from making the decision in the first place.[21] Arbitral tribunals are generally allowed to continue with the arbitral proceeding and even render an award while the jurisdictional challenge is pending before the court. For example, Article 8(2) and Article 16(3) of the Model Law allow the arbitral tribunal to continue the arbitration proceedings and render an award while the jurisdictional issue is pending before the court.

3.1.2 Chinese Practice

On the issue of arbitral jurisdiction, the Chinese approach deviates substantially from transnational standards. The principle of competence-competence is notably absent from arbitration legislation in China. The power to decide on

---

[14] Paris Court of Appeal, 9 March 1972, *Lefrère v SA Les Pétroles Pursan*: Revue trimestrielle de droit commercial 1972, p 344; Paris Court of Appeal, 7 December 1994, *V2000 v Renault*: Revue de l'arbitrage 245 (1996), and Charles Jarrosson's note; Revue trimestrielle de droit commercial 401 (1995), and Jean-Claude Dubarry and Eric Loquin's note; affirmed by Cour de cassation, 1 civil chamber, 21 May 1997: Revue de l'arbitrage 537 (1997), and Emmanuel Gaillard's note.

[15] Federal Tribunal, 29 April 1996, *Fondation M v Banque X*, Swiss: ASA Bulletin 527 (1996).

[16] *Pacific International Lines (pte) Ltd v Tsinlien Metals and Minerals Co Ltd* (Hong Kong Supreme Court, 30 July 1993) XVIII Yearbook Commercial Arbitration 180 (1993).

[17] *Rio Algom Ltd v Sammi Steel Corp Ltd*, Ontario Court of Justice, 1 March 1991, XYIII Yearbook Commercial Arbitration 16 (1993).

[18] ICCA's Guide (2011) 40.

[19] Gaillard and Savage, *Fouchard Gaillard Goldman on International Commercial Arbitration*, para 675.

[20] S 32 of the English Arbitration Act 1996.

[21] Hunter et al, *Redfern and Hunter on International Arbitration*, 346.

jurisdiction does not lie within the arbitral tribunals but with the courts and the arbitration institutions, according to Article 20 of the Arbitration Law:

> If a party challenges the validity of the arbitration agreement, it may request the arbitration institution to make a decision or the People's Court to give a ruling. If one party request the arbitration institution to make a decision and the other party applies to the people's court for a ruling, the people's court shall give a ruling.[22]

The Chinese approach is peculiar compared to transnational standards in two ways: on the one hand, arbitration institutions supersede an individual arbitral tribunal to rule on the tribunal's jurisdiction; and on the other hand, the court prevails over the arbitration institution in determining arbitral jurisdiction.[23] We shall now examine these issues in turn.

A. Arbitration Institution v Arbitral Tribunal

Given the contractual nature of arbitration, the arbitral tribunal is the only authority entrusted and empowered by the parties' agreement to decide the disputes between them. In institutional arbitration, the role of the arbitration institution is essentially administrative, assisting the parties and the arbitral tribunals to organise their arbitration proceedings. The existence of an arbitration institution should not affect the arbitral tribunal's power to rule on its own jurisdiction. The ICC Court, for example, only makes a prima facie determination as to whether an arbitration agreement *may* exist. The arbitral tribunal decides whether the arbitration agreement is valid and whether the objection against arbitral jurisdiction is justified.[24]

In contrast, pursuant to the Arbitration Law, the arbitration institution, not the arbitral tribunal, is authorised to rule on the arbitrators' jurisdiction. Clearly, the fact that arbitrators are ousted from making a final decision on their jurisdiction is contrary to the competence-competence principle. Arbitration institutions, as administrative bodies, have no legal basis to make the decision on jurisdictional challenges. This improper enlargement of the power of the institution provided under the Arbitration Law is contrary to the contractual nature of arbitration, and restricts the principle of party autonomy. Unfortunately, no subsequent legislation or judicial interpretations have addressed this issue to introduce the competence-competence principle.

Given China's unitary institutional arbitration system,[25] institutional practice plays a very important part in the promotion of arbitration in China. The CIETAC, as a leading arbitration institution in China, has been endeavouring to develop the tribunal's jurisdictional autonomy in China through a series of institutional reforms.

---

[22] Art 20 of the Arbitration Law.
[23] For a discussion, see Kun Fan, 'Arbitration in China: Practice, Legal Obstacles and Reforms' (2008) 19 *ICC Bulletin* 2, 27–29.
[24] See Arts 6(4) and 6(5) of the ICC Rules 2012.
[25] See ch 2, s 2.2.2-B above.

58   *Arbitral Tribunal*

The first step of the CIETAC's reform was to make informal adaptations to its internal practice. Generally, if the jurisdictional objection is easy to decide, the CIETAC will make a ruling directly without consulting the arbitral tribunal. If the jurisdictional objection raises more complex issues, such as (i) where the jurisdictional objection is raised before an arbitral tribunal is constituted, the CIETAC issues a preliminary ruling on jurisdiction based on a prima facie assessment – this is similar to the ICC's practice; (ii) where the jurisdictional objection is raised after the arbitral tribunal is constituted, the CIETAC will consult with the tribunal before it renders a preliminary ruling. In either of the two circumstances, should the arbitral tribunal find that it has no jurisdiction after a substantive hearing, it will express its opinions on the jurisdictional issue to the CIETAC, which will confirm, revise or reverse the preliminary ruling, and render a new jurisdictional decision.[26] According to the CIETAC arbitrators, such approach generally works well in practice, because the CIETAC will generally respect the tribunal's opinions.[27] However, what if the arbitral tribunal and the arbitration institution have conflicting views on the jurisdictional issue? For instance, if the CIETAC decides that the tribunal has jurisdiction, but the tribunal is of the opposite view, then the only solution for the arbitrators would be to resign. This is certainly not a satisfactory solution.

As a second step, the CIETAC officially endorsed this internal practice of joint rulings on arbitral jurisdiction in its Rules of 2005, and such practice is maintained in its amended Rules of 2012. Article 6(2) of the CIETAC Rules 2012 provides that 'where CIETAC is satisfied by prima facie evidence that an arbitration agreement providing for arbitration by CIETAC exists, it may make a decision based on such evidence that it has jurisdiction over the arbitration case, and the arbitration shall proceed'. This provision mirrors the practice at the ICC Court.[28] It allows the CIETAC to make a decision that it has jurisdiction over the arbitration case and to proceed with the arbitration, based on prima facie evidence that an arbitration agreement providing for arbitration by the CIETAC exists. However, Article 6(2) of the CIETAC Rules 2012 continues to provide that 'such a decision shall not prevent the CIETAC from making a new decision on jurisdiction based on facts and/or evidence found by the arbitral tribunal during the arbitration proceedings that are inconsistent with the *prima facie* evidence'. Different from the practice of the ICC Court, where the subsequent decision on jurisdiction lies *solely* with the arbitral tribunal,[29] Article 6(2) of the CIETAC Rules 2012 allows the CIETAC to make a new decision on jurisdiction should the proceedings later show that the initial prima facie decision was not well-founded. The real reason behind this provision is

---

[26] According to the Chinese arbitrators interviewed during the research trip in China in March–April 2007, see Introduction, fn 18 above.
[27] ibid.
[28] Art 6(4) of the ICC Rules 2012.
[29] Art 6(5) of the ICC Rules 2012.

that Article 20 of the Arbitration Law grants the power to decide jurisdiction to the arbitration institution, not the arbitral tribunal.

Despite the legislative drawback, the CIETAC made a further step in advancing the tribunal's competence-competence jurisprudence. Article 6(1) of the CIETAC Rules 2012 vests the arbitral tribunal with the power to determine its own jurisdiction, upon the CIETAC's 'delegation':

> The CIETAC shall have the power to determine the existence and validity of an arbitration agreement and its jurisdiction over the arbitration case. The CIETAC may, if necessary, delegate such power to the arbitral tribunal.[30]

The CIETAC has made such delegation to the arbitral tribunal in a few cases.[31] This development is certainly to be welcomed as an institutional adaptation towards a higher degree of party autonomy and arbitral autonomy. Under the current legislative regime, the CIETAC's efforts face both theoretical and practical challenges: theoretically, the delegation of such power to the individual arbitral tribunal provided in Article 6(1) of the CIETAC Rules 2012 may be considered to be in conflict with Article 20 of the Arbitration Law. On a practical level, it is unclear under what circumstances the power to rule on jurisdiction may be delegated, that is, when delegation is 'necessary'. In the long run, CIETAC's above efforts may serve to stimulate legislative reforms, either by revision of the Arbitration Law or through judicial interpretations by the SPC. However, these efforts are only temporary measures as an institutional struggle towards arbitral autonomy, limited by the restriction of the Chinese legislation.[32] In consensual arbitration, 'the authority or competence of the arbitral tribunal comes from the agreement of the parties'.[33] Accordingly, the arbitral tribunal's power to rule on its own jurisdiction should not be dependent on the delegation from the arbitration institution. Further clarifications and reforms are needed in the legislation expressly to recognise the principle of competence-competence in China.

B. Court v Arbitration Institution

Pursuant to Article 20 of the Arbitration Law, if one party requests the arbitration institution to make a decision on the issue of arbitral jurisdiction and the other party requests the people's court for a ruling, the people's court will rule. In 1998, the SPC issued a notice to clarify this provision. Where applications of

---

[30] Art 6(1) of the CIETAC Rules 2005.
[31] According to an interview with a CIETAC official in Beijing on 27 March 2007, and discussions with the CIETAC's case managers.
[32] For a discussion, see Weixia Gu, *Arbitration in China: Regulation of Arbitration Agreements and Practical Issues* (Hong Kong, Sweet & Maxwell, 2012) 109–14.
[33] Hunter et al, *Redfern and Hunter on International Arbitration*, para 5.85.

jurisdictional challenge are made to both bodies, the people's court must not accept the case where the arbitration institution has already accepted the application and has made a decision. However, if the arbitration institution has not yet made a decision, the people's court should accept the case and inform the arbitration institution to suspend the arbitration.[34] The SPC Interpretation 2006 takes the matter one step further by providing that after an arbitration institution has made its decision on the validity of an arbitration agreement, the people's court shall not entertain any application by a party either to determine the validity of the arbitration agreement or to set aside the decision of the arbitration institution.[35]

The above provisions reflect the unique court control system in China over the arbitrators' jurisdiction, which is different from transnational standards. According to transnational standards, even when a jurisdictional challenge is filed before the court, the arbitral tribunals are generally allowed to continue with the arbitral proceeding. From a practical standpoint, this rule is to ensure that a party cannot succeed in delaying the arbitral proceedings by alleging that the arbitration agreement is invalid or non-existent. Such delay is avoided by allowing the arbitrators to rule on this issue, subject to subsequent review by the courts. Under this approach, the arbitral tribunals take the risk that the award may not be enforced if the court subsequently finds an arbitration agreement to be invalid. In contrast, the Chinese approach grants the people's court a *prevailing* power over the arbitration institution's (in lieu of the arbitral tribunal) jurisdictional decision. The court's involvement is not through judicial review after the jurisdiction decision is made by the arbitration institution, but through *direct* participation when a challenge of the arbitral tribunal's jurisdiction is made, provided that the arbitration institution has not made a decision. Furthermore, where the arbitration institution has not made a ruling on the jurisdictional challenge, the people's court *should* notify the arbitration institution to *suspend* the arbitration proceeding. This Chinese approach may minimise the risk at the enforcement stage, if the court takes an opposite view to the arbitral tribunal after an award is rendered. However, the court's early intervention raises much concern insofar as it generates an inherent control, which could easily remove the arbitration institution's jurisdictional power. It may also create opportunities for the reluctant party to create tactical delays: unless the tribunal has accepted the case and has made a ruling on the validity of the arbitration agreement before the court's action, all the arbitral proceedings will be stayed until the court has announced its decision.

---

[34] SPC Reply on Several Questions Regarding the Determination of the Validity of Arbitration Agreements (*Fa Shi* No 27 of 1998) issued on 26 October 1998.
[35] Art 13 of the SPC Interpretation 2006.

3.2 CONSTITUTION OF THE ARBITRAL TRIBUNAL

The freedom of the parties to choose arbitrators in whom they have confidence in is one of the main advantages of arbitration. Is the parties' choice of arbitrators subject to any limitations? How do national laws address the issue of the constitution of the arbitral tribunal? We shall first examine the transnational standards (section 3.2.1) and then compare them with the Chinese approach (section 3.2.2).

3.2.1 Transnational Standards

Since arbitration is contractual in nature, the parties are in principle free to choose their arbitrators. Most international conventions and national laws allow the parties a great deal of freedom to choose members of the arbitral tribunal. For instance, Arts 10(1) and 11(2) of the Model Law allow the parties the freedom to choose the number of arbitrators, and to agree on a procedure for appointing the arbitrator or arbitrators. Article 1508 of the French Code of Civil Procedure provides that 'arbitration agreements may, directly or by reference to arbitration rules, appoint the arbitrator or arbitrators or provide for a mechanism for their appointment'.[36] Article 179 of the Swiss PIL 1987 states that 'the arbitrators shall be appointed . . . in accordance with the agreement of the parties'. Similar provisions can be found in Sections 15 and 16 of the English Arbitration Act 1996. There is generally no substantive rule governing the appointment of the arbitrators other than the parties' freedom of choice. The emphasis is that the arbitration agreement takes precedence, with the parties either choosing the arbitrators directly, or indirectly by adopting pre-existing arbitration rules usually drawn up by an arbitration institution. The constitution of the arbitral tribunal is thus a matter for the parties alone, and the only limitation is the independence and impartiality of the arbitrators, and respect for the fundamental principles of due process. There is generally no specific requirement as to the qualification of arbitrators, apart from being independent and impartial. Even though some arbitration institutions maintain a panel list of arbitrators to facilitate the parties' choice, the parties are not obliged to choose arbitrators from any particular panel list. We will use the ICC Court as an example to illustrate the actual practice of the constitution of the arbitral tribunal at arbitration institutions in terms of (A) the appointment mechanism; and (B) the independence, impartiality and availability of arbitrators.[37]

---

[36] Translated by the author. Art 1508 of the French Code of Civil Procedure provides: 'La convention d'arbitrage peut, directement ou par référence à un règlement d'arbitrage ou à des règles de procédure, désigner le ou les arbitres ou prévoir les modalités de leur désignation'.

[37] For a discussion of the ICC Court's establishment, nature, development, structure, personnel and financial management, the relationship between the institution and arbitrators, see ch 5, s 5.2 below.

A. The Appointment Mechanism

Arbitrators are assigned to the ICC proceedings upon (i) confirmation by the Court (or its Secretary General) of nominations made by parties or arbitrators, or (ii) appointment by the Court.[38] The ICC Court does not maintain a compulsory panel list of arbitrators. The parties enjoy the widest freedom to nominate arbitrators, so long as the requirements of independence and impartiality are met. The arbitrators nominated by the parties sign a declaration of independence, subject to the confirmation of the ICC Court or the Secretary General.[39] In practice, more than 70 per cent of the arbitrators are nominated by the parties, and confirmed by the Court or the Secretary General. The Court's role in the constitution of the arbitral tribunal by appointing a party-appointed arbitrator is limited to situations where a party defaults.[40]

When the ICC Court is required to appoint a sole arbitrator or the Chairman of the arbitral tribunal (Articles 12(3) and 12(5) of the ICC Rules 2012), or a co-arbitrator on behalf of the defaulting party (Article 12(4) of the ICC Rules 2012), the Court takes advantage of the extraordinary network of its national committees to propose a candidate, and then decides whether or not to appoint the person proposed by the national committee. National committees represent the ICC in some 90 different countries around the world, which gives the ICC Court immense reach and diversity of choice when appointing arbitrators. In 2011, the arbitrators confirmed or appointed came from 78 countries.[41] Although delays may occur with some national committees, the system works well with most of them. It offers a means of integrating promising young arbitrators into the arbitration community and provides an opportunity for regional officers to open the allegedly closed circle of international arbitrators and promote arbitration in their countries.[42] In selecting a national committee, the Court will take into account all material aspects of the case, including the subject matter in dispute, the place and language of arbitration, the applicable law etc. The Court's goal is to select a national committee that has suitable candidates for the case.

B. Independence, Impartiality and Availability of Arbitrators

The ICC Rules 2012 do not contain any specific requirement as to the qualifications of the arbitrators. The parties are given a broad discretion in their nomi-

---

[38] For a discussion of the ICC Court's practice concerning the constitution of the Arbitral Tribunal, see Anne Marie Whitesell, 'Independence in ICC Arbitration: ICC Court Practice concerning the Appointment, Confirmation, Challenge and Replacement of Arbitrators' (2007) *ICC Bulletin* Independence of Arbitrators, Special Supp, 7–41.

[39] Art 13(2) of the ICC Rules 2012.

[40] From 2006 to 2010, the total number of arbitrators appointed by the Court accounts for 27%, 30%, 29%, 28.2%, and 27.2% respectively of the total arbitrators involved in ICC proceedings. See ICC Statistical Reports from 2006 to 2010, published in the *ICC Bulletins*.

[41] ICC 2011 Statistical Report.

[42] Pierre Tercier, 'ICC Rules of Arbitration: A Decade of Use' (2008) 19 *ICC Bulletin* 1, 40.

nation of arbitrators, which is not subject to any compulsory panel list of the ICC Court. There is one limitation on the parties' choice of arbitrators with respect to their nationalities, in order to ensure the impartiality of the arbitral tribunal. The ICC Rules 2012 expressly provide that the sole arbitrator or the Chairman of the arbitral tribunal shall be of 'a nationality other than those of the parties', except in exceptional circumstances with no objections from the parties.[43]

The arbitrators nominated by the parties or appointed by the Court are required to be independent and impartial and have the required availability. Pursuant to Article 11(2) of the ICC Rules 2012, before appointment or confirmation, a prospective arbitrator is required to sign a statement of independence and disclose in writing to the Secretariat

> any facts or circumstances which might be of such a nature as to call into the question the arbitrator's independence *in the eyes of the parties*. The Secretariat shall provide such information to the parties in writing and fix a time limit for any comments from them (emphasis added).

An arbitrator's duty to disclose potential conflicts of interest is continuous throughout the arbitration proceeding. Article 11(3) of the ICC Rules 2012 provides that '[a]n arbitrator shall immediately disclose in writing to the Secretariat and to the parties any facts or circumstances of a similar nature which may arise during the arbitration'. Since January 2010, the ICC Court has required a prospective arbitrator to declare his or her 'availability' when filling in the ICC Arbitrator Statement of Acceptance, Availability and Independence form.[44] Upon signing the form, the prospective arbitrator agrees to serve as an arbitrator in accordance with the ICC Rules and agrees to be remunerated in accordance therewith. The prospective arbitrator is required to declare that he or she can devote the time necessary to conduct the arbitration diligently, efficiently and in accordance with the time limits in the Rules, subject to any extensions granted by the ICC Court. In declaring his or her independence, the prospective arbitrator is required to take into account, pursuant to Article 11(2) of the ICC Rules 2012, whether there exists any past or present relationship, direct or indirect, with any of the parties, their related entities or their lawyers or other representatives, whether financial, professional or of any other kind. Any doubt must be resolved in favour of disclosure.[45] Finally, to ensure independence, the President and the members of the Secretariat of the Court may not act as arbitrators or as counsel in cases submitted to ICC arbitration. Although the Court members may not be appointed by the ICC Court as arbitrators in ICC arbitrations, they may be nominated by the parties, or by any other procedure agreed

---

[43] Art 13(5) of the ICC Rules 2012.
[44] The earlier form used was the Arbitrators' Declaration of Acceptance and Statement of Independence (amended in December 2008).
[45] Arbitrator's Declaration of Acceptance and Statement of Independence (amended in January 2010).

64   Arbitral Tribunal

upon by the parties, subject to confirmation.[46] Moreover, if the President, a Vice-President, or a member of the Court or of the Secretariat is involved in any way whatsoever in a case that comes before the ICC Court, such person may not receive any documents related to that case or participate in the discussions or the decisions of the ICC Court and must leave the room whenever the case is considered.[47]

3.2.2 Chinese Practice

What is the practice in China in terms of the constitution of the arbitral tribunal? Is it consistent with transnational standards? We will examine the Chinese practice in terms of (A) the appointment mechanism; and (B) the independence and impartiality of arbitrators.

A. The Appointment Mechanism

In terms of the appointment mechanism, the parties' freedom to choose arbitrators is restricted in China in two ways: (a) the strict statutory requirements regarding arbitrators' qualifications and (b) institutional control by means of the so-called 'compulsory panel system'.

a. Strict Statutory Qualification of Arbitrators

While modern arbitration laws generally do not stipulate or only set out minimum qualifications of arbitrators, such as civil capacity to be appointed, Article 13 of the Arbitration Law details strict qualifications necessary to be appointed to the panel of arbitrators of any arbitration institution in China:

> Arbitration institutions shall appoint their arbitrators from among righteous, upright persons. An arbitrator shall meet one of the conditions set forth below:
>
> (i)   to have been engaged in arbitration work for at least eight years;
> (ii) to have worked as a lawyer for at least eight years;
> (iii) to have been a judge for at least eight years;
> (iv) to have engaged in legal research or legal teaching in senior positions; or
> (v)   to have legal knowledge and be engaged in professional work relating to economics and trade, possessing a senior professional title or having an equivalent professional level.

This provision imposes both moral qualifications (righteous, upright) and a relatively high level of professional qualifications in law (with sufficient years of

---

[46] Arts 2(1) and 2(2) of the Internal Rules of the International Court of Arbitration, app II of the ICC Rules 2012.
[47] Arts 2(3), 2(4) and 2(5) of the Internal Rules of the International Court of Arbitration, app II of the ICC Rules 2012.

experience in a particular field). To the extent that 'an arbitration is as good as the arbitrators', the above provision could be considered to be a legislative attempt at quality control of arbitrators. Nevertheless, the consensual nature of arbitration implies the professional or other personal characteristics of the arbitrators should be left to the parties to agree, if they wish to include such conditions at all, either directly or by reference to institutional arbitration rules. As commentators have argued:

> It is a major advantage of arbitration that the parties can submit the settlement of their dispute to a tribunal of their choice. They do not have to rely on an appointee of the state as in a national court, where they have no influence on who is dealing with their dispute. The parties can appoint persons in whom they have confidence, and who have the necessary legal and technical expertise for the determination of the particular dispute.[48]

Chinese legislation, however, imposes statutory qualification requirements of arbitrators on behalf of the parties, which can be viewed as an improper restriction on party autonomy to define the qualifications of their own private judges. This defeats the very purpose of the parties in selecting arbitration in order to settle their disputes by private judges of their choice, rather than by state judges chosen by the state.

It should be noted that such stringent requirements do not apply to foreign arbitrators. Chapter 7 of the Arbitration Law, which deals specifically with foreign-related arbitrations, contains the following provision about the appointment of foreign specialists to foreign-related arbitration panels: '[f]oreign-related arbitration institutions may appoint their arbitrators from among foreigners with special knowledge in the fields of law, economy and trade, science and technology, etc'.[49] This provision does not make reference to the requirements in Article 13 of the Arbitration Law. In view of the different treatment of foreign-related arbitration, appointments of foreign-nationals as arbitrators (including in Hong Kong, Macao and Taiwan) are not subject to the specific criteria, such as established years of experience, set out in Article 13; it is sufficient for them to have special knowledge in the field.

b. Compulsory Panel System

Apart from the requirements relating to the qualification of arbitrators, Article 13 of the Arbitration Law further requires each arbitration institution to draw up its own panel of arbitrators according to different professions. This requirement is generally seen as creating a compulsory panel system in China.[50] There are more than 200 arbitration institutions throughout China,[51] and each individual

---

[48] Lew, Mistelis and Kröll, *Comparative International Commercial Arbitration*, para 10-4.
[49] Art 67 of the Arbitration Law.
[50] See Fung and Wang, *Arbitration in China: A Practical Guide*, 159.
[51] See ch 1, s 1.2.2, fn 32.

arbitration institution maintains its own panel list. Only those persons whose names are on a particular arbitration institution's panel are eligible to be appointed as an arbitrator by that institution. For instance, an arbitrator on the CIETAC's panel list cannot be appointed for an arbitration conducted by the BAC unless he or she is also on the BAC's panel list. One study on arbitral power explained the reasons for the compulsory panel system in China. These reasons included the following: China is not a mature arbitration community; the parties may not be able to make 'rational' decisions regarding appointments; and arbitrators may not conscientiously observe professional ethics. As such, the compulsory panel system may help to guarantee the high quality of arbitration via the institution's strict control of arbitrator qualifications.[52]

Based on this background, the CIETAC's reforms allow parties greater freedom in choosing arbitrators. Under the CIETAC rules before 2005, the panel list was compulsory in that the parties could appoint arbitrators only from the panel list of the respective arbitration institution. The CIETAC maintains an impressive list of 998 arbitrators, most of whom are renowned experts in the field of arbitration, and 28.26 per cent of whom are foreigners coming from over 30 countries around the world.[53] Nevertheless, parties expecting the greatest possible freedom in their choice of arbitrators will remain unsatisfied, as the panel list neither provides expertise for every technical field nor represents nationalities from each jurisdiction. In an effort to bring its practice in line with transnational standards, the CIETAC Rules have, since 2005, allowed the parties to choose arbitrators outside its panel list, subject to approval of the Chairman of the CIETAC.[54] This approach is maintained in the CIETAC Rules 2012.[55] In this sense, the CIETAC panel list is no longer compulsory, but suggestive. However, the tendency so far has been to continue appointing arbitrators from the CIETAC's panel list. Mr Yu Jianlong, Secretary General of the CIETAC, noted that 'it takes a while for the legal and business community to become aware of and take advantage of the change in the Rules'.[56] He has observed that some parties are already beginning to take advantage of the change in the procedure. For instance, in a series of high-value contracts between a major state-owned enterprise of China and a German conglomerate, it was expressly specified that all disputes arising out of or in connection with the contracts should be submitted to the CIETAC for arbitration, with each party being entitled to appoint an arbitrator *off the panel*.[57]

---

[52] Wenying Wang, *Arbitral Power in the People's Republic of China: Reality and Reform*, thesis for the degree of SJD at the University of Hong Kong, 2004.
[53] See the Domestic and Foreign-related Panel Lists of Arbitrators, promulgated by the CIETAC, effective as of 1 May 2011, available at www.cietac.org.
[54] Art 21(2) of the CIETAC Rules 2005.
[55] Art 24(2) of the CIETAC Rules 2012.
[56] Michael Moser and Jianlong Yu, 'CIETAC and its Work – An Interview with Vice Chairman Yu Jianlong' (2007) 24 *Journal of International Arbitration* 6, 559.
[57] Jianlong Yu, 'The Arbitrators' Mandate: Private Judge, Service-Provider or Both?' (2007) 3 *Stockholm International Arbitration Review*, 559.

B. Independence and Impartiality of Arbitrators

With respect to the independence and impartiality of arbitrators, Professor Jerome Cohen presented an example of a conflict of interest which he had experienced:

> The advocate for the respondent, had, without prior public announcement, become a vice chairman of the CIETAC shortly before the hearing. This meant that the presiding arbitrator, a deputy secretary general of the CIETAC, was the subordinate of the other side's advocate. Nevertheless, at the outset of the hearing, when the presiding arbitrator asked whether the parties wished to disqualify any arbitrator, neither the presiding arbitrator nor the advocate thought it necessary to reveal this crucial fact.[58]

To address this concern, the CIETAC Rules 2012 require that before accepting the case, an arbitrator must sign a declaration of impartiality and independence and disclose to the CIETAC in writing 'any facts or circumstances likely to give rise to justifiable doubts as to his/her impartiality or independence'.[59] They further provide that, if circumstances that need to be disclosed arise during the arbitration proceedings, the arbitrators must promptly make such disclosure.[60] The CIETAC will then communicate the declaration and the disclosure of the arbitrator to the parties.[61] In addition to this latter improvement, the CIETAC also established in 2004 a supervisory department to monitor the arbitrators' compliance with the Rules.

Another concern is the CIETAC's frequent appointment of its own personnel as arbitrators, especially as presiding arbitrators. This is done with a view to ensuring the quality of the arbitration.[62] This practice is criticised as creating an opportunity for the CIETAC to 'exercise administrative influence and even control over the arbitral tribunal and its decisions' and as involving its staff 'in conflicts of interest even when no CIETAC influence is exercised behind the scenes'.[63] A related issue is the CIETAC's appointment of government officials as arbitrators. The impartiality of the official is questionable if state assets or a state-owned enterprise (SOE) is involved. Even if no government interest is involved, the presence of a government official on the arbitral tribunal may exert undue influence on the decision-making of the other members of the tribunal. In light of these concerns, the CIETAC has introduced a number of reforms to enhance the CIETAC's status as a fair forum that offers user-friendly procedures. One improvement is the restriction imposed upon the appointment of staff members as arbitrators in CIETAC cases since 2006. A staff member may no longer sit as a party-appointed arbitrator, and may only be appointed as arbitrator by the Chairman of the CIETAC for small claim cases. The CIETAC

---

[58] Jerome Cohen, 'Time to Fix China's Arbitration' (2005) 168 *Far Eastern Economic Review* 31.
[59] Art 29(1) of the CIETAC Rules 2012.
[60] Art 29(2) of the CIETAC Rules 2012.
[61] Art 29(3) of the CIETAC Rules 2012.
[62] John Mo, *Arbitration Law in China* (Sweet & Maxwell Asia, 2001) para 5.03.
[63] Cohen, 'Time to Fix China's Arbitration', 32.

68   *Arbitral Tribunal*

is considering an end to the practice of appointing CIETAC staff as arbitrators completely in the near future, so as to bring CIETAC arbitration into further compliance with transnational standards.[64]

Concerns have also been raised about the appearance of imbalance in the arbitral tribunal. Unlike the ICC Rules, the CIETAC Rules do not exclude a person from the nationality of a party from being confirmed or appointed as the sole arbitrator or the chairman of the arbitral tribunal. Previous versions of the CIETAC Rules provided for the default power of the CIETAC Chairman to appoint the chairman of the arbitral tribunal if no agreement was reached by the parties. This default power has raised concerns because, as Mr Tao Jingzhou observed, 'the Chairman usually, with very few exceptions, appoints Chinese nationals as [the] presiding arbitrator'.[65] As a matter of fact, only a small portion of foreign arbitrators on the panel have actually served as arbitrators in CIETAC proceedings. In 2006, for instance, foreign panelists were appointed to sit as arbitrators in only about 10 per cent of the CIETAC's foreign-related cases.[66] If the Chinese party has already appointed a Chinese national (which is usually the case), there will be two Chinese arbitrators sitting on the panel. The fact that two of the three arbitrators share the same cultural, linguistic and legal background as one of the disputing parties may create an appearance of imbalance in the arbitral tribunal.

The main reason for the CIETAC's reluctance to appoint foreign arbitrators is the financial restraints, as the remuneration is often too low for foreign arbitrators.[67] Some arbitrators accept the CIETAC's appointment in order to keep abreast of recent developments in Chinese arbitration. However, other foreign nationals nominated by the Chairman of CIETAC are known to have declined appointments due to the level of compensation. To deal with the difficulty, Mr Yu Jianlong detailed current practice in terms of appointment of foreign arbitrators:

> For appointment of a non-Chinese arbitrator or tribunal chair (presiding arbitrator), the Secretariat collects from parties an additional amount defined as 'actual expense', usually ranging from US$ 6,000 to US$ 12,000 according to the geographical location of the foreign arbitrator being appointed. The 'actual expense' will be paid to the foreign arbitrator as in a lump sum to cover both his or her remuneration and actual expenses (travel and lodging) for attending the oral hearing(s).[68]

This practice does not appear to be a perfect solution. It means that the party nominating a foreign arbitrator must pay an extra fee in advance (although these fees will be considered in the allocation of costs in the final award). The requirement of such an advance may be a disincentive for parties to nominate a foreign arbitrator. More importantly, the different treatment may put the foreign arbitrator's impartiality into question, knowing that the party appointing him has paid

---

[64] Moser and Yu, 'CIETAC and its Work – An Interview with Vice Chairman Yu Jianlong', 564.
[65] Tao, *Arbitration Law and Practice in China*, 123.
[66] Yu, 'The Arbitrators' Mandate: Private Judge, Service-Provider or Both?', 561.
[67] An interview with a CIETAC official at the CIETAC, in Beijing, on 27 March 2007.
[68] Moser and Yu, 'CIETAC and its Work – An Interview with Vice Chairman Yu Jianlong', 559–60.

extra fees for the appointment.[69] Eventually, the fee schedule of the CIETAC should be adjusted to conform to transnational standards, in order to attract more foreign arbitrators to serve on its panels. In light of the criticisms, the CIETAC has improved its appointment procedure concerning the presiding arbitrator since its Rules of 2005, by allowing each party to recommend one to three arbitrators as candidates for the presiding arbitrator. Where there is only one common candidate on the lists, such candidate will act as the presiding arbitrator jointly appointed by the parties. Where there is more than one common candidate on the lists, the Chairman of the CIETAC will choose a presiding arbitrator from among the common candidates based on the specific nature of the case. Where no common candidate is listed, the Chairman of the CIETAC will make an appointment from outside of the lists of recommended arbitrators.[70] This novel approach is intended to limit the CIETAC's role in the appointment of the presiding arbitrator, which is expected to 'help deflect persistent criticisms that CIETAC's role in the selection of the Chairman under the 2000 Rules allowed it to "stack" tribunal membership in favour of Chinese nationals'.[71] Another improvement was made in Article 28 of the CIETAC Rules 2012, which describes the criteria which the Chairman of CIETAC may take into consideration when appointing arbitrators in the absence of party agreement. In addition to the applicable law, the seat of arbitration, language of the arbitration (and any other factors considered to be relevant), the Chairman can also take into account the 'nationalities of the parties'. However, the new rules do not require that the presiding or sole arbitrator is of a different nationality to the parties.

To summarise, the above comparison demonstrates the overwhelming restrictions on party autonomy in the process of constitution of the arbitral tribunal in China. The Chinese legislature considers that dispute resolution relates to 'social order' and is 'public' in nature. As a result, the state controls the channels for the appointment of arbitrators by imposing statutory requirements as to the qualifications of arbitrators and authorising arbitration institutions to set up compulsory panel lists, so as to ensure the quality of arbitrators.[72] Such attitude is reflected in a high degree of 'control' in Chinese legislation over arbitration. This institutional control over party autonomy goes against the general idea that the parties control and the institutions facilitate:

> If a minimum of trust is to be maintained between the parties and their judges in international arbitration, the appointment of arbitrators must be left to the parties. It is up to them to exercise that right or, if they so choose, to delegate it to an arbitral institution.[73]

---

[69] This issue was addressed by two of the interviewees during the research trip in 2007.
[70] See Art 22(3) of the CIETAC Rules 2005 and Art 25(3) of the CIETAC Rules 2012.
[71] Michael Moser and Peter Yuen, 'The New CIETAC Arbitration Rules' (2005) 21 *Arbitration International*, 391–403.
[72] See 乔欣, 《仲裁权研究-仲裁程序公正与权利保障》 (北京, 法律出版社, 2001) 第三章 (Xin Qiao, The Research on Power of Arbitration – The Due Process of Arbitration and the Right Protection (Beijing, Legal Press, 2001) ch 3).
[73] Gaillard and Savage, *Fouchard Gaillard Goldman on International Commercial Arbitration*, 453.

Furthermore, given that 'the network of *guanxi* could be very wide within the relatively small group from which advocates, arbitrators and administrators are drawn',[74] the independence of arbitrators in China has aroused great concerns. While institutions such as the CIETAC have made impressive reforms, further efforts are needed to improve the impartiality and independence of arbitrators in China.

[74] Cohen, 'Time to Fix China's Arbitration'.

4

Recognition and Enforcement of Arbitral Awards

'For this relief much thanks; "tis bitter cold".'
Francisco to Barnardo, Hamlet

THE WINNING PARTY in an arbitration may echo Francisco's sentiment – 'for this relief much thanks' – as arbitrators render the award. Once a decision has been made in the form of an award, it is an implied term of every arbitration agreement that the parties will carry it out.[1] Indeed, most awards are voluntarily performed by the parties without the need to go to state courts. According to a survey of corporate attitudes and practices on international arbitration conducted by PricewaterhouseCoopers and the School of International Arbitration, Queen Mary, University of London (QMUL) in 2008, participants only needed to proceed to enforce an award in 11 per cent of cases.[2] Our discussions on recognition and enforcement of arbitral awards should be understood in this wider perspective of the performance of the awards.

However, this is not the end of the story. What if the losing party fails to carry out an award? Unless at the end of the arbitration proceedings the award can be enforced if not complied with voluntarily, any favourable award will only be a nominal victory. The arbitrators fall short of the power to enforce an award against a reluctant party. Being made by private judges, 'arbitral awards have no authority in national laws other than that which those laws choose to confer upon them'.[3] In consequence, the enforcement of awards always takes place through a national court operating under its own procedural rules. The detailed procedures adopted in these courts vary from country to country. In this chapter we will examine the recognition and enforcement of arbitral awards. We will first look at the law and practice of transnational standards on this matter (section 4.1) and then discuss the current status in China (section 4.2).

---

[1] Michael Mustill and Stewart Boyd, *Mustill & Boyd: Commercial Arbitration*, 2nd edn (London, Butterworths, 1989) 47.
[2] PricewaterhouseCoopers LLP and QMUL, 'International Arbitration: Corporate Attitudes and Practices 2008' 6 *Transnational Dispute Management* 1 (March 2009).
[3] Gaillard and Savage, *Fouchard Gaillard Goldman on International Commercial Arbitration*, 885.

4.1 TRANSNATIONAL STANDARDS

International enforceability conferred on arbitral awards by national legal systems would be inconceivable without some form of guarantee that state courts may review the award if a party has a good reason to be aggrieved by the arbitration and the way in which the award was rendered. This guarantee inspires the confidence of the parties in the arbitration process.

Generally, if dissatisfied with an award and unwilling to accept its effect voluntarily, an unsuccessful party may (i) challenge the award in the courts of the place where the award was made; and/or (ii) wait until the successful party initiates enforcement proceedings before a court, at which stage it can seek to resist enforcement. To put it in other terms, the judicial review of awards occurs both at the seat of arbitration (where, as a general rule, actions to set aside will take place) (section 4.1.2); and in all countries where enforcement of the award may be sought (section 4.1.1).

4.1.1 Recognition and Enforcement of Arbitral Awards

The effect of the international conventions has been to secure a considerable degree of uniformity in the recognition and enforcement of awards around the world.[4] The New York Convention was the result of an international effort to make arbitration a more efficient means of resolving international disputes. It facilitates and safeguards the enforcement of arbitration agreements and arbitral awards, and in doing so it serves international trade and commerce. Since the New York Convention became available for ratification in 1958, 146 nations have ratified or acceded to it.[5] The New York Convention significantly simplifies the enforcement of foreign awards and harmonises national rules for the enforcement of foreign awards.[6] It is thus considered as 'the most successful international instrument in the field of arbitration, and perhaps could lay down the most effective instance of international legislation in the entire history of commercial law'.[7] Thanks to the publication of the ICCA Yearbook Commercial Arbitration since 1976, an effective worldwide system of reporting cases applying the Convention has contributed to the application of the New York Convention in an 'increasingly unified and harmonized fashion'.[8] On 3 July 2012, the UNCITRAL announced the launch of an online platform which supplements the forthcoming Guide on the New York Convention. Professor

---

[4] Hunter et al, *Redfern and Hunter on International Arbitration*, para 11.36.
[5] For a list of signatories to the New York Convention, see www.uncitral.org/uncitral/en/uncitral_texts/arbitration/NYConvention_status.html.
[6] Lew, Mistelis and Kröll, *Comparative International Commercial Arbitration*, para 26-21.
[7] Michael Mustill, 'Arbitration: History and Background' (1989) 6 *Journal of International Arbitration* 2, 49.
[8] ICCA, *ICCA's Guide to the Interpretation of the 1958 New York Convention: A Handbook for Judges*, 6.

Emmanuel Gaillard, Professor George Bermann and their research teams, with the support of UNCITRAL, has established a website to make the information gathered in preparation of the Guide on the New York Convention publicly available. The website constitutes a platform which reflects the evolution of case law on the New York Convention[9].

Article III of the New York Convention provides clearly that 'each contracting state shall recognise arbitration awards as binding and enforce them in accordance with the rules of procedure of the territory where the award is relied on'. In addition, Article III mandates that '(. . .) there shall not be imposed substantially more onerous conditions or higher fees or charges on the recognition or enforcement of arbitral awards to which this Convention applies than are imposed on the recognition or enforcement of domestic arbitral awards'. Article V of the New York Convention gives an 'exhaustive' list of grounds for refusal to enforce arbitral awards that *may* be invoked by national courts. Enforcement may be refused 'only if' the party against whom the award is invoked is able to prove one of the grounds listed in Article V(1), or if the court finds that the enforcement of the award would violate its (international) public policy (Article V(2)). Except for the public policy ground, the second look at the award during the enforcement stage is confined to the procedural issues listed in Article V(1). The New York Convention does not allow a re-examination of the merits of the award because of a mistake of fact or law by the arbitral tribunal.[10] The overall objective of the New York Convention is the facilitation of the enforcement of the award. This objective reflects a pro-enforcement bias. Accordingly, the grounds enumerated in Article V must be construed *narrowly* by national courts.

It should be emphasised that the New York Convention does not create a uniform standard for enforcement. Rather, it sets the *minimum standards* that the national courts must respect to facilitate recognition and enforcement of foreign arbitral awards. The 'most favourable regime' principle expressed in Article VII(1) of the New York Convention means that the Convention does not prevent the Contracting States from restricting the grounds for refusal enumerated in Article V and thereby creating a more favourable law for enforcement. A good example of a more favourable law for enforcement is that of France, which, for instance, allows enforcement of a foreign award even if it is set aside in its country of origin.[11] In fact, foreign awards have for years been enforced in France without reference to the New York Convention, given that French law itself is more favourable to enforcement than is Article V of the New York Convention.[12] In the discussions of transnational standards, we will focus primarily on the minimum standards set out in the New York Convention.

---

[9] See www.newyorkconvention1958.org.
[10] Lew, Mistelis and Kröll, *Comparative International Commercial Arbitration*, para 26–66; Gaillard and Savage, *Fouchard Gaillard Goldman on International Commercial Arbitration*, 983.
[11] See s 4.1.1-A.e(ii) below.
[12] Jan Paulsson, 'Towards Minimum Standards of Enforcement: Feasibility of a Model Law' in Albert Jan van den Berg (ed), *ICCA Congress Series no 9* (The Hague, Kluwer Law International, 1999).

A. Grounds which Must be Raised by the Party Resisting Recognition or Enforcement

a. Incapacity or Invalid Arbitration Agreement (Article V(1)(a) of the New York Convention)

Article V(1)(a) of the New York Convention provides that:

> the parties to the agreement were, according to the law applicable to them, under some incapacity, or the said agreement is not valid under the law to which the parties have subjected it or, failing any indication thereon, under the law of the country where the award was made.

This provision allows refusal of recognition and enforcement on the grounds that the arbitration agreement on which the award is based is invalid, whether as a result of the incapacity of a party or because circumstances such as mistake or duress invalidate the consent to arbitrate.

b. No Proper Notice of Appointment of Arbitrator or of the Proceedings; Lack of Due Process (Article V(1)(b) of the New York Convention)

Article V(1)(b) of the New York Convention allows recognition or enforcement to be refused if it is established that:

> [t]he party against whom the award is invoked was not given proper notice of the appointment of the arbitrator or of the arbitration proceedings or was otherwise unable to present his case.

This ground is directed at ensuring that the arbitration itself is properly conducted, with proper notice to the parties and procedural fairness. It requires the arbitrator to conduct the arbitration in such a manner that each party has a fair opportunity to present its case. It is often taken into account by the arbitrator in decisions with respect to the production and admission of evidence, the scheduling of hearings and the time allowed for direct and cross-examination of witnesses. In general, the arbitrators have broad discretion as to how they may conduct proceedings, and this defence has been narrowly construed.

c. Ultra Vires (Article V(1)(c) of the New York Convention)

Under Article V(1)(c) of the New York Convention, recognition or enforcement of an arbitral award may be refused if it is established that:

> [t]he award deals with a difference not contemplated by or not falling within the terms of the submission to arbitration, or it contains decisions on matters beyond the scope of the submission to arbitration, provided that, if the decisions on matters submitted to arbitration can be separated from those not so submitted, that part of the award which contains decisions on matters submitted to arbitration may be recognised and enforced.

What is at issue under this ground is not the existence of the arbitration agreement but the scope of the arbitral tribunal's jurisdiction and authority over the dispute. There are essentially two situations in which this ground may be invoked. First, if the arbitrators exceed the scope of a valid arbitration agreement – rendering an award relating to differences beyond the ambit of such agreement – enforcement may be refused for want of jurisdiction. Second, should the arbitrators act within the scope of the valid arbitration agreement but exceed their authority by dealing with claims that the parties have not submitted to them, enforcement may be refused for transgression of the arbitrators' mandate.[13] This ground reflects the principle that the arbitral tribunal only has the jurisdiction to decide the issues that the parties have agreed to submit to it for determination.[14] When it is alleged that the tribunal exceeded its jurisdiction in some respects, but not in others, the courts have discretion to grant partial enforcement of an award. In such a situation, even if partial excess of authority is proved, that part of the award that concerns matters submitted to arbitration may be saved and enforced.[15]

d. Composition of Tribunal or Procedure not in Accordance with Arbitration Agreement or the Relevant Law (Article V(1)(d) of the New York Convention)

Article V(1)(d) of the New York Convention allows recognition or enforcement to be refused if it is established that:

> the composition of the arbitral tribunal or the arbitral procedure was not in accordance with the agreement of the parties, or, failing such agreement, was not in accordance with the law of the country where the arbitration took place.

This ground provides two types of potential violations, concerning (i) the composition of the arbitral tribunal; and (ii) the arbitral procedure.

The first option of Article V(1)(d) is applicable if a party is deprived of its right to appoint an arbitrator or to have its case decided by an arbitral tribunal whose composition reflects the parties' agreement. Cases where one party refuses to appoint an arbitrator and the arbitrator is then appointed by a court, or where arbitrators are successfully challenged and replaced in accordance with the applicable rules chosen by the parties and the applicable law, would not succeed under this ground.[16]

---

[13] Mercédeh Azeredo da Silveira and Laurent Lévy, 'Transgression of the Arbitrators' Authority: Article V(a)(c) of the New York Convention' in Emmanuel Gaillard and Domenico di Pietro (eds), *Enforcement of Arbitration Agreements and International Arbitral Awards: The New York Convention in Practice* (London, Cameron May, 2008) 641.

[14] ICCA, *ICCA's Guide to the Interpretation of the 1958 New York Convention: A Handbook for Judges*, 93; Robert B von Mehren, 'Enforcement of Foreign Arbitral Awards in the United States' (1998) 1 *International Arbitration Law Review* 6, 202.

[15] Hunter et al, *Redfern and Hunter on International Arbitration*, para 11.79; ICCA, *ICCA's Guide to the Interpretation of the 1958 New York Convention: A Handbook for Judges*, 94.

[16] ICCA, *ICCA's Guide to the Interpretation of the 1958 New York Convention: A Handbook for Judges*, 95.

76 *Recognition and Enforcement*

The second option of Article V(1)(d) is not aimed at refusing to recognise or enforce an award if the court called upon has a different legal view to the arbitrators regarding whether or not to hear a witness, to allow re-cross-examination or how many written submissions they would like to allow. Rather, this option is aimed at 'more fundamental deviation from the agreed procedure', which include situations in which the parties agreed to use the rules of one institution but the arbitration was conducted under the rules of another, or even where the parties have agreed that no institutional rules would apply.[17]

e. Award not Binding, Suspended, or Set Aside (Article V(1)(e) of the New York Convention)

The fifth ground for refusal of recognition and enforcement under the New York Convention is as follows:

> The award has not yet become binding on the parties, or has been set aside or suspended by a competent authority of the country in which, or under the law of which, that award was made.

(i) Award not Binding

The drafters of the New York Convention intentionally chose the word 'binding', instead of 'final', which was used in the Geneva Convention on the Execution of Foreign Arbitral Awards of 1927 (Geneva Convention 1927).[18] The reason was to avoid the problem of '*double exequatur*', so that a party did not need to obtain *exequatur* or leave for recognition and enforcement from the court of the state in which, or under the law of which, the award was made.[19] The fact that no double *exequatur* is required under the New York Convention is 'universally recognised by courts and commentators'.[20]

However, national courts differ over the question of whether the binding force is to be determined under the law applicable to the award or independently of the applicable law.[21] Some national courts consider it necessary to investigate the law applicable to the award to see if it is binding under that law.[22] Other courts interpret the word 'binding' without regard to an applicable law, as

---

[17] ibid.
[18] Convention on the Execution of Foreign Arbitral Awards, Geneva, 26 September 1927, League of Nations, Treaty Series, vol 92, 301.
[19] Albert Jan van den Berg, 'New York Convention of 1958: Refusals of Enforcement' (2008) 18 ICC Bulletin 2, 29; Hunter et al, *Redfern and Hunter on International Arbitration*, para 11.85.
[20] ICCA, *ICCA's Guide to the Interpretation of the 1958 New York Convention: A Handbook for Judges*, 101.
[21] For a commentary, see Berg, 'New York Convention of 1958: Refusals of Enforcement', 30; ICCA, *ICCA's Guide to the Interpretation of the 1958 New York Convention: A Handbook for Judges*, 101–02.
[22] Strasbourg Tribunal of First Instance, 9 October 1970, *Animalfeeds International Corp v SAA Becker & Cie*, II Yearbook Commercial Arbitration (1977) 244 (France No 2).

meaning that the award can no longer be appealed on the merits in further proceedings before another arbitral tribunal or in a court.[23]

(ii) Award is Set Aside

Ground (e) also allows national courts to refuse enforcement of an award if the party against whom the award is invoked proves that the award has been 'set aside' (annulled, vacated) by a court in the country where, or under the law of which, the award was made. Notwithstanding this provision, a court in another country may still grant recognition and enforcement of an award that has been set aside in the country of origin. This is allowed under the 'more-favourable-right' provision under Article VII(1) of the New York Convention, which allows courts to apply an enforcement regime that is more favourable to enforcement than the New York Convention.[24]

France is the best-known example of a jurisdiction that has declared an award enforceable notwithstanding the fact that it had been set aside in the country of origin. In *Hilmarton*,[25] the French Cour de cassation decided to enforce an award by a tribunal in Switzerland even though it was set aside by the Geneva Court of Appeal. In *Putrabali*,[26] the French Cour de cassation enforced an award set aside in England. The court held that 'an international arbitral award, which does not belong to any state legal system, is an international decision of justice and its validity must be examined according to the applicable rules of the country where its recognition and enforcement are sought'.[27]

In the United States, the US Federal Court for the District of Columbia reached a similar conclusion in *Chromalloy*,[28] holding an award set aside in Egypt (the country of origin) to be enforceable in the United States. In doing so, the court relied on the resisting party's contractual commitment not to appeal

---

[23] For instance, *Compagnie X SA v Federation Y, Tribunal Fédéral, First Civil Chamber*, Switzerland, 9 December 2008, XXXIV Yearbook Commercial Arbitration (2009) 810–16 (Switzerland No 40).

[24] Hunter et al, *Redfern and Hunter on International Arbitration*, para 11.91.

[25] Cour de cassation, 1 civil chamber, 23 March 1994, *Hilmarton*: Revue de l'arbitrage 376 (1997), and Philippe Fouchard's note; *Journal du droit international (Clunet)* (1997) 1033, and Emmanuel Gaillard's note. See also, in the same vein: Cour de cassation, 1 civil chamber, 9 October 1984, *Norsolor*: Revue de l'arbitrage (1985) 431, and Berthold Goldman's note; *Journal du droit international (Clunet)* (1985) 679, and Philippe Kahn's note; *Recueil Dalloz* (1985) 101, and Jean Robert's note. See also Berthold Goldman, 'Une bataille judiciaire autour de la *lex mercatoria*: l'affaire Norsolor', *Revue de l'arbitrage* (1983) 379; Cour de cassation, 1 civil chamber, 10 March 1993, *Polish Ocean Line*: Revue de l'arbitrage (1993) 255 (second decision), and Dominique Hascher's note; *Journal du droit international (Clunet)* (1993) 360 (first decision), and Philippe Kahn's note.

[26] Cour de cassation, 1 civil chamber, 29 June 2007, *Putrabali: Bulletin de la Cour de cassation I*, no 251; XXXII *Yearbook Commercial Arbitration* 299–302 (France, no 42); partial English translation extracted in Philippe Pinsolle, 'The Status of Vacated Awards in France: The Cour de cassation Decision in *Putrabali*', (2008) 24 *Arbitration International* 2, 294; *Revue de l'arbitrage* (2007), 507, and Jean-Pierre Ancel's report and Emmanuel Gaillard's note; *Journal du droit international (Clunet)* (2007) 1236, and Thomas Clay's note; *Revue trimestrielle de droit commercial* (2007) 682, with Eric Loquin's note.

[27] ibid.

[28] *Chromalloy Aeroservices Inc v Arab Republic of Egypt*, 939 F Supp 907 (DDC 1996).

78 *Recognition and Enforcement*

the arbitral award and the strong US public policy favouring arbitration. The court expressly distinguished the permissive nature of Article V of the New York Convention with the mandatory nature of Article VII:

> While article V provides a discretionary standard, article VII of the Convention *requires* that, 'the provisions of the present Convention *shall not* . . . deprive any interested party of any right he may have to avail himself of an arbitral award in the manner and to the extent allowed by the law . . . of the count[r]y where such award is sought to be relied upon'.[29]

Notwithstanding *Hilmarton, Chromalloy* and *Putrabali*, enforcement of arbitral awards that have been set aside by the courts in the country of origin remains controversial. There are a number of examples where the courts declined to enforce annulled awards.[30] In *Termorio*, for instance, the US Court of Appeals for the District of Columbia denied the enforcement of a Colombian arbitral award that had been set aside by the Colombian courts on the ground that Colombian law in effect at the date of the agreement did not expressly permit the use of ICC procedural rules, which the parties had designated in their arbitration clause.[31] The Court of Appeals for the District of Columbia subsequently upheld the decision,[32] stating that:

> the Convention does not endorse a regime in which secondary States (in determining whether to enforce an award) routinely second-guess the judgment of a court in a primary State, when the court in the primary State has lawfully acted pursuant to 'competent authority' to 'set aside' an arbitration award made in its country . . . It takes much more than a mere assertion that the judgment of the primary State 'offends the public policy' of the secondary State to overcome a defense raised under article V(1)(e).[33]

(iii) Award is Suspended

Article VI of the New York Convention provides that a court may adjourn its decision on enforcement if the respondent has applied for suspension of the award in the country of origin. The term 'suspension' is not defined in the New York Convention. Courts have generally construed it to refer to suspension of the enforceability of the award by a court in the country of origin.[34]

---

[29] ibid, 909–10.
[30] See, for instance, *Baker Marine Ltd (Nig) v Chevron Ltd (Nig)*, 191 F3d 194 (2nd Cir 1999); *Spier v Tecnica*, 71 F Supp 2d 279 (SDNY 1999); *Termorio SAESP v Electranta SP*, 487 F3d 928 (DC Cir 2007).
[31] *Termorio SAESP v Electranta SP*, 421 FSupp2d 87 (DDC2006).
[32] *Termorio*, 487 F3d.
[33] ibid, 938.
[34] ICCA, *ICCA's Guide to the Interpretation of the 1958 New York Convention: A Handbook for Judges*, 104.

B. Grounds which can be Raised by the Courts on their Own Motion

Article V(2) of the New York Convention provides grounds which can be raised by the courts on their own motion for the refusal of recognition and enforcement of arbitral awards, if the court finds that:

a. the subject matter of the difference is not capable of settlement by arbitration under the law of that country; or
b. the recognition or enforcement of the award would be contrary to the public policy of that country.[35]

a. Arbitrability (Article V(2)(a) of the New York Convention)

Article V(2)(a) of the New York Convention allows a national court to refuse to recognise and enforce an award where the dispute involves a subject matter reserved for the courts. The issue of 'arbitrability' may also arise at an early stage of arbitration, when the court will examine whether an issue is 'capable of being referred to arbitration' pursuant to Article II of the New York Convention. 'Subject matter capable of settlement by arbitration' is generally understood to mean 'arbitrable'.[36] The issue of 'arbitrability' under this provision of the Convention is a question to be determined under the law of the country where the application for recognition and enforcement is being made.[37] Each state has its own concept of what disputes should be reserved for courts of law and what disputes may be resolved by arbitration, governed largely by questions of public policy. For example, criminal cases are clearly non-arbitrable; similarly, cases reserved exclusively for the courts of a jurisdiction are non-arbitrable, including: (i) divorce; (ii) custody of children; (iii) property settlements; (iv) wills; (v) bankruptcy; and (vi) winding up of companies.[38] The modern trend is towards a smaller category of non-arbitrable matters as a consequence of the growing acceptance of arbitration.[39]

In any event, arbitrability standards should be interpreted with regard to the presumptive validity of international arbitration agreements enshrined in the Convention, which requires 'any doubts concerning the scope of arbitral issues . . . be resolved in favor of arbitration'.[40] Thus, a finding that a dispute is non-arbitrable under a country's domestic law does not necessarily prevent the recognition in that country of a foreign award dealing with the same subject matter.[41]

---

[35] New York Convention, Arts V(2)(a)–(b).
[36] ICCA, *ICCA's Guide to the Interpretation of the 1958 New York Convention: A Handbook for Judges*, 63.
[37] ibid.
[38] ibid.
[39] ibid.
[40] *Moses H Cone Mem'l Hosp v Mercury Constr Corp*, 460 US 1, 24–25 (1983).
[41] Gaillard and Savage, *Fouchard Gaillard Goldman on International Commercial Arbitration*, 995; ICCA, *ICCA's Guide to the Interpretation of the 1958 New York Convention: A Handbook for Judges*, 64.

b. Public Policy (Article V(2)(b) of the New York Convention)

In accordance with Article V(2)(b) of the New York Convention, arbitral awards can be refused enforcement and recognition where it would be contrary to public policy.[42] However, this provision does not define the term 'public policy'. In theory, there are three levels of public policy; domestic, international and transnational.[43]

(i) **Domestic public policy:** When only one country is associated with the arbitration, then the laws and standards that form the domestic public policy of that country apply.[44]
(ii) **International public policy:** As an extension of domestic public policy, international public policy consists of the rules of a country's domestic public policy applied in an international context.[45]
(iii) **Transnational public policy:** Unlike international public policy, which relies on the laws and standards of specific countries, transnational public policy represents the international consensus on accepted norms of conduct,[46] a 'genuinely international public policy rooted in the law of the community of nations'.[47]

The case law generated by the various courts which have applied Article V(2)(b) of the New York Convention supports the view that this provision refers to 'international public policy' and not 'domestic public policy'. Emmanuel Gaillard made the following comments:

> Not every breach of a mandatory rule of the host country could justify refusing recognition or enforcement of a foreign award. Such refusal is only justified where the award contravenes principles which are considered in the host country as reflecting its *fundamental convections, or as having an absolute, universal value* (emphasis added).[48]

Furthermore, as the New York Convention's own wording indicates 'the recognition or enforcement of the award would be contrary to *the public policy of that country* (emphasis added)', Article V(2)(b) refers to the host country's concept of international public policy, not transnational public policy.[49] The latter is only relevant to arbitrators who, having no forum, are required to apply only genuinely transnational concepts.[50] The logic for this provision is different: it is to enable the

---

[42] New York Convention Art V(2)(b).
[43] Mark A Buchanan, 'Public Policy and International Commercial Arbitration' (1988) 26 *American Business Law Journal* 511, 513.
[44] Kenneth-Michael Curtin, 'Redefining Public Policy in International Arbitration of Mandatory National Laws' (1997) 64 *Defence Counsel Journal* 271, 281.
[45] Buchanan, 'Public Policy and International Commercial Arbitration', 514.
[46] ibid.
[47] Gaillard and Savage, *Fouchard Gaillard Goldman on International Commercial Arbitration*, 997.
[48] ibid.
[49] Buchanan, 'Public Policy and International Commercial Arbitration', 515–16.
[50] Gaillard and Savage, *Fouchard Gaillard Goldman on International Commercial Arbitration*, para 1712.

country where recognition or enforcement is sought to refuse to accept into its legal order an award which contravenes its fundamental convictions.[51]

Although the New York Convention refers to the host country's conception of international public policy, that country must nevertheless apply it with caution. For instance, the US Court of Appeals for the Second Circuit has held that public policy under the Convention is limited to 'the forum state's most basic notion of morality and justice', and 'the Convention's public policy defense should be construed narrowly'. Similarly, the Court of Justice of the Canton of Geneva held that a violation of public policy implies 'a violation of fundamental principles of the Swiss legal order, hurting intolerably the feeling of justice'.[52] Despite the fact that this defence is frequently raised by the parties, it has rarely been accepted by national courts as justifying a refusal of recognition and enforcement.

4.1.2 Setting Aside of Arbitral Awards

The actions governed by the New York Convention do not include the setting aside (annulment, vacation) of an arbitral award. The New York Convention may, however, have an influence on the action for setting aside the award in at least two respects.

First, it is a generally accepted rule that the setting aside of an arbitral award pertains to the exclusive jurisdiction of the courts in the country of origin (ie, the country in, or, rather theoretically, under the law of which the award was made) and is to be adjudicated on the basis of the arbitration law of that country. The courts in the other contracting states may only decide under the New York Convention whether or not to grant enforcement of the award within their jurisdiction. The consequence is that the setting aside of an award in the country of origin may have 'extra-territorial effect' as the award loses the benefit of contracting state enforcement provided by virtue of Article V(1)(e) of the New York Convention. In contrast, a refusal of enforcement is limited to the jurisdiction within which a court refuses enforcement, and courts in other contracting states are in principle not bound by such refusal.

Second, many jurisdictions with modern arbitration legislation have provided a procedure for setting aside an award made within its jurisdiction, which mirrors the grounds for refusal of enforcement set forth in Article V of the Convention. The extent of the review performed by the court still varies considerably from one country to the next, but with very few exceptions the principle of such review is accepted in comparative law. For instance, the grounds for setting aside arbitral awards listed in Article 34 of the Model Law are virtually identical to the grounds for refusal of enforcement listed in Article V of the

---

[51] ibid.
[52] *Léopold Lazarus Ltd v Chrome Resources SA* (Court of Justice of the Canton of Geneva, 17 September 1976) IV Yearbook Commercial Arbitration 311 (1979) 312.

82 *Recognition and Enforcement*

New York Convention (except for ground (1)(e)). Article 34 of the Model Law also unequivocally suggests that judicial review in the context of an application to set aside an award can only be based on natural justice and legality grounds. There can be no review on the merits. The provisions on setting aside in the Model Law are also considered as the minimum standard. Certain states take a more liberal approach by eliminating, in certain circumstances, any action to set aside at the seat of arbitration. For instance, the Swiss PIL 1987 allows the parties, by express agreement, to waive any action to set aside at the seat of arbitration, by stating that:

> where none of the parties has its domicile, its habitual residence, or a business establishment in Switzerland, they may, by an express statement in the arbitration agreement or by a subsequent agreement in writing, exclude all setting aside proceedings, or they may also limit such proceedings to one or several of the grounds [on which an award can be set aside].[53]

4.2 CHINESE PRACTICE

What, then, is the situation in China with respect to the recognition and enforcement of arbitral awards? While foreign investors and reports have often claimed that enforcement in China is equivalent to the survival of the fittest in the jungle, official and semi-official PRC sources present a much more positive view. This section endeavours to present to readers an objective picture of the enforcement of arbitral awards in China, based on existing literature,[54] case studies, field interviews and some empirical information. We shall first review the legal regime (section 4.2.1), then assess statistical information concerning China's

---

[53] Art 192 of the Swiss PIL 1987.
[54] See, for instance, Matthew D Bersani, 'Enforcement of Arbitration Awards in China: Foreigners Find the System Solely Lacking' (1992) 19 *China Business Review* 5; Tang Houzhi, 'Conciliation in China (updated)' (2000); Tang Houzhi, 'Combination of Arbitration with Conciliation: Arb-Med' in *New Horizons in International Arbitration and Beyond* (The Hague, Kluwer Law International, 2005); Jin Huang and Huanfang Du, 'Chinese Judicial Practice in Private International Law: 2003' (2008) 7 *Chinese Journal of International Law* 1; Sarah Catherine Peck, 'Playing by a New Set of Rules Will China's New Arbitration Laws and Recent Membership in the ICC Improve Trade with China?' (2004) 12 *Journal of International Arbitration* 4; Guiguo Wang, 'One Country, Two Arbitration Systems: Recognition and Enforcement of Arbitral Awards in Hong Kong and China' (1997) 14 *Journal of International Arbitration* 1; Tao, *Arbitration Law and Practice in China*, 63; Dejun Cheng, Michael Moser and Shengchang Wang, *International Arbitration in the People's Republic of China: Commentary, Cases and Materials* (Butterworths Asia, 1995) 73–84; Tao, *Arbitration Law and Practice in China*, 155–209; Wang, 'The Practical Application of Multilateral Conventions Experience with Bilateral Treaties Enforcement of Foreign Arbitral Awards in the People's Republic of China', 461–504; Yeoh and Yu, 'The People's Courts and Arbitration – A Snapshot of Recent Judicial Attitudes on Arbitrability and Enforcement', 635–49; Stanley Lubman and Gregory Wajnowski, 'International Commercial Dispute Resolution in China: A Practical Assessment' (1993) 4 *American Review of International Arbitration* 2; Randall Peerenboom, 'Seek Truth From Facts: An Empirical Study of Enforcement of Arbitral Awards in the PRC' (2001) 49 *American Journal of Comparative Law* 249, 249–327; Clarisse von Wunschheim, *Enforcement of Commercial Arbitral Awards in China*, 2nd edn (New York, Thomson Reuters business, 2012).

enforcement record (section 4.2.2) and, finally, conduct a case analysis to examine judicial attitudes towards recognition and enforcement of arbitral awards (section 4.2.3).

4.2.1 The Legal Regime

A. Legal Framework

The Arbitration Law and Civil Procedure Law set out different standards with respect to the setting aside, or recognition and enforcement, of 'domestic', 'foreign-related' and 'foreign' awards.[55] From a practical point of view, a losing party can either (a) initiate an action to set aside the award (within six months from the date the award has been received); or (b) wait for the winning party to apply for enforcement (within two years) and to file an action to resist recognition and enforcement of the award. An action for setting aside as a judicial remedy is applicable to domestic and foreign-related arbitral awards, but not to foreign awards; an action for resisting the recognition and enforcement of an arbitral award in China is applicable to any type of arbitration.

a. Setting Aside of Arbitral Awards

(i) Domestic Awards

Article 58 (1) of the Arbitration Law sets out the grounds on which domestic awards may be set aside by the people's court:

(1) there is no arbitration agreement;
(2) the matters decided exceed the scope of the agreement or are beyond the authority of the arbitration institution;
(3) the formation of the tribunal or the arbitral procedure was not in conformity with the statutory procedure;
(4) evidence on which the award was based was forged;
(5) the other party withheld evidence sufficient to affect the impartiality of the arbitration; or
(6) the arbitrators have committed embezzlement, accepted bribes, conducted malpractice for their personal benefit or perverted the law. It further provides that, if the People's Court determines that the arbitral award is contrary to the social and public interest, it shall rule to set aside the award.

Article 58(3) further provides that where the court determines that the award is contrary to social and public interest, it shall rule to set aside the award.

The merits of the dispute may be reviewed to some extent in both setting aside and enforcement procedures of domestic awards. Pursuant to grounds (4) and (5) of Article 58(1) of the Arbitration Law stated above, a Chinese court

---

[55] As discussed earlier, the distinction is not clearly defined. See ch 1, s 1.4.1 above.

84 *Recognition and Enforcement*

may, during the proceedings for annulment of an award, examine and investigate the evidence submitted in the arbitration, which is considered an issue of merits.

(ii) Foreign-related Awards

Article 70 of the Arbitration Law sets out the grounds for setting aside foreign-related awards, making reference to Article 260(1) of the Civil Procedure Law 1991.[56] The grounds for the setting aside of a foreign-related award read as follows:

(1) there is no arbitration clause in the parties' contract and no subsequent written arbitration agreement between them;
(2) the party against which the application for enforcement is made was not given notice of the appointment of an arbitrator or of the initiation of the arbitration proceedings or was unable to present its case due to causes beyond its responsibility;
(3) the formation of the arbitral tribunal or the arbitration procedure was not in conformity with the rules of arbitration; or
(4) matters decided in the award exceed the scope of the arbitration agreement or are beyond the authority of the arbitration institution.

Article 260 (2) of the Civil Procedure Law 1991 further provides that '[i]f the people's court determines that the enforcement of the arbitral award is against social and public interest, it shall rule against enforcement'.[57] Chinese courts will not review the merits of an award while considering an application for setting aside a foreign-related award, except for the social and public interest consideration which can be substantive in nature.

b. Recognition and Enforcement of Arbitral Awards

(i) Domestic Awards

Pursuant to Article 63 of the Arbitration Law, making reference to Art 217 (2) of the Civil Procedure Law 1991,[58] the grounds for refusal to enforce domestic awards are:

(1) the parties have neither included an arbitration clause in their contract nor subsequently reached a written arbitration agreement;
(2) the matters decided exceed the scope of the agreement or are beyond the authority of the arbitration institution;
(3) the formation of the tribunal or the arbitral procedure was not in conformity with the statutory procedure;
(4) the main evidence for ascertaining the facts was insufficient;
(5) application of law was incorrect; or

---

[56] The corresponding provision now is Art 274(1) of the Civil Procedure Law revised in 2012.
[57] The corresponding provision now is Art 274 (2) of the Civil Procedure Law revised in 2012.
[58] The corresponding provision now is Art 237 (2) of the Civil Procedure Law revised in 2012.

(6) while arbitrating the case, the arbitrators have committed embezzlement, accepted bribes, conducted malpractice for their personal benefit or perverted the law.

Article 217 (3) of the Civil Procedure Law 1991 further provides that '[i]f the people's court determines that the enforcement of the arbitral award is against social and public interest, it shall rule against enforcement'.[59] Grounds (4) and (5) under Article 217(2) of the Civil Procedure Law allow a Chinese court to examine the evidence and the application of the law; this goes beyond procedural review and touches the merits of the disputes.

(ii) Foreign-related Awards

Article 71 of the Arbitration Law stipulates grounds for resisting enforcement of foreign-related awards, making reference to Article 260(1) of the Civil Procedure Law 1991,[60] which are identical to those for setting aside the same:

(1) there is no arbitration clause in the parties' contract and no subsequent written arbitration agreement between them;
(2) the party against which the application for enforcement is made was not given notice of the appointment of an arbitrator or of the initiation of the arbitration proceedings or was unable to present its case due to causes beyond its responsibility;
(3) the formation of the arbitral tribunal or the arbitration procedure was not in conformity with the rules of arbitration; or
(4) matters decided in the award exceed the scope of the arbitration agreement or are beyond the authority of the arbitration institution.

Article 260 (2) of the Civil Procedure Law 1991 further provides that '[i]f the people's court determines that the enforcement of the arbitral award is against social and public interest, it shall rule against enforcement'.[61] Similar to the setting aside procedure, Chinese courts will not review the merits of an award while considering an application for enforcement of a foreign-related award, except for the public policy consideration which can be substantive in nature.

(iii) Foreign Awards

- Awards made in a foreign country

The legal basis for the recognition and enforcement of foreign awards in China is international treaties to which China has acceded or the principle of reciprocity.[62] The principle of reciprocity has never been invoked so far for the recognition and enforcement of foreign awards. The relevant international treaties include (i) bilateral treaties on civil and commercial judicial assistance;[63]

---

[59] The corresponding provision now is Art 237 (3) of the Civil Procedure Law revised in 2012.
[60] The corresponding provision now is Art 274 (1) of the Civil Procedure Law revised in 2012.
[61] The corresponding provision now is Art 237 (3) of the Civil Procedure Law revised in 2012.
[62] Art 267 of the Civil Procedure Law.
[63] China has signed bilateral civil and commercial judicial assistance treaties with more than 30 countries, such as Belgium, France, Bulgaria, Egypt, Hungary and Korea.

86 Recognition and Enforcement

and (ii) multilateral international conventions that China has acceded to with respect to the recognition and enforcement of foreign awards. With the widespread adoption of the New York Convention, most of the bilateral treaties on judicial assistance provide that the recognition and enforcement of arbitral awards made in the other country should make reference to the New York Convention. The New York Convention is the principal international treaty applicable for this purpose in China. China decided to ratify the New York Convention on 2 December 1986 at the 18th Session of the 6th NPC Standing Committee, which came into effect in China on 22 April 1987. On 10 April 1987, the SPC issued the Notice of the SPC on the Implementation of the New York Convention, which has the effect of implementing legislation and provides the basis for implementation of the New York Convention in China. The notice also declares that China makes the reciprocal reservation[64] and commercial reservation[65] pursuant to Article I(3) of the Convention.

- Hong Kong awards

To solve the problem of reciprocally enforcing arbitral awards after the handover in 1997, the SPC and the Justice Department of Hong Kong entered into the Arrangement.[66] In 2000, the Arrangement was adopted in mainland China by the SPC Notice Concerning the Arrangement for Mutual Enforcement of Arbitral Awards between Mainland China and the Hong Kong Special Administrative Region.[67] Among other things, the grounds for refusing enforcement set out in Article 7 of the Arrangement borrow to a large extent from those set out in Article V of the New York Convention. Practically speaking, the effect of the Arrangement is that the enforcement of a Hong Kong award is treated like the enforcement of an arbitral award rendered in any country which is a signatory to the New York Convention.[68]

- Macao awards

Likewise, on 30 October 2007, Macao and mainland China signed the Arrangement Concerning Mutual Recognition and Enforcement of Arbitral Awards between the Macao Special Administrative Region and the Mainland, which entered into effect on 1 January 2008. The enforcement regime provided

---

[64] With the reciprocal reservation, China will apply the New York Convention only to the recognition and enforcement of awards made in the territory of another contracting state.

[65] With the commercial reservation, China will apply the New York Convention only to differences arising out of legal relationships, whether contractual or not, which are deemed commercial under the national law of the state making such declaration.

[66] www.legislation.gov.hk/intracountry/eng/pdf/mainlandmutual2e.pdf.

[67] See ch 2, s 2.2.2-B.a, fn 60.

[68] For a discussion of the mutual enforcement of arbitral awards between mainland China and Hong Kong, see generally, Langfang Fei, 'Enforcement of Arbitral Awards between Hong Kong and Mainland China: A Successful Model?' (2009) 8 *Chinese Journal of International Law* 3; Xianchu Zhang, 'The Agreement between Mainland China and the Hong Kong SAR on Mutual Enforcement of Arbitral Awards: Problems and Prospects' (1999) 29 *Hong Kong Law Journal* 463.

therein is very similar to the regime applicable to Hong Kong awards and Convention awards.

- Taiwan awards

In 1998, the SPC promulgated the Regulation for Recognition of Civil Judgments of the Courts of the Taiwan Region, which became effective on 26 May 1998 (SPC Regulation on Taiwan Judgments). The SPC Regulation on Taiwan Judgments is primarily intended to deal with the recognition of civil court judgments, but Article 19 extends its applicability to arbitral awards rendered in Taiwan. It should be noted that the SPC Regulation on Taiwan Judgments only sets out a mechanism for 'recognition', and only in relation to those applicants whose permanent domicile, habitual residence or involved properties are in mainland China or its Special Administrative Regions.[69]

B. Unique Features of the Legislation

Compared with transnational standards, the unique features of the Chinese legislation with respect to the recognition and enforcement of arbitral awards can be summarised as follows: (a) the court's review of domestic awards includes substantive issues; (b) the courts have no discretion to enforce awards on the existence of one of the grounds for non-enforcement; (c) the Report System applies on the enforcement of foreign-related and foreign awards; and (d) the Arbitration Law creates a dual supervision mechanism.

a. Substantive Review for Domestic Awards

In international practice, with the exception of public policy, the grounds for refusing enforcement or setting aside listed in the New York Convention, the Model Law and most modern legislation are limited to procedural grounds, based on natural justice and legality. National courts are prohibited from reviewing the merits of the awards, which is meant to support the finality of the arbitral awards.[70]

The Arbitration Law, by contrast, allows Chinese courts to review certain substantive issues, such as grounds (4) and (5) in setting aside domestic awards and grounds (4) and (5) in refusals to enforce domestic awards.[71] Although the law limits such review to domestic arbitration, it may impose some practical consequences on international arbitration: one consequence is for disputes involving FIEs. As explained above, FIEs are considered domestic companies,

---

[69] See José Alejandro Carballo Leyda, 'A Uniform, Internationally Oriented Legal Framework for the Recognition and Enforcement of Foreign Arbitral Awards in Mainland China, Hong Kong and Taiwan?' (2007) 6 *Chinese Journal of International Law* 2.
[70] See ss 4.1.1 and 4.1.2 above.
[71] See s 4.2.1-A.a(i) and A.b(i) above.

even if they are 100 per cent held by foreign investors.[72] Accordingly, arbitral awards rendered in such arbitrations would be subject to Chinese courts' substantive review for enforcement.

In addition, with different standards applied to the enforcement of different types of cases, some judges, inexperienced with international arbitration, have erroneously set aside or denied the enforcement of foreign-related or foreign awards after having reviewed the substance of an award. For instance, in *Hong Kong Wah Hing v Xiamen Dongfeng*,[73] the Xiamen IPC denied enforcement of a CIETAC award on the ground that the main evidence for ascertaining the facts was insufficient under Article 217 of the Civil Procedure Law 1991. In this case, a 'foreign element' was involved: one party was a company domiciled in Hong Kong (which is considered a 'foreign' jurisdiction in this context). Therefore, provisions regarding foreign-related arbitration should apply. The grounds for denying enforcement of foreign-related awards are clearly set forth in Article 260(1) of the Civil Procedure Law 1991, and are limited to procedural matters. However, the court erroneously applied the standards of review for domestic awards by invoking Article 217(4) of the Civil Procedure Law 1991, and denied enforcement after reviewing the merits.

b. No Discretion for the Court to Decide upon Enforcement

The New York Convention provides that recognition and enforcement of the award *may* be refused under listed grounds, which affords judicial *discretion* to enforce awards notwithstanding that one or more of the grounds for non-enforcement are established. In contrast, Articles 70 and 71 of the Arbitration Law provide that the court *shall* rule to set aside or deny enforcement of the awards if a ground listed in Article 260 of the Civil Procedure Law 1991 (now Article 274 of the Civil Procedure Law 2012) is established. Unlike transnational standards, the Chinese courts are not afforded any discretion to decide upon enforcement.

c. Report System for Foreign-related and Foreign Awards

One major concern relating to enforcement of awards in China is the local protectionism practised by some lower courts. To reduce the risk of decisions being invalidated because of local protectionism and lower court corruption, a Report System was established to ensure that an international award may not be set aside by a lower court without the prior examination and confirmation of the SPC.[74]

---

[72] See ch 1, s1.4.3-D above.
[73] *Hong Kong Wah Hing Development Company v Xiamen Dongfeng Rubber Manufacturing Company*, cited in Wang, 'The Practical Application of Multilateral Conventions Experience with Bilateral Treaties Enforcement of Foreign Arbitral Awards in the People's Republic of China', 487–88.
[74] See ch 1, s 1.4.3-D above.

Domestic awards, however, do not enjoy the benefit of the Report System. More importantly, the decision making process of the reporting mechanism is not transparent. The parties are not afforded a right to participate in the hearing by the HPC or the SPC to decide whether to enforce the award. They are not even provided the right to be notified about the hearing or to submit written documents in support of their position. Professor Peerenboom made the following comments, based on a series of interviews conducted with lawyers and parties in China:

> On more than one occasion lawyers were surprised to find out the reason the IPC was dragging its feet was that the case had been submitted to the higher courts for review. Some parties complained that they were severely disadvantaged by the court's reliance on the presentation of the facts and legal issues by the lower level court. They felt the lower courts did not provide a fair and accurate presentation of the case, either due to incompetence or local protectionist bias, and suggested that they be allowed to make their case directly to the higher courts.[75]

Moreover, as no time limit is set for the completion of the reporting process, there are concerns that it may lead to significant delays in proceedings.[76] On a few occasions, it took the court more than two years to hand down its decision to the lower court in the process of reporting.[77]

Despite its limits, the Report System has had a positive effect in practice. It is said to 'have significantly bolstered the confidence of investors in fear of local protectionism'.[78] Most of the arbitration experts whom the author interviewed during the research trip in 2007 viewed the Report System positively, in terms of ensuring the quality of judges, avoiding local protectionism, and protecting foreign investors. One interviewee described the Report System as a 'positive violation of law' (*liang xing wei fa*), as it was not consistent with the Civil Procedure Law and the constitutional law in theory, but has its positive effects in arbitration practice. However, it can only be a transitional method and will eventually be removed with the improvement of the arbitration system in China.[79] After all, the Report System can only be viewed as a temporary measure to protect foreign investors under the current legal regime. The existence of the system itself reflects the unbalanced development of courts in various regions and at different levels in China. The final liberalisation of arbitration depends on the improvement of the quality of judges at all levels.

---

[75] Peerenboom, 'Seek Truth From Facts: An Empirical Study of Enforcement of Arbitral Awards in the PRC', 289.
[76] These concerns were addressed by a number of practitioners, arbitrators, and academics that the author interviewed during the research trip in China conducted in March–April 2007. See Introduction, fn 18 above.
[77] See s 4.2.3 below.
[78] Tao, *Arbitration Law and Practice in China*,176.
[79] Introduction, fn 18 above. The specific comments of the interviewees have been kept anonymous.

d. Dual Supervision Mechanism

The Arbitration Law follows a dual supervision mechanism, under which the parties have two chances to challenge an award, by applying to set aside the award in China and/or by resisting enforcement of the award in China.

Such dual mechanism is also the approach under the Model Law. Although the Model Law provides that 'recourse to a court against an arbitral award may be made *only* by an application for setting aside,'[80] it does not prevent the losing party from resisting enforcement in another jurisdiction. In that sense, the losing party has two bites of the apple to challenge an arbitral award against it, (i) by an application to set aside the award in the country of origin, and/or (ii) by an action to resist enforcement of the award *in another jurisdiction* before the court where the winning party attempts to enforce it.[81] As the court in another jurisdiction might apply a different standard of review, the losing party may still have a second chance to resist enforcing the award even if its setting aside application failed at the seat of arbitration.

In China, however, the losing party has two bites of the apple even within the same jurisdiction. In other words, if the seat of arbitration is in China, the losing party has two chances to challenge the award before the Chinese courts, (i) by an application to set aside the award to the IPC 'in the place where the arbitration institution is located' (Court A), and (ii) by an action to resist enforcement of the award before the court in the place where the winning party started the enforcement action (Court B). In practice, Court A and Court B may be located in different regions in China. As courts at different regions may apply different standards of review, this gives the losing party the chance to try its luck twice before two different courts both within the territory of China. The dual mechanism in China is particularly problematic, as it may lead to inconsistent judicial decisions within the same legal order.

In practical terms, if the application for enforcement is lodged by the winning party within six months of the date of the award, the losing party may also have initiated judicial proceedings for setting aside the award within that period. In such a case, the court must stay any proceedings for enforcement and focus on the setting aside application. While the Model Law grants the court discretion to suspend the enforcement proceedings where there is an application to set aside an award as it deems proper,[82] an application to set aside an award before the Chinese court will automatically result in the suspension of any enforcement proceedings pertaining to the award in

---

[80] Art 34 of the Model Law.

[81] See s 4.1 above.

[82] Art 36(2) of the Model Law provides that 'if an application for setting aside or suspension of an award has been made to a [competent] court, the court where recognition or enforcement is sought *may*, if it considers it proper, adjourn its decision and *may* also, on the application of the party claiming recognition or enforcement of the award, order the other party to provide appropriate security (emphasis added)'.

China.[83] This automatic suspension opens the door for a reluctant party purposefully to delay the enforcement proceedings by taking advantage of the dual supervision mechanism. Furthermore, since the grounds for setting aside and the grounds for non-enforcement of domestic awards are slightly different, the procedure used may affect the outcome.

In light of the potential problems, the SPC Interpretation 2006 offers a partial reform to this dual supervision mechanism in China, by providing that where a party's application to set aside an award is refused, the courts will not entertain an application by the same party to resist enforcement on the same ground.[84] However, in practice, a losing party may still raise one ground for the setting aside application, and invoke a different ground later in the action to resist enforcement if the first application fails. Further reform is needed to eliminate completely the dual supervision mechanism within the same jurisdiction, so that if the seat of arbitration is in China, the only recourse against the award in China should be an action to set aside the award.

4.2.2 Statistical Assessment of the Enforcement Record

In reality, how difficult is it to enforce an arbitral award before the Chinese courts? What is the overall enforcement rate in China? What are the major difficulties at the enforcement stage? To put the situation in perspective, the survey conducted by PricewaterhouseCoopers and QMUL shows that judicial recognition and enforcement of arbitral awards are usually granted. The challenges encountered in the enforcement process tend to be practical, such as debtor solvency, rather than legal. When enforcement was needed, corporations were able to enforce arbitral awards within one year, and 84 per cent of those corporations have recovered more than 75 per cent of the value of the award following the enforcement and execution proceedings. Most participating corporations revealed no major difficulties in achieving recognition and enforcement of their arbitral awards. Where difficulties were encountered, they usually related to the circumstances of an award debtor, typically a lack of assets or an inability to identify relevant assets (70 per cent). Local enforcement and execution proceedings were the reasons why corporations encountered complications. 10 per cent of the respondents cited difficulties arising from corruption of local courts. Many corporate counsel cited countries in Africa and Central America, as well as China, India and Russia, as states that they perceive as hostile to enforcement of foreign arbitral awards.[85] Is corporate counsels' concern about the hostility of Chinese courts to the enforcement of foreign awards a real one?

---

[83] Art 64 of the Arbitration Law provides that 'if one party applies to enforce an arbitral award and the other party applies to set aside the award, the People's Court *shall* suspend the enforcement proceedings (emphasis added)'.
[84] Art 26 of the SPC Interpretation 2006.
[85] n 2 above.

92 *Recognition and Enforcement*

To get a sense of the enforcement statistics in China, the following two investigations are worth examining; one made through official channels, and the other through informal channels. The Arbitration Research Institute of the China Chamber of International Commerce (ARI) conducted two surveys, in 1994 and 1997 respectively, to investigate the enforcement of arbitral awards in China. The second investigation in 1997 was conducted by a survey of 310 IPCs and Maritime Courts throughout China (out of which 43 responded) about their experience of enforcing foreign-related and foreign awards. The statistics show that up to 1996 there were 164 applications for enforcement of CIETAC awards, 37 of which were denied enforcement, which yielded a 77.4 per cent enforcement rate. There were a mere 14 applications for enforcement of foreign arbitral awards, of which three were denied enforcement and one was still pending, which yielded a 71.4 per cent enforcement rate. On the basis of the responses received, the ARI concludes that the Chinese courts had recognised and enforced approximately 77 per cent of the awards (40 awards were denied enforcement and one was pending out of 178 applications).[86] Another important investigation was conducted by Professor Peerenboom, through the survey of 89 applications for the enforcement of arbitral awards in China during the period from 1991–1999 (the assessment of enforcement was based on 72 of these cases). His survey found an enforcement rate of 47 per cent for CIETAC awards and 52 per cent for foreign awards, with an overall enforcement rate of 49 per cent (a total of 37 cases was refused enforcement out of the 72 cases analysed).[87]

The difference in results between the two surveys may be explained by the different methodology adopted in the investigation. Rather than relying on an official channel like the people's courts (ARI only had responses from 14 per cent of the 310 courts approached), Professor Peerenboom's survey was conducted principally by way of direct interviews with lawyers and companies doing business in China, as well as published cases by the SPC and press reports. The reliance on information from lawyers may have resulted in a focus on cases with sizeable awards, or cases that are legally or politically more difficult to enforce (for which reason the parties decided to engage a lawyer). Furthermore, ARI's survey also includes cases which took place before the Civil Procedure Law was implemented in 1991. The Civil Procedure Law (Trial Implementation) then in force did not list any grounds for refusal to enforce arbitral awards.[88] Lastly, the difference may partially be due to the tendency on the part of the courts to report only good news.

Despite the respective limitations and the different results, the two surveys together give a general picture of the enforcement status in China. It is neither

---

[86] Wang, '*The Practical Application of Multilateral Conventions Experience with Bilateral Treaties Enforcement of Foreign Arbitral Awards in the People's Republic of China*', 478–84.

[87] Peerenboom, 'Seek Truth From Facts: An Empirical Study of Enforcement of Arbitral Awards in the PRC', 249–327.

[88] Art 167 of the Civil Procedure Law (Trial Implementation).

as hopeless as some foreign investors and reporters are wont to suggest, nor as trouble-free as official and semi-official sources allege. First, both surveys reveal that, while the overwhelming number of arbitral awards are voluntarily complied with by the parties concerned, in those cases where there is an enforcement failure, it is often practical reasons that prevent the court from enforcing the award, such as the respondent's lack of assets. This seems to be a common problem with enforcement all over the world. In light of this, parties should be advised to contract with proper partners with a good credit record, or to file timely applications for interim measures of protection to secure enforcement. Second, both surveys suggest that local protectionism may be an important impediment to enforcement. Local government officials may put pressure on a court to deny applications for enforcement against the assets of a local company or just drag out the enforcement process, usually by requesting additional documents or leaving a case pending. ARI's study shows that, out of the 37 non-enforcement awards, nine were not enforced due to 'some other difficulties' and three for 'grounds unknown'. According to the reporter of the ARI,

> while to give an accurate background calls for further investigation, it is generally presumed that the so-called 'difficulties' may be either the influence of local protectionism or otherwise the courts had reviewed the merits of the case, contrary to the stipulations of law.[89]

Peerenboom found that the parties attributed difficulties in enforcement at least partly to local protectionism in almost 60 per cent of the non-enforcement cases.[90] Lastly, the above surveys also indicate the uneven development of legal consciousness in various parts of China. Professor Peerenboom's survey provides statistical evidence to support the assumption that the likelihood of enforcement is higher in the major investment centres such as Beijing, Shanghai and Guangzhou, whilst less likely in smaller cities.

Chart 2: Probability of Enforcement in Large and Small Cities, by Amount of Award (Probabilities Calculated from Logistic Regression Coefficients)[91]

Amount of Award	Total (%)	Large City (%)	Other Cities (%)
$20,000	72	85	63
$200,000	59	74	49
$2,000,000	47	60	38
$20,000,000	39	46	32

---

[89] Wang, 'The Practical Application of Multilateral Conventions. Experience with Bilateral Treaties. Enforcement of Foreign Arbitral Awards in the People's Republic of China', 481–82.
[90] Peerenboom, 'Seek Truth From Facts: An Empirical Study of Enforcement of Arbitral Awards in the PRC', 277.
[91] ibid.

94 *Recognition and Enforcement*

As indicated in the above chart, an applicant would have an 85 per cent chance of enforcing an award for under $20,000 in Beijing, Shanghai or Guangzhou but only a 63 per cent chance in other, smaller, cities. When the amount of the award is between $200,000 and $2 million, the applicant's chances of enforcing the award fall to 60 per cent in the three major investment centres and to just 38 per cent in other cities.[92]

The Fourth Civil Division of the SPC conducted a sample survey in 2007 on the judicial review of foreign-related and foreign arbitration by the people's courts,[93] involving courts in 17 provinces or municipalities.[94] The sample survey covers the following types of cases: (i) applications for the confirmation of the validity of an arbitration agreement; (ii) applications for setting aside foreign-related arbitral awards; (iii) applications for the recognition and enforcement of foreign-related awards from one party and applications for refusal of enforcement from the other; and (iv) applications for the recognition and enforcement of foreign awards. Hong Kong, Macau and Taiwan awards are not included in the survey. The survey reviewed a total of 610 cases heard by the investigated courts between 2002 and 2006. According to the survey, of the 95 cases for the confirmation of the validity of arbitration agreements, 24 were denied validity (25.26 per cent of the total cases). Of the 337 cases applying for the setting aside of foreign-related awards, 16 awards were set aside (4.75 per cent of the total cases). Of the total 104 cases for the recognition and enforcement of foreign-related awards, only four were refused enforcement (3.85 per cent of the total cases). Of the 74 cases for the recognition and enforcement of foreign arbitral awards heard by the Chinese courts, rulings to reject recognition and enforcement of such awards were made in only five of these cases (6.76 per cent of the total cases).[95] These figures may indicate judicial attitudes supporting arbitration in recent years. The courts have made affirmative conclusions in the majority of these cases, in other words, confirmed the validity of arbitration agreements in 63.16 per cent of the total applications, rejected 85.16 per cent of the setting aside applications, enforced foreign-related awards in 96.15 per cent of the total applications, and enforced foreign awards in 78.38 per cent of the total applications.[96] Furthermore, the survey also reflects the importance of the Report System in current judicial practice. In the applications for recognition and enforcement of foreign awards, nine were rejected by the lower level courts. Thanks to the Report System, four of these rejected cases were overruled by the SPC, accounting for 44 per cent of the total reported cases.[97]

[92] ibid.
[93] 杨弘磊,《人民法院涉外仲裁司法审查情况的调研报告'》(2009) 9 武大国际法评论, (Honglei Yang, Report on the Judicial Review of International Arbitration by Chinese Courts).
[94] The 17 provinces or municipalities include: Beijing, Shanghai, Tianjin, Jiangsu, Guangdong, Liaoning, Fujian, Shandong, Hubei, Zhejiang, Heilongjiang, Hunan, Guangxi, Hainan, Shanxi, Sichuan and Chongqing.
[95] Yang, 'Report on the Judicial Review of International Arbitration by Chinese Courts', 306–08.
[96] ibid.
[97] ibid.

According to a report by two SPC judges, from January 2000 to September 2011, a total of 56 cases has been reported to the SPC in which lower courts refused to recognise and enforce foreign awards. The SPC has confirmed the refusal of recognition and enforcement of foreign awards in 21 of these reported cases: eight cases due to the lack of a valid arbitration agreement; nine cases on the ground of no proper notice of the appointment of arbitrator or of the proceedings or violation of due process; two cases of partial refusal of recognition and enforcement due to partial ultra vires, and one case due to non-arbitrability under Chinese law. In three cases the claimant's request was dismissed due to the expiration of the time limit for enforcement.[98]

4.2.3 Case Analysis

After a review of the statutory framework and statistical assessment, we shall now examine the 'real stories' by way of case analysis. After all, the proper functioning of an enforcement mechanism relies heavily on the court's interpretation of the statutory grounds against enforcement of arbitral awards. As this book is focused on international arbitration in China, we will only examine cases concerning (i) enforcement of foreign-related awards; and (ii) enforcement of foreign awards.

A. Setting Aside/Recognition and Enforcement of Foreign-related Awards

a. Lack of a Valid Arbitration Agreement (Article 274 (1)(1) of the Civil Procedure Law)

Article 274(1)(1) of the Civil Procedure Law (revised in 2012) provides that a court may set aside/refuse to enforce a foreign-related award if 'there is no arbitration clause in the parties' contract and no subsequent written arbitration agreement between them'. As discussed earlier, lacking a general principle of a pro-validity interpretation, the Chinese courts often take a very restrictive view of the arbitration agreement in case of ambiguity.[99] In addition, some courts systematically applied Chinese law to interpret the arbitration agreement, even when a foreign law should have applied and would have upheld its validity. If the arbitration agreement was ruled to be invalid, the award rendered thereof will necessarily be refused enforcement.

Despite the increasing number of multi-contract and multi-party arbitrations, the Chinese courts maintain a very restrictive approach to the issue of joinder and intervention, and are very reluctant to extend the arbitration clause

---

[98] 刘贵祥、沈红雨,《我国承认和执行外国仲裁裁决的司法实践述评》, 2011年"国际私法全球论坛", 2011年10月22–23日, 北京。(Guixiang Liu and Hongyu Shen, 'Recognition and Enforcement of Foreign Arbitral Awards in China: A Reflection on the Court Practices', report presented at Private International Law Global Forum, held in Beijing, 22–23 October 2011).

[99] See ch 2, s 2.2.2-A above.

to non-signatories. On a few occasions, a people's court has refused enforcement of arbitral awards rendered against a non-signatory. In *Bao Yangbo v Shangqiao*,[100] Bao Yangbo, Shangqiao and Sha-ping signed a joint venture (JV) contract (containing a CIETAC arbitration clause), which provided for the right of first refusal for venture parties, and that any share transfer had to be approved by a government body before it became effective. Later, a series of share transfer agreements occurred between Shangqiao, Sha-ping and a third party, Chengguang, without the approval of the government body. Bao attempted to invalidate these share transfer agreements before the CIETAC according to the arbitration clause contained in the JV contract. The CIETAC confirmed its jurisdiction against the third party based on the following ground:

> The third party has accepted the equity of the JV enterprise, thereby becoming a party to the JV enterprise in form or substance and has participated in the business management of the JV enterprise, it follows that the method for resolving any disputes arising from the above issues shall undoubtedly have to be dealt with according to the stipulations of the JV contract, that is such disputes shall be resolved through arbitration.

The tribunal thus proceeded with the matter and rendered a final award in favour of Bao Yangbo. In contrast to the attitude of the CIETAC, the SPC was not prepared to look beyond a strict 'contractual construct' to take into account the interconnectedness between the interests of the parties. As a result, the SPC refused to enforce the award against the third party, despite the third party's acceptance of the equity of the JV enterprise, and its participation in its business management. The SPC reasoned that:

> As Bao Yangbo, Shangqiao and Sha-ping were parties to the JV contract and the arbitration agreement therein, an award concerning the effectiveness of any transfer of shares between them was enforceable. In contrast, Chengguang had not been a party to the said contract, accordingly, to the extent the award sought to bind Chengguan, it was unenforceable.[101]

b. Violation of Due Process (Article 274(1)(2) of the Civil Procedure Law)

The second ground for refusing to enforce a foreign-related award is when

> the party against which the application for enforcement is made was not given notice of the appointment of an arbitrator or of the initiation of the arbitration proceedings or was unable to present its case due to causes beyond its responsibility,

pursuant to Article 274(2) of the Civil Procedure Law. Chinese courts generally interpreted this ground narrowly, and will support enforcement as far as the parties concerned have been afforded sufficient opportunities to present their

---

[100] *Bao Yangbo v Chongqing Shangqiao Industrials Co et al*, [2002] Min Si Ta Zi No 39 (SPC, 27 May 2003), reproduced in Exiang Wan (ed), *Guide on Foreign-Related Commercial and Maritime Trials*, People's Court Press, vol 5 (2003), 30–42.
[101] ibid.

case. The ARI's 1997 survey revealed that by the end of 1996 only three foreign-related awards were refused enforcement on the grounds that the party was not properly notified (two cases) or that the party was unable to present its case (one case).[102]

The court has held that a properly informed party that fails to appear at a hearing was not denied due process. In *China Leasing v Shenzhen Zhongji*,[103] the Shenzhen IPC rejected the applicant's argument for violation of due process due to the respondent's absence from the second oral hearing. The court held that the respondent received the notice for hearing, and had been afforded with sufficient opportunity to present its case; accordingly, no rule of procedure was violated.

The fact that the arbitration institution did not provide an interpreter during the hearing where the party did not make such a request was not sufficient ground to set aside the award under Article 274(1)(2) of the Civil Procedure Law. In *Materials & Machinery v New Makasu*,[104] the SPC rejected the applicant's argument that it was unable to present its case since the CIETAC did not provide it with a Chinese-Japanese interpreter during an oral hearing. The court reasoned that under the CIETAC Rules, the respondent had discretion to decide whether an interpreter was needed. However, in the present case, it did not request interpretation, and submitted a bundle of supplementary documents and evidence after the hearing, in addition to its previous statement of defence and counter-claim without objecting to the absence of interpretation. As a result, the court ruled that the respondent was not unduly precluded from presenting its case.

One disappointing decision is the Jiangmen IPC's ruling in *Pan Asia v Newport*.[105] The Court held that the respondent did not receive the notice for arbitration and was convinced that the respondent was deprived of the opportunity to present its case. However, there was only *ex parte* communication between the enforcing court and the respondent. The claimant was thus unable to furnish proof to refute the respondent's assertion and unable to plead in favour of enforcement.

c. Irregularities in the Composition of the Arbitral Tribunal or in the Arbitral Procedure Pursuant to the Rules of Arbitration (Article 274(1)(3) of the Civil Procedure Law)

The third ground under Article 274(1)(3) of the Civil Procedure Law is 'the formation of the arbitral tribunal or the arbitration procedure was not in conformity

---

[102] Wang, '*The Practical Application of Multilateral Conventions Experience with Bilateral Treaties Enforcement of Foreign Arbitral Awards in the People's Republic of China*', 481.
[103] *China Leasing Company Limited v Shenzhen Zhongji Industry & Development Center* (Shenzhen IPC, 30 October 1996), unreported, cited in ibid.
[104] *Xi'an New Materials & Machinery Research Institute (China) v New Makasu Co Ltd (Japan)* (Xiamen IPC), cited in ibid.
[105] *Pan Asia Trading Co, Ltd (China) v Newport Trading Co (HK)* (Jiangmen IPC), cited in ibid.

with the rules of arbitration'. It should be noted that, pursuant to the New York Convention, the standard of regularity is measured by the agreement of the parties, or, failing such agreement, by the law of the country where the award was made.[106] In China, however, the standard of regularity is reviewed by reference to the 'rules of arbitration'. Arbitration institutional rules thus play an essential part in Chinese courts' reviews of irregularity.

With respect to arbitral procedure, CIETAC Rules 2005 and 2012, for instance, provide that the arbitral tribunal shall hold an oral hearing when examining the case. Only if the parties so request or agree, and the tribunal also deems that oral hearings are unnecessary, can the oral hearing be omitted.[107] Relying on this provision, there are a few applications to set aside an award based on the arbitral tribunal's objection to holding a second hearing in respect of new claims or new evidence. The courts have consistently held that the decision to hold a subsequent hearing will be at the absolute discretion of the tribunal, provided that the tribunal granted sufficient opportunity to the parties to present their argument at the first hearing. For instance, in *Beijing Yayun v Lin Dunye*,[108] the Beijing IPC rejected Beijing Yayun's application to set aside the award based on the tribunal's failure to hold a supplementary hearing for the claimant's amended claims, ruling that Beijing Ya-yun had been afforded a sufficient opportunity to reply to the supplementary opinions, and the tribunal had no obligation to hold a second hearing. Similarly, in *Jiajun v Jinyu*,[109] the Beijing IPC dismissed the application to set aside the award based on the arbitral tribunal's refusal to hold a second hearing with respect to new evidence submitted after the first hearing, holding that the decision to hold a second hearing to deal with new evidence was entirely within the discretion of the arbitral tribunal.

In another case, an application to set aside the award based on the tribunal's acceptance of supplementary submissions after the expiration of the time limit was rejected. The Beijing No 2 IPC held in *Dalian Dongda v Dalian Liangshi*[110] that 'it is within the remit of the tribunal to accept documents after the time limit has elapsed, as such acceptance is not expressly prohibited by the Arbitration Law or the CIETAC Rules'.

This case analysis shows that the courts generally interpret this ground in a very narrow fashion, in light of the arbitral tribunal's broad procedural powers granted under the arbitral rules.

---

[106] Art V(1)(d) of the New York Convention.

[107] Art 29(2) of the CIETAC Rules 2005. Art 33(2) of the CIETAC Rules 2012 maintained similar wordings.

[108] *Beijing Yayun Garden Real-Estate Development Co Ltd v Lin Dunye (a Hong Kong citizen)*, [2002] Er Zhong Min Te Zi No 05139 (Beijing IPC, 20 June 2002), cited in Tao, *Arbitration Law and Practice in China*, 180.

[109] *Jiajun Development Co, Ltd v Beijing Jinyu Group Co, Ltd*, [2001] Er Zhong Min Te Zi No 1679 (Beijing No 2 IPC, 29 November 2001), cited in ibid.

[110] *Dalian Dongda Clothing Co, Ltd v Dalian Liangshi Clothing Co Ltd*, [2002] Er Zhong Min Te Zi No 01312 (Beijing No 2 IPC, 15 April 2002), cited in ibid.

d. *The Matters Decided in the Award Exceed the Scope of the Arbitration Agreement or the Authority of the Arbitration Institution (Article 274(1)(4) of the Civil Procedure Law)*

Ground (4) set out in Article 274(1) of the Civil Procedure Law allows the courts to set aside or refuse to enforce a foreign-related award if the matters decided in the award either exceed the scope of the arbitration agreement (ultra vires) or are beyond the authority of the arbitration institution.

On the ground of ultra vires, the Civil Procedure Law, unlike the New York Convention, did not provide for occasions when partial enforcement could be ascertained with respect to the matters decided within the scope of the arbitration agreement. In practice, this omission has resulted in refusal of enforcement of the entire award, even when only part of it was ultra vires. For instance, in *Knives v Ruibo Knives*, the award ordered the respondent to pay damages and return a car to the claimant. The Chengdu IPC found that the car did not belong to the respondent (which itself was a review on the merits), and concluded that the award had dealt with a matter beyond the scope of the arbitration agreement. Consequently, enforcement was *totally* refused by the court, including the part relating to damages.[111]

The ground of going 'beyond the authority of the arbitration institution' is rather unusual compared to transnational standards. Generally, the parties should be free to agree to have their case administered by any arbitration institution in which they put their confidence. Where does this limitation to the authority of arbitration institutions arise? It may be explained by the fact that when the Arbitration Law was promulgated in 1995, domestic arbitration institutions could only handle domestic cases, while foreign-related arbitrations were handled by the two so-called 'foreign-related arbitration institutions', namely the CIETAC and the CMAC. However, such limitation to the authority of arbitration institutions no longer exists today. Since 2000, the CIETAC is authorised to handle domestic cases. Domestic arbitration institutions are also allowed to hear foreign-related cases.[112] In light of these changes, this ground concerning the authority of arbitration institutions should be removed. Unfortunately, the Civil Procedure Law revised in 2012 failed to take into account these changes and maintained the same wording.[113] In *CICCC v Lido*,[114] the Beijing IPC invoked this ground to refuse enforcement of the CIETAC award. The court ruled as follows:

---

[111] *Chengdu Zhongshan Knives Development Institute (China) v Chengdu Zhongshan Ruibo Knives Co, Ltd (a Sino-foreign Joint Venture)* (Chengdu IPC), cited in Wang, 'The Practical Application of Multilateral Conventions. Experience with Bilateral Treaties. Enforcement of Foreign Arbitral Awards in the People's Republic of China', 487–88.

[112] See ch 1, s 1.3.2 above.

[113] Art 274(1)(4) of the Civil Procedure Law.

[114] *China International Construction and Consultant Corporation (CICCC) v Beijing Lido Hotel Company (Lido)*, Beijing IPC, unreported, cited in Wang, 'The Practical Application of Multilateral Conventions. Experience with Bilateral Treaties. Enforcement of Foreign Arbitral Awards in the People's Republic of China', 489.

After examination and verification, this court holds that both parties to the award, *ie*, CICCC and Lido, are Chinese legal persons; in addition, the contract of construction between them has no foreign element. Hence, this dispute is not a dispute arising from international economy and trade. According to the Rules of Arbitration of CIETAC, it is clear that *the dispute does not belong to the scope of case handled by CIETAC*. According to Article 260(1)(4) of the Civil Procedure Law 1991, the application for enforcement of the award submitted by CICCC shall therefore be denied (emphasis added).[115]

Given that the CIETAC has expanded its reach to domestic cases since 2000, this ground should no longer be applicable in practice.

e. Social and Public Interest (Article 274(2) of the Civil Procedure Law)

Pursuant to Article 274(2) of the Civil Procedure Law, conflict with social and public interest is another ground for setting aside or refusal to enforce a foreign-related award. The Chinese legislation does not use the commonly used term 'public policy', and has not provided a clear definition with respect to 'social and public interest'. A document issued by the SPC in 2004 titled Answers to Practical Questions in the Trial of Foreign-related Commercial and Maritime Cases (SPC Answers 2004)[116] may provide some guidance for the courts in defining the scope of 'social and public interest'. According to the SPC Answers 2004, the 'social and public interest' reservation can be applied where there is a violation of 'the fundamental principles of Chinese law, the State Sovereignty or national security, or the Chinese customs and basis moral standards'.[117] Although this explanation of 'social and public interest' is made in the context of the application of foreign law, it may also provide some guidance for courts when interpreting the 'social and public interest' ground under Article 274(2) of the Civil Procedure Law.

There is a risk that this ground may be misinterpreted by courts in order to protect local interests when they fear that the enforcement of an arbitral award could result in economic ruin for a small or medium-sized town. In the case of *Dongfeng Garments*,[118] the Zhengzhou IPC denied enforcement on the ground of violation of 'social and public interest'. The court did not contest the findings of the arbitrators that the defendant had breached the contract, but simply stated that:

---

[115] ibid.

[116] 涉外商事海事审判实务问题解答 (一). (Answers to Practical Questions in the Trial of Foreign-related Commercial and Maritime Cases, vol 1). Available in Chinese at www.shewai.com/news_info.asp?classcode=0&keyno=0&prono=107. (The English version is the unofficial translation by the author.)

[117] Para 43 of the SPC Answers 2004.

[118] *Dongfeng Garments Factory of Kai Feng City and Tai Chun International Trade (HK) Co, Ltd v Henan Garments Import and Export Group Company* (Zhenzhou IPC), cited in Cheng, Moser and Wang, *International Arbitration in the People's Republic of China: Commentary, Cases and Materials*, 131; Wang, 'The Practical Application of Multilateral Conventions. Experience with Bilateral Treaties. Enforcement of Foreign Arbitral Awards in the People's Republic of China', 491.

According to current State policies and regulations, enforcement . . . would seriously harm the economic influence of the State and public interest of the society, and adversely affect the foreign trade order of the State.[119]

Commentators raised concerns that the court used this ground to protect the local party since the defendant was the major local economic concern.[120] This case typically reflects one of the obstacles hindering the enforcement of awards in China – local protectionism. Fortunately, this decision was later reversed by the SPC. The SPC seems to take a very restrictive approach in its review of the social and public interest ground.

B. Recognition and Enforcement of Foreign Awards

With respect to the recognition and enforcement of foreign awards, the courts shall make reference to the New York Convention. The Notice of the SPC on the Implementation of the New York Convention provides further guidance on the application of the New York Convention in China, including the scope of application, competent courts, time limit for application, and standards of review. The courts' application of each ground of Article V of the New York Convention will be examined in turn.

a. Incapacity or Invalid Arbitration Agreement (Article V(1)(a) of the New York Convention)

The invalidity of an arbitration agreement is perhaps the most frequently invoked ground to oppose enforcement of a foreign award. Despite the exclusion of ad hoc arbitrations in China[121] and the unclear status of foreign arbitration institutions conducting arbitration in China,[122] Chinese courts are required to enforce foreign awards rendered by an ad hoc tribunal or a foreign arbitration institution outside China, in accordance with the New York Convention. A case review demonstrates that Chinese courts generally respect this commitment. In *Aiduoladuo (Mongolia) v Zhejiang Zhancheng Construction Group*,[123] the SPC specifically held that under Article V(1)(a) of the New York Convention, only if the arbitration agreement is not valid under the law to which the parties have subjected it or, failing any indication thereon, under the law of the country where the award was made, can an award be refused to be recognised and enforced. The SPC rejected the Zhengjiang HPC's reasoning to refuse enforcing an arbitral award on the ground that arbitration agreement was invalid pursuant to Chinese law.

---

[119] ibid.
[120] Michael Moser, 'China and the Enforcement of Arbitral Awards' (1995) 2 *Arbitration*, 50–51.
[121] On the exclusion of ad hoc arbitration in China, see ch 2, s 2.2.2-B above.
[122] On the unclear status of foreign arbitration institutions conducting arbitration in China, see ch 2, s 2.2.2-C above.
[123] *Aiduoladuo (Mongolia) Co, Ltd v Zhejiang Zhancheng Construction Group Co, Ltd*, [2009] Min Si Ta Zi No 46 (SPC, 8 December 2009), reproduced in Exiang Wan (ed), Guide on Foreign-related Commercial and Maritime Trial, People's Court Press, Vol 1, (2010), 87–93.

However, the attack on the validity of the arbitration agreement may cause significant delays for the enforcement procedure. The lower courts' reporting obligation under the Report System may have further contributed to the delays.

In the most widely cited case of *Revpower v SFAIC*,[124] the Shanghai No 2 IPC delayed the enforcement of an award rendered in Sweden for almost two years, based on the then-pending jurisdictional challenge before the court. The dispute resolution clause provides that 'should either party, after 60 days after the dispute arises, believe that no solution to the dispute can be reached through friendly consultation, such party has the right to initiate and require arbitration in Stockholm, Sweden, in accordance with the Statute of the Arbitration Institute of the Stockholm Chamber of Commerce'. On 29 June 1991 Revpower filed a request for arbitration to the Arbitration Institute of the Stockholm Chamber of Commerce (SCC). The SCC accepted the case and notified the request to the SFAIC, who raised jurisdictional objections to the SCC on 5 October 1991 but nominated an arbitrator. An arbitral tribunal was constituted in accordance with the SCC arbitration rules and rendered an interim award in July 1992, confirming its jurisdiction over the claims brought by the claimant. Before the scheduled hearing in June took place, the SFAIC filed a lawsuit for the same dispute before the Shanghai IPC in March 1993.

The court, instead of referring the matter to arbitration, accepted the case on the ground that the arbitration clause contained in the agreement was ambiguous and incapable of being performed because the arbitration clause did not refer to the SCC. Revpower promptly challenged the court's jurisdiction over the case. Surprisingly, it took the court almost two years to render a decision on its jurisdiction. While the lawsuit was pending before the Shanghai IPC, the respondent refused to participate further in the arbitration proceedings. The tribunal declared that the oral hearing scheduled to commence on 14 June 1993 would take place as planned and informed the respondent that if it would not attend the hearing, the tribunal would base its award on what the parties had stated in their respective written pleadings and documentation as well as on what would be presented by the claimant during the hearing. The respondent did not participate in the hearing. The arbitral tribunal rendered a final award on 13 July 1993, which ordered SFAIC to pay Revpower US$6,500,000. Revpower filed an application for enforcement of the award before the Shanghai IPC on 29 December 1993. However, the enforcement action was not accepted by the court

---

[124] *Revpower Ltd (Hong Kong) v Shanghai Far East Aerial Technology Import and Export Corporation* (SFAIC) (Shanghai No 2 IPC, 1 March 1996), unreported, cited in Wang, '*The Practical Application of Multilateral Conventions. Experience with Bilateral Treaties. Enforcement of Foreign Arbitral Awards in the People's Republic of China*', 496–98; Guiguo Wang, 'The Unification of the Dispute Resolution System in China Cultural Economic and Legal Contributions' (1996) 13 *Journal of International Arbitration* 2, 29; Alberto More, 'The Revpower Dispute: China's Breach of the New York Convention?' in Chris Hunter (ed), *Dispute Resolution in the PRC: A Practical Guide to Litigation and Arbitration in China* (Hong Kong, Asia Law and Practice Ltd, 1995) 151–58; Zhang, 'The Agreement between Mainland China and the Hong Kong SAR on Mutual Enforcement of Arbitral Awards: Problems and Prospects', 468; Tao, *Arbitration Law and Practice in China*, 196–98.

due to the fact that the jurisdiction issue of SFAIC's lawsuit was pending before the court. To enforce this award, the US consulate in Shanghai, high level official contacts with the Ministry of Foreign Trade and Economic Cooperation and the CIETAC have made political and diplomatic efforts. With China being openly accused of failing to honour its commitments under the New York Convention, the issue has further implications in terms of foreign trade and investment in China. Numerous US congressmen, the Office of the US Trade Representative and the US–China Joint Commission on Commerce and Trade also raised their concerns about this matter. Under these pressures, two years later, on 18 May 1995, the Shanghai IPC rendered its decision to dismiss the SFAIC's claims for lacking jurisdiction. The SFAIC appealed to the Shanghai HPC, which upheld the Shanghai IPC's ruling. Revpower resumed its application for enforcement to the Shanghai IPC on 29 February 1996. Finally, on 1 March 1996, the Shanghai IPC rendered its ruling on the recognition and enforcement of the award:

> The award, which was made by the arbitral tribunal composed of Lars Rahmn, Jerome Cohen and J. Gillis Wetter under the auspices of the Arbitration Institute of the Stockholm Chamber of Commerce, had satisfied the conditions for the recognition of foreign awards in accordance with the Convention on the Recognition and Enforcement of Foreign Arbitral Awards to which our country is a party and the laws of our country. Based on article 269 of the Civil Procedure Law of the People's Republic of China (1991), this court rule to recognise the validity of the arbitral award.[125]

Even though the court finally enforced the award in accordance with the New York Convention, there was a significant delay of almost two and a half years since the enforcement application was made on 29 December 1993. Unfortunately, while Revpower was waiting for the court's final ruling, SFAIC had successfully filed for bankruptcy, which made Revpower finally unable to enforce the award. The substantial delays in the court proceedings made the award in favour of the foreign investor meaningless.

Similar delays occurred in the *Nautilus* case,[126] in which the Dalian Maritime Court decided to enforce the ad hoc award rendered in London in accordance with the New York Convention more than two years after the application of enforcement.

Again, in *Norbok v China Navigation*,[127] it took two and a half years for the Beijing IPC to enforce a foreign award rendered by the London Maritime Arbitrators Association. Although the court's final decision was positive as no

---

[125] ibid.
[126] *Nautilus Transport and Trading Co, Ltd (Hong Kong) v China Jilin Province International Economic and Trade Development Corporation (China)* (Dalian Maritime Court, 25 April 1997), unreported, cited in Wang, 'The Practical Application of Multilateral Conventions. Experience with Bilateral Treaties. Enforcement of Foreign Arbitral Awards in the People's Republic of China', 499–501.
[127] *Norbok Cargo Transport Services Co, Ltd (Hong Kong) v China Navigation Technology Consultation & Services Company (China)* (Beijing IPC, 26 August 1992), reproduced in *Selected Cases of the SPC* (consolidated 1992–1996) No 1, 2179.

grounds listed in Article V of the New York Convention were found, the delay in rendering it overshadowed the desirable efficiency essential to enforcement. In the course of the enforcement proceedings, the parties reached a settlement agreement pursuant to which the claimant accepted the payment of US$160,000 to end the dispute.

To continue the story of the famous *Züblin* case,[128] after the SPC denied the validity of the arbitration agreement on 8 July 2004, the matter experienced further complications when the court was asked to address the issue of enforcement of arbitral awards rendered in accordance with such clause. While the issue of the validity of the arbitration agreement was still pending, the arbitral tribunal constituted in accordance with the ICC Rules proceeded with the arbitration proceedings and issued an arbitral award in favor of Züblin (the award was dated 30 March 2004). After Züblin subsequently applied to the Wuxi IPC in August 2004 for the enforcement of the award, Woco resisted enforcement on the basis that the SPC found the arbitration agreement invalid. In July 2006, almost two years after the application for the enforcement, the Wuxi IPC denied the recognition and enforcement of the award. It reasoned as follows:

1. As the arbitral award was made by the Court of Arbitration of the ICC, and confirmed by the seal of its Secretariat, it ought to be regarded as a 'non-domestic award';
2. Since Article I(1) of the New York Convention provides that the Convention 'shall also apply to arbitral awards not considered as domestic awards in the State where their recognition and enforcement are sought', the Convention would apply in determining the enforceability of this award;
3. Nevertheless, as the arbitration clause had been held by the SPC to be invalid, the award should be refused recognition and enforcement in accordance with Article V(1) of the New York Convention.[129]

Before the Wuxi IPC made a ruling on the enforcement, on 18 May 2006, Züblin applied to the Berlin Court of Appeal for a writ of execution of the arbitral awards, that is, a motion to declare the arbitral award executable in accordance with sections 1060(1), 1061 and 1062 of the German Code of Civil Procedure. However, the Berlin Court of Appeal held that, since the Chinese courts had already dismissed the application for the determination of the validity of the arbitration clause, the application for registration should be rejected in consequence, as the Chinese court decision had to be recognised in Germany.[130]

---

[128] See ch 2, s 2.2.2-C.b, fn 74.

[129] *Züblin International GmbH v Wuxi Woco-Tongyong Rubber Engineering Co Ltd*, [2003] Xi Min San Zhong Zi No 1 (Wuxi IPC ruling, 19 July 2006), cited in Nadia Darwazeh and Friven Yeoh, 'Recognition and Enforcement of Awards under the New York Convention: China and Hong Kong Perspectives' (2008) 25 *Journal of International Arbitration* 6, 841–42; Yeoh and Yu, 'The People's Courts and Arbitration – A Snapshot of Recent Judicial Attitudes on Arbitrability and Enforcement', 648.

[130] For more discussions of the proceedings before the German court, see Gotz-sebastian Hok, 'Chinese Arbitration Requirements – A Trap For FIDIC–ICC Arbitration?' (2008) 25 *The International Construction Law Review* 190, 190–97.

b. No Proper Notice of Appointment of Arbitrator or of the Proceedings; Lack of Due Process (Article V(1)(b) of the New York Convention)

As stated earlier, arbitrators have a broad discretion as to how they may conduct proceedings, and this defence has been narrowly construed.[131] The Chinese courts have followed the transnational approach and have held that there was no violation of due process under the New York Convention, as far as the means of notice or service met the requirements of the applicable arbitration law and arbitration rules.

In *Haimalu v Daqing Properties*,[132] the Korean Commercial Arbitration Board (KCAB) had delivered the arbitral notice and the arbitral award to the respondent in the Korean language without Chinese translation. The respondent requested the court to refuse enforcement, on the ground that it was not given proper notice of the proceedings in accordance with Article V(1)(b) of the New York Convention. The SPC ruled that:

> It does not constitute a violation of Korea's Arbitration Act and the Arbitration Rules of KCAB that the tribunal sent to the respondent the notice of hearing and the award without the Chinese translation attached. The applicant does not furnish any evidence to prove that there exists any circumstances stipulated in article V(1)(b) of NYC. Therefore, the award should be enforced.[133]

In *Boertong v Beijing Liantaichang*,[134] the KCAB sent the notice of arbitration and the arbitral award by mail to the Chinese party's registered address. The respondent did not receive them because his address had changed. The SPC ruled that the service was proper, for it did not violate the Arbitration Rules of the KCAB.

However, if the tribunal proceeded with the hearing when notification of the hearing date was not properly delivered to the respondent, the award rendered thereafter may be refused to enforcement. In *Aiduoladuo (Mongolia) v Zhejiang Zhancheng Construction Group*,[135] notification of the hearing date could not be delivered to the respondent, and the sender confirmed to abandon the delivery when contacted by the DHL. The tribunal continued with the hearing in the absence of the respondent and rendered an award. Based on the evidence presented, the SPC refused to recognise and enforce an arbitral award in accordance with Article V(1)(b) of the New York Convention.

---

[131] s 4.1.1-A.b above.

[132] *TS Haimalu Co Ltd v Daqing PoPeyes Food Co Ltd*, [2005] Min Zi Ta Si No 46 (SPC, 3 March 2006), reproduced in Exiang Wan (ed), *Guide on Foreign-related Commercial and Maritime Trials*, People's Court Press, vol 12 (2006) 51–57.

[133] ibid.

[134] *Boertong Corp (Group) v Beijing Liantaichang Trade Co Ltd*, [2006] Min Si Ta Zi No 36, (SPC, 14 December 2006), reproduced in Exiang Wan (ed), *Guide on Foreign-related Commercial and Maritime Trials*, People's Court Press, vol 14 (2007) 94–96.

[135] *Aiduoladuo (Mongolia) Co, Ltd v Zhejiang Zhancheng Construction Group Co, Ltd,* (SPC, 8 December 2009), n 125.

It should be noted that the Chinese courts take a cautious view with respect to notification by emails, as the email address is not the parties' place of business operation, habitual residence or correspondence address. The Chinese courts tend to take the standard of 'actual knowledge' to determine adequate notice when delivery is made by email, unless the applicable arbitration rule or the arbitration law at the seat of arbitration contains express provisions otherwise. In *Cosmos v Tianjin Kaiqiang*,[136] the SPC refused to enforce an arbitral award made in London on the ground that the claimant could not provide evidence that the respondent had received adequate notice. The English Arbitration Act 1996 does not specify the requirements of delivery by email. The SPC ruled that as the claimant did not provide any evidence of the respondent's confirmation of receiving the notification or any other evidence to prove the receipt by the respondent of the email notification, the notification was not adequate, and enforcement should be rejected according to Article V(1)(b) of the New York Convention.

c. Ultra Vires (Article V(1)(c) of the New York Convention)

For a similar ground provided under Article 274(1)(3) of the Civil Procedure Law, no partial enforcement is specified. This legislative gap has resulted in total refusal to enforce a foreign-related award even if only part of the award was declared ultra vires.[137] When it comes to enforcement of foreign awards, partial enforcement should be allowed 'if the decisions on matters submitted to arbitration can be separated from those not so submitted, that part of the award which contains decisions on matters submitted to arbitration may be recognised and enforced'.[138] In *Gerald Metals v Wuhu Smeltery*,[139] the Anhui HPC held that the whole award should be refused recognition because the arbitration award exceeded the scope of the arbitration clause. The case was then reported to the SPC. The SPC agreed that the arbitration award went beyond the scope of the arbitration clause. However, since the arbitration award could be separated into the part falling within the scope of the arbitration clause and the part going beyond the scope of the arbitration clause, the former should be recognised. The SPC's ruling properly applied Article V(1)(c) of the New York Convention.

---

[136] *Cosmos Marine Management SA v Tianjin Kaiqiang Trade Co Ltd*, [2006] Min Si Ta Zi No 34 (SPC, 10 January 2007), reproduced in Exiang Wan (ed), *Guide on Foreign-related Commercial and Maritime Trials*, People's Court Press, vol 14 (2007) 83–86.

[137] *Chengdu Zhongshan Knives Development Institute (China) v Chengdu Zhongshan Ruibo Knives Co, Ltd (a Sino-foreign Joint Venture)* (Chengdu IPC), see s 4.2.3-A.d, n 108.

[138] Art V(1)(c) of the New York Convention. See s 4.1.1-A.c above.

[139] *Gerald Metals Inc (US) v Wuhu Smeltery* (China), [2003] Min Zi Ta Si No 12 (SPC, 12 November 2003), reproduced in Exiang Wan (ed), *Guide on Foreign-related Commercial and Maritime Trials*, People's Court Press, vol 7 (2004) 30–35.

d. Composition of Tribunal or Procedure not in Accordance with Arbitration Agreement or the Relevant Law (Article V(1)(d) of the New York Convention)

As stated earlier, this ground under the New York Convention is aimed at 'more fundamental deviation from the agreed procedure'. The SPC has invoked this ground to refuse enforcement of arbitral awards on the basis that the parties failed to comply with the pre-arbitral consultation requirements under the respective arbitration clauses, which has aroused much criticism. In *PepsiCo v Sichuan Pepsi* and *Pepsi China v Sichuan Yun Lu*,[140] two awards rendered by the SCC tribunal in Sweden ruled in favour of Pepsi Co and Pepsi China. When the winning parties attempted to enforce the awards, the Chinese parties Sichuan Pepsi and Sichuan Yun Lu filed respective applications to resist enforcement of the two awards in Sichuan, arguing that (i) the tribunal permitted the arbitrations to proceed before the parties had the opportunity to exhaust the requisite period of 'friendly consultation', a violation of Article V(1)(d) of the New York Convention; (ii) they were not given adequate opportunities to present their cases, a violation of Article V(1)(b) of the New York Convention; (iii) matters went beyond the scope of the parties' submission to arbitration (ie, in relation to Sichuan Pepsi's profit distribution), a violation of Article V(1)(c) of the New York Convention; (iv) the criminal charges against Wang Shengchang[141] should result in his replacement; (v) the composition of the arbitral tribunal was not in accordance with the law of the seat (Sweden), a violation of Article V(1)(d) of the New York Convention; and (vi) the awards were decided under questionable circumstances and by questionable characters and their enforcement was against China's public policy, a violation of Article V(2)(b) of the New York Convention.

In its enforcement ruling, the Chengdu IPC dismissed the argument of bias, and held that Wang Shengchang's arrest would not qualify as a ground under Article V(1)(d) of the New York Convention or the public policy violation ground under Article V(2)(b) of the New York Convention. Further, the allegations of lack of impartiality were not supported by evidence to justify refusal of enforcement. However, the Court did refuse to enforce the two awards on the basis that failure to comply with the pre-arbitral consultation requirements under the respective arbitration clauses fell within Article V(1)(d) of the New York Convention. The Court reasoned as follows:

---

[140] *PepsiCo Inc v Sichuan Pepsi-Cola Beverage Co Ltd*, [2008] Cheng Min Chu Zi No 912 (Chendu IPC, 30 April 2008); *PepsiCo Investment (China) Ltd v Sichuan Province Yun Lu Industrial Co Ltd*, [2008] Cheng Min Chu Zi No 36 (Chengdu IPC, 30 April 2008), both cited in Darwazeh and Yeoh, 'Recognition and Enforcement of Awards under the New York Convention – China and Hong Kong Perspectives', 842–46; 邹晓乔, 《浅析四川百事合作经营合同案中的几个法律问题》, 《北京仲裁》第56辑, 第69–76页 (Xiaoqiao Zou, A Brief Analysis of Legal Issues in the *Pepsi Co* Case).

[141] Wang Shengchang, former Secretary General of the CIETAC, was arrested in March 2006. He was in detention for more than two years until 7 July 2008, when Tianjin IPC rendered the decision to sentence him to prison for five years for corruption and abuse of state assets. For further discussion about the Wang Shengchang case, see Wu Ming, 'The Strange Case of Wang Shengchang' (2007) 24 *Journal of International Arbitration* 2, 63–68.

The evidence presented by PepsiCo and Pepsi China could not establish that they had issued any notice to resolve the dispute through consultation, nor that consultation had been carried out for the requisite number of days. The awards must accordingly be refused enforcement because the arbitral proceedings were not in accordance with the parties' agreement.[142]

The court's refusal to allow enforcement on the basis of Article V(1)(d) in the above two cases is rather curious. Generally, the key issue arising from whether any precondition to arbitration is satisfied is whether the tribunal had rightly conferred jurisdiction, and not whether the 'arbitral procedures' themselves were defective. In addition, in *Pepsi China v Sichuan Yun Lu*, Sichuan Yun Lu failed to raise any objections in relation to the tribunal's jurisdiction or to any procedural irregularity, and the tribunal had assumed jurisdiction accordingly. Thus, Sichuan Yun Lu should have been held before the arbitral tribunal to have waived its rights to, and/or be estopped from, challenging the recognition and enforcement of the award under Article V(1)(d) of the Convention. The Court's unconvincing reasoning raises suspicions that this ground may be invoked as an ex post justification of a predetermined outcome,[143] to serve the court's political motivation to protect state-owned entities.

In *First Investment Corp of Marshall Islands v the Fujian respondents*,[144] the SPC refused to recognise and enforce an arbitral award made when one of the arbitrators did not fully participate in the arbitral proceedings and was not fully involved in the deliberation of the decision. First, the court ruled that the composition of the tribunal was not in accordance with the arbitration clause, which provided that an arbitral tribunal composed of three arbitrators should determine all future disputes arising out of the contract, and required the three arbitrators to participate fully in the arbitration procedure, such as the hearing of all evidence provided by the parties, the hearing of the cross-examination of all evidence, and the whole deliberation of the arbitral award. In reality, however, Wang Shengchang, a co-arbitrator, did not fully participate in the deliberation of the arbitral awards. The Court ruled that the fact that Wang participated in the deliberation of the first draft of the award of 21 January 2006 did not mean that the tribunal had finished the whole deliberation. Indeed, Wang was arrested on 20 March 2006, and was not able to read the second draft of the award sent by the president of the tribunal on 25 March 2006 and the final draft of 31 March 2006. Thus, Wang had not fully participated in the deliberation of the arbitral award, contrary to the provision that 'the decision shall be made by a tribunal composed of three arbitrators' in the arbitration clause. Second, the

---

[142] *PepsiCo Inc v Sichuan Pepsi-Cola Beverage Co Ltd*, [2008] Cheng Min Chu Zi No 912 (Chendu IPC, 30 April 2008); *PepsiCo Investment (China) Ltd v Sichuan Province Yun Lu Industrial Co Ltd*, [2008] Cheng Min Chu Zi No 36 (Chengdu IPC, 30 April 2008), n 142.

[143] Darwazeh and Yeoh, 'Recognition and Enforcement of Awards under the New York Convention – China and Hong Kong Perspectives', 849.

[144] *First Investment Corp of Marshal Island v Fujian Mawei Shipbuilding Ltd and Fujian Shipbuilding Industry Group Corp (collectively 'the Fujian Respondents')*, [2007] Min Si Ta Zi No 35 (SPC, 27 February 2008).

court held that the composition of the tribunal was not in accordance with the procedural law of the seat of arbitration (English law). Pursuant to the English Arbitration Act 1996, when an arbitrator refuses, or is unable, to continue performing his or her function as an arbitrator, the parties have the power to cure the defects in the composition of the tribunal by (i) revoking the arbitrator's authority;[145] (ii) applying to the court for the removal of the arbitrator;[146] or (iii) filing the vacancy by appointing a replacement arbitrator.[147] In this case, Wang was not able to continue participating in the arbitration proceedings and performing his function as an arbitrator since he had been arrested. Before the parties take one of the above statutory measures provided by the English Arbitration Act 1996, the two remaining arbitrators cannot constitute a valid arbitral tribunal to continue arbitration. Accordingly, the court concluded that the composition of the tribunal was not in accordance with the arbitration agreement and the relevant law, and refused to recognise and enforce the award in accordance with Article V(1)(d) of the New York Convention.

In *North American Foreign Trading Corporation v Shenzhen Laiyingda et Al*,[148] SPC rejected the respondents' application to refuse recognition and enforcement of the award on the ground that tribunal's postponement of the hearing date was in violation of the arbitration rules. The Guangdong HPC ruled that even though the parties agreed on a hearing date, they did not specify that the tribunal could not change the hearing date. The timetable the parties agreed on 4 January 2005 does not constitute an amendment of the arbitration rules, and cannot exclude the tribunal's discretion in postponing the hearing date. The tribunal's extension of the hearing date upon the claimant's request is not in violation of the arbitration rules. The SPC agreed with the Guangdong HPC's ruling and held that respondents had not provided evidence to prove that they were not aware of the extended hearing date, and the arbitration procedure was in accordance with the arbitration rules.

e. Award not Binding, Suspended, or Set Aside (Article V(1)(e) of the New York Convention)

ARI's finding indicates that none of the refusals to enforce foreign awards was based on ground (e) of the New York Convention. After a comprehensive review of the recent cases available, the author has not found any instance when the Chinese courts have refused to enforce a foreign award by invoking this ground to date.

---

[145] Art 23 of the English Arbitration Act 1996.
[146] Art 24 of the English Arbitration Act 1996.
[147] Art 27 of the English Arbitration Act 1996.
[148] *North American Foreign Trading Corporation v Shenzhen Laiyingda Co, Ltd, Shenzhen Laiyingda Technology Co, Ltd, Shenzhen Cangping Import & Export Co, Ltd, Shenzhen Light Industry Import & Export Co, Ltd*, [2009] Min Si Ta Zi No 30, (2 September 2009): reproduced in Exiang Wan (ed), *Guide on Foreign-related Commercial and Maritime Trial*, People's Court Press, vol 2 (2009), 87–92.

110 *Recognition and Enforcement*

f. *Arbitrability (Article V(2)(a) of the New York Convention)*

On the issue of arbitrability, the Arbitration Law has both positive and negative provisions. Article 2 of the Arbitration Law provides that 'contractual disputes and other disputes over rights and interests in property between citizens, legal persons and other organisations that are equal subjects may be arbitrated'. Article 3 makes an exclusive provision on non-arbitrable matters:

1. Marital, adoption, guardianship, support and succession disputes; and
2. Administrative disputes that laws require to be handled by administrative authorities.

In *ED&F v China Sugar*,[149] the respondent argued that the contract between the parties involved fraudulent option transactions and was thus illegal; accordingly, it did not belong to the arbitrable commercial disputes recognised under Chinese law. The Beijing HPC ruled that there was no provision under Chinese law that illegal option contracts did not belong to a contractual or non-contractual commercial legal relationship. The SPC confirmed the ruling of the Beijing HPC and held that the dispute arising out of an option contract was arbitrable under Chinese law.

g. *Public Policy (Article V(2)(b) of the New York Convention)*

The ground of public policy under the New York Convention is generally construed as referring to 'international public policy', and is narrowly construed by national courts.[150] The SPC has held that the notion of 'public policy' in the context of Article V(2)(b) must be narrowly construed, and that a breach of mandatory provisions of Chinese law does not equate with a public policy violation so as to justify refusal of enforcement. In *ED&F v China Sugar*,[151] the SPC decided to enforce an award under the New York Convention, despite the fact that the contract should have been held invalid for breach of mandatory Chinese laws (which prohibit Chinese companies from engaging in futures trading overseas without the approval of Chinese authorities). The SPC ruled that 'a breach of mandatory provisions of Chinese law did not "completely equate with a breach of public policy" so as to justify non-enforcement under article V(2)(b) of the New York Convention'.[152]

This approach was reaffirmed by the SPC in *Mitsui v Hainan Textile*.[153] Although the SPC agreed with the Hainan HPC that the assumption of foreign

---

[149] *ED&F Man (HK) Co, Ltd v China National Sugar & Wines Group Corp*, [2003] Min Si Ta Zi No 3 (SPC, 1 July 2003), reproduced in Exiang Wan (ed), *Guide on Foreign-related Commercial and Maritime Trials*, People's Court Press, vol 7 (2004) 12–17.
[150] See s 4.1.1-B.b above.
[151] n 149 above.
[152] ibid.
[153] *Mitsui & Co (Japan) v Hainan Province Textile Industry Corporation*, [2001] Min Si Ta Zi No 12 (SPC, 13 July 2005), reproduced in Exiang Wan (ed), *Guide on Foreign-related Commercial and Maritime Trials*, People's Court Press, vol 11 (2005) 109–12.

debt by Hainan Textile without proper approval violated mandatory regulations regarding foreign debt approval and registration, as well as foreign exchange policy, it ruled that such violation did not necessarily constitute a violation of the public policy of the PRC. On that basis, the application to refuse enforcement was rejected.

The first case in which the SPC invoked the public policy ground to refuse enforcing a foreign award was its ruling in *Hemofarm v Jinan Yongning*,[154] on the basis of the violation of China's judicial sovereignty and the jurisdiction of the Chinese courts. In this case, Hemofram and Jinan Yongning signed a contract to establish a JV company (the Company), which provided for ICC arbitration in Paris. Despite the arbitration clause, Jinan Yongning commenced litigation against the Company in the Jinan IPC to recover rentals for land and machinery leased to the Company. The Company challenged the Court's jurisdiction based on the arbitration clause. The Court rejected the jurisdictional objection, holding that as the Company was not a party to the JV contract, the Court had jurisdiction. It then proceeded to rule in favour of Jinan Yongning, and allowed its application to freeze the Company's assets. In parallel, relying on the arbitration clause, Hemofarm commenced ICC arbitration against Jinan Yongning, alleging that the latter had breached the JV contract by mismanaging the Company, and that Hemofarm was unable to continue with the JV as a result of the Chinese litigation which led to property preservation measures imposed on the Company. The ICC tribunal ruled in favour of Hemofarm, ruling that: (1) the Chinese litigation and the remedies awarded by the court prejudiced Hemofarm's rights and benefits arising out of the JV, leading to the cessation of operation and eventual closure of the Company; (2) Jianan Yongning's action in having the property preservation measures imposed upon the Company was a breach of the JV contract and therefore Hemofarm could pursue its claims for damages against Jinan Yongning in the ICC proceedings; and that (3) Jinan Yongning was in breach of the JV agreement by bringing the claim before the people's court, when the contract provided for ICC arbitration. The SPC refused to enforce the ICC award rendered in Paris on the following grounds:

1. the arbitration clause only governed disputes in connection with the JV contract between the parties to the JV and did not cover disputes between the Company (not a party to JV contract) and a JV party, which can only be properly litigated before the People's Courts;
2. The tribunal had exceeded the scope of the arbitration agreement by 're-adjudicating' and issuing an award to the dispute that had been heard before the People's court; and
3. The tribunal had *violated China's judicial sovereignty and the jurisdiction of the Chinese courts* by re-adjudicating upon the legality of the property preservation measured awarded by the Chinese courts and the issue of the Chinese court's

---

[154] *Hemofarm DD et al v Jinan Yongning Pharmaceutical Co*, [2008] Min Si Ta Zi No 11 (SPC, 27 June 2008), cited in People's Court Daily, available at rmfyb.chinacourt.org/public/detail.php?id=120776.

jurisdiction over the dispute. Accordingly, the enforcement was rejected (emphasis added).[155]

This decision may be viewed as setting a dangerous precedent, particularly in relation to JV disputes between Chinese and foreign parties. Although JV contracts frequently provide for arbitration with a foreign seat, the arbitration agreement often only covers the JV partners, not the JV company itself. To circumvent the arbitration clause, Chinese parties may seek to have the dispute resolved before the people's court, by including both the JV counterpart and the JV company which is not a party to the arbitration agreement. Given that the SPC has taken a restrictive approach to issues of third-party joinder and intervention, it is likely that the court will assume jurisdiction over the entire dispute. In view of *Hemofarm*, any ruling by the people's court relating to the rights and obligations between the JV partners under the JV contract would then preclude a tribunal from rendering an enforceable award governing the rights and obligations.[156]

Despite the decision in *Hemofarm*, the Chinese courts have generally interpreted the ground of public policy narrowly, and only apply this ground in extreme cases when the recognition and enforcement of an award is against the basic principles of Chinese law, violates state sovereignty, threatens national and social security, or violates the fundamental social and public interest of China. In the refusal of recognition and enforcement of Award No 07-11 of the Japan Commercial Arbitration Association,[157] the SPC stated that 'if other circumstances exist which support a refusal of recognition and enforcement of the award, the public policy ground will not be invoked'.

C. Further Observations Arising From the Case Analysis

From the above case analysis, further observations can be made with respect to enforcement of foreign-related and foreign awards in China regarding: (a) inconsistent decisions due to uneven developments in courts at different levels and locations in China; (b) the influence of local protectionism; and (c) problems of delay in enforcement.

a. Inconsistent Decisions

Given the uneven development of judicial practice in various parts of China, the Chinese courts are not always consistent in construing the grounds for setting aside or refusing to enforce arbitral awards. Differences exist among different hierarchical levels of courts, and various geographical locations of courts at the same level. Some lower-level courts, unfamiliar with international arbitration

---

[155] ibid.
[156] Darwazeh and Yeoh, 'Recognition and Enforcement of Awards under the New York Convention – China and Hong Kong Perspectives', 488–89.
[157] [2010] Min Si Ta Zi No 32.

norms, have rendered surprising decisions without providing sufficient reasoning. Judges at higher level courts are generally more experienced with international arbitration. On a few occasions, the SPC has corrected errors made by lower courts under the Report System. Consistent with Professor Peerenboom's findings, the success of enforcement also depends on the location of the court. Generally, courts in more economically developed municipalities (such as Beijing, Shanghai and Shenzhen) take a more liberal attitude towards enforcement than their counterparts in less developed areas.

b. Local Protectionism

The case review also indicates that enforcement becomes more difficult when a state-owned enterprise is involved or local interests may be affected. This is explained by the influence of local protectionism, which may hinder the enforcement of awards in accordance with the Arbitration Law or the New York Convention. Certain lower-level people's courts are subject to the considerable influence of local government, particularly in terms of financial resources and personnel management. On a few occasions, fearing that enforcement of an arbitral award could result in the economic ruin of a small or medium-sized town, the courts have refused to enforce the award by invoking the public policy ground without giving much legal analysis (eg, the *Dongfeng Garments Factory* case[158]), or by seeking a statutory ground to justify an outcome to protect the local interest (eg, the *PepsiCo* case[159]).

c. Problems of Delays

In certain cases, local protectionism did not result in the court's refusal to enforce the award eventually, but has caused problems for the applicant such as significant delays or difficulties discovering assets. Based on the case review mentioned above, a few cases lasted for more than two years. In certain of them, the court's delay in enforcement has finally made the successful party unable to enforce the award, due to the debtor's declaration of bankruptcy or transfer of assets (eg, *Revpower* case[160]). Some parties had to reach an enforcement settlement with the debtor despite an award in their favour, in the hope of collecting at least some of the money due (eg, *Norbok* case[161]). This observation is consistent with Professor Peerenboom's finding that in the 35 cases out of 72 where applicants were able to enforce the award at all, they were only able to recover the total amount of the award in 34 per cent of the cases. Meanwhile, in 17 per cent of these successful cases the applicant recovered less than half of the award.[162]

[158] n 120 above.
[159] n 142 above.
[160] n 126 above.
[161] n 129 above.
[162] Peerenboom, 'Seek Truth From Facts: An Empirical Study of Enforcement of Arbitral Awards in the PRC', 255.

5

The Practice of Arbitration Institutions

'The proof of the pudding is in the eating. By a small sample we may judge the whole piece.'

Miguel de Cervantes Saavedra

PROFESSOR JARROSSON COMPARED institutional arbitration to a 'theatre', at which the arbitrator and the parties are the actors and the arbitration institutions are the organisers of the performance. The arbitration institution functions as an organiser or facilitator, which helps to ensure the smooth progress of the arbitration proceedings. The real players in the arbitration are the parties and the arbitrators.[1] How do arbitration institutions organise these theatrical performances? What is the actual practice of arbitration institutions in China?

There are more than 200 arbitration institutions all over China,[2] and we will not be able to examine the practice of each institution in turn: 'By a small sample we may judge the whole piece'. This chapter intends to illustrate the current status of Chinese arbitration institutions through the example of the CIETAC and an overall review of local arbitration institutions. We shall start with a discussion of the legislative background for the establishment of arbitration institutions in China (section 5.1). With this background information, we will examine contemporary practice of Chinese arbitration institutions in detail: first by comparing the practice at the CIETAC – the leading arbitration institution in China – to the ICC Court, one of the most renowned arbitration institutions in the world (section 5.2); and then discussing the general status of local arbitration institutions in China (section 5.3).

5.1 LEGISLATIVE BACKGROUND OF THE ESTABLISHMENT OF ARBITRATION INSTITUTIONS IN CHINA

To better understand the current status of arbitration institutions in China, it is helpful to examine earlier legislative history. China's modern arbitration system

---

[1] See Charles Jarroson, 'Le rôle respectif de l'institution, de l'arbitre et des parties dans l'instance arbitrale' (1990) *Revue de l'arbitrage* 381, 381.
[2] Ch 1, s 1.2.2, fn 32.

has its origins in the early 1950s, when the Chinese government began actively to promote arbitration and mediation as the preferred means for resolving economic disputes. Initially, China developed a domestic administrative arbitration system substantially different from its system of foreign-related arbitration. Domestic arbitration in China was essentially administrative arbitration. This system was drawn from the experience in the Union of Soviet Socialist Republics (USSR). Under the USSR model, arbitration was compulsory without the need for an arbitration agreement between the parties; the parties did not have the right to choose the arbitrators; arbitration institutions were established within administrative bodies; the leading positions within the institutions were assumed by administrative officials; the staff of administrative bodies acted as arbitrators; the arbitral decision was essentially made by administrative bodies exercising their administrative powers; and the arbitral awards were not final as the parties had a right to appeal to the courts. Such an arbitration system was a product of the 'planned economy' (sometimes called 'centralised economy') – an economic system controlled by administrative bureaus. The administrative arbitration system is completely different from the modern international commercial arbitration system in that the arbitration is not based on party autonomy, but on administrative control. Foreign-related arbitration, on the other hand, was dominated by the CIETAC and the CMAC, under the auspices of the CCPIT. As early as the early 1950s, the founders of the CIETAC decided not to follow the USSR model, but to take the road of arbitration pursuant to transnational standards.[3]

With an attempt to reform the past administrative arbitration system thoroughly for domestic arbitration, on 30 August 1994, the Standing Committee of the NPC passed the Arbitration Law. The core of the reform was to transform the arbitration bodies attached to administrative bodies into independent arbitration institutions of a private nature. To achieve this goal, the Arbitration Law contains a number of specific provisions with reference to restoration of the private nature of arbitration. The legislative purpose can be understood in the context of the historical development of the arbitration system in China. These provisions are specifically addressed to the former administrative arbitration system.

On the nature of arbitration institutions, Mr Fei Zongyi, a reputable Chinese arbitration expert who was involved in the drafting of the Arbitration Law, proposed specifying that an arbitration institution should be defined as an organisation of a private nature during the discussions on the drafting of the Arbitration Law. The opponents to his proposal argued that there was no other arbitration law that contained a similar provision. Fei Zongyi responded that 'it is because the problem does not exist in other countries. Our arbitration system was transformed from administrative arbitration, and this clarification is necessary

---

[3] The history of the CIETAC is discussed in s 5.2.1-B below.

to avoid future confusion'.[4] Finally, Mr Fei's proposal was adopted. Article 14 of the Arbitration Law provides:

> [A]rbitration institutions shall be independent from administrative authorities and there shall be no subordinate relationships between arbitration institutions and administrative authorities. There shall also be no subordinate relationship between arbitration institutions.

With respect to the composition of the arbitration institution, Article 12 of the Arbitration Law stipulates as follows:

> The offices of chairman, vice chairman and member of an arbitration institution shall be held by experts in the field of law, economy and trade and by persons with practical working experience. At least two-thirds of the persons forming an arbitration institution shall be experts in the field of law, economy and trade.

In other words, arbitration institutions shall not have more than one third of government officials as their members. This legislative limitation to the percentage of government officials within the arbitration institutions demonstrates the legislator's intention to reform the administrative arbitration based on the USSR model and to ensure the independence of arbitration institutions from administrative intervention.[5]

To implement the restructuring of arbitration institutions, the Arbitration Law provides that:

> [A]rbitration institutions in the municipalities directly under the central government, in the municipalities that are the seats of the People's Governments of provinces and autonomous regions and in other municipalities with districts that were established prior to the implementation of this Law shall be reorganized in accordance with this Law. Those of such arbitration institutions that are not reorganized shall cease to exist one year from the date of implementation of this Law. Other arbitration institutions established prior to the implementation of this Law that do not comply with the provisions of this Law shall cease to exist from the date of implementation of this Law.[6]

The practical impact of this provision is often underestimated. In 1994, there were 3,640 arbitration institutions of various types in China, and more than 20,000 related personnel. From 1983 to 1994, 2,580,000 cases were resolved by administrative arbitration – this translates into an average of 250,000 arbitration cases per year.[7] The restructuring of 3,640 existing arbitration institutions in the old system meant a significant number of such institutions needed to be eliminated, related personnel need to be rearranged, and total numbers of cases

---

[4] See 费宗祎,《费宗祎先生谈仲裁法的修改》《北京仲裁》第62辑, 2007年 (Zongyi Fei, 'Comments on the Reforms of the Arbitration Law by Mr Fei Zongyi', (2007) 62 *Beijing Arbitration*).

[5] As we will see later, such legislative intention, however, is not fully implemented in practice.

[6] Art 79 of the Arbitration Law.

[7] 王红松,《中国仲裁面临的机遇和挑战》,《北京仲裁》第64期, 2008年(Hongsong Wang, The Opportunities and Challenges of Chinese Arbitration', (2008) 62 *Beijing Arbitration*).

needed to be reduced. Thus, this provision demonstrates the legislators' determination to reform the old arbitration system in China following the USSR model, and to build up a new arbitration system in line with transnational standards.

The question was, who was to be in charge of the restructuring? There were suggestions to refer this to the chambers of commerce, as many foreign arbitration institutions were established within the structures of chambers of commerce. However, there were no truly independent chambers of commerce at local levels in China. Given the strong connections between the existing arbitration institutions and administrative bodies, the government was probably better positioned to take the lead role in the restructuring process. Against this background, the Arbitration Law specified that the function of the government in the establishment of arbitration institutions was to arrange for the relevant departments and chambers of commerce to organise the arbitration institutions in a unified manner.[8] The State Council issued a notice to provide some further guidance on this issue:

> In the initial period of establishment, the municipal government shall refer to relevant provisions concerning 'companies for public interest' to resolve the arbitration institutions' personnel, finance and renting issues. The arbitration institutions shall gradually achieve its financial independence from government support.[9]

The purpose was to provide some governmental support in the initial period – as the Chinese say, to help them get on the horse (*fu shang ma, song yi cheng*). The arbitration institutions were supposed to operate independently after the transitional period. Have the above legislative objectives been achieved in arbitration practice? What is the current status of arbitration institutions throughout China?

5.2 COMPARISON BETWEEN THE CIETAC AND THE ICC COURT

The CIETAC is the oldest arbitration institution in China dealing with foreign-related arbitrations and remains the leading one. Thus, before discussing the status of local arbitration institutions throughout China, we shall first examine the historical development and the current status of the CIETAC. To have a better illustration of its Chinese characteristics, comparison will be made with the ICC Court, one of the oldest and most prestigious arbitration institutions in the world. Comparisons between the CIETAC and the ICC Court will be made in the following aspects: establishment and nature (section 5.2.1); structure and personnel management (section 5.2.2); financial management (section 5.2.3); and the relationship between the arbitration institution and the arbitrators

---

[8] Art 10(2) of the Arbitration Law.
[9] Circulation Concerning the Re-establishment of the Arbitration Institutions issued by the State Council on 1 August 1995, [1995] Guo Ban Fa No 44.

118   *The Practice of Arbitration Institutions*

(section 5.2.4). The following discussions will not only be based on the current arbitration rules, the existing literature concerning the practice of the CIETAC and the ICC, and the official information published on their websites and journals, but also on first-hand knowledge that the author obtained through her personal observations working at the Secretariat of the ICC Court (the Secretariat) in Paris in 2008–2009, discussions with the staff at the Secretariat and members of the ICC Court, interviews with officials and arbitrators from the CIETAC during the above-mentioned research trip in 2007,[10] and informal conversations with the case managers of the CIETAC.

5.2.1 Establishment, Nature, and Development

A. *The ICC Court*

Shortly after World War I, in 1919, prominent members of the business communities of the United States, the United Kingdom, France, Belgium and Italy met and established a business organisation to promote world peace. These men, who referred to themselves as 'the merchants of peace', believed that by fostering international commerce they could promote friendly relations between nations, and avoid wars. This was the birth of the ICC. Very early in the ICC's inception and central to its philosophy was, and remains, the belief that an effective method of dispute resolution is necessary to facilitate trade. The founding fathers of the ICC quickly adopted a plan for mediation and arbitration, leading to a set of procedural rules in 1922 and, a year later, to the creation of the body now known as the International Court of Arbitration.[11]

Since its founding in 1923, the ICC Court has been at the forefront of the development of arbitration as the method of choice for resolving international business disputes. 'The dispute resolution mechanisms developed by the ICC have been conceived specifically for business disputes in an international context'.[12] Since its creation, the Court has handled more than 15,000 international arbitrations all over the world involving parties and arbitrators from more than 180 different countries or independent territories.[13] Over the past 10 years, the Court's workload has grown by 40 per cent. Growth has been particularly strong since 2007, with the number of cases handled by the Court rising by 15 per cent between 2007 and 2010.[14] In 2011, 796 new requests for arbitration were filed with the ICC Court. Those requests concerned 2,293 parties from 139 countries and independent territories with 63 different countries being nomi-

---

[10] Introduction, fn 18.
[11] See Overview of the International Chamber of Commerce, available at www.iccwbo.org/uploadedFiles/ICC/ICC_Home_Page/pages/ICC%202007-1-complete.pdf.
[12] ICC Publications, *International Court of Arbitration, Resolving Business Disputes Worldwide*, 2, available at www.iccbookshop.com/more/downloads/resolvin.pdf.
[13] ibid.
[14] See ICC Statistical Reports.

nated as the place of arbitration. Arbitrators of 78 nationalities were appointed or confirmed under the ICC Rules.[15]

In terms of its nature, the ICC Court is attached to the ICC, a non-governmental organisation, whose fundamental objective is to further the development of an open world economy with the firm conviction that international commercial exchanges are conducive to both greater global prosperity and peace among nations. The ICC Court is registered as a not-for-profit association in France, and is subject to French law. Since its very establishment, the ICC Court was intended to serve the international business community and to promote international trade.

B. *The CIETAC*

Almost 30 years later than the establishment of the ICC Court, the CIETAC was created in the 1950s, under the regime of a planned economy. At that time, there was no concept of private ownership, and all property belonged to the state or the community. Consequently, all economic activities were handled by highly centralised state institutions, and administrative control could be exercised over all economic activities, including dispute resolution. Meanwhile, at the beginning of the 1950s, the PRC was still at the toddler stage with everything starting anew. The USSR model served as the basis for the foreign trade system. Foreign trade was at insignificant levels and commercial dealings were, in the main, consummated with Soviet countries.[16] This Sino-Soviet trading regime served as the impetus by which international commercial arbitration took root in China. In April 1950, a Protocol for General Conditions of Delivery of Goods was signed by the USSR and the PRC. The Protocol provided that any dispute arising from a contract should be settled through arbitration and should not be filed with a court. Where the respondent was a Soviet enterprise or organisation, the arbitration would be conducted in the USSR; where the respondent was a Chinese enterprise or organisation, the arbitration would take place in the PRC. In order to implement such an undertaking, it was necessary to establish a dedicated arbitration body, separate and distinct from the traditional domestic arbitration institutions.[17] Against this background in 1952, when the CCPIT was established as a 'non-private-non-government' organisation charged with promoting China's foreign trade, Nan Hanchen, then president of the CCPIT, and Ji Chaoding, then Secretary General of the CCPIT, advocated the establishment of an arbitration department within the CCPIT to be responsible for international arbitration in China.[18]

---

[15] '2011 Statistical Report', 23 *ICC Bulletin* 1 (2012).
[16] See Gemmell, *Western and Chinese Arbitration: The Arbitral Chain*, 151.
[17] Tao, *Arbitration Law and Practice in China*, 8.
[18] See Houzhi Tang, 'The Arbitration Road – In Commemoration of the 50th Anniversary of the Founding of CCPIT' in CIETAC and CMAC (ed), *China International Commercial Arbitration Yearbook* (2000–2001) 92–98.

As discussed earlier, domestic arbitration in China was essentially administrative arbitration following the USSR model, which was fundamentally different from modern commercial arbitration.[19] Under the circumstances, what form would CCPIT arbitration take? After careful consideration, the CCPIT decided to develop its arbitration organisation mirroring transnational standards. The staff at the arbitration department of the CCPIT collected arbitration materials from abroad, and studied advanced arbitration laws and institutional rules. On this basis, it worked out a plan to set up an arbitration organisation within the CCPIT, which was submitted to the Government Administration Council of the Central People's Government for approval.[20] On 6 May 1954, with the support of Premier Zhou Enlai and Deng Xiaoping, the Government Administration Council issued a decision establishing an arbitration institution within the CCPIT, as an official institution for arbitrating disputes that may arise from contracts and transactions in foreign trade, particularly disputes between foreign firms, companies, or other economic organisations.[21] The Decision laid down the basic principles for foreign-related arbitration in China, including: (i) arbitration shall be based on the arbitration agreement between the parties; (ii) the parties shall have the freedom to choose the arbitrators; (iii) the award rendered by the arbitration institution shall be final and the people's court shall enforce it at the request of a party. According to the Decision, the CCPIT, at its fourth committee session on 31 March 1956, adopted the Provisional Arbitration Rules for Arbitration Procedures of the Foreign Trade Arbitration Commission under the auspices of the CCPIT. The CCPIT selected 21 members in the fields of foreign trade, commerce, industry, agriculture, transport, insurance, and law to compose the first committee and to act as arbitrators concurrently. From then on, the first international arbitration institution of China – Foreign Trade Arbitration Commission (the FTAC, later renamed as the CIETAC) – came into being.

The CIETAC's development can be divided into five periods, namely, the founding period (1956–1966), the adjustment period (1967–1979), the growth period (1980–1988), the acceleration period (1989–1994), and the expansion period (1995–present).[22]

---

[19] s 5.1 above.
[20] Tang, 'The Arbitration Road – In Commemoration of the 50th Anniversary of the Founding of CCPIT', 92–98.
[21] See Decision of the Government Administration Council of the Central People's Government Concerning the Establishment of a Foreign Trade Arbitration Commission within CCPIT, issued on 6 May 1954.
[22] On CIETAC's history and development, see Tang, 'The Arbitration Road – In Commemoration of the 50th Anniversary of the Founding of CCPIT', 92–98. Tao, *Arbitration Law and Practice in China*, 20–23; 仲裁研究所, '中国国际经济贸易仲裁委员会五十年回顾和展望' (2004) 92 仲裁与法律, 73-90页 (Arbitration Research Center, 'Looking Back and Forward of the Fifty Years of the CIETAC', (2004) 92 Arbitration and Law, 73–90).

a. Founding Period (1956–1966)

During its founding period, the FTAC was not known to the international community, due to the underdevelopment of international trade in China at the time. Very few international trade disputes were settled through arbitration; most were settled by mediation or negotiations. From 1956 to 1966, the FTAC only accepted 27 cases involving foreign trade disputes.

b. Adjustment Period (1967–1979)

Since the restoration of the lawful rights of the PRC in the United Nations in 1971,[23] the FTAC began to establish connections with foreign international institutions, and its contacts with the outside world increased dramatically after the mid-1970s. However, the caseload remained low, with a total of 81 arbitration cases accepted from 1967 to 1979.

c. Growth Period (1980–1988)

Since the end of 1978, when reforms and opening up policies were implemented in China, economic development in China embarked on a new era. In July 1979, the Law on Chinese-Foreign Equity Joint Ventures was promulgated. Special Economic Zones including Shenzhen, Zhuhai, and Shantou were successively established. The environment for foreign investment was greatly improved, and trade and disputes increased accordingly. Under this background, on 26 February 1980, the State Council issued a notice with the following decisions: (i) to change the name of the FTAC to the CIETAC, (ii) to enlarge the scope of cognisance of the CIETAC to cover disputes arising from various kinds of China – foreign economic cooperation, such as JVs, foreign investment in China, credits and loans between Chinese and foreign banks, etc, and (iii) to increase the number of members of the CIETAC to cope with the additional work. This corresponds to a drastic increase in the caseload of the CIETAC. The complexity of the cases and the magnitude of the amounts in dispute were unprecedented. The annual caseload increased in multiples, from 37 in 1985 to 310 in 1988. Between 1980 and 1988, the CIETAC accepted 403 cases (according to estimated calculations), involving parties from 23 countries from the five continents.[24]

---

[23] United Nations General Assembly Resolution 2758, Twenty Sixth Session of 25 October 1971, which decided to restore all its rights to the PRC and to recognise the representatives of its government as the only legitimate representatives of China to the United Nations and to expel forthwith the representatives of Chiang Kai-shek from the place which they unlawfully occupied at the United Nations and in all organisations related to it.

[24] 'Looking Back and Forward of the Fifty Years of the CIETAC'.

d. Acceleration Period (1989–1994)

The CIETAC accelerated its development in the period from 1988 to 1994. The CIETAC Rules were amended in 1988, which responded better to China's reform and opening-up policy. Sub-commissions were established in 1989 and 1990 in Shenzhen and Shanghai respectively. The CIETAC's Articles of Association and the Code of Ethics for Arbitrators were adopted in 1993. In 1993, the CIETAC accepted 486 cases, ranking first among all international arbitration institutions in terms of caseload.

e. Expansion Period (1995–present)

From 1995 to the present, the CIETAC entered into its expansion period. The implementation of the Arbitration Law in 1995 played an important role in reforming China's domestic arbitration, promoting internationalisation and modernisation of foreign-related arbitration, and establishing a market-orientated arbitration system. Since 1995, the CIETAC has revised its arbitration rules four times to bring them closer in line with international practice. On 30 June 2003, the CIETAC completed an institutional reform, and was officially separated from the CCPIT, to become a 'not-for-profit company' (*shi ye dan wei*). The number of foreign-related cases reached a record of 902 cases.

While the CIETAC experienced continued growth, it faced serious challenges at the same time. Due to the competition from local arbitration institutions in China, which began to accept foreign-related cases, the economic crises in South East Asian countries in 1997, and the intensified competition by foreign arbitration institutions in Asia, the CIETAC's caseload dropped to 778 in 1996. Nevertheless, the amounts in dispute continued to grow, and the institution was becoming increasingly international. From 2000 to 2010, the CIETAC handled 10,749 cases, of which 5,280 were foreign-related.[25] In 2011, the CIETAC had a record of 1,435 new cases filed (470 foreign-related cases),[26] which was more than the ICC Court, the London Court of International Arbitration (LCIA), and the American Arbitration Association (AAA). Despite the challenges, the CIETAC remains the leading arbitration institution in China in terms of foreign-related cases, and the CIETAC'S work has earned wide recognition at home and abroad.

In terms of its nature, the CIETAC is an organisation set up within the CCPIT, with the aim of meeting the demands of foreign trade. The CIETAC is functionally independent from the CCPIT and administers arbitration proceedings at its own discretion. Despite the *non-governmental* status in theory, the CIETAC still appears to maintain some governmental links: its creation itself was a decision made by the Government Administration Council, and it remains to some extent influenced by government bodies.

---

[25] See CIETAC Statistics, available at www.cietac.org.
[26] See CIETAC Statistics 2011, available at www.cietac.org.

5.2.2 Structure and Personnel Management

A. *The ICC Court*

The ICC Court is composed of 125 members from 90 countries. One of them serves as Chairman and nine as Vice-Chairmen. Currently, the Chairman is from the United Kingdom, the Vice-Chairmen are from Algeria, Australia, Belgium, China, France, France–Mauritius, France–Sweden, Germany, India, Italy, Mexico, Russia, Switzerland–Brazil, United Kingdom, and the United States (since the appointment of June 2009).[27] The diversity of the Court's members gives the ICC Court unparalleled collective expertise. The court members are appointed for renewable three-year terms by the supreme governing body of the ICC (World Council), upon the proposal of the ICC's constituent national committees. Court members are not employees of the ICC Court, and most of them are practitioners from international law firms or law professors. The court members cannot be appointed as arbitrators by the Court; they can, however, act as arbitrators nominated by the parties.[28] The court members make decisions at the weekly committee sessions (where only three court members are present, with either the Chairman or one of the Vice-Chairmen presiding) or, for important decisions, at the plenary sessions (where all Court members are invited, with an average number of 30 to 50 court members present).

The day-to-day administration of the cases is handled by the Secretariat, which is located at the ICC's headquarters in Paris. The Secretariat is headed by the Secretary General, assisted by the Deputy Secretary General and the General Counsel. Within the Secretariat there are eight legal teams to manage the Court's caseload. The teams roughly correspond to different geographic or cultural regions around the world.[29] To deal with a constantly growing caseload, the Secretariat has increased in size. The number of staff members has doubled in 10 years, rising from 35 to 70, including 35 lawyers. The origins of staff members have also broadened, reflecting the increasing internationalisation of the cases. More than 20 nationalities are represented among the Secretariat staff, who are able to monitor cases in most of the world's major languages, including English, French, Arabic, Chinese, German, Italian, Portuguese, and Spanish. In light of the growing demand for arbitration services in Asia, the ICC opened its first branch office in Hong Kong in 2008.

In the meantime, the significant development of institutional arbitration in recent years has imposed great challenges to the ICC at management level. Mr Simon Greenberg, the former Deputy Secretary General of the Secretariat has made the following remarks:

---

[27] A list of the Court's members is available on the ICC Court's website at www.iccwbo.org/court/arbitration/id4086/index.html.
[28] App II, Art 2(2) of the ICC Rules 2012.
[29] For more comments on the structure of the ICC Court and its Secretariat, see Jennifer Kirby, 'The ICC Court: A Behind-the-Scenes Look' (2005) 16 *ICC Bulletin* 2; Robert Smith, 'An Inside View of the ICC Court' (1994) 10 *Arbitration International* 1; Tercier, 'ICC Rules of Arbitration: A Decade of Use'.

124 *The Practice of Arbitration Institutions*

The environment has changed at the level of management at the ICC. On the one hand, arbitration has become more sophisticated, and the parties require a speedy settlement of their dispute at the same time, which requires adjustment of the working style of the staff. On the other hand, the ICC is facing more and more competition from arbitration institutions all over the world, such as the LCIA, the SIAC, the HKIAC, the SCC, and the CIETAC, etc. These changes make the work at the Secretariat more demanding. Facing the challenges, we need to retain competent staff, and to ensure sufficient training for the staff, etc.[30]

B. *The CIETAC*

In terms of institutional structure, the CIETAC is composed of a Chairman, a number of Vice-Chairmen, and members, all of whom are arbitration specialists appointed according to the Articles of Association of the CIETAC. Within the CIETAC, three committees are set up to perform different functions: (i) the arbitrators' qualification review committee, responsible for recruiting new arbitrators and ensuring CIETAC arbitrators' compliance with the Code of Ethics (currently 12 members); (ii) the case editing committee, responsible for editing awards that are selected for publication (currently 11 members); and (iii) the expert consultation committee, responsible for providing advice on complex legal matters, substantive and procedural, relating to the CIETAC arbitration (currently 37 members).[31] The day-to-day work of the CIETAC is conducted through the Secretariats in the Beijing headquarters and in the Shanghai and Shenzhen sub-commissions. Each Secretariat has a Secretary General and two or three Deputy Secretaries General. There are about 100 staff members in the Secretariats of the CIETAC, 70 of whom are lawyers who work as case managers. The staff at the Secretariat of the CIETAC are hired on a competitive basis from all over China. All of them are bilingual in Chinese and English, and many of them have studied abroad or are even admitted to the bar in a foreign state. The Secretariat in the Beijing headquarters consists of various departments, including the registration and consultation department, the first (foreign-related) business department, the second (domestic) business department, the development department, the supervisory department and the administrative department. Aside from the committees and Secretariats, the CIETAC has two other divisions, namely the arbitration research institute, and the domain name resolution centre.[32]

The CIETAC conducts regular training to improve the quality of service of the staff. The retention of competent staff has always been on the agenda of the CIETAC, and as a result, CIETAC maintains a relatively stable staff. The

---

[30] Interview with Simon Greenberg, who was Deputy Secretary General of the Secretariat of the ICC Court at the time of the interview, Paris, 21 May 2009.

[31] For a list of the CIETAC's members, see *The CIETAC Organizational Structure*, available on the CIETAC website at cn.cietac.org/AboutUS/AboutUS2.shtml.

[32] On the structure of the CIETAC, see ibid. See also, Yu, 'The Arbitrators' Mandate: Private Judge, Service-Provider or Both?', 1–13.

CIETAC faces major challenges about the remuneration of CIETAC personnel, in light of the competition from private sector employment and especially foreign companies where the market rates are much higher. The CIETAC has endeavoured to make the salaries at the Secretariat competitive in order to attract the best graduates from China's top law schools, and has introduced a new internal mechanism for improving the quality and efficiency of the CIETAC staff's work in administering arbitration cases since 2006.[33]

5.2.3 Financial Management

A. *The ICC Court*

The ICC Court is registered as a not-for-profit association in France, and is subject to French law. It enjoys full financial independence over its funds and budget and is not subject to the intervention of any government. The Court's revenue comes mainly from its administrative fees for arbitration cases. There is also other income, such as the national committees' membership fees from their members. As a sub-branch of the ICC, the revenue generated by the ICC Court is redistributed within the ICC as a whole based on the overall revenue among different departments for expenditure, including payment of the staff, renovation, marketing, facilities, etc.[34]

B. *The CIETAC*

With respect to the financial system of the CIETAC, Mr Yu Jianlong, the Secretary General of the CIETAC has made the following statement:

> Before 2002, CIETAC was financially independent and not affiliated to any government agency. As a result, it could freely spend and allocate all of its own revenues. However, a government regulation issued in 2002 required all arbitration institutions to hand up their revenues to the Ministry of Finance or its local branches, and to make an annual budget for their expenditures, which has to be submitted to the Ministry or its branches for approval.[35]

The above statement by Yu Jianlong explained the so-called 'separation of distribution and income' financial system. According to Circular No 29 Concerning the Amendment of the Arbitration Fee for 'the Separation of Distribution and Income' Financial System issued by four departments of the State Council in 2003 (Circular No 29), the 'arbitration fee' is defined as an 'administrative fee', and is therefore characterised as a 'state asset'. The Circular No 29 requires all income of the CIETAC to be 'handed over' to the Ministry of Finance, which will then fix and allocate the distribution of such income according to reported expenditure.

---

[33] Moser and Yu, 'CIETAC and its Work – An Interview with Vice Chairman Yu Jianlong', 564.
[34] Interview with Simon Greenberg, n 30 above.
[35] Moser and Yu, 'CIETAC and its Work – An Interview with Vice Chairman Yu Jianlong', 5577.

The budgetary allocation by the state is reported often to be much less than the revenue that the CIETAC has remitted, which has caused much difficulty for the CIETAC in upgrading its facilities, improving case management, hiring competent staff for its Secretariat, and improving its profile in the market to ensure that it can compete with other international arbitration institutions.[36]

The Circular No 29 appears to be in conflict with Circular No 44 Concerning the Method of Collecting Arbitration Fees by Arbitration Institutions issued by the General Office of State Council in 1995 (Circular No 44), according to which arbitration institutions must allocate expenditure based on their own revenues (*zi shou zi zhi*). Furthermore, Circular No 29 is inconsistent with the promises that China made when entering into the WTO on 10 January 2001. In the WTO negotiations, the Chinese government expressly stated that arbitration fees fell into the category of 'commission service fees' and would be dealt with in accordance with the Regulations Concerning the Commission Service Fees issued by six central government departments,[37] pursuant to which the arbitration institutions would allocate expenditure based on their own revenues. Such promise is clearly recorded in the Report of the Working Party on the Accession of China to the WTO.[38]

In light of China's WTO commitment, much effort has been made to change the current system of separation of distribution and income. In March 2007, at the 5th Session of the 10th People's Political Consultative Conference, many well-known legal experts and People's delegation members submitted a proposal for changing the current system.[39] On 31 October 2007, the Ministry of Finance replied to the People's delegate members as follows:

> Due to historical reasons, the reform of the arbitration system was not fully completed, and a certain number of arbitration institutions are still managed as not-for-profit companies [with an administrative nature or with administrative support], which affects their independence, and is inconsistent with transnational standards.
>
> Further research and studies will be carried out with respect to the establishment and the financial management of arbitration institutions, by referring to international customs and the promises China made when entering the WTO and the suggestions and opinions expressed by the delegate members will be carefully considered.[40]

The lack of financial independence turns out to be the main obstacle to the management of the CIETAC. As Yu Jianlong stated, 'this practice [of separation of distribution and income] not only gives rise to doubts about the CIETAC's independence, but also undermines the development of the CIETAC

---

[36] Ming, 'The Strange Case of Wang Shengchang', 65.

[37] 六个中央政府部委关于印发《中介服务收费管理办法》的通知, 国家发展计划委员会、国家经济贸易委员会、财政部、监察部、审计署、国务院纠风办文件 计价格[1999] 2255号。(Regulations Concerning the Commission Service Fees).

[38] See Report of the Working Party on the Accession of China in document WT/ACC/CHN/49.

[39] 提案第3667号, 财政金融类第381号。(Proposal No 3667, Finance and Economics No 381.)

[40] Cited *in* 王红松, '贯彻党的十七大精神, 加快推进仲裁机构体制改革' (2008) 65 北京仲裁, 79页(Hongsong Wang,'Implementing the Spirits of the Communist Party's Seventeenth Conference and Promoting the Structural Reform of Arbitration Institutions' (2008) 65 Beijing Arbitration, 79).

in the long run'.[41] Since 2010, these restrictions imposed on the CIETAC's financial management are said to have been lifted.[42]

5.2.4 Relationship Between the Arbitration Institution and Arbitrators

The relationship between arbitration institutions and arbitrators is often described as 'a contract of arbitral collaboration', where each party independently promises and performs services for the benefit of the other and particularly for the benefit of third parties (the parties to the arbitration).[43] This concept of a contractual relationship is recognised by many Chinese academics, practitioners and officials working in the domain of arbitration. Yu Jianlong addressed the contractual relationship between the parties, the arbitrators, and arbitration institutions. Yu explained that in institutional arbitration, the institution administers the disputes for the parties and engages the arbitrator to perform services, and the arbitrator performs the services for and administers justice to the parties. He describes the relationship between the arbitration institution and the arbitrators as a kind of 'arbitrator assignment agreement or management agreement':

> The arbitrator is the legal professional engaged in providing arbitration services and is qualified to provide such services. The institution is an administrator of arbitration under its arbitration rules. Both are independent contractors, acting each at its own direction and control in the performance of the obligation under this agreement . . . The institution administers the disputes for the parties and engages the arbitrator to perform services, and the arbitrator performs the services for and administers justice to the parties.[44]

How is this concept translated into the respective institutional practices of the ICC and the CIETAC? Specifically, what role do the ICC Court and the CIETAC play in their relationships with the arbitrators in terms of (A) case management; (B) allocation of fees; and (C) scrutiny of arbitral awards? We shall examine these issues in turn.

A. *Institution's General Role in Case Management*

a. *The ICC Court*

The ICC Rules 2012 clearly indicate that the Court does not settle disputes, but has the function of ensuring the application of the ICC Rules.[45] Specifically, the ICC Court's main function includes deciding to set the arbitration in motion,

---

[41] Moser and Yu, 'CIETAC and its Work – An Interview with Vice Chairman Yu Jianlong', 557.
[42] Speech of Yu Jianlong, Secretary General of the CIETAC at the Annual Banquet of the CIETAC for Spring Festival, 2011.
[43] Clay, *L'arbitre*, para 1055 s.
[44] Yu, 'The Arbitrators' Mandate: Private Judge, Service-Provider or Both?', 1–13.
[45] Art 1(2) of the ICC Rules 2012.

fixing the advance on costs, constituting the arbitral tribunal, scrutinising drafting awards, and fixing the costs of the arbitration.[46]

In terms of case management, the ICC's role is probably between very light administration, such as that of the LCIA and the HKIAC, and heavy administration such as that of the CIETAC. The ICC Secretariat plays an important role in the administration of the case before the file is transferred to the arbitrators. For instance, the ICC Secretariat serves as the parties' point of contact with the ICC Court, invites submissions from the parties on the contested procedural issues, prepares issues for the Court, and assists in the constitution of the arbitral tribunal, etc. Once the arbitral tribunal is fully constituted, the work of the Secretariat decreases and generally consists of keeping track of the time limits prescribed by the ICC Rules, monitoring the financial aspects of the case, and answering procedural questions from the arbitral tribunal and the parties. When the draft arbitral award is rendered, the Secretariat and the Court again play an important role in scrutinising the award. No award can be notified to the parties without the Court's approval.

b. The CIETAC

The CIETAC is reported to be the busiest arbitration institution in the world.[47] One may wonder what makes the CIETAC so busy. Indeed, the CIETAC Secretariat provides significant services throughout the arbitration proceedings and maintains a close relationship with the arbitrators. When the reception department deems that the claimant has completed all formalities required for arbitration, it transfers the file to the procedural administration department, which then sends the notice of arbitration to the parties and appoints a case manager to be in charge of the subsequent procedural matters. Usually, the number of cases handled by each case manager ranges from 10 to 30. The case managers play an active role in assisting the arbitral tribunal on procedural issues. They even provide services that are often performed by administrative secretaries, such as arranging hearings, taking notes during the hearings and providing translations, arranging deliberations between the arbitrators, taking part in site inspections and collection of evidence, and conducting research under the arbitral tribunal's instruction.[48] Thus, the CIETAC is said to be more 'institutional' than many other arbitration institutions. The CIETAC's heavy administration has also aroused criticisms on the improper enlargement of the power of the CIETAC as an institution, on the basis that it has exercised some of the functions that arbitrators should exercise.[49] For instance, it has been asserted that 'the CIETAC staff draft awards

---

[46] Kirby, 'The ICC Court: A Behind-the-Scenes Look', 8–18.
[47] On the caseload of the CIETAC, see s 5.2.1-B.e above.
[48] Information is based on the conversations with the case managers of the CIETAC.
[49] See Lianbin Song, Jian Zhao and Hong Li, 'Approaches to the Revision of the 1994 Arbitration Act of the People's Republic of China' (2003) 20 *Journal of International Arbitration* 2, 178–79.

for some Chinese arbitrators, thereby enabling them to handle many more cases than they otherwise would'.[50]

B. Allocation of Fees

a. The ICC Court

The costs of ICC arbitration include the fees of the arbitrators, their out-of-pocket expenses, if any, and the ICC's administrative expenses. The costs are calculated based on the amount in dispute in accordance with the scale in force at the time of the commencement of the arbitral proceedings.[51]

The parties are requested to pay the costs in advance in a few steps. First, when filing a request for arbitration, the claimant is required to pay a non-refundable filing fee of US$3,000.[52] Second, after receiving a request for arbitration, the Secretary General will generally fix a provisional budget, known as the provisional advance, payable by the claimant, in order to cover the costs of arbitration until the arbitral tribunal has drawn up a document setting forth the scope of its mission, known as the Terms of Reference.[53] The Secretariat will only transfer the file to the arbitral tribunal once the provisional advance has been fully paid. Third, soon after the Secretary General has fixed the provisional advance, on the basis of the amount in dispute, the ICC Court fixes a budget for the entire case that is designed to cover (i) the fees of the arbitrators; (ii) the reimbursement of the arbitrators' expenses; and (iii) the administrative fees for the ICC's services in administering the arbitration. This budget is known as the 'advance on costs'.[54] The advance on costs is in principle payable in equal shares by the parties.[55] The claimant's initial US$3,000 filing fee and its payment of the provisional advance are credited towards its half of the advance on costs.[56] At the end of the case, the Court will fix the final costs of the arbitration. When the arbitration ends with a final award on the merits, the Court usually decides to pay the arbitrators the full amount budgeted to cover their fees, and the ICC the full amount budgeted to cover the cost of administering the case. Where the arbitration ends before a final award is rendered, the Court fixes the arbitration costs taking into account the stage of the proceedings, the work done, and any other relevant circumstances.[57] It is not uncommon to refund part of the advance on costs to the parties.

---

[50] Cohen, 'Time to Fix China's Arbitration'.
[51] See fee schedules in app III of the ICC Rules 2012 – Arbitration Costs and Fees.
[52] Art 1(1) of app III of the ICC Rules 2012 – Arbitration Costs and Fees.
[53] Art 36(1) of the ICC Rules 2012; Art 1(2) of app III of the ICC Rules 2012 – Arbitration Costs and Fees.
[54] Art 36(2)–36(7) of the ICC Rules 2012; Art 1(3)–1(13) of app III of the ICC Rules 2012 – Arbitration Costs and Fees.
[55] Art 36(2) of the ICC Rules 2012.
[56] Arts 1(1) and 1(2) of app III of the ICC Rules 2012 – Arbitration Costs and Fees.
[57] Art 2 of app III of the ICC Rules 2012 – Arbitration Costs and Fees.

The arbitrators' fees and the ICC administrative expenses are fixed by the Court at the end of the proceedings in accordance with the fee schedules set out in the ICC Rules. In deciding how much the arbitrators are to be paid within the range, the Court takes into account their diligence, the number of hours spent on the case, the expediency of the proceedings, and the complexity of the dispute.[58] Separate fee arrangements between the parties and the arbitrators are expressly prohibited.[59]

b. The CIETAC

The CIETAC charges the arbitration fees on an *ad valorem* basis. The arbitration fee, which is calculated according to the fee schedule,[60] includes both the administrative fee of the CIETAC and the costs of the arbitrators' fees and expenses.

The method of collecting the fees differs between the two institutions. While in the ICC arbitration the parties are invited to share the advance on costs *equally* in several steps (US$3,000 when filing the request of arbitration paid by the claimant, a provisional advance until Terms of Reference are drafted paid by the claimant, and finally the total advance on costs to be paid equally by the parties), in the CIETAC arbitration, *the claimant alone* is required to pay the *total* arbitration fees at the very beginning of the proceedings, when filing the request for arbitration.

Generally, the total cost of a CIETAC arbitration is much lower than that of an ICC arbitration. According to its Secretary General, a CIETAC case on average involves a claim of approximately RMB9.38 million yuan (US$1.2 million). For a foreign-related case of this value, the CIETAC charges RMB210,700 yuan (US$27,012) as the arbitration fee, which covers both the arbitrators' remuneration and the CIETAC's administration fees.[61] By contrast, for a dispute involving the same amount, the fees for a three-member arbitral tribunal would be in the range of US$48,015–US$214,014, and the ICC's administrative fees would be US$23,615. The total cost of the ICC arbitration would be approximately US$154,613 on average, without taking into account the arbitrators' expenses.[62] The fees for a sole arbitrator for this amount in dispute would be in the range of US$16,005–US$71,338, and the ICC's administrative fees would be US$23,615. The total cost of the ICC arbitration is approximately US$67,287, without taking into account the arbitrator's expenses.[63] The above comparison demonstrates a much lower total cost incurred in a CIETAC arbitration than in an ICC arbitration.

---

[58] Art 2(2) of app III of the ICC Rules 2012 – Arbitration Costs and Fees.
[59] Art 2(4) of app III of the ICC Rules 2012 – Arbitration Costs and Fees.
[60] Fee Schedule in the CIETAC Rules 2012.
[61] See Moser and Yu, 'CIETAC and its Work – An Interview with Vice Chairman Yu Jianlong', 561. See also the fee schedules of the CIETAC Rules 2012.
[62] See ICC Scales for Administrative Expenses and Arbitrators' Fees, effective as of 1 May 2010; ICC cost calculator, available at www.iccwbo.org/court/arbitration/id4097/index.html.
[63] ibid.

However, the CIETAC's low cost advantage will be diluted as the amount in dispute increases. For instance, the CIETAC arbitration fee will be higher than that of the ICC when the amount in dispute is over US$50 million. In cases involving such large amounts in dispute, the CIETAC's method will result in the claimant paying a very large up-front fee, which is said to have a 'chilling' effect on otherwise valid claims. According to Mr Yu Jianlong, the CIETAC has realised the problem and will change the fee rate for cases involving very high amounts in dispute in due course.[64]

With respect to the division between the arbitrators' remuneration and the CIETAC's administrative fees, the remuneration of the arbitrators is a percentage of the total arbitration fees collected, the amount being determined by the CIETAC and being generally much lower than transnational standards. Chinese arbitrators are paid in local currency and foreign arbitrators in foreign exchange. According to Yu Jianlong, the CIETAC is considering reforming its fee system to make it more competitive internationally.[65]

C. Scrutiny of Arbitral Awards

a. The ICC Court

The ICC Rules require that the arbitral tribunal submit all arbitral awards (be they partial, interim or final) in draft to the ICC Court for scrutiny and approval.[66] Only after the Court has approved a draft award may the arbitral tribunal sign and send it to the Secretariat for notification to the parties. Although the Court's scrutiny of awards is designed to capture problems of both substance and form, the Court's power to require changes to draft awards is limited. With respect to the form, the Court may 'lay down modifications as to the form of the award',[67] to ensure that the award complies with the requirements at the place of arbitration. With respect to the substance, the Court may only 'draw [the arbitral tribunal]'s attention to points of substance',[68] but cannot require the arbitral tribunal to make changes to the substance of the award. The power to decide the substantive issues rests with the arbitral tribunal alone, and nothing in the scrutiny process can affect the arbitral tribunal's liberty of decision. The majority of the draft awards are submitted for scrutiny to the Court's weekly committee sessions. Certain awards involving large amounts in dispute, complex or novel legal issues, state parties or dissenting opinions[69] are submitted to the Court's monthly plenary sessions for scrutiny. When scrutinising a draft

---

[64] Moser and Yu, 'CIETAC and its Work – An Interview with Vice Chairman Yu Jianlong', 564.
[65] ibid.
[66] Art 33 of the ICC Rules 2012.
[67] Art 33 of the ICC Rules 2012.
[68] ibid.
[69] When a draft award with a dissenting opinion is presented for scrutiny, the Court receives a copy of the dissenting opinion for its information only. The Court does not scrutinise the dissenting opinion and makes no comments on it.

award, the Court may effectively make three decisions: (i) to approve the draft award; (ii) to approve the draft award but invite the arbitral tribunal to make changes to the award when finalising it for notification to the parties; or (iii) to invite the arbitral tribunal to make changes to the draft award and to submit a revised draft for scrutiny by the Court at a future session. As mentioned above, the Court's comments on the merits of the awards are only suggestive. Yet in most of the cases, the arbitral tribunal takes into account the Court's comments. Since the arbitral tribunal has the final word on the awards, the Court may not refuse to approve the draft award if the arbitral tribunal chooses to ignore the Court's comments.

b. The CIETAC

Similar to the ICC practice, the arbitral tribunal is requested to submit its draft award to the CIETAC for scrutiny before signing the award. Article 49 of the CIETAC Rules 2012 provides that 'the CIETAC may remind the arbitral tribunal of issues in the award on condition that the arbitral tribunal's independence in rendering the award is not affected'.

At the CIETAC, a scrutinising team, composed of several case managers at the CIETAC Secretariats, carries out the scrutiny process of the draft award. The scrutinising team may make comments on the procedure as well as on the substance for the arbitrators' consideration. The CIETAC arbitrators are at liberty to maintain their original position and disregard the suggestions of the scrutiny team, although most arbitrators do consider them carefully. When complicated legal matters are involved, the award will be submitted to the expert consultation committee for discussions. There are currently 33 members of the expert consultation committee, all of whom are experienced arbitrators at the CIETAC. The expert consultation committee will render its opinion on certain legal issues for the arbitral tribunal's reference. The arbitral tribunal is free to disregard the opinion of the expert consultation committee. Usually, the arbitral tribunal takes the committee's ideas into careful consideration before deciding whether to accept them or not.[70]

Based on the above comparison between the practice of the ICC Court and the CIETAC, two main features of the CIETAC practice can be observed: first, given the background and nature of the establishment of the CIETAC, despite its non-governmental nature, some administrative taints and governmental links remain. Second, these administrative taints further make the CIETAC arbitration more 'institutional' than other arbitration institutions. On the positive side, the CIETAC renders more services throughout the proceedings of arbitration, which makes it one of the most efficient arbitration institutions in the world. On the negative side, the heavy administration of the CIETAC is criti-

---

[70] According to a telephone interview with a case manager at the Secretariat of the CIETAC in Beijing, 17 November 2010.

cised as improperly enlarging its power as an institution and interfering with the independence of the arbitral tribunal.

5.3 STATUS OF LOCAL ARBITRATION INSTITUTIONS IN CHINA

The review of the practice of the CIETAC gives us a vivid picture of features of a Chinese arbitration institution compared to international practice. One may argue that the example of the CIETAC may not be representative of the various arbitration institutions in different regions of China. To present a full picture of arbitration institutions in China, we need to examine the status of local arbitration institutions in China.

As explained earlier, prior to the enactment of the Arbitration Law, domestic arbitration institutions were administrative agencies affiliated with their relevant governmental superiors.[71] This was partly due to the highly centralised planned economy, where the administrative powers dominated all economic activities, and partly owing to the legislative vacuum at that time. One of the main objectives of the Arbitration Law was to change the old domestic administrative arbitration into arbitration of a private nature. This requires restructuring the 3,640 arbitration institutions existing in the old system and re-employing their 20,000 employees. Mr Hu Kangsheng, Chairman of the Legal Commission of the Standing Committee of the NPC, who was involved in the drafting of the Arbitration Law, made the following statement at the meeting for the 10th anniversary of the Arbitration Law in October 2004:

> The Arbitration Law drafted ten years ago was a law of reforms. At the time there was clear intention to establish the system of 'socialist market economy'. At the initial stage, the drafters of the Law took into account China's actuality, made reference to generally accepted transnational standards, and were determined to reform the old administrative arbitration into commercial arbitration of a private nature. The Arbitration Law expressly provided that there was no hierarchical relationship between arbitration institutions and administrative bodies, or among arbitration institutions. This provision fully reflected the reform spirit, and provided the legal basis for the independence of the arbitration institutions.[72]

The private nature of arbitration requires that the restructured or newly established local arbitration institutions are (i) independent in terms of organisation and personnel constituents, and free from administrative interference, and (ii) financially independent from government control. In reality, is the private nature of arbitration respected? What is the current status of local arbitration

---

[71] See s 5.1 above.

[72] The Speech of Hu Kangsheng, the Chairman of the Commission of Legislative Affairs of the Standing Committee of the NPC, at the 10th Anniversary of Arbitration Law in October 2004, cited in 肖峋,《在仲裁机构民间化建设座谈会上的发言》,《北京仲裁》第63辑,年, 第6页 (Xun Xiao, 'The Speech at the Symposium of Establishing Arbitration Institutions of a Private Nature', (2007) 63 *Beijing Arbitration*, 6).

institutions in China? Have they achieved full independence? Are there any remaining administrative taints within local arbitration institutions?

5.3.1 The Establishment: Government Support

Local arbitration institutions are established by local government. Although in a market economy it is evident that arbitration institutions as service providers should be established to respond to the demands of the market for dispute resolution, the Arbitration Law emphasised this principle by providing that arbitration institutions *may* be established 'according to need' in other cities divided into districts (not directly under central government or seats of the people's governments of provinces or autonomous regions).[73] This specification was made to avoid confusion about compulsory establishment rooted in concepts of planned economy. Unfortunately, such legislative intent was not fully respected in practice. In some cities where international trade is not developed, there are very few commercial disputes even before the courts, and hence there is no such need to establish a local arbitration institution. Nevertheless, local governments established local arbitration institutions not 'according to need', but to serve local government's interest. A number of local arbitration institutions receive insufficient caseloads, and could not survive without the government's continued financial support.

5.3.2 The Government's Interference Continues After the Establishment

The initial government financial support was intended to help the arbitration institutions go through the transitional period, after which the arbitration institutions should gradually achieve financial independence. In reality, a number of local governments did not end their engagement after the transition period. This continued support and involvement is contrary to the legislative intent, which was for the government to help the arbitration institutions get on the horse (*fu shang ma, song yi cheng*), but not to help them run the whole course (*fu shang ma, song quan cheng*).[74]

In May and June 2007, the BAC conducted a survey, during which a number of questionnaires were distributed to arbitration institutions in various cities and regions in China, with 80 responses (42.6 per cent response rate).[75] An analysis of the geographical allocation of survey samples and the actual geographical alloca-

---

[73] Art 10 of the Arbitration Law.

[74] 谭兵,《中国仲裁制度研究》, (北京, 法律出版社, 1995) 第178页 (Bing Tan, *Research on the Arbitration System in China*, (Beijing, Legal Press, 1995) 178).

[75] See 王亚新,《关于仲裁机构问卷调查的统计分析》,《北京仲裁》第63辑, 2007年, 第6-11页 (Yaxin Wang, 'The Statistical Analysis on the Questionnaires to Arbitration Institutions', (2007) 63 *Beijing Arbitration*, 6–11).

tion of arbitration institutions indicates that the survey results are representative of the status quo of local arbitration institutions all over China.[76] The survey shows much confusion among local arbitration institutions as to their legal status: 48.8 per cent of the arbitration institutions define themselves as 'not-for-profit association[s] with [an] administrative nature or administrative support', another 30 per cent as 'not-for-profit association[s] for social and public interest', and some 2.5 per cent even as 'administrative bodies'. These institutions tend to emphasise the 'public' nature of arbitration. Only 13.8 per cent consider themselves to belong to the private sector, as 'not-for-profit association[s] with [an] entrepreneur and service nature'.[77]

In terms of personnel, it is very common for officials of administrative bodies also to assume the leading positions at arbitration institutions – often referred to as the 'same groups of staff, two different official titles' phenomenon (*yi tao ban zi, liang kuai pai zi*).[78] Also, a number of leadership positions are assumed by party members. As a result, many local arbitration institutions are subject to administrative intervention from government officials. The administrative features of arbitration institutions may have further implications for the independence of arbitrators, who to some extent were 'grandfathered' by the arbitration institutions. What is worse, when the arbitration cases involve parties related to local government or its affiliated bodies, even if the arbitrators have no conflict of interest, their impartiality may be jeopardised because of pressures exercised by the arbitration institution. Half of the arbitration institutions have achieved financial equilibrium without governmental support, while 42.5 per cent still largely rely on governmental aid. With respect to the financial system, 47 arbitration institutions out of 80 that responded (58.8 per cent) are subject to the system of Separation of Distribution and Income, pursuant to which the institutions' income is remitted to government agencies, which deprives the arbitration institutions of financial independence.[79]

A review of domestic arbitration institutions in various regions of China shows significant imbalances in their development. In less developed regions, especially in the inner areas, the administrative taints are often more pronounced. There the establishment of arbitration institutions caters for administrative needs rather than for market demand for dispute resolution. As a result, many of them face a situation of 'looking for rice to cook' and cannot survive in the market economy without government support. To increase the caseload,

---

[76] 陈福勇,《直面仲裁机构现状的复杂性－关于问卷调查的几点补充说明与思考》,《北京仲裁》第63辑, 2007年, 第18–23页 (Fuyong Chen, 'Facing the Complexity of the Current Status of Arbitration Institutions – Several Supplements and Thoughts on the Questionnaire' (2007) 63 *Beijing Arbitration*, 18–23).

[77] See Yaxin Wang, 'The Statistical Analysis on the Questionnaires to Arbitration Institutions', 6–11.

[78] See 王红松,《仲裁行政化的危害及应对之策》,《北京仲裁》第62辑, 2007年, 第14–21页 (Hongsong Wang, 'The Detriments of and Measures Against the Administrative Influence on Arbitration', (2007) 62 *Beijing Arbitration*, 14–22).

[79] Yaxin Wang, 'The Statistical Analysis on the Questionnaires to Arbitration Institutions', 6–11.

some local governments require various administrative bureaus and local banks to impose standard contracts which contain an arbitration clause designating the local arbitration institution. Such practice is obviously contrary to party autonomy. For instance, a report on arbitration published by the Legal Department of the State Council in December 2000 refers to the method of promoting the use of arbitration in Xiangfan City, Hubei Province. That city requires various government departments to adopt standard contracts with an arbitration clause designating the local arbitration institution, including the construction commission, the foreign trade commission, the people's bank, the transportation bureau, the agriculture bureau, the insurance companies, the real estate bureaus, and the pharmaceutical bureaus.[80] In the bigger cities such as Beijing, Shanghai, Wuhan, Guanzhou, Shenzhen, Qingdao, where the local governments are more inclined to respect the consensual nature of arbitration, local arbitration institutions have achieved independence from administrative interference. The BAC is a good example of the success of local arbitration institutions which have benefited from the 'non-interference' approach adopted by the Beijing municipal people's government. Given such unequal development, whether an arbitration institution can operate independently depends to a major extent on the attitude towards arbitration of the local people's government. The difficulties experienced in the reform of arbitration institutions also come from the arbitration institutions themselves. Some local arbitration institutions are reluctant to engage in reforms as they fear market competition and prefer to continue to rely on government support.

To summarise, despite legislative attempts to respect institutional independence and restore the private nature of arbitration, their goal of achieving full independence of Chinese arbitration institutions at the national and at the local levels has not been achieved in reality. The difficulties come from government control and intervention, institutional reluctance to face the competition in a market economy, as well as the remaining 'control' mentality rooted from the planned economy. Nevertheless, positive adaptations are taking place in Chinese arbitration institutions due to the increased exposure to transnational arbitration norms such as the participation of foreign parties and arbitrators in the arbitration activities in China. The successful reforms undertaken by the CIETAC and the BAC are particularly impressive,[81] which may be a driving force for further reforms at local arbitration institutions throughout China.

---

[80] Notice on the Implementation of the Arbitration System, issued by Xiangfan City, Hubei Province, cited in Bing Tan, *Research on the Arbitration System in China*, 180–81.

[81] For further discussion of the reforms of Chinese arbitration institutions, see ch 10, s 10.1.2.

6

The Combination of Mediation with Arbitration

'Persuade your neighbors to compromise whenever you can. Point out to them how the nominal winner is often the real loser – in fees, expenses and waste of time'.

Abraham Lincoln

THE FOREGOING ANALYSIS demonstrates the differences between transnational standards and Chinese practice in terms of the arbitration agreement, arbitral tribunal, recognition and enforcement of arbitral awards, and the practice of arbitration institutions. In this chapter, we will explore another important difference: the role of arbitrators in facilitating settlement. In the Western world, the culture of dispute resolution is traditionally characterised as litigious or confrontational. By contrast, in the Oriental world, especially in the Far East, there is a strong mediation culture. In the context of this cultural clash, there has been much discussion recently on integrating mediation and other alternative dispute resolution (ADR) methods into arbitration proceedings, in order to improve the efficiency of dispute resolution. Various combinations have long been practised in certain parts of the world. However, due to the different legal cultures and views towards the roles of the arbitrators, there is no transnational consensus yet on whether one neutral party can serve as both an arbitrator and a mediator in the same proceeding.

Divergent opinions on this issue arise from different perceptions of the role of an arbitrator: in the West, the arbitrator is viewed as an unbiased fact-finder unconnected to the parties, uninfluenced by previous knowledge of the facts of the dispute, who renders a decision based solely on the application of the law to proven facts, without regard to the effect on the parties' relationship. As a result, there is a clear distinction between the role of an arbitrator and that of a mediator, and the combination of the two roles is not viewed favourably. In China, on the other hand, parties tend to seek an arbitrator who is familiar with them, and who will not only end their dispute, but do so in a mutually agreeable fashion, with as little loss of face as possible. Thus, the distinction between the function of the arbitrator and that of the mediator is blurred.[1]

---

[1] See M Schott Donahey, 'Seeking Harmony: Is the Asian Concept of the Conciliator/Arbitrator Applicable in the West?' (1995) 50 *Dispute Resolution International* 2.

138 *Arb-Med*

A system merging the two roles appears to work well in China. In this respect, the Chinese experience may contribute to the development of international arbitration elsewhere. For this reason, we will devote a separate chapter to the role of arbitrators in promoting settlement within arbitration proceedings that are already pending, in other words, on the combination of mediation with arbitration (arb-med). It is characterised by the fact that *the same person* acts as both an arbitrator and a mediator in *the same* proceeding. This chapter starts with the theoretical debates on whether arbitrators can and should facilitate settlement (section 6.1). On this basis, we will review the law and practice of arb-med in different legal traditions and cultures (section 6.2). Lastly, the Chinese practice of arb-med will be examined in detail (section 6.3).

6.1 THE THEORETICAL DEBATES ON THE ARBITRATORS' ROLE IN SETTLEMENT FACILITATION

Over the past few decades there has been an ongoing, heated debate on the issue of whether a mediation process can be integrated into an arbitration proceeding, and whether an arbitrator can play the role of a settlement facilitator in a pending arbitration.[2] The debate give rises to the delicate ethical issues, and

---

[2] Klaus-Peter Berger, 'Integration of Mediation Elements into Arbitration: Hybrid Procedures and "Intuitive" Mediation by International Arbitrators' (2003) 19 *Arbitration International* 3; Christian Buhring-Uhle, *Arbitration and Mediation in International Business* (The Hague, Kluwer Law International, 1996); James Carter, 'Issues Arising From Integrated Dispute Resolution Clauses' in Albert Jan van den Berg (ed), *ICCA Congress series no 12* (The Hague, Kluwer Law International, 2005); Michael Collins, 'Do International Arbitral Tribunals Have Any Obligations to Encourage Settlement of the Disputes Before Them?' (2003) 19 *Arbitration International* 3; Renate Dendorfer and Jeremy Lack, 'The Interaction Between Arbitration and Mediation: Vision v Reality' (2007) 1 *Dispute Resolution International* 1; Michael Hoellering, 'Comments on the Growing Inter-Action of Arbitration and Mediation' in Albert Jan van den Berg (ed), *ICCA Congress series no 8* (The Hague, Kluwer Law International, 1998); Martin Hunter, 'Commentary on Integrated Dispute Resolution Clauses' in Albert Jan van den Berg (ed), *ICCA Congress series no 12* (The Hague, Kluwer Law International, 2005); Michael Hwang, 'The Role of Arbitrators as Settlement Facilitators: Commentary' in Albert Jan van den Berg (ed), *ICCA Congress series no 12* (The Hague, Kluwer Law International, 2005); Gabrielle Kaufmann-Kohler, 'When Arbitrators Facilitate Settlement: Towards a Transnational Standard' (2009) 25 *Arbitration International* 2; Consultation Document for CEDR Commission on Settlement in International Arbitration (2009); Pierre Lalive, 'The Role of Arbitrators as Settlement Facilitators: A Swiss View' in Albert Jan van den Berg (ed), *ICCA Congress series no 12* (The Hague, Kluwer Law International, 2005); Julian Lew, 'Multi-Institutionals Conciliation and the Reconciliation of Different Legal Cultures' in Albert Jan van den Berg (ed), *ICCA Congress series no 12* (The Hague, Kluwer Law International, 2005); Arthur Marriott, 'Arbitrators and Settlement' in Albert Jan van den Berg (ed), *ICCA Congress series no 12* (The Hague, Kluwer Law International, 2005); Carlos Nehring Netto, 'The Brazilian Approach to Arbitrators as Settlement Faciliators' in Albert Jan van den Berg (ed), *ICCA Congress series no 12* (The Hague, Kluwer Law International, 2005); David Plant, 'The Arbitrators as Settlement Facilitator' (2000) 17 *Journal of International Arbitration* 1; Toshio Sawada, 'Hybrid Arb-Med: Will West and East Never Meet?' (2003) 14 *ICC Bulletin* 2; Michael Schneider, 'Combining Arbitration with Conciliation' in Albert Jan van den Berg (ed), *ICCA Congress series no 8* (The Hague, Kluwer Law International, 1996); Houzhi Tang, 'Is There an Expending Culture that Favors Combining Arbitration with Conciliation or Other ADR Procedures?' in Albert Jan van den Berg (ed), *ICCA Congress Series no 8* (The Hague, Kluwer Law International, 1996); Houzhi Tang,

touches the very core of arbitration, that is, the mission of arbitrators. If the arbitrator is supposed to resolve a dispute by handing down a binding decision, then facilitating settlement is not compatible with that role. On the other hand, if the arbitrator's role is simply to resolve a dispute, by any means necessary, then he or she could promote settlement.[3]

6.1.1 Supporters of Arb-Med

Arguments in support of arb-med can be summarised as follows, (A) it is the mission of arbitrators to resolve disputes in the most efficient way, (B) the parties act of their own free will and use the process voluntarily, and (C) it is an efficient means of dispute resolution.

A. *Mission of Arbitrators to Resolve the Dispute in the Most Efficient Way*

If the arbitrators are considered to have the responsibility of ensuring that arbitration in general provides the parties with a menu of processes that may assist the parties in resolving their disputes in the most effective way, which includes assisting the parties in reaching a fair resolution of their differences at the earliest practical time, then the arbitrators' role will include the facilitation of settlement.

The supporters of the combination hold the view that the mission of arbitrators is not merely to adjudicate the dispute, but also to help to resolve it amicably with the cooperation of the parties. Hence,

> a well-structured and conducted arbitration can facilitate and even encourage a constructive dialogue between the parties, thereby providing the parties, possibly with the active support of the tribunal, not only with the resolution of a pathological dispute but with a service for the future.[4]

In addition, as in court proceedings, arbitrators may even order the parties to appear in person for the purpose of providing information or for attempts to arrive at a settlement at any stage of the proceedings.[5] Professor Pieter Sanders has made the following comments:

'Combination of Arbitration with Conciliation: Arb/Med' in Albert Jan van den Berg (ed), *ICCA Congress Series no 12* (The Hague, Kluwer Law International, 2005); Shengchang Wang, 'Combination of Arbitration with Conciliation and Remittance of Awards – with Special Reference to the Asia-Oceania Region' (2002) 19 *Journal of International Arbitration* 1.

[3] See Kaufmann-Kohler, 'When Arbitrators Facilitate Settlement: Towards a Transnational Standard', 187.

[4] Berger, 'Integration of Mediation Elements into Arbitration: Hybrid Procedures and "Intuitive" Mediation by International Arbitrators', 403.

[5] Pieter Sanders, 'The 1996 Alexander Lecture, Cross-Border Arbitration: A View on the Future' (1996) 62 *Arbitration* 3, 173.

In case arbitrators take the initiative to order such a meeting to discuss possibilities of a settlement it seems to me that it is not excluded that arbitrators would invite the parties to use one of the available means of ADR to settle their dispute. Such an invitation is not outside the mission of the arbitrators. Arbitration is a service industry in the interest of the parties. Why should arbitrators not suggest, in appropriate cases, to use one of the available means of ADR?[6]

Furthermore, the arbitrator does not formulate his or her decision in one instant; rather, he or she forms a view gradually during the arbitration process. The views formed by the arbitrator are provisional and evolve as the proceedings advance. 'Why should the arbitrator leave the parties in the dark about this evolution and surprise them at the end with his award?'[7] Engaging in settlement discussions may allow the arbitrator, before rendering a final decision, to discuss the case with the parties or at least identify to the parties the points on which the arbitrator has difficulties in accepting the parties' positions. Practice has shown that the approach is welcomed even by counsel and arbitrators from a cultural background where such discussions are not admitted or practised.[8]

B. Free Will and Voluntariness of the Parties

Another justification for the arbitrators to facilitate settlement is based on the parties' freedom of choice.[9] Party autonomy is the essence of arbitration. If the parties want the arbitrators to carry out a conciliatory role, to use caucus in mediation, or to put their arbitration hats back on if the mediation fails, such choices should be respected. Professor Tang Houzhi, a strong advocate for arb-med, made the following statements at the International Council for Commercial Arbitration (ICCA) conference in Beijing in 2004:

> Conciliation, like arbitration, is private business. Its basis is the agreement of the parties and its essence is the parties' autonomy (the freewill and voluntariness of the parties). If the parties want conciliation to be conducted by arbitrators in the arbitration proceedings, if the parties agree to have 'caucus' without disclosing from one party to the other party all the information received by the arbitration tribunal (the arbitrators-turned-conciliators) in the course of caucusing, if the parties wish to have the same person to act as an arbitrator and at the same time as a conciliator or first act as a conciliator and later as an arbitrator and vice versa, how could a third person (a lawyer, a law-maker, a judge, a law professor, etc.) say this is not appropriate and unfair to the parties and this is running counter to 'natural justice'? . . . The third

---

[6] ibid.
[7] Schneider, 'Combining Arbitration with Conciliation', 76.
[8] ibid.
[9] See, for instance, Tang, 'Is There an Expending Culture that Favors Combining Arbitration with Conciliation or Other ADR Procedures?', 113; Berger, 'Integration of Mediation Elements into Arbitration: Hybrid Procedures and "Intuitive' Mediation by International Arbitrators', 387–403; Lew, 'Multi-Institutionals Conciliation and the Reconciliation of Different Legal Cultures', 421–29.

person may not worry about this because this is just what the parties want and this is not contrary to 'public policy' or 'public order' or 'public interests'.[10]

In addition, the combined approach may give the parties a greater psychological satisfaction than a decided outcome. It offers the parties more control over the process than they would have in pure arbitration, giving the parties the feeling of having been heard. Moreover, due its greater flexibility (as compared to pure arbitration), arb-med has the capacity of reaching solutions that are more acceptable to all parties involved. In an arb-med process, the parties may focus on current issues and future interest-based solutions instead of solely discussing past events and the allocation of blame.

C. *Efficiency of Dispute Resolution*

Furthermore, settlement facilitation by arbitrators can be a useful tool to enhance the efficiency of arbitration and improve the administration of justice.[11] One of the decisive advantages that arbitration has over regular courts is 'the possibility of achieving an economically sound settlement which does justice to the parties' interests and expectations'.[12] Therefore, it is argued that 'arbitration must never be considered as excluding from its purview the settlement of a dispute before the arbitrator, because this is of the essence of the spirit of arbitration'.[13]

Sir Michael Kerr argued that the future of dispute resolution lies in ADR, as it is faster, simpler, and conducive to higher success rates and better results for the parties. Mediation does not decide what is 'right' or 'wrong' according to the law, which requires complex legal proceedings to conduct a thorough analysis of the commercial disputes before resolving the disputes. The time spent on the thorough investigation is often not worthwhile, except for exceptional cases. Mediation, on the other hand, may produce a satisfactory result acceptable to both parties.[14] With respect to costs, Sir Michael Kerr referred to the statement by the head of the legal department of Shell Company: 'the biggest cost of arbitration is the loss of operation and management time'. These costs may become unbearable as arbitration is as time consuming as litigation to achieve the 'correct' result – to distinguish 'right' and 'wrong' according to the law. Modern business management has thus been trying to avoid overly complicated processes, and to replace them with faster and easier methods of ADR.[15]

---

[10] Tang, 'Is There an Expending Culture that Favors Combining Arbitration with Conciliation or Other ADR Procedures?', 113.
[11] Kaufmann-Kohler, 'When Arbitrators Facilitate Settlement: Towards a Transnational Standard', 205.
[12] Berger, 'Integration of Mediation Elements into Arbitration: Hybrid Procedures and "Intuitive" Mediation by International Arbitrators', 387–403.
[13] ibid.
[14] Michael Kerr, 'Reflections on 50 Years' Involvement in Dispute Resolution' (1998) 64 *Arbitration*, 175.
[15] ibid.

142   *Arb-Med*

In this respect, the use of mediation in the proceedings encompasses all the benefits which are usually attributed to *settled*, rather than *decided*, outcomes, such as cost savings, efficiency gains, and the maintenance of a friendly cooperative relationship between the disputing parties. Combining the two processes also improves efficiency.[16] First, in the event that mediation fails or was only partially successful, the parties need not educate another neutral fact-finder, with the inevitable duplication of work, additional expenses, and delays. The neutral party who has been serving as mediator already knows much, if not all, of the information she or he will need to make a decision, and will have a broader range of options to consider, given the focus on the future interests of the parties. Second, in an arb-med process, the arbitrator is the master of the timing of the proceedings, and is in the best position to choose the appropriate moment in the course of the proceedings to offer the tribunal's services for settlement purposes. Third, settlement agreements entered into by the parties in stand-alone mediation proceedings are enforceable only as private contracts. By contrast, arb-med may produce a directly enforceable instrument: a settlement agreement entered into in the course of a pending arbitration may form part of a consent award and become enforceable under the New York Convention. Finally, the Chinese experience also shows that mediation conducted in the course of arbitration proceedings is more likely to be successful than if the mediation is conducted separately.[17] Even if no settlement is reached, a combined proceeding may enable the parties to narrow their disputes substantially during the mediation phase, often leaving only a few remaining issues to be arbitrated. By agreeing to arbitrate the remaining issues, the parties can preserve the fruits of their partial agreements. Indeed,

> the more complex the dispute – in terms of subject matter, numbers of issues, numbers of parties, numbers of related proceedings, numbers of relationships among the parties and their affiliates, and the like – the greater may be the need, and concomitant benefits, of facilitated settlement discussions.[18]

6.1.2 Opponents of Arb-Med

Criticism of arb-med boils down to the following three aspects: (A) the mission of arbitrators to render a binding decision; (B) a risk of failure to achieve due process and natural justice; and (C) impartiality of arbitrators.

---

[16] Kaufmann-Kohler, 'When Arbitrators Facilitate Settlement: Towards a Transnational Standard', 197.
[17] See Wang, 'Combination of Arbitration with Conciliation and Remittance of Awards – with Special Reference to the Asia-Oceania Region', 51–66.
[18] David Plant, 'ADR and Arbitration' in Lawrence Newman and Richard Hill (ed), *The Leading Arbitrators' Guide to International Arbitration* (New York, JurisNet, LLC, 2008) 263.

A. Mission of Arbitrators to Render a Binding Decision

If the role of arbitrators is considered as solely to assure that the arbitral process results in an *enforceable* award arrived at in a fair way, then promoting settlement would fall beyond the mission of the arbitrators. Michael Collins QC, for instance, holds the view that the arbitrators' obligations are to resolve disputes by a process of adjudication, and to produce a binding decision which finally determines the legal rights of the parties.[19] He does not object to the practice that an international arbitrator should 'encourage settlement whenever the opportunity to do so presents itself'. This encouragement, he believes, should take the form either of inviting the parties to discuss the matter among themselves, or to engage in mediation, or both. However, the encouragement should not,

> except in very rare circumstances, involve the arbitrator playing a personal role in the settlement discussions, or assuming the role of a mediator; and they should do so only once the ground rules have been clearly established, and the written consent of the parties obtained.[20]

B. Due Process and Natural Justice

The main argument against arbitrators facilitating settlement is the risk of a breach of due process and natural justice. Fundamental to the notion of natural justice is the right to know and be able to answer an opponent's case. The rule of due process governing fair hearing of disputes on the merits forbids ex parte communications with the decision maker. However, the process of mediation often involves a separate meeting between the mediator and each party (caucusing). During these caucuses, information communicated confidentially to the mediator is not known to the opposing party, and is not subject to a response or clarification by the opposing party. As a consequence, the other party may be deprived of its due process right to rebut that information.[21]

C. Impartiality of Arbitrators

Another drawback to the combined approach is the fear that, in the event that the settlement fails and the arbitration continues, the impartiality of the mediator-turned-arbitrator may be affected because of the confidential information he or she obtained during the mediation phase that is not part of the record. By the same token, there is the concern that if the parties anticipate that the mediator may revert to being an arbitrator and decide the case if the mediation fails,

---

[19] Collins, 'Do International Arbitral Tribunals Have Any Obligations to Encourage Settlement of the Disputes Before Them?', 333–43.
[20] ibid.
[21] See Kaufmann-Kohler, 'When Arbitrators Facilitate Settlement: Towards a Transnational Standard', 197; Emilia Onyema, 'The Use of Med-Arb in International Commercial Dispute Resolution' (2001) 12 *American Review of International Arbitration* 3–4, 415.

they might be less candid than they would be with a 'pure' mediator. This may weaken the effectiveness of the mediation process. Professors Alan Redfern and Martin Hunter put forward their concerns as follows:

> To a lawyer, it raises many questions. For example, how frank are the parties likely to be in their discussions with the mediator (for instance, by indicating what settlement proposals they would accept), whilst knowing that, if there is no settlement, that same person will change hats and appear as an arbitrator? And how can the arbitrator satisfy (or appear to satisfy) the requirements of 'impartiality' and 'a fair hearing' if he has previously held private discussions with the parties separately and indicated his views to them?[22]

6.2 COMPARATIVE STUDY OF THE LAW AND PRACTICE OF ARB-MED

How are the theoretical debates perceived in the law and practice of international arbitration?[23] We shall answer the question by reviewing, in turn, relevant provisions in national laws (section 6.2.1); the approaches in institutional rules (section 6.2.2); and actual arbitration practice from the practitioners' view (section 6.2.3).

6.2.1 National Laws

Experience and empirical research show that the way arbitrators conduct proceedings is greatly influenced by the way judges in their home jurisdiction conduct court proceedings.[24] Therefore, when examining national laws, we will look at general procedural rules as well as arbitration statutes.

A. *Civil Law Jurisdictions*

In the Romano-Germanic tradition, it is part of a court's mission to promote settlement. In Germany, the Code of Civil Procedure (ZPO) requires judges to explore opportunities for an amicable settlement of the dispute or any of the

---

[22] Hunter et al, *Redfern and Hunter on International Arbitration*, 48.
[23] For a discussion of the national laws and institutional rules on this topic, see Kaufmann-Kohler, 'When Arbitrators Facilitate Settlement: Towards a Transnational Standard', 189–97. See also Tang, 'Is There an Expending Culture that Favors Combining Arbitration with Conciliation or Other ADR Procedures?', 101–20. 王生长, 《仲裁与调解相结合的理论与实务》, (北京, 法律出版社, 2001) 第 136–51页 (Shengchang Wang, The Combination of Arbitration and Mediation: Theory and Practice, (Beijing, Legal Press, 2001) 136–51); Alexander Petsche and Martin Platte, 'The Arbitrator – The Arbitrator as Dispute Settlement Facilitator' in Peter Klein, Christian Klausegger et al (eds), *Austrian Arbitration Yearbook* (Vienna, CH Beck, Stämpfli & Manz, 2007) 89–93.
[24] See Gabrielle Kaufmann-Kohler and Victor Bonnin, 'Arbitrators as Conciliators: A Statistical Study of the Relation between an Arbitrator's Role and Legal Background' (2007) 18 *ICC Bulletin* 2, 79–85. Kaufmann-Kohler, 'When Arbitrators Facilitate Settlement: Towards a Transnational Standard', 189.

contentious issues throughout the proceeding.[25] This provision is considered to apply to arbitration by analogy.[26] Under German law an arbitrator is thus authorised, and even obliged in some circumstances, to attempt a settlement between the parties. This view is also consistent with what is regarded in Germany as one of arbitration's primary aims, the achievement of economically sensible and equitable settlements.[27]

In Switzerland, there is also a trend to resolve civil disputes by settlement. The Zurich Code of Civil Procedure stipulates that the judge can at any time summon the parties to attend a mediation hearing. At that hearing, the judge generally sets out his understanding of the relevant facts, carries out a detailed legal analysis and concludes with his proposal for a settlement.[28] The unified Swiss Code of Civil Procedure, which entered into force on 1 January 2011,[29] places greater emphasis on ADR mechanisms. According to the Swiss Code of Civil Procedure, mediation proceedings are now mandatory, with limited exceptions.[30] Furthermore, for certain disputes, the 'mediation authority'[31] can submit a decision proposal to the parties,[32] which will become final and binding unless one party objects to it within a period of 20 days.[33] Such a practice has been carried out by Swiss arbitrators in arbitration proceedings.

Apart from the Romano-Germanic tradition, ADR methods are also increasingly incorporated into the judicial system in other civil law countries. Article 21 of the French Code of Civil Procedure, for instance, expressly states that conciliation falls within the scope of the judge's mission.[34] Pursuant to Article 1464 of the French Code of Civil Procedure, the governing principles of proceedings provided for under Article 21, among others, always apply to arbitration proceedings.[35]

---

[25] Art 278 of the German Code of Civil Procedure (ZPO). See Kaufmann-Kohler and Bonnin, 'Arbitrators as Conciliators: A Statistical Study of the Relation between an Arbitrator's Role and Legal Background', 84; John Langbein, 'The German Advantage in Civil Procedure' (1985) 52 *University of Chicago Law Review* 4, 823–24; Schneider, 'Combining Arbitration with Conciliation', 79.

[26] Petsche and Platte, 'The Arbitrator – The Arbitrator as Dispute Settlement Facilitator', citing Fritz Nicklisch, *Schiedsgerichtsverfahren mit integrierter Schlichtung*, Recht der Internationalen Wirtschaft (1998) 169; Eugen Bucher, *Die Rolle des Schiedsrichters bei der vergleichsweisen Beilegung des Streits*, ASA Bulletin (1995) 574.

[27] ibid.

[28] Art 62 of the Zurich Code of Civil Procedure (Zurich ZPO). On this practice, see Werner Wenger, 'The Role of the Arbitrator in Bringing about a Settlement' (2006) *Best Practices in International Arbitration, ASA Special Series*, 139.

[29] Before the SCCP came into force, each of the 26 cantons in Switzerland had its own code of civil procedure. These codes could differ substantially from each other given the varying influence of the Germanic and French legal traditions prevailing in Switzerland. The SCCP aims to eliminate these obstacles by way of a uniform civil procedural law. It is a relatively concise code of 408 articles regulating civil procedure and domestic arbitration.

[30] Arts 197 and 198 of the SCCP.

[31] Defined in Art 200 of the SCCP.

[32] Art 210 of the SCCP.

[33] Art 211 of the SCCP.

[34] Art 21 of the French Code of Civil Procedure provides that '*il entre dans la mission du juge de concilier les parties*'. Unofficial translation by the author.

[35] Para 2 of Art 1464 of the French Code of Civil Procedure.

Therefore, arbitrators in France are also authorised to encourage parties to settle their disputes. In practice, French judges are reluctant to conciliate the cases they are adjudicating, but rather choose to refer cases to other judges for settlement.[36] Influenced by the tradition in the court, French arbitrators also tend to be less willing to facilitate settlement themselves in a pending arbitration.

In the Netherlands, arbitration law expressly states that arbitrators may at any stage of the proceedings order the parties to appear in person for the purpose of providing information or for attempts to arrive at a settlement.[37]

In China, given the long mediation tradition, Chinese judges customarily promote settlement to relieve the heavy judicial caseload and to reduce judicial costs. The legal basis for the judges to mediate the disputes can be found in the Civil Procedure Law, which provides that 'when adjudicating civil cases, the people's courts may mediate the disputes according to the principles of voluntariness and lawfulness. If a mediation agreement cannot be reached, the courts shall render a judgment without delay'.[38] Following court practice, promotion of settlement by arbitrators is also admissible and encouraged under the Arbitration Law.[39]

B. *Common Law Jurisdictions*

Common law courts have traditionally been entrusted with adjudicating, not settling, disputes.[40] Nevertheless, this traditional hostility towards mediation is changing. Recent developments indicate a movement in favour of settlement and away from adjudication in order to promote efficiency. In the United Kingdom, for instance, Lord Woolf's reform of civil procedure in 1996 promoted the development of ADR. Lord Woolf essentially proposed that the courts should encourage and assist the parties to settle cases or, at least, to agree on particular issues and to encourage the use of ADR.[41] This proposal was codified in the English Civil Procedure Rules 1998, which provide as follows:

(1) The court must further the overriding objective by actively managing cases.

(2) Active case management includes:

... (e) encouraging the parties to use an alternative dispute resolution procedure if the court considers that appropriate and facilitating the use of such procedure; and

(f) helping the parties to settle the whole or part of the case.[42]

---

[36] See Bruno Oppetit, 'Arbitrage, médiation et conciliation' (1984) *Revue de l'arbitrage* 308.

[37] Art 1043 of the Dutch Arbitration Law, effective on 1 December 1986 (as amended on 1 January 2002 and 30 June 2004).

[38] Art 9 of the Civil Procedure Law 2012.

[39] Art 51 of the Arbitration Law.

[40] See generally John Coons, 'Approaches to Court Imposed Compromises – The Uses of Doubt and Reason' (1964) 58 *Northwestern University Law Review* 750, 750–94.

[41] Woolf, Access to Justice, Final Report, 1996, s I, para 9; s II, ch I, para 7(d), para 16(b)–(c), available at www.dca.gov.uk/civil/final/index.htm.

[42] Art 1.4 of the English Civil Procedure Rules 1998.

In Canada, the Canadian Arbitration Act allows an arbitrator to conduct mediation with the parties' consent and to resume his or her function as an arbitrator if the mediation attempt fails.

In Singapore, courts have resorted to mediation for many years on an informal basis in cases where the judges saw a potential for settlement. Judges normally first explore with counsel whether the parties have been in negotiations and, if so, why and when the process broke down. They will then, in appropriate cases, either before the hearing or even after the hearing, speak to counsel (often with the parties present) to facilitate a settlement. This tradition has now been institutionalised in the lower courts by a procedure known as Court Dispute Resolution where all cases passing through the lower courts (generally, cases with monetary values of less than US$150,000) need to go through a court-assisted mediation process before a judge (the 'Settlement Judge') after pleadings have been filed. If the mediation is unsuccessful, as a matter of policy, a different judge will be assigned to hear the case on its merits.[43] Following the tradition of court-assisted mediation, the International Arbitration Act of Singapore expressly provides that the arbitrator may act as a conciliator, if all the parties consent in writing and for so long as no party withdraws its consent in writing.[44]

In Hong Kong, mediation is one of the main objectives of the Civil Justice Reform of 2009. In the Practice Direction on Mediation, which came into effect on 1 January 2010, one of the underlying objectives of the Rules of the High Court and the District Court was precisely to facilitate the settlement of disputes.[45] The new Hong Kong Arbitration Ordinance (Ordinance),[46] which borrowed and enhanced the old regime, also contains express provisions on the power of an arbitrator to act as a mediator. Under the Ordinance, an arbitrator may act as a mediator after the arbitration proceedings have commenced, provided that all parties give their written consent.[47] If an arbitrator acts as a mediator, the arbitration proceedings are to be stayed in order to afford the mediation the maximum chance of success.[48] If the mediation fails, the arbitrator-mediator is required to disclose to all parties any confidential information obtained during the mediation which he or she considers to be 'material to the arbitral

---

[43] Hwang, 'The Role of Arbitrators as Settlement Facilitators: Commentary', 576–77.
[44] Section 17(1) of the International Arbitration Act of Singapore 2002.
[45] PD 31 – Practice Direction on Mediation, effective from 1 January 2010, available at www.hklii.org/hk/other/pd/en/PD31.doc. For a commentary, see Kun Fan, 'Mediation and Civil Justice Reform in Hong Kong' (2011) 27 *International Litigation Quarterly* 2, 11–14.
[46] The new Hong Kong Arbitration Ordinance (ch 609) was approved by the Hong Kong Legislative Council on 10 November 2010. It came into effect on 1 June 2011, replacing the existing Arbitration Ordinance (ch 341). The Ordinance draws heavily on the Model Law, with certain modifications (and additions) which reflect the specific features of arbitration in the region. For a discussion on the new Ordinance, see eg John Choong and Romesh Weeramantry (eds), *The Hong Kong Arbitration Ordinance, Commentary and Annotations* (Hong Kong, Sweet & Maxwell, 2011).
[47] Section 33(1) of the Ordinance.
[48] Section 33(2) of the Ordinance.

proceedings'.[49] The Ordinance further provides that no challenge shall be made to the arbitrator solely on the ground that the person had acted previously as a mediator in connection with some or all of the matters relating to the dispute submitted to arbitration.[50]

To summarise, in Germany, Switzerland, and France, although arbitration law does not expressly allow arbitrators to promote settlement, it is generally considered acceptable for arbitrators to carry out such a role, by analogy to the provisions and similar practice in their national courts. In the Netherlands and China, arbitration statues expressly allow arbitrators to promote settlement. Even in traditional common law countries where judges are traditionally meant to adjudicate and not to settle disputes, there is a movement in favour of settlement in the court system with a view to promoting efficiency, such as the United Kingdom. Following this trend, the arbitration laws of Canada, Singapore and Hong Kong now expressly permit arbitrators to carry out the role of mediator.

6.2.2 Institutional Rules

How do institutional rules address the admissibility of arbitrators to promote settlement? Although institutional rules do not carry the force of law, they do play an important role in guiding arbitration practice. We will thus examine the relevant provisions in various institutional rules.

In Germany, the arbitration rules of the Deutsche Institution für Schiedsgerichtsbarkeit (German Institution of Arbitration or DIS) provide that 'at every stage of the proceedings, the arbitral tribunal should seek to encourage an amicable settlement of the dispute or of individual issues in dispute'.[51]

The Swiss Rules of International Arbitration do not directly address the issue of whether arbitrators may act as mediators. They do provide, however, that in case the parties reach a settlement before the award is made, the arbitral tribunal shall terminate the arbitration proceedings or, if requested by both parties and accepted by the tribunal, record the settlement in the form of an arbitral award on agreed terms.[52] The LCIA Rules similarly allow arbitrators to record the parties' settlement in a consent award.[53]

In China, most institutional rules expressly allow the combination of mediation and arbitration. The CIETAC Rules 2012, for instance, allow the arbitral tribunal to commence mediation in the process of arbitration proceedings upon the parties' agreement.[54] Similarly, the BAC Rules 2008 allow the arbitral tribu-

---

[49] Section 32(4) of the Ordinance.
[50] Section 32(3)(a) of the Ordinance.
[51] Art 32(1) of the DIS Rules, promulgated by the German Institution of Arbitration on and effective from 1 July 1998.
[52] Art 34(1) of the Swiss Rules of Arbitration 2004, applicable for Chambers of Commerce and Industry of Basel, Bern, Geneva, Ticino, Vaud and Zurich (collectively the 'Swiss Chambers').
[53] Art 26.8 of the LCIA Rules, effective from 1 January 1998.
[54] Art 45(1) of the CIETAC Rules 2012.

nal to mediate the case in a manner that it considers appropriate at the request of both parties or upon obtaining the consent of both parties.[55]

In Japan and Korea, the practice of arb-med is endorsed in the institutional rules. The Rules of the Japan Commercial Arbitration Association (JCAA) stipulate that 'an arbitral tribunal may attempt to settle the dispute in the arbitral proceedings if all of the parties consent, orally or in writing, thereto'.[56] The Arbitration Rules of the Korea Commercial Arbitration Board (KCAB) allow mediation to be conducted by a mediator listed on the KCAB's panel of arbitrators before arbitration proceedings start. If mediation is successful, the mediator shall then be regarded as an arbitrator appointed by agreement of the parties and the result of the mediation will have the same effect as an award. If mediation fails, the mediation will terminate and arbitration proceedings will commence, with the mediator remaining as an arbitrator to adjudicate the dispute.[57] The head of KCAB said that 'in keeping with global trend[s] to solve trade disputes fairly and rapidly, KCAB will further develop the ADR sector and play its key role in solving disputes amicably'.[58] It should be noted that the Korean approach is essentially a *pre-arbitration* mediation, in that (i) the mediation is generally conducted before arbitral proceedings start, and (ii) although the arbitrator is not barred from acting as a mediator, he or she does usually not mediate during the process of arbitration.

The World Intellectual Property Organization (WIPO) Arbitration and Mediation Center expressly supports the combination of arbitration with mediation. The WIPO Arbitration Rules provide that 'the tribunal may suggest that the parties explore settlement at such times as the tribunal may deem appropriate'.[59] If settlement is reached before the award is rendered, the tribunal will terminate arbitration and, if requested jointly by the parties, record the settlement in the form of a consent award.[60] It is interesting to note that arb-med is also allowed under the WIPO Mediation Rules. It stipulates that the mediator may propose, for the consideration of the parties, procedures or means for resolving the disputes which the mediator considers the least costly and the most productive for settlement of those issues, including 'arbitration', or 'arbitration in which the mediator will, with the express consent of the parties, act as sole arbitrator'.[61]

At the ICC, arbitration and other ADR proceedings are dealt with separately. The ICC Arbitration Rules do not have express provisions with respect to the appropriateness of arbitrators promoting settlement in a pending arbitration proceeding. They simply provide that where the parties have settled before an

---

[55] Art 39 of the BAC Rules 2008.
[56] Art 49 of the JCAA Rules, amended and effective from 1 January 2008.
[57] Art 18 of the KCAB Rules, amended by the Supreme Court on 13 December 2004.
[58] 'KCAB Strives to Become Arbitration Hub of Northeast Asia', *Korea IT Times*, 27 May 2009.
[59] Art 65(a) of the WIPO Arbitration Rules 2002, effective from 1 October 2002.
[60] Art 65(b) of the WIPO Arbitration Rules 2002.
[61] Art 13(b)(ii) and (iv) of the WIPO Mediation Rules 2002.

award is rendered, such agreement can be recorded in an award by consent.[62] According to the ICC ADR Rules, the neutral person (mediator) in the ADR proceedings is generally discouraged from acting as an arbitrator in a later arbitration or similar proceedings relating to the dispute which is or was the subject matter of ADR proceedings.[63] That said, arb-med is possible if all of the parties agree in writing.[64]

A development initiated by the International Bar Association (IBA) deserves attention in this context. The IBA Guidelines on Conflicts of Interest provide that an arbitrator's impartiality is not affected by his involvement in settlement, but that if settlement fails and the arbitration continues, the arbitrator should resign if he considers that he cannot perform his duties objectively as a result of his involvement in the settlement attempts.[65] This development is interesting because the IBA Guidelines were drafted on the basis of reports on national laws by a working group of practitioners in which all legal traditions were represented. It can thus be viewed as a synthesis of the different legal traditions involved. Similarly, the IBA Rules of Ethics for International Arbitrators accept that a tribunal as a whole or the presiding arbitrator 'make proposals for settlement to both parties simultaneously and preferably in the presence of each other', where 'the parties have so requested or consented to a suggestion to this effect by the arbitral tribunal'.[66]

To sum up, some institutional rules expressly allow or even encourage the conduct of mediation by the arbitrators (eg, CIETAC, BAC, KCAB, JACC, WIPO, and DIS); some are silent on the practice of combination (eg, LCIA and the Swiss Chambers), while others generally keep the proceedings separate but do not exclude the combination with the parties' consent (eg, ICC). Two common aspects can be identified in our examination of institutional rules: (i) all institutional rules allow the arbitrators to record the settlement in a consent award; (ii) none of the institutional rules prohibits the same mediator to act as an arbitrator if the parties so agree.

---

[62] Art 32 of the ICC Rules 2012.
[63] Art 3 of the ICC ADR Rules 2001, effective from 1 July 2001.
[64] Art 3 of the ICC ADR Rules 2001.
[65] See IBA Guidelines on Conflicts of Interest in International Arbitration, s 4(d): 'An arbitrator may assist the parties in reaching a settlement of the dispute at any stage of the proceedings. However, before doing so, the arbitrator should receive an express agreement by the parties that acting in such a manner shall not disqualify the arbitrator from continuing to serve as arbitrator. Such express agreement shall be considered to be an effective waiver of any potential conflict of interest that may arise from the arbitrator's participation in such process or from information that the arbitrator may learn in the process. If the assistance by the arbitrator does not lead to final settlement of the case, the parties remain bound by their waiver. However, consistent with General Standard 2(a) and notwithstanding such agreement, the arbitrator shall resign if, as a consequence of his or her involvement in the settlement process, the arbitrator develops doubts as to his or her ability to remain impartial or independent in the future course of the arbitration proceedings'.
[66] Art 8 of the IBA Rules of Ethics for International Arbitrators.

6.2.3 Actual Arbitration Practice: Some Empirical Studies

The above review of the national laws applied in courts, arbitration laws and institutional rules demonstrates that arb-med is not only widely practised in China, but also accepted in other parts of the world, especially in continental Europe, where judges traditionally promote settlement. This trend is also expanding to common law jurisdictions, such as Hong Kong and Singapore perhaps somehow influenced by the Chinese tradition. In international arbitration practice, how often do the international arbitrators facilitate settlement? What is the overall settlement rate in arbitration proceedings? To what extent do arbitrators actively engage in promoting a voluntary settlement between the parties? What, if any, are the different attitudes and practices between practitioners from different legal backgrounds and cultures? To answer these questions, we will need to examine the results of a few empirical studies on the view of arbitration practitioners.

A. *Two Surveys of Arbitration and Mediation Practitioners (1994, 2004)*

One of the first comprehensive empirical studies on the practice of international business dispute resolution was presented by Professor Christian Bühring-Uhle in *Arbitration and Mediation in International Business: Designing Procedures for Effective Conflict Management* (1996).[67] Ten years later, this survey was supplemented by a second survey, presented in the second edition of *Arbitration and Mediation in International Business* (2006).[68] The new survey was started in the autumn of 2001 and completed in 2004. Some of the questions of the earlier survey were repeated to see whether the practices and/or the attitudes had changed. Some new questions were added, such as the different roles of different members of an arbitral tribunal in trying to help the parties, the use of separate mediators during arbitral proceedings, the use of mediation clauses and the role of arbitration institutions in proposing mediation to the parties to an arbitration. The quantitative analysis is based on 53 completed questionnaires. The 53 respondents came from 14 countries representing all six continents, 20 from the USA, eight from Germany, 11 from other continental European countries and another 11 from other common law countries. The group included both users and providers of dispute resolution services, that is, in-house counsel, advocates, arbitrators, and mediators who had participated in aggregate in more than 2,500 arbitrations and more than 600 mediations. The

---

[67] Buhring-Uhle, *Arbitration and Mediation in International Business*. As reported in his study, close to 150 questionnaires were distributed to practitioners all over the world in the first survey, which was completed in 1994. A total of 91 arbitrators, lawyers and in-house counsel from 17 countries responded, 67 of which (from 8 countries) were interviewed in person, while the rest responded in writing.

[68] Christian Buhring-Uhle, Lars Kirchhoff and Gabriele Scherer, *Arbitration and Mediation in International Business*, 2nd edn (The Hague, Kluwer Law International, 2006).

main research findings of the two surveys of 1994 and 2004 are summarised below.

First, in terms of the role of arbitrators, a large majority of the respondents (86 per cent) thought that facilitating settlement was one of the functions of the arbitral process (a slight increase in comparison to the first survey where the figure was 83 per cent). This view was universal among the German and the non-American respondents with a common law background, whereas 26 per cent of the Americans and 15 per cent of the non-German civil law practitioners thought that voluntary settlement was not a goal of arbitration.

Second, on the settlement rate, the survey showed that 43 per cent of the cases were settled before an arbitral decision. The average figure varies markedly according to the background of the respondents. A large divergence of experience exists between German and American practitioners: 69 per cent of the Germans settled as opposed to only 33 per cent of the Americans. This may be explained by the different practices and traditions in the respective judicial systems, particularly with regard to the function of judicial proceedings and the role of judges: German procedural laws require settlement attempts by the judges, whilst the traditional American image of the judge is one of a detached and impartial decision maker.

Last, on the timing of settlement, settlement occurs at all stages of the arbitral procedure but the likelihood of an agreement increases as the process evolves. 29 per cent of settlements occurred before the first meeting of the tribunal with the parties. 33 per cent of the settlements occurred during the written phase before the main evidence hearing. The largest group of settlements occurred fairly late: well over one third of settlements (37 per cent) were achieved after the hearing on evidence had begun (ie, during the evidence hearings or in the post-hearing phase).

B. Corporate Attitudes and Practices about International Arbitration (2008)

Another survey was conducted by PricewaterhouseCoopers LLP and QMUL with respect to corporate attitudes and practices on international arbitration.[69] The research was conducted between 15 November 2007 and 15 April 2008 in two phases: (i) an online questionnaire completed by 82 respondents (ie, general counsel, heads of legal departments or counsel on the authority of the general counsel) between 15 November 2007 and 28 February 2008; and (ii) 47 face-to-face or telephone interviews with corporate counsel between 1 February 2008 and 15 April 2008 in the United Kingdom, USA, Sweden, Switzerland, Greece, Japan, Mexico and Brazil. This survey demonstrates a lower settlement rate than Professor Bühring-Uhle's findings: 25 per cent of interviewees reported achieving a settlement before receiving an arbitral award, while a further seven per cent reported settlements that were followed by an arbitral award by

---

[69] Ch 4, fn 2.

consent. With respect to the timing of settlement, almost three quarters of settlements occurred before the hearing on the merits (ie, 43 per cent were settled before the first hearing in the arbitration proceedings, and 31 per cent were settled after the procedural hearing but before the hearing on the merits). Four main reasons were raised for pre-award settlements: to preserve the business relationship (27 per cent), to avoid high costs (23 per cent), a weak case (21 per cent), and to avoid excessive delay (17 per cent). The incentive to settle in order to preserve business relationships was particularly evident where the parties had been doing business together for a considerable period of time or where the market did not offer a wide range of alternative suppliers.

C. *A Survey of Arbitration and Settlement in International Commercial Disputes in Asia (2006–2007)*

The above surveys have apparently not included the parallel attitudes of arbitrators working in the Far East region where a strong consensual culture is present. In his original study, Professor Bühring-Uhle notes that other distinct practices exist, particularly in the Far East, and notes that such practices represent a unique approach to international arbitration that are of particular importance for continued research.[70] To fill in the gap, Professor Shahla Ali's 2006–2007 survey covers practitioners across the region, with a focus on practitioners from East Asia (77 respondents, 75 per cent[71]) and a small portion from the United States and Europe (26 respondents, 25 per cent[72]). Close to 250 surveys were distributed to arbitrators, academics, attorneys and in-house counsel, and a total of 115 individuals responded. Professor Ali's survey was essentially based on the questionnaires developed by Professor Bühring-Uhle, and provides valuable information on the attitudes of practitioners working in East Asia regarding the role of arbitrators in the settlement process:[73]

First, in terms of the role of arbitrators, a significantly higher number of respondents working in East Asia (82 per cent) saw the facilitation of voluntary settlement as one of the goals of arbitration, in comparison to 62 per cent of practitioners working in the West.[74]

Second, on the settlement rate, quite counter-intuitively, the result shows a lower settlement rate in East Asia (30 per cent) than that reported in European

---

[70] Buhring-Uhle, Kirchhoff and Scherer, *Arbitration and Mediation in International Business*, 131.
[71] Shahla Ali, *Resolving Disputes in the Asia-Pacific Region: International Arbitration and Mediation in the East Asia and the West* (London, Routledge, 2011) 96, app A.
[72] ibid.
[73] For a discussion, see Shahla Ali, 'The Morality of Conciliation: An Empirical Examination of Arbitrator "Role Moralities' in East Asia and the West' (2011) 16 *Harvard Negotiation Law Review* 1; Ali, *Resolving Disputes in the Asia-Pacific Region: International Arbitration and Mediation in the East Asia and the West*.
[74] Ali, *Resolving Disputes in the Asia-Pacific Region: International Arbitration and Mediation in the East Asia and the West*, 53–54.

and American regions (48 per cent). An explanation offered is that arbitrators working in East Asia make greater efforts before the arbitration to settle disputes (38 per cent believed that settlement options were exhausted prior to initiating arbitration) than their Western counterparts (28 per cent).[75]

Last, the survey found the highest degree of regional variation in the arbitrators' use of settlement interventions. While all arbitrators surveyed shared the view that it was appropriate to suggest settlement negotiations to parties and to participate actively in settlement negotiations at the parties' request, the result reveals 'a greater proclivity on the part of arbitrators working in the East Asian region to effectively carry out settlement'.[76] More than 40 per cent of practitioners working in East Asia report regularly suggesting settlement negotiations to the parties, in comparison with 16 per cent of their counterparts working in the West. Over 30 per cent of practitioners working in East Asia reported that arbitrators regularly participate in settlement negotiations in comparison with 16 per cent of those surveyed working in the West. Meeting separately with parties to discuss settlement is another technique used more frequently by practitioners working in East Asia (26 per cent) compared to counterparts working in the West (8 per cent). Finally, 17 per cent of East Asian practitioners reported regularly suggesting a settlement formula in comparison with 4 per cent of practitioners surveyed working in the West.

D. Summary of the Empirical Findings

These empirical studies evidence that, despite the theoretical controversies on the appropriateness of the same person acting as a mediator and an arbitrator, the majority of practitioners agree that it is acceptable for arbitrators to facilitate settlement. According to Bühring-Uhle's surveys, 86 per cent of the respondents saw settlement facilitation as one of the goals of arbitration. Ali's survey shows a higher rate of acceptance among practitioners in East Asian regions (82 per cent) than their counterparts working in the Western region (62 per cent).

Given the 'judicialisation' of arbitration proceedings and associated high costs, quite a number of cases are settled amicably before an award is rendered (32 per cent in Pricewaterhouse and QMUL's survey, an average of 43 per cent in Bühring-Uhle's surveys, and an average of 35 per cent in Ali's survey). The experience varies markedly depending on the legal background of the practitioners. The settlement rate tends to be higher in civil law jurisdictions where judges customarily facilitate settlement than common law jurisdictions where courts have traditionally been entrusted with adjudicating, not settling, disputes (69 per cent of the Germans settled as opposed to only 33 per cent of the Americans). Practitioners working in East Asia were reported to make greater

[75] ibid.
[76] ibid.

efforts to exhaust settlement options prior to initiating arbitration. The overall settlement rate in East Asia (30 per cent) was, however, slightly lower than that in the West (48 per cent).

The main incentives for the parties to consider a settlement are to preserve business relationships and to avoid high costs or delays. Settlement occurs at all stages of the arbitral procedure; a number of cases were settled after the procedural hearing but before the hearing on the merits, while others settled at a fairly late stage of the process, that is, after the taking of evidence. A settlement can lead to important savings, which are larger the earlier the settlement is achieved.

Finally, the degree of settlement intervention varies significantly across the region. East Asian arbitrators tend to play a more active role in promoting settlement. This is achieved through suggesting settlement negotiations to the parties, actively participating in settlement negotiations (at both parties' request), meeting with the parties separately to discuss settlement options (with both parties' consent) and proposing a settlement formula (at both parties' request). On average, the frequency of participation in these techniques by practitioners working in East Asia was more than double that reported by counterparts working in Europe and the United States.

6.3 THE CHINESE EXPERIENCE OF COMBINING MEDIATION WITH ARBITRATION

In China, the combined mechanism is used frequently and enjoys a high degree of success. In practice, why does such a combined practice work well in China? How do Chinese arbitrators carry out the role of a settlement facilitator? Is the Chinese practice exportable elsewhere? What impact, if any, may Chinese practice have on the formation of a transnational rule on this issue? In order to answer these questions, the Chinese combination of mediation with arbitration will be examined in further detail. Before addressing the practice of mediation within arbitration proceedings (section 6.3.2), we shall first look at the general development of mediation in China (section 6.3.1).

6.3.1 Mediation in General

A. Historical Development

Mediation has a long history in China. It emphasises amicable dispute resolution and the avoidance of confrontation in conformity with the Confucian values that dominated political philosophy in traditional Chinese society. For the Chinese, a dispute is considered an evil in that it disturbs the harmony that should govern all social life. The Chinese believe that if it is impossible to avoid a dispute in the long run, it is imperative for the parties (either by themselves or with the aid of a mediator) to take the necessary steps early on to remove the root causes of the potential dispute amicably.[77] To trace the formation and use of mediation in ancient China, we may refer to the following official or semi-official records, such as laws – *Lü* (legal code), *Ling* (administrative procedures), *Ge* (orders from the emperor) and *Shi* (guidance of implementations); judges' decisions (*shu pan*); Emperor's sacred edicts; other official documents such as handbooks for government (*zheng shu*), official correspondence (*an du*), veritable records of emperors (*shi lu*) and public notices issued by local officials.[78]

By reviewing these historical records, we may not find the explicit use of the term 'mediation system', but there are descriptions about *tiaoren*, village elders and community leaders who are charged with the duty to resolve disputes amicably outside of court and to restore harmony. The earliest record on the use of mediation can be traced back to China's pre-state tribes and clans. The book of Hanfeizi described the practice during the Yao and Shun period as follows:

> When farmers in Lishan encroached on each other's land, King Shun went there to farm with them. A year later, no one crossed the land boundaries. When fishermen fought to fish upstream, Shun went there to fish with them. A year later, the fishermen gave up the upstream to the elderly. When potters in Dongyi made shoddy pottery, Shun went there to work with them. A year later, potters made sturdy pottery.[79]

In Western Zhou dynasty (1027BC–771BC), the concept of *tiaoren* (mediators) was officially recognised. According to the Rites of Zhou:

> Tiaoren were persons responsible for investigating and resolving the people's grievances to restore peace and harmony . . . 'Trivial affairs' such as marriage and land disputes were amicably resolved. Criminal offences such as manslaughter may also be mediated. If mediation failed, the dispute would be documented, and no party was allowed to carry the dispute further. Any party who caused further trouble would be punished under the law.[80]

Based on such description, it seems that the role of a *tiaoren* was essentially mediation, with the aim of resolving grievances and restoring harmony. In the meantime, they also played the role of an investigator, and even to some extent an adjudicator who might impose punishment on the party who 'causes further trouble'. Furthermore, compared to consensual mediation, the outcome of the process did not seem to be voluntary: if the parties did not accept a mediated outcome, they had no other recourse to solve their disputes.

Legal historians generally believe that, 'despite the practice in ancient China, mediation rules were "codified" (*ru lü*) and held legal significance only during the Yuan Dynasty (1271–1368)'.[81] Such records could be found in the Li min

---

[77] For more discussions on the philosophical basis of mediation tradition in China, see ch 8, s 8.3.1 below.

[78] These official documents reveal local officials' responsibilities and the social life of ancient times. See Xianyi Zeng, 'Mediation in China – Past and Present' (2009) 17 *Asia Pacific Law Review* Special Issue on Mediation.

[79] 《韩非子・卷十五・难一第三十六》, 第795 页(Hang Feizi: Vol 15, Nan Yi No 36, p 795.)

[80] 《周礼・地官司徒》, 第13 页。(Rites of Zhou: Land Officers, p 13).

[81] Zeng, 'Mediation in China – Past and Present', 4.

article of the 'Clauses and Paragraphs of the Unified System of Yuan', which reads as follows:

> for complaints about marriage, family property, farmland, home and debts that are not major violations of the law, disputing parties shall listen to their community leader's reasoning for clarification and resolution, to avoid hindering or neglecting farm work, or disturbing the government.[82]

During the Ming dynasty (1368–1644), a specialised institution called the Pavilion for Extending Clarity was established. According to the Ming Code, 'village elders are permitted to mediate and settle minor affairs concerning family, marriage and land matters in the pavilion'.[83] The roles of the *shenmingting* and village elders in settling disputes and maintaining social order were discussed in detail in Gu Yanwu's (1613–1682) *Record of Daily Study*. Gu referred to the Veritable Records of the Emperor Taizu,[84] according to which officials were ordered to select righteous and capable village elders and charge them with the duty of handling complaints in the village community. Gu's description of the official post of the *xiangting* (mediators) revealed that mediation has always been the main responsibility of junior officials.[85] The function of the elders was also made to the public via the Announcement for Educating the General Public issued in the period of Hongwu (1388), which read as follows:

> Disputes of trivial matters concerning family affairs and marriage, land and housing shall not be filed with the county magistrate, but must be first decided (*duan jue*) by the village elders. Serious matters such as theft, fraud and manslaughter can be reported to the officials. Those who bypassed the elders to sue will be canned 60 strokes and sent back to the elders to decide (*li duan*).[86]

The practice of establishing *shenmingting* was maintained in the Qing dynasty (1644–1911) as evidenced in the Qing Code:

> A Pavilion for Extending Clarity shall be erected in every village (*li*) in all prefectures and counties (*xian*) . . . Village elders shall be permitted to mediate and settle minor affairs concerning family, marriage and land matters in the pavilion. This is the system of extending clarity and admonition.[87]

---

[82] 《通制條格・卷第十六・田令・理民》, 第 184 頁, (Clauses and Paragraphs of the Unified System of Yuan, vol 16, Edits on Land, Edits on the People, p 184).

[83] 《大明律集解附例卷之二十六・刑律・雜犯》, 学生书局印刷 1974 年, 第五卷, 第 186 頁, (The Great Ming Code vol 26, Criminal Code, Miscellaneous Crimes, reprinted by Student Books Press, 1974, vol 5, p 1863).

[84] 《明實錄・太宗・卷一百四十六》, 第 579 頁 (The Veritable Records of Ming Emperor, Tai Zong, vol 146, p 579).

[85] 85 顧炎武,《日知錄・卷十一・鄉亭之職》, 第 230 頁。(Yanwu Gu, Record of Daily Study, Vol 12, The Function of Elders, p 230.)

[86] 張鹵(編), 《皇明制书・卷九》,《教民榜文》,《续修四库全书》影印本, 上海古籍出版社 1999年版, 第 352–53 頁, (Lu Zhang (ed.) Veritable Records of the Emperors, Vol 9, Announcement for Educating the General Public, reprinted by Shanghai Ancient Works Press, 1999, p 352–53).

[87] 《大清律例卷三十四・雜犯第三百七十六・拆毀申明亭・條例》, 天津古籍出版社 1993年影印, 第 560 頁。(The Qing Code, vol 34, Miscellaneous Crimes No 376, Destruction of the Pavilion for Clarity and Admonition, the Annotation, p 560).

The government, particularly under the Ming and Qing dynasties, frequently demanded the populace to settle the disputes without recourse to the official magistrate. A reply from Emperor Kangxi to a memorial drawn by the cantons against country tribunals reflected such attitude:

> The Emperor considering the immense population of the Empire, the great division of territorial property, and the notoriously law-loving character of the Chinese, is of the opinion that lawsuits would tend to increase, to a frightful amount, if people were not afraid of the tribunals, and if they felt confident of always finding in them ready and perfect justice. As man is apt to delude himself concerning his own interests, contests would then be interminable, and the half of the Empire would not suffice to settle the lawsuits of the other half. I desire, therefore, that those who have recourse to the tribunals should be treated without any pity, and in such a manner that they shall be disgusted with law, and tremble to appear before a magistrate. In this manner the evil will be cut up by the roots; the good citizens, who may have difficulty between themselves, will settle them like brothers, by referring to the arbitration of some old man, or the mayor of the commune. As for those who are troublesome, obstinate, and quarrelsome, let them be ruined in the law-courts – that is the justice that is due to them.[88]

Instead of referring to mediation as a 'system' of regulations, 'perhaps it is more appropriate to think of mediation as a set of socially accepted customary laws. These customary laws had gained not only popular acceptance but support from the State'.[89] To a certain extent, mediation can be said to be an essential and integral part of the dispute resolution system in traditional China.[90] It should be noted, however, that the notion of *tiaojie* in ancient China does not have the same connotations as the term 'mediation' as defined in the West, that is, a voluntary process in which the mediator assists disputing parties in reaching a mutually agreeable resolution without coercion. First, the start of the process was not voluntary: for minor matters, the disputants had to submit them to a neutral party (village elder or community leader) before resorting to a formal means of resolution. Failure to do so could result in corporal punishment. Second, the dispute resolvers were not voluntarily selected by the parties, but appointed by officials from within the village elders. Third, village elders or community leaders performed an official function by handling minor disputes within the community. They were charged with a facilitative role to 'mediate and settle' minor affairs, but at the same time an adjudicatory role to 'decide' the matters. Lastly, the outcome of the process was not voluntary. The dispute resolver was able to impose a decision by his seniority and standing in the community. Such decisions, although not directly enforceable as a judgment, were often 'listened to' by the disputing parties.[91]

---

[88] Thomas Jernigan, *China in Law and Commerce* (New York, The Macmillan Company, 1905) 191–92; Sybille Van der Sprenkel, *Legal Institutions in Manchu China* (London, The Athlone Press, 1966) 77; John R Watt, *The District Magistrate in Late Imperial China* (New York, Columbia University Press, 1972) 305, n 7.

[89] Zeng, 'Mediation in China – Past and Present', 5.

[90] The reasons for the popularity of mediation in Chinese history will be explored in ch 8, s 8.3 below.

[91] For a discussion, see, Kun Fan, 'Glocalisation of Arbitration: Transnational Standards Struggling with Local Norms' (2013) *Harvard Negotiation Law Review*, forthcoming.

B. Contemporary Practice

Now that China's legal system has greatly evolved and commercial disputes are burgeoning, mediation still permeates every corner of modern Chinese society where disputes arise. In this setting, mediation is used on its own and in combination with adversarial procedures such as litigation and arbitration. In general, the modern mediation system in China can be divided into five categories: (a) people's mediation, or mediation undertaken by people's mediation committees (PMC); (b) administrative mediation, or mediation conducted by local people's governments or administrative departments; (c) institutional mediation, or mediation conducted by permanent mediation centres; (d) mediation within litigation proceedings; and (e) mediation within arbitral proceedings.[92]

a. People's Mediation

People's mediation is mediation undertaken by the PMC. It came into being during the period of land revolution, and was formally established in 1954 when the Government Administration Council issued the Provisional Organic Rules of People's Mediation Committees (the 1954 Rules).[93] During the early days after this declaration, the PMC were mainly used to 'articulate and apply the ideological principles, values, and programs of the Communist Party and help mobilize the people to increase their commitment to Party policies and goals',[94] by correcting the disputants' views in terms of Communist tenets, and resolving disputes in a way that ensured that the result was consistent with national policy. The PRC Constitution of 1982 confirmed the legal status of people's mediation,[95] and a new set of Regulations on the Organisation of the People's Mediation Committees was promulgated in 1989 to replace the 1954 Rules,[96] the major themes of which were 'the pre-eminence of law and the resulting need for accountability to the law'.[97]

In 2002, the Ministry of Finance issued Some Provisions Concerning the Work of People's Mediation,[98] which clarifies among other things, the tasks of

---

[92] See Gabrielle Kaufmann-Kohler and Kun Fan, 'Integrating Mediation into Arbitration: Why It Works In China?' (2008) 25 *Journal of International Arbitration* 4.

[93] Promulgated by the Government Administration Council of the Central People's Government on and effective from 22 March 1954, abolished as of 17 June 1989.

[94] Stanley Lubman, 'Mao and Mediation: Politics and Dispute Resolution in Communist China' (1967) 55 *California Law Review* 5, 1339.

[95] Adopted at the Fifth Meeting of the Fifth NPC on and effective as of 4 December 1982. It was subsequently revised on 12 April 1988, 29 March 1993, 15 March 1999, and 14 March 2004. According to Art 111 of the PRC Constitution, PMC are one of the work committees under the basic self-governing organisations such as residents' committees or villagers' committees, and they are specifically responsible for conciliating civil disputes.

[96] Issued by the SPC on 16 September 2002, and effective from 1 November 2002; adopted at the 1240th meeting of the Judicial Committee of the SPC; Interpretation No 29 [2002] of the SPC.

[97] Eric Glassman, 'The Function of Mediation in China: Examining the Impact of Regulations Governing the People's Mediation Committees' (1992) 10 *UCLA Pacific Basin Law Journal*, 478.

[98] Promulgated by the Ministry of Justice on 26 September 2002, and effective from 11 November 2002.

the PMC and the principles of mediation that the PMC should observe.[99] The PMC must observe certain principles in the mediation of private disputes. They must conduct mediations on the basis of laws, regulations, administrative rules and policies and, lacking such rules, socialist morality. They must further conduct mediations on the basis of the free will and equality of both parties concerned. Finally, they must respect the litigation rights of the parties concerned, and may not prevent them from lodging lawsuits with the people's court because of the failure to settle the dispute through mediation.[100]

Currently, the PMC are far less politicised than their Maoist predecessors. They continue to play an important role in settling civil disputes and in maintaining stability in Communist China. People's courts also have a role in promoting people's mediation, at a time when China is experiencing an explosive growth in litigation, by providing guidance for the daily work of the PMC, by encouraging parties who file civil lawsuits to try people's mediation first, by visiting communities to work with people's mediators, and by having people's mediators watch court proceedings.[101] On 29 August 2010, the first national legislation on mediation – the People's Mediation Law – was adopted by the Standing Committee of the NPC, which came into effect on 1 January 2011. The People's Mediation Law is promulgated pursuant to the Constitution, in order to 'improve the people's mediation system, regulate the people's mediation activities, timely solve civil disputes and maintain social harmony and stability'.[102] It contains provisions on the regulation of the PMC and its mediators and the mediation procedure as well as the mediation agreement. According to the statistics released by the Ministry of Justice on 22 June 2010, there are now 4,900,000 mediators in China working in more than 800,000 mediation committees. These organisations handled 7.67 million civil disputes in 2009, up 54 per cent year-on-year. Among the total disputes, 97.2 per cent were settled, and only 1 per cent of the settled cases was later brought to the court, as highlighted by Justice Minister Wu Aiying when introducing the draft law to the bimonthly session of the Standing Committee of the NPC.[103]

b. Administrative Mediation

Administrative mediation is conducted by administrative bodies within their authorities according to the law, for the purpose of resolving disputes. Generally, two organs in China conduct administrative mediation: the basic-level people's governments and the administrative organs. Administrative mediation can be utilised in China to resolve civil disputes, commercial disputes, and certain

---

[99] Art 3 of Some Provisions Concerning the Work of People's Mediation.
[100] Art 4 of Some Provisions Concerning the Work of People's Mediation.
[101] See Aaron Halegua, 'Reforming the People's Mediation System in Urban China' (2005) 35 *Hong Kong Law Journal*, 744.
[102] Art 1 of the People's Mediation Law.
[103] 'New Law to make Conflict-solving Neighborhood Issue', *China Daily*, 22 June 2010, available at www.chinadaily.com.cn/china/2010-06/22/content_10005266.htm.

criminal disputes, and must be conducted in accordance with particular administrative regulations. For example, the Measures of Using Administrative Mediation to Resolve Contract Disputes[104] grants the administrative organs for industry and commerce the power to mediate the disputes arising from contracts.[105] However, if a court or arbitration institution accepts a dispute, or if a party to a dispute refuses to mediate, the administrative organ cannot then conduct mediation.[106]

c. Institutional Mediation

The China Council for the Promotion of International Trade (CCPIT), also known as the China Chamber of International Commerce (CCOIC), was the first Chinese institution to offer commercial mediation services. It set up its first mediation centre, the Beijing Mediation Center, in 1987, renamed as the CCPIT/CCOIC Mediation Center (CCPIT Mediation Center) in 2000. Over 40 mediation centres have been set up within its sub-councils in various provinces, municipalities, and autonomous regions throughout the country,[107] constituting a nationwide mediation network.

The CCPIT Center implements uniform guidance and administration with regard to the business of local centres within the network. One important aspect of such uniformity is the adoption of the uniform mediation rules, that is, the CCPIT Mediation Rules. In terms of the scope of disputes, the CCPIT network mediates disputes concerning trade, investment, finance, securities, intellectual property, real estate, construction, transportation, insurance and other commercial and maritime business. Each mediation centre has its own list of mediators, from which the parties choose. The mediators on the list are selected and appointed by the CCPIT and its sub-councils respectively from professionals with knowledge of the law or of a specific trade. So far, the mediation network has taken up disputes involving different trades and over 30 countries and regions; over 80 per cent of the cases have been successfully settled through conciliation. The Mediation Center handles, through conciliation, about 400 cases of different kinds of commercial disputes annually, and in addition, offers other dispute resolution options such as early neutral evaluation and expert opinion.[108]

One interesting aspect of the CCPIT Center is its joint mediation with international partners. Under Article 6 of the CCPIT Mediation Rules, the CCPIT Center may, upon the parties' agreement, conduct mediation jointly with other

---

[104] Issued by the State Administration for Industry and Commerce on and effective on 3 November 1997.
[105] Art 6 of the Measures of Using Administrative Mediation to Resolve Contract Disputes.
[106] Art 8 of the Measures of Using Administrative Mediation to Resolve Contract Disputes.
[107] For a complete list of sub-council mediation centres, see www.adr.ccpit.org/typeinfo.aspx?t2=32&t3=116.
[108] Statistics are based on the information from CCPIT's official website, lad.ccpit.org/english.aspx?tid=115&mid=4.

dispute settlement organisations. The CCPIT Center has set up seven joint mediation centers with partners from Germany, Argentina, Korea, the United States and Italy, and the cooperation is expanding.[109]

d. Mediation within Litigation Proceedings

Developing in parallel with the PMC, mediation was also widely conducted within the people's court system itself. The practice of combining mediation with litigation was started in the 'Liberated Areas'[110] to alleviate the pressure on courts and reduce costs, especially during a time when the revenue of judicial functionaries was cut under a policy of 'trimming staff and simplifying administration' (*jing bing jian zheng*) at the Shan-Gan-Ning (Shanxi-Gansu-Ningxia) border region before the establishment of the PRC. A pioneer in promoting this practice was Judge Ma Xiwu, who became president of the High Court of the Shan-Gan-Ning region in 1946. He had handled a large number of civil disputes by encouraging settlement between the parties themselves. This practice is thus referred to as 'Ma Xiwu Style Adjudication'.[111]

The practice of mediation within litigation was further pursued by the Communist Party after the establishment of the PRC. The Trial Implementation of the Civil Procedure Law of the PRC in 1982[112] provides that 'the People's Court shall emphasize mediation when hearing cases'. When the Civil Procedure Law 1991 was promulgated, the principle of 'emphasising mediation' in the Trial Implementation was amended by the provision that 'the court shall conduct mediation on the principle of party autonomy and legality'.[113] The principles of party autonomy and legality are further elaborated as follows: (i) the settlement agreement must be made of the parties' free will and without compulsion;[114] (ii) the settlement agreement shall not be contrary to the law;[115] and (iii) if no agreement is reached through mediation or if either party backs out of the settlement agreement before the mediation statement is served, the

---

[109] For a discussion on institutional mediation, see Lijun Cao, 'Combining Conciliation and Arbitration in China: Overview and Latest Development' (2006) 9 *International Arbitration Law Review* 3, 86; Wenying Wang, 'The Role of Conciliation in Resolving Disputes: A PRC Perspective' (2005) 20 *Ohio State Journal on Dispute Resolution* 2, 427–31.

[110] The term 'Liberated Areas' refers to the areas that were controlled by the Communist Party during the new-democratic revolution period (1910–1949).

[111] For a discussion on Ma Xiwu Style Adjudication, see 张希坡·韩延龙 (编), 中国革命法制史 (北京, 中国社会科学出版社, 2007) 437–52 (Xipo Zhang and Yanlong Han, The History of Chinese Revolution and Law); 强世功, '权利的组织网络与法律的治理化 – 马锡五审判方式与中国法律的新传统', in 强世功 (编), 调解·法制与现代性: 中国调解制度研究 (北京, 中国法制出版社, 2001) 204–63 (Shigong Jiang, The Network of Power and Regulation of Law – The Ma Xiwu Style and New Tradition in Chinese Law).

[112] Adopted at the 22nd Meeting of the Standing Committee of the Fifth NPCs and promulgated by Order No 8 of the Standing Committee of the National People's Congress on 8 March 1982, and implemented on a trial basis as of 1 October 1982.

[113] Art 9 of the Civil Procedure Law 1991.

[114] Art 88 of the Civil Procedure Law 1991.

[115] Art 88 of the Civil Procedure Law 1991.

court must render a judgment without delay.[116] The same principles are reinforced in the latest amendment of the Civil Procedure Law, which was adopted by the Standing Committee of the National People's Congress in October 2007 and entered into force on 1 April 2008.[117]

Following the promulgation of the SPC Provisions on Court's Civil Mediation Work in 2004,[118] courts have been revising their incentive mechanisms to encourage court-mediation; many have set up a target settlement rate of civil litigation for the judges to achieve. As a result, an increasing number of cases accepted by the courts is *settled*, rather than *adjudicated*. The percentage of civil cases resolved through mediation in China increased from 31 per cent in 2004[119] to 65.29 per cent in 2010[120], doubling within six years.

6.3.2 Mediation within Arbitration Proceedings

A. *Historical Development*

Deeply influenced by the practice in the Chinese courts, the CIETAC empowered its arbitral tribunals to mediate arbitration cases from the beginning. Prior to the enactment of the Arbitration Law, the CIETAC attempted to mediate its cases, even though the first arbitration rules of the CIETAC did not contain specific provisions on mediation, only a provision stating that an arbitration must be dismissed if the parties reached an amicable settlement agreement.[121] Mediation was first provided in the CIETAC Rules 1989. They provided that the CIETAC and its arbitral tribunals may mediate cases accepted by the CIETAC and, if an amicable settlement is reached, the arbitral tribunal must render a consent award – an arbitral award recording the content of the settlement.[122]

The CIETAC's early mediation practice must be understood in the context of the historical development of the arbitration system at the time. Although the modern commercial arbitration process is a product of the market economy, the Chinese arbitration system emerged and developed in the environment of a planned economy. As a consequence, there were few laws in China that could be applied to commercial disputes before the 1980s. In such a legal vacuum, the arbitral tribunals could only decide cases in accordance with the principles of fairness and reasonableness, or they could encourage the parties to resolve their disputes by mediation with the assistance of the arbitral tribunal. In addition, the disputes submitted to the CIETAC in the early days were relatively easy to

---

[116] Art 91 of the Civil Procedure Law 1991.
[117] Arts 85, 88 and 91 of the Civil Procedure Law 2007.
[118] Adopted at the 1321st meeting of the Judicial Committee of the Supreme People's Court on 18 August 2004, and became effective as of 1 November 2004. The Provision requests that 'all cases that can be mediated should be mediated'.
[119] The SPC Work Report of 2005.
[120] The SPC Work Report of 2011.
[121] See Wang, 'The Combination of Mediation and Arbitration: Theory and Practice', 84.
[122] Art 37 of the CIETAC Rules 1989.

settle, given their simplicity and low amounts as well as the relatively stable business relations.[123]

Driven by the CIETAC's initiative, the Arbitration Law now permits and encourages the combination of mediation with arbitration.[124] The CIETAC has also amended its rules several times and improved the provisions concerning mediation. The CIETAC Rules 2012 have established a relatively comprehensive system of combining mediation with arbitration.[125]

B. Contemporary Practice

In actual practice, how is the role of arbitrators perceived in China? What are the features of the Chinese practice of arb-med? Apart from some general guidance in the legislation and institutional rules, our perceptions about the conduct of arbitrators are often driven by anecdotes. Numerous practitioner-orientated symposia, workshops, conferences and roundtables are organised annually, where one hears an array of anecdotes from personal experiences of counsel and arbitrators, either confirming best practices or underscoring problem areas. This is partly because arbitration is private and does not involve public court proceedings. The problem with anecdotes is that it is difficult to evaluate whether the event described is typical or atypical, frequent or infrequent, ordinary or extreme, or as Professor Drahozal puts it, as common as a rabbit or as rare as a rhinoceros.[126] Some further research is needed in order to supplement anecdotes with empirical data.[127]

Dr Wang Shengchang conducted two empirical studies on the attitudes of arb-med in China.[128] In the first study, Dr Wang made an analysis of the cases settled at the CIETAC's Beijing headquarters between 1993 and 2000,[129] and concluded that arb-med had been widely welcomed by parties from different legal backgrounds.[130] Parties from Asian regions more easily accepted a settlement. The analysis also showed a relatively higher settlement rate in joint venture disputes (an average of 40 per cent of the settled cases involved joint venture disputes). This finding may be explained by the parties' strong appreciation of maintaining a friendly cooperative relationship and their potential long term interests. A second study was an informal survey, conducted by the CIETAC in September 2000, among experienced Chinese arbitrators who participated in

---

[123] Wang, 'The Role of Conciliation in Resolving Disputes: A PRC Perspective', 436.
[124] Arts 51and 52 of the Arbitration Law.
[125] Art 45 of the CIETAC Rules 2012.
[126] Christopher R Drahozal, 'Of Rabbits and Rhinoceri: A Survey of Empirical Research on International Commercial Arbitration' (2003) 20 *Journal of International Arbitration* 1, 23.
[127] See Jack Coe, 'From Anecdote to Data: Reflections on the Global Center's Barcelona Meeting' (2003) 20 *Journal of International Arbitration* 1.
[128] Wang, 'The Combination of Mediation and Arbitration: Theory and Practice', 177–87.
[129] ibid.
[130] In the arbitration cases accepted by the CIETAC between 1993 and 2002, the parties came from 45 different countries and regions.

the seminar on the practice of arbitrators in Beijing.[131] 56 of the participants completed the questionnaire. The survey shows that the respondents unanimously considered that it was appropriate for arbitrators to facilitate settlement. Most of the respondents considered that this practice was appropriate because it was based on the parties' consent. They believe that the parties' trust in the arbitrator is the main reason for their willingness for the arbitrator to conduct mediation. A majority of arbitrators had made efforts to mediate during arbitration proceedings and 37 per cent of them had conducted mediation in more than 50 per cent of their cases. A majority of the arbitrators (71 per cent) believed that the combination of mediation and arbitration would evolve to be accepted and practised in more and more countries.

There are unanswered questions that need to be explored further in order to get a full picture of the actual practice of arb-med in China. Who raises the idea of mediation, the parties or the arbitral tribunal? When is the mediation proposal made? When does the settlement offer occur? What kind of mediation techniques are often used by arbitrators? In a series of interviews conducted during the above research trip in 2007, the Chinese arbitrators explained in detail how arb-med is typically conducted in China. The arbitrators' use of mediation, determined through these interviews, suggests that the influence from people's mediation or mediation conducted by the courts remains strong, although more emphasis is placed on party autonomy. Their practice is summarised as follows:[132]

a. Who Raises the Idea of Mediation during the Arbitration Proceedings, the Parties or the Arbitral Tribunal?

Either the parties or the arbitral tribunal can raise the idea of mediation, notwithstanding commencement of the arbitration proceedings. The Arbitration Law provides that the arbitral tribunal *may* carry out mediation prior to rendering an award. If the parties request mediation, the arbitral tribunal *must* carry out mediation proceedings.[133] In practice, although not obligated to do so by law, Chinese arbitrators will systematically take the initiative of asking the parties if they wish the tribunal to assist them in reaching an amicable solution. If, and only if, the responses from both parties are positive, the arbitral tribunal will commence the mediation proceedings.

Depending on the experience of the arbitrators, positive responses from both parties range from 10 per cent to 90 per cent. Generally, the percentage is higher in domestic arbitrations, as Chinese parties are used to this practice and willing to cooperate to avoid making a bad impression on the tribunal. By contrast,

---

[131] Wang, 'The Combination of Mediation and Arbitration: Theory and Practice', 180–87.
[132] The results of the interviews on the actual practice of arb-med in China were originally published in Kaufmann-Kohler and Kun Fan, 'Integrating Mediation into Arbitration: Why It Works In China?'.
[133] Art 51 of the Arbitration Law.

foreign parties are less receptive because they expect to argue the case and obtain an award.

b. When do Arbitrators make the Mediation Proposal?

The best moment to propose mediation is ultimately a case-by-case assessment. Chinese arbitrators tend to believe that parties may be more prepared to consider settlement when they begin to realise the weaknesses of their position and the strengths of the other side's position through the process of pleading and the exchange of documentary evidence and witness statements. Furthermore, when the parties have completed their written submissions, certain issues also tend to crystallise and the core issues in disputes are narrowed down. The mediation process conducted thereafter is generally believed to be more effective, as the process will have focused the parties on the core issues.

It is important to understand that mediation attempts are often made during the *ongoing process of arbitration*. If the first mediation proposal is unsuccessful, the arbitrators, after taking some evidence and hearing certain witnesses, may make another attempt to mediate. If those efforts at mediation fail, they may return to the receipt of evidence and the hearing of witness, ready to attempt mediation again at another time during the course of the proceedings. The mediation proposal can be raised several times *at any stage* of the proceedings before an arbitral award is rendered. In general, there is no clear distinction between the 'mediation phases' and the 'arbitration phases'. This differs from other Asian countries (eg, South Korea and Indonesia) where an arbitrator only attempts to mediate at the outset of the arbitration, or if the parties seek mediation during the course of arbitral proceedings; an arbitrator will suspend the arbitration during the period that mediation is attempted. The Chinese model thus represents the most complete integration of mediation and arbitration.[134]

c. How do Arbitrators Facilitate Settlement?

(i) Facilitative or Evaluative

In the case of a combined practice, arbitrators are not likely to be purely facilitative during the mediation process. Consciously or subconsciously, an element of evaluation is always involved when arbitrators engage in settlement activities.

(ii) Meeting the Parties Separately or Caucusing

Chinese practitioners have no hesitation in meeting parties privately, known as 'caucusing', as long as both parties give their consent. They believe that caucuses are the best way of clarifying the points which matter to facilitate a settlement.

---

[134] See Donahey, 'Seeking Harmony: Is the Asian Concept of the Conciliator/arbitrator Applicable in the West?', 74–78.

During the caucus, the arbitrators will ask for each party's bottom line separately, so as to have a better understanding of their real interests. If the difference between the parties' bottom line is considerable, then the arbitrators terminate the mediation and render an award; if the difference is less important, then they may try to narrow the gap in an effort to reach settlement. Meeting parties separately also allows arbitrators to conduct a so-called 'reality check' that can encourage a party with an overly optimistic view of its chances of success to reconsider its case on its merits, and thereby increase the possibility that the parties reach a settlement.

(iii) Giving Opinions on the Merits

Interestingly enough, even though evaluation is always present, all the Chinese arbitrators interviewed were very cautious not to express any opinion on the merits to the parties. Arbitrators do sometimes indicate to the parties the strengths and weaknesses of their respective positions in order to draw the parties' positions closer together. However, the analysis is limited to a party's 'possible' deficiencies; arbitrators will not pronounce on the outcome of the arbitration. Expressing views as to the merits of the dispute are taken with extreme caution by Chinese arbitrators, as they think it may affect their impartiality.[135]

(iv) Proposing a Settlement Formula

Among Chinese arbitrators who participate in mediation, there is some controversy about whether it is suitable for them to make a settlement proposal. Some rarely make formal proposals unless so requested by the parties. Others believe a quantified proposal may speed up the process if the gap between the parties is not huge. Generally, arbitrators would not make a concrete settlement proposal before the facts were about 90 per cent clear. Usually, a concrete settlement proposal is made at the last stage of the mediation when the gap between the parties has been narrowed to the minimum extent.[136]

If an arbitrator does make a settlement proposal, it may be specific and state amounts to be paid and actions to be taken, but more frequently it provides a range of numbers within which he or she suggests the final solution should lie. On certain occasions, the arbitrator may also propose a business arrangement, so as to encourage the parties to compromise and continue their business relationship. Whatever the form of the proposal may be, arbitrators are careful not to give any party the impression that a refusal of their proposal will upset them and elicit an unfavourable award.

---

[135] The practice of Swiss and German arbitrators is quite different. They are very reluctant to use caucus for concerns of due process, but easily give evaluations of the possible outcome.

[136] See Tang, 'Is There an Expending Culture that Favors Combining Arbitration with Conciliation or Other ADR Procedures?', 555.

d. Chinese Approaches to the Concerns of Arb-Med

Regarding concerns about due process and natural justice, Chinese arbitrators think that the problem of caucusing is much less serious in practice than it is in theory, as they believe that the parties are not very likely to reveal facts to the mediator during the mediation phase that the mediator/arbitrator could not have found out himself by a thorough study of the file. During the interviews, a few CIETAC arbitrators shared their personal experience with respect to the impact on the impartiality of the arbitrator. They stated that the information obtained during the caucus would not affect their view on the merits if they later had to make a binding decision, as this would be based solely on proven facts. The view is that caucusing is not the only situation in which the arbitrator has to disregard information received. There are cases where improperly submitted documents or arguments are rejected or discarded after the arbitrators have taken cognisance of them. There are occasions when jurors need to make a decision after having heard inadmissible evidence. Arbitrators are legally trained to make a decision based on proven facts according to applicable law, and their brains should be less likely to be contaminated than the juries who are layman.

Regarding the concern that parties may withhold relevant information from the mediator knowing that the same person may later arbitrate the dispute if mediation fails, Professor Tang Houzhi commented that there is no need to have all the cards on the table:

> Mediation is not arbitration; you don't need all the cards of the parties put on the table; when about 80% or even less than 80% of the cards of the parties have been put on the table, you would be able to have a good conduct of mediation; as a mediator, your job is to bring about an amicable settlement and not to make an award.[137]

Furthermore, Chinese practitioners believe that following a failed mediation, the mediator 'is the best person to be appointed as an arbitrator just because he knows everything of the case'.[138] This is particularly true in arbitral proceedings (as compared to litigation), because trust is built up between the parties and the arbitrators whom they have voluntarily appointed. If the parties have gained such strong confidence in the mediator during the course of the mediation that they would actually prefer to have him or her arbitrate the remaining issues despite any caucusing that might have taken place, this choice should be respected, notwithstanding concerns about the possible confusion of roles.

To summarise, there has been no established transnational consensus as to whether arbitrators should facilitate settlement, despite the strong wave of harmonisation of the law and practice of arbitration across borders. In East Asia, where there are strong traditions of encouraging the settlement of disputes by

---

[137] Houzhi Tang, 'The Use of Conciliation in Arbitration', *WIPO Conference on Mediation*, Geneva (1996).

[138] Houzhi Tang, 'Combination of Arbitration with Conciliation – Arb-Med' in Albert Jan van den Berg (ed), *ICCA Congress series no 12* (The Hague, Kluwer Law International, 2005) 13.

mediation, the idea of arbitrators facilitating settlement is easily accepted and widely practised. In the West, civil law lawyers (especially those from jurisdictions where the judges traditionally promote settlement) more easily accept the combination of mediation and arbitration, whereas common law lawyers are more reluctant to accept the concept that the functions of settlement facilitator and adjudicator can be assumed by the same person. Discussions in this chapter demonstrate China's preference for resolving disputes through amicable means. In its various forms, mediation has played and does play an essential role in dispute resolution in traditional and modern China, serving the objectives of social harmony and the restoration of harmonious long-term relations. The Chinese concept and practice of arb-med may be of valuable reference for other jurisdictions at a time when efficiency is the core of dispute resolution. As Abraham Lincoln said of the role of lawyers: '[p]ersuade your neighbors to compromise, whenever you can. Point out to them how the nominal winner is often the real loser – in fees, expenses and waste of time'.[139] Professional arbitrators may well assume this role as well to improve the efficiency of justice. Greater efforts still need to be made in order to familiarise arbitrators with the practice of facilitating settlement and implementing the necessary procedural safeguards,[140] so that such integration can be used effectively to improve the efficiency of the dispute resolution.

---

[139] Abraham Lincoln, 'Notes for a Law Lecture', 1 July 1850.
[140] For a discussion of the safeguards, see Harold Abramson, 'Protocols For International Arbitrators Who Dare to Settle Cases' (1999) 10 *American Review of International Arbitration* 1; Kun Fan, 'The Risks of Apparent Bias When An Arbitrator Act As a Mediator: Remarks on Hong Kong Court's Decision in Gao Haiyan' (2011) 13 *Yearbook of Private International Law* 93; Kaufmann-Kohler, 'When Arbitrators Facilitate Settlement: Towards a Transnational Standard'.

7
Chinese Characteristics in Arbitration Law and Practice

'For many years, China has been "crossing a river by feeling the stones". Now China has crossed the "river", and felt many "stones". China is still a low income country'.

Joseph E Stiglitz

HAVING EXAMINED THE current law and practice of arbitration in China, in terms of the legislation and the practice of the courts (chapters two to four), the practice of the arbitration institutions (chapter five), and the use of mediation in arbitration proceedings (chapter six), it is now time to turn back to our starting point: is arbitration in China a game of Chinese chess, which 'shares a common ancestry with international arbitration standards, but also has differences that make it unique'?[1] If so, what are the commonalities between Chinese and transnational standards, and what are the features that make it uniquely Chinese?

One the one hand, one should acknowledge the remarkable progress that China has been made in a short period of time. The business environment is now considerably more favourable to both foreign and domestic investors. China has looked westwards in promoting arbitration. In terms of legislation, many of the internationally accepted principles of modern arbitration have been adopted, such as party autonomy, independence of arbitration institutions, and the finality of arbitral awards. The Arbitration Law and the relevant judicial interpretations are generally business-friendly and pro-arbitration. In terms of judicial practice, while enforcement is often portrayed as difficult in China, recent studies have shown a more positive picture. In fact, ARI's investigation reveals that 77 per cent of the awards were enforced.[2] Professor Peerenboom's research finds a 49 per cent rate of enforcement.[3] The result is, of course, far from perfect, but it is hardly the situation suggested by the criticisms one often finds in the media. In terms of arbitral practice, arbitration institutions have made significant progress in recent years in increasing independence

[1] Ch 1, fn 1.
[2] Ch 4, s 4.2.2, fn 88.
[3] Ch 4, s 4.2.2, fn 89.

and improving efficiency, and are gaining significance in the international arbitration market. The CIETAC has been regularly reviewing and revising its arbitration rules, so as to keep them in line with modern transnational standards. As a result, the CIETAC's caseload has risen dramatically from a mere 37 cases in 1985 to over 1,000 per year today, topping the list of arbitration centres worldwide in terms of caseload. Local arbitration institutions, such as the BAC and the WAC, are also gaining international recognition.

On the other hand, the Chinese arbitration system is still in a relatively early stage of development. Unlike in many Western countries, the Chinese arbitration system was born under an environment of a planned economy, in the absence of the concept of private ownership, when all economic activities were under administrative control. Since the late 1970s, great reforms have taken place in China, in an effort to open the door and build up a market-based economy. Nevertheless, 'Rome was not built in a day'. In the transition towards a market economy, public ownership still plays a larger role than in other such economies. Administrative bureaucracy continues to be influential in Chinese social and economic life, and as a result administrative interference can still be felt in the practice of arbitration. These, together with cultural and historical reasons, have contributed to the formation of what has been understood as 'Chinese characteristics', with both positive and negative elements. The 'Chinese characteristics' can be summarised as follows: deficiencies in the legislation (section 7.1), inconsistencies in the implementation of the laws (section 7.2), administrative intervention (section 7.3), conceptual differences (section 7.4), and an emphasis on amicable resolution of disputes (section 7.5).

7.1 DEFICIENCIES IN THE LEGISLATION

Despite China's great efforts to create a viable legal framework for arbitration, ambiguous provisions and gaps remain. First of all, many provisions in the Arbitration Law are too simple and vague, without clear guidance on specific application. Secondly, the inconsistent provisions in the Arbitration Law and the Civil Procedure Law call for clarifications. The Civil Procedure Law was implemented in 1991 before a formal arbitration system was established in China. By the time the Arbitration Law was promulgated in 1995, the arbitration concepts had undergone significant improvements in China, but the law still made references to the Civil Procedure Law 1991 on several occasions. Such references have caused great confusion in practice. For instance, the Arbitration Law of 1995 made reference to Article 260(1) of Civil Procedure Law 1991 with respect to setting aside, and resisting recognition and enforcement, of foreign-related awards. Article 260(1)(4) of the Civil Procedure Law 1991 provides an unusual ground for refusal of enforcement or setting aside foreign-related awards if 'matters decided in the award are outside the authority of the arbitration institution'. Now that there is no longer any distinction in the scope of cases that an arbitration institution can handle, the reference to 'foreign-related arbitration institution[s]' should be eliminated and the ground related to the 'authority of the arbitration institution' accordingly deleted. Unfortunately, the legislation failed to take into account these developments. To fill the remaining loopholes in the national laws, the SPC and the HPCs in major cities have been publishing a number of notices and interpretations relating to various aspects of arbitration. The courts' efforts at central and provincial levels responded to business needs with a more sensible approach than national legislation, and have served to promote arbitration and create a friendlier legal environment for investors. However, these interpretations remain isolated texts, and there is no systematic judicial effort to reconcile them. In practice, this has caused inconsistencies in judicial decisions, which makes arbitration in China somewhat unpredictable.

These imperfections in the legislation are not surprising given the speed of reform and the variety of challenges. The flurry of notices and interpretations by the SPC and the HPCs relating to various aspects of arbitration indicates that Chinese leaders are well aware of the shortcomings in the regulatory framework, and are making efforts to fill the loopholes. However, these interpretations are not always consistent with each other, which leads to difficulties in their implementation. Further reforms at the legislative level are needed to bring Chinese rules more in line with transnational standards.

Another feature of the legislation is the rigidity of the arbitration system, which leaves little flexibility to the parties in the arbitral process. The notion of control can be found throughout the arbitration proceedings, which restricts party autonomy – the core element of modern arbitration. Administrative powers interfere with the key players of the arbitration proceedings, that is, the parties and the arbitral tribunal. The following are examples of these rigidities and of control instances:

(i) Very strict requirements are set out by law as a condition for an arbitration agreement to be valid (ie, the designation of an arbitration institution). No general guidance is given on the interpretation of the arbitration agreement in case of ambiguities. Instead there is a series of interpretations by the SPC and the HPCs for each specific circumstance. As a result, the parties' real intention to arbitrate may be easily distorted due to poorly drafted arbitration clauses.
(ii) Instead of giving the parties the widest pool from which to choose their arbitrators, significant statutory qualifications restrict the choice of arbitrator, and a closed panel system is imposed in an attempt to control the quality of arbitrators.
(iii) The parties' choice to opt for ad hoc arbitration is effectively rebutted in the legislation, for the purpose of ensuring control over the quality of arbitration.
(iv) The power to rule on jurisdictional issues is shared by the court and arbitration institutions, instead of being left to the arbitrators, who are the private judges of the parties' choice.

As a result of these rigidities in the legal framework, party autonomy in China is reduced to a bundle of specific freedoms within a regulated regime, as opposed to the Western tradition of a general principle of party autonomy, subject to specific restraints.

7.2 INCONSISTENCIES IN THE IMPLEMENTATION OF THE LAW

In terms of the implementation of the law, discussions in chapters two to four demonstrate a wide gap between the laws on paper and their implementation in actual practice. It is true that in every system, practice does not necessarily mirror the written law. The distance, however, seems to be wider in China than elsewhere. The ambiguities and vagueness in the law perhaps contribute to the inconsistencies in practice. A further possible reason is the unbalanced development of the economy, legal consciousness and the quality of judges in different regions of China, where different standards are applied in the application of law. This imbalance exists at different hierarchical levels of the courts, as well as in various geographical locations of the courts at the same level. The SPC generally takes a pro-arbitration approach, and has endeavoured to pay more attention to party autonomy. However, not all lower level courts follow suit. Generally, courts in booming municipalities take a more liberal attitude towards arbitration than their counterparts in less developed areas. Certain local courts are still subject to local government control, and are influenced by 'local protectionism', taking away from the effectiveness of arbitration law. Local courts would do well to realise that short term advantages gleaned for local interest will in the long run negatively affect the Chinese economy.

7.3 ADMINISTRATIVE INTERVENTION

Apart from the regulatory shortcomings, the bigger obstacle to a viable arbitration regime is *institutional* in nature. Although the Arbitration Law attempts to establish an independent arbitration system so that party autonomy will not be interfered with by the administrative powers, in reality, arbitration is still largely subject to administrative control. Traces of excessive state control can be found along the whole process of arbitration – from the arbitration agreement, to the constitution of the arbitral tribunal, and local protectionism during court review of arbitral awards.

An examination of the practice of Chinese arbitration institutions at the national and local levels in chapter five reveals their strong administrative features. The starting point of institutional arbitration in China is the role of the *institution*, which acts as the guardian of rights and of the quality control of the arbitration. This practice is not entrusted to *individuals* in the person of the arbitrators. As a result, government control and administrative influence can be gleaned in several aspects of institutional arbitration in China:

(i) Unilateral institutional arbitration makes it impossible for parties to escape institutional control through ad hoc arbitration.
(ii) Chinese arbitration institutions are generally more 'institutional' than any other international arbitration institutions. The broad powers of Chinese arbitration institutions are said to infringe upon the independence of arbitrators, some of whom are even appointed from institutions' internal staff. If we compare institutional arbitration to a 'theatre',[4] Chinese arbitration institutions are not merely setting the stage: they are also *directors* of the play, giving instructions to the real actors, the parties and the arbitrators throughout the show, as well as deciding on jurisdictional issues, the constitution of arbitral tribunals, procedural details, allocation of fees, and even, to some extent, the outcome of the proceedings.
(iii) Furthermore, Chinese arbitration institutions are still subject to administrative influence and government control in terms of their establishment, financial resources, and personnel: first, arbitration institutions largely rely upon government support for their establishment, and some arbitration institutions are established by local government for administrative purposes rather than to meet market demand for dispute resolution; second, the government retains strong financial control over many arbitration institutions even after they have been established: the income of arbitration institutions is considered a state asset and must be remitted to the government, which decides on its allocation according to reported expenditure; and third, many of the leading positions in arbitration institutions are held by government officials.

Chart 3 illustrates the features of institutional structure in China. State control over institutional practice can be better explained by the metaphor 'bird in a cage',[5] where the state functions as a cage and captures all business activities (the birds) within the cage. In other words, the freedom to contract only extends to the boundaries of the cage established by the state.[6] The individuals' rights are not inherent, but granted.

7.4 CONCEPTUAL DIFFERENCES

Although the Arbitration Law has *textually* incorporated many modern arbitration principles and practices, the core value of consensual arbitration in Western society has not been integrated into the Chinese system. This is rooted

---

[4] See Charles Jarroson, 'L'instance arbitrale : Le rôle respectif de l'institution, de l'arbitre et des parties dans l'instance arbitrale' (1990) *Revue de l'arbitrage* 381.
[5] Stanley Lubman, *Bird in a Cage: Legal Reform in China After Mao* (Palo Alto, Stanford University Press, 1999).
[6] ibid.

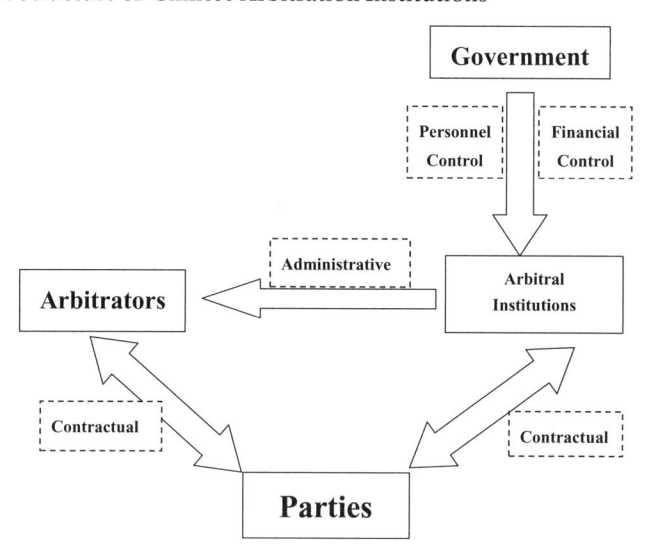

Chart 3: Structure of Chinese Arbitration Institutions

```
                          ┌──────────────┐
                          │  Government  │
                          └──────────────┘
                      ┌─────────┐ ┌─────────┐
                      │Personnel│ │Financial│
                      │ Control │ │ Control │
                      └─────────┘ └─────────┘
                                │
                                ▼
                      ┌──────────────┐
                      │Administrative│    ┌──────────────┐
  ┌────────────┐      └──────────────┘    │   Arbitral   │
  │ Arbitrators│◄─────────────────────────│ Institutions │
  └────────────┘                          └──────────────┘
          ▲                                      ▲
          │                                      │
   ┌────────────┐                          ┌────────────┐
   │ Contractual│                          │ Contractual│
   └────────────┘                          └────────────┘
              ▲                            ▲
               ┌──────────────┐
               │   Parties    │
               └──────────────┘
```

in conceptual differences between the contractual nature of arbitration in the West and the administrative character of arbitration in China.

7.4.1 The Western Concept of Consensual Arbitration – Bottom-up

According to the general theory of arbitration in the West, despite the quasi-judicial role of the arbitrators, the source of their status remains contractual; they assume that role as a result of a contract with the parties, under which they accept a well-defined brief, usually for remuneration.[7] In essence, the arbitrators' role as private judges comes from below, that is, from the intentions of private parties. The existence of a contract between the parties and the arbitrators is universally recognised, in both ad hoc and institutional arbitration. The choice of an arbitration institution to organise the proceedings does not change the nature of the contract between the parties and the arbitrators. The contractual theory of arbitration is illustrated as follows:[8]

---

[7] Gaillard and Savage, *Fouchard Gaillard Goldman on International Commercial Arbitration*, para 1101 et seq.

[8] For a discussion of the contractual nature of arbitration, see ibid; Jarrosson, 'Le rôle respectif de l'institution, de l'arbitre et des parties dans l'instance arbitrale'; Clay, *L'arbitre*, para 764 et seq; Lew, Mistelis and Kröll, *Comparative International Commercial Arbitration*, para 5-16 et seq; Hunter et al, *Redfern and Hunter on International Arbitration*, 315.

Contract for Organisation of Arbitration between the Parties and Arbitration Institutions

An initial contract of organisation is concluded between the parties and the arbitral institution. By publishing its arbitration rules, the arbitral institution puts out a permanent offer to contract, aimed at an undetermined group of persons (those potential litigants operating in the field or fields covered by the institution), and made upon fixed conditions. By concluding their arbitration agreement and referring to the institution's rules, the parties accept that offer and agree to empower their chosen institution to organise and oversee the arbitration in the event that a dispute arises between them. When the request for arbitration is submitted to the institution and it begins to organise the proceedings, the contract is perfected.[9]

Contract of Arbitral Collaboration between the Arbitration Institution and Arbitrators

There is also a contract of arbitral collaboration between the arbitral institution and the arbitrators, where each party independently promises to perform services for the benefit of the other, and particularly for the benefit of third parties (the parties to the arbitration).[10] The institution appoints or confirms the appointment of the arbitrators after verifying their suitability; it agrees to play an organisational and administrative role in the arbitration proceeding; it undertakes to reimburse the arbitrators' expenses and to pay the arbitrators' fees. As for the arbitrators, by accepting the appointment they agree to conduct the arbitration proceeding under the auspices of, and in accordance with, the rules of the institution. They agree that the institution shall exercise its functions under those rules, such as its powers to challenge or remove an arbitrator, grant extensions of time, monitor the proceedings, examine a draft version of the award before it is rendered, and determine the arbitrators' fees.

Contract of Arbitration between the Parties and Arbitrators

Finally, the involvement of an arbitral institution does not affect the contractual relationship between the parties and the arbitrators. The parties agree that the arbitrators should carry out a judicial role to resolve their disputes. Arbitrators' rights and obligations are not fundamentally different according to whether they are dealing with or without arbitration institutions, although the way in which those rights and obligations are exercised is affected by the presence and the rules of the institution. The arbitrators consent to their appointment by

---

[9] Clay, *L'arbitre*, para 1066 et seq; Gaillard and Savage, *Fouchard Gaillard Goldman on International Commercial Arbitration*, para 1103-10.

[10] Clay, *L'arbitre*, para 1055; Gaillard and Savage, *Fouchard Gaillard Goldman on International Commercial Arbitration*, para 1111.

signing the submission agreement, by drawing up terms of reference, or by any manifestation of an intention to perform the functions conferred on them by the parties.

Judicial Nature of Arbitration: The Role of State Control

Despite the contractual nature of arbitration, there must be a regulatory framework that controls the legal status and effectiveness of arbitration in a national and international legal environment[11]. In other words, arbitration is based on party autonomy, as well as national laws giving effect to that party autonomy. Professor Emmanuel Gaillard has categorised the legal sources of the legitimacy of the party autonomy into three representations of international arbitration:

(i) international arbitration is based on the national legal system at the seat of arbitration, pursuant to which parties can only submit to arbitration to the extent expressly allowed or accepted implicitly by the law of the seat of arbitration;
(ii) international arbitration is founded on plural national legal systems, which considers that the orders at the place of enforcement authorise the legitimacy of the arbitral awards retroactively; or
(iii) international arbitration is based on a transnational theory, according to which the legitimacy of arbitrators' judicial role is based not on a national legal system (be it at the seat or at the places of enforcement), but based on an a national legal system, an arbitral legal system.[12]

Leaving aside the theoretical debates as to the sources of party autonomy, it is observed that the traditional role of national legislation in international arbitration is evolving as a result of globalisation. The power to regulate arbitration has shifted from states to private actors.[13] According to Professor Kaufmann-Kohler,

> a transnational consensus on the core principles of arbitration law has emerged. That consensus encompasses broad party autonomy. The states have enacted new legislation – or the courts have interpreted existing statutes – making party autonomy a genuine source of arbitration law.[14]

One can conclude that there is a general trend among national courts to move to the position in favour of arbitration giving priority to party autonomy and

---

[11] On the judicial nature of arbitration, *see* Gaillard and Savage, *Fouchard Gaillard Goldman on International Commercial Arbitration*, para 12; Hunter, et al, *Redfern and Hunter on International Arbitration*, para 5.01 et seq; Charles Jarrosson, *La Notion d'Arbitrage* (Paris, LGDJ, 1987), para 785; Lew, Mistelis and Kröll, *Comparative International Commercial Arbitration*, para 55-1 et seq. Clay, *L'arbitre*, para 60 et seq.

[12] Emmanuel Gaillard, *Aspects philosophiques du droit de l'arbitrage international* (Leiden, Martinus Nihoff Publishers, 2008).

[13] Gabrielle Kaufmann-Kohler, 'Global Implications of the US Federal Arbitration Act: The Role of Legislation in International Arbitration' (2005) 20 *ICSID Review* 2, 339–56.

[14] ibid.

178 *Chinese Characteristics*

eschewing intervention.[15] Charts 4 and 5 below summarise the relationship between the various players in international arbitration, in which the main players are the private parties, with party autonomy being the core of arbitration:

Chart 4: Ad hoc Arbitration

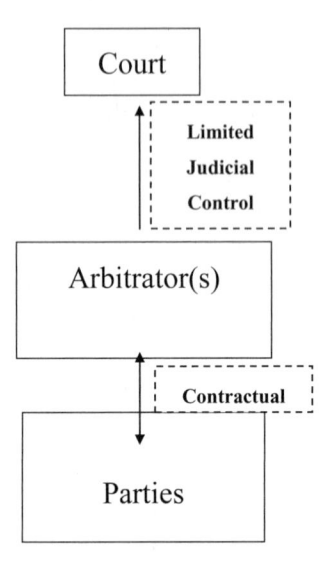

```
        Court
          ↑
          ↓   Limited Judicial Control
    Arbitrator(s)
          ↑
          ↓   Contractual
       Parties
```

Chart 5: Institutional Arbitration

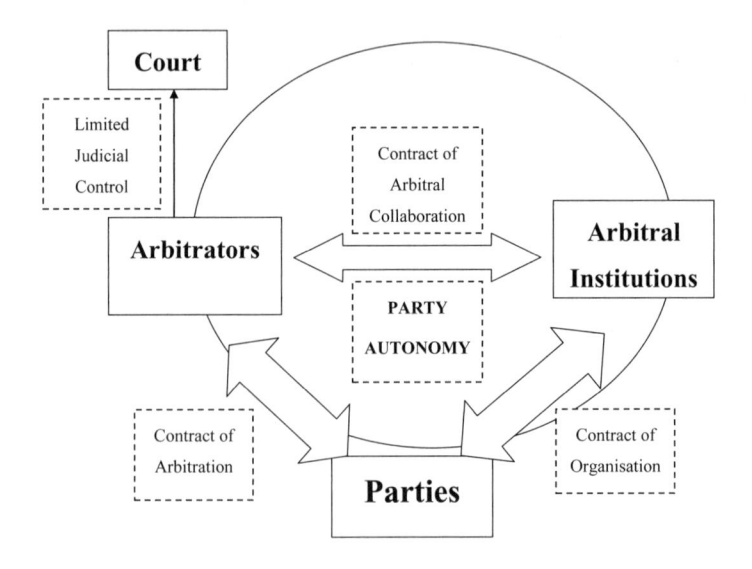

```
         Court
           ↑
    Limited Judicial Control

                    Contract of
                    Arbitral
                    Collaboration
   Arbitrators  ⇔                  ⇔  Arbitral Institutions
                    PARTY
                    AUTONOMY

   Contract of                        Contract of
   Arbitration                        Organisation
                    Parties
```

---

[15] See Lew, Mistelis and Kröll, *Comparative International Commercial Arbitration*, para 15-5.

7.4.2 The Chinese Notion of Arbitration – Top-down

In China, however, the nature of arbitration remains more administrative than contractual. The concept of party autonomy is traditionally foreign to Chinese minds. On the basis of international experience, the private nature of arbitration and its core principle of party autonomy have been much addressed by academics and other arbitration experts in China. However, legislation and arbitration practice still lags behind. Although the Arbitration Law sets forth party autonomy as one of the basic principles for the development of arbitration in China, in reality this principle is neither fully implemented in substantive provisions of the law, nor fully respected in arbitral practice. A number of restrictions on the parties' choices in law and practice derive from the procedural rules of the courts. The restrictions on party autonomy permeate the whole process of arbitration:

(i) the principle of severability of the arbitration agreement is applied with limited scope;
(ii) the parties' choice of ad hoc arbitration or of a foreign arbitration institution is denied if the arbitration is to be conducted in China;
(iii) the power to rule on jurisdictional issues is not conferred on the private judges of the parties' choice, but shared by the court and arbitration institutions; and
(iv) the parties' choice of arbitrators is limited to a closed panel list drafted by arbitration institutions including only individuals with strict statutory qualifications.

Chart 6 below demonstrates the relationship between various players of arbitration, in which *top-down* administrative governance is the main feature, instead of party autonomy.

Chart 6: The Chinese Arbitration Structure

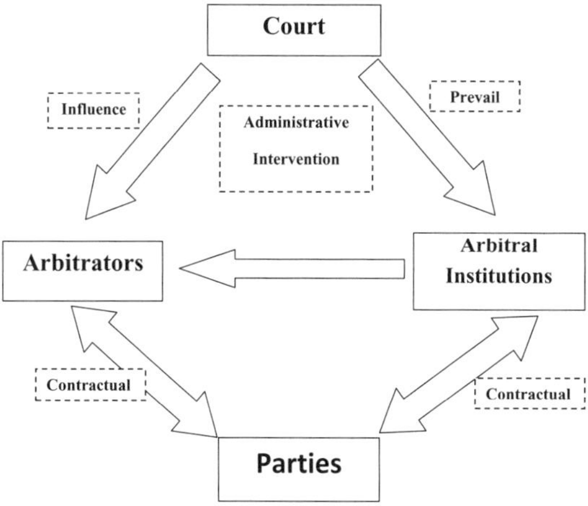

From the charts above, we can see the major difference in the notion of arbitration, and more generally, the sources of law, between the Chinese and international norms: law, in Western minds, comes from below. In China, it comes from above. The Western system takes as its starting point the rights claimed by the *individual*; party autonomy runs through the whole procedure of arbitration, as a 'private' means of dispute resolution. The Chinese system begins with the *state* as the guardian of rights, and quality control of the arbitration, as a 'public' means of dispute resolution. This 'top-down' (state-controlled) notion, in contrast to the essentially 'bottom-up' (contractual) notion of Western arbitration, casts a long shadow on the way arbitration is conducted in China.

7.5 THE EMPHASIS ON AMICABLE RESOLUTION OF DISPUTES

Somewhat paradoxically, given the rigidity of Chinese law, a notion of 'finding flexible ways around laws' (*biantong*) seems to make the normative force of law somewhat weaker in China than elsewhere. Furthermore, it seems that the network of *guanxi* still plays an important role in arbitration practice, especially given that the 'club' of arbitration practitioners is relatively small.

Another aspect of Chinese *biantong* is the doctrine of 'finding the middle way' (*zhong yong*), or the art of compromise. This paves the way for the role of mediation, an intrinsic part of which is the settlement of the dispute through compromise and finding the 'middle way'. In its various forms, mediation has played and still plays an essential role in dispute resolution in China, serving the objectives of social harmony and the restoration of harmonious long-term relations. Chapter six demonstrates the widely adopted practice of arb-med in China. This practice is featured by the fact that the same person acts as both arbitrator and mediator in one and the same proceedings. So far, there is no transnational consensus as to whether it is appropriate for the arbitrators to facilitate settlement, due to the different legal cultures and views towards the roles of the arbitrators. Despite the theoretical debates and divergent practice worldwide, most Chinese arbitrators consider that facilitating settlement is consistent with the mission of arbitrators; and thus, in practice, they will almost systematically take the initiative of asking the parties if they wish the tribunal to assist them in reaching an amicable solution.

8

Traditional Legal Culture and its Influence on Contemporary Arbitration Practice

'To enter a court of law is to enter a tiger's mouth'.
'Avoid litigation; for once you resort to law there is nothing but trouble'.

Chinese proverbs

IN THE REAL world, there are no legal systems that exist independently of a particular political, economic, social and cultural context. From the epistemological point of view, law is so closely linked to other disciplines that legal knowledge is best acquired through an interdisciplinary lens, through understanding of other fields such as psychology, sociology, economy and history.[1] Professor Lawrence Friedman identified three central components of the legal system: (a) the social and legal forces that, in some way, press and make 'the law'; (b) 'the law' itself – structures and rules; and (c) the impact of law on behaviour in the outside world.[2] Putting law into a social context may help us to understand better where the law comes from and what the law accomplishes.

To name the 'social forces . . . constantly at work on the law', Professor Friedman introduced the concept of 'legal culture'. He defines it as 'those parts of general culture – customs, opinions, way[s] of doing and thinking – that bend social forces toward or away from the law and in particular ways'.[3] As an example of variations within legal cultures, Professor Friedman distinguished the 'internal legal culture' of professionals working in the system from the 'external legal culture' of citizens interacting within the system.[4] On a similar note, Professor Huang Yuansheng, a legal historian, suggests that legal culture is a special cultural regime composed of the legal system, legal regulations, legal thoughts, legal awareness and legal implementation. It includes tangible

---

[1] Christian Atias, *Épistémologie juridique* (Paris, Dalloz, 2002) 106.
[2] Lawrence M Friedman, *The Legal System: A Social Science Perspective* (New York, Russell Sage Foundation, 1975) 3.
[3] ibid.
[4] Lawrence M Friedman, 'The Concept of Legal Culture: A Reply' in David Nelken (ed), *Comparing Legal Cultures* (Aldershot, Dartmouth, 1997) 34.

external factors such as legislation and judicial practice, as well as internal factors such as the attitudes towards law and the judiciary among the general public.[5] There is a necessary interaction and harmony between the legal system and legal culture. 'For the law to be effective, it must be meaningful in the context in which it is applied so citizens have an incentive to use the law and to demand institutions that work to enforce and develop the law'.[6]

The choice of a dispute resolution mechanism, whether mediation, arbitration or litigation, within the forum designed and established by a particular society, is strongly influenced by the tradition, culture and legal evolution of that society. Thus, in addition to examining the current laws and practice of arbitration in China, this study must aim to understand Chinese legal culture, its traditional values, and special features and evolutions in society, in order to determine the historical spectrums that can explain the present state of arbitration phenomenon.

From the perspective of legal culture, Chinese legal history can be divided into three periods: (i) the period of the 'traditional' Chinese legal system – from the law of Yu in the Xia dynasty to the Qing dynasty – when the values and features of law were self-originated and local (*gu you fa*); (ii) the period of legal 'reception' (*jishou*) – from 1840 to 1949, when the form and essence of law were imported from the West; and (iii) the period of the construction of the socialist legal system – from 1949 to the present, since the People's Republic of China was established.[7] To facilitate the reader's understanding of the time frames in Chinese history, an abbreviated chronological chart is provided below:

Chart 7: Timeline of Chinese History

Dates	Dynasty	朝代
2000–1500 BC	Xia	夏
1700–1027 BC	Shang	商
1027–771 BC	Western Zhou	西周
770–221 BC	Eastern Zhou	东周
	770–476 BC – Spring and Autumn period	春秋
	475–221 BC – Warring States period	战国
221–207 BC	Qin	秦
206 BC–AD 24	Western Han	西汉
AD 25–220	Eastern Han	东汉

[5] 黄源盛，《法律继受与近代中国法》,(台北，元照出版有限公司，2007), 第6页(Yuansheng Huang, *Legal Transplant and Recent Chinese Law* (Taipei, Yuanzhao Press, 2007), 6).

[6] Daniel Berkowitz, Katharina Pistor and Jean-Francois Richard, 'The Transplant Effect' (2003) 51 *American Journal of Comparative Law* 163, 167.

[7] Xianyi Zeng, Ding Zheng and Xiaogeng Zhao (eds), *A History of Chinese Law* (Beijing, People's University Press, 2004) 1–18.

AD 220–280	Three Kingdoms	三国
AD 265–316	Western Jin	西晋
AD 317–420	Eastern Jin	东晋
AD 420–588	Southern and Northern Dynasties	南北朝
AD 581–617	Sui	隋
AD 618–907	Tang	唐
AD 907–960	Five Dynasties	五代
AD 907–979	Ten Kingdoms	十国
AD 960–1279	Song	宋
	960–1127: Northern Song	北宋
	1127–1279: Southern Song	南宋
AD 1279–1368	Yuan	元
AD 1368–1644	Ming	明
AD 1644–1911	Qing	清
AD 1911–1949	Republic of China	中华民国
AD 1949–	People's Republic of China	中华人民共和国

The question is, after the Western concepts of law were introduced in China, when Chinese law began to experience a process of 'modernisation', whether and to what extent are Chinese traditions carried out in the present? 'Traditional' and 'modern' are relative concepts, and there is no clear line between the two. However, 'tradition' can be used as a mirror to reflect and explain the process of 'modernisation', and to help us further understand where the current legal reforms should be directed. Before discussing the evolution of legal culture and legal system in contemporary society (chapter nine), we will first step back and search for the main features and values of traditional legal culture in China's imperial history in this chapter.

To define the features of traditional legal culture in imperial China is not an easy task, as we will never be able to see the law of ancient China precisely as would someone living in the past. Professor William Alford raised the limits of using the 'grand theory' in comparative law.[8] In order to make a fair and meaningful assessment of traditional legal culture in China, we need to be careful not to look simply for the presence or absence of the values and norms from the West. Otherwise, we will 'run the risk of failing to understand on their own terms the people we are studying'.[9]

In fact, if we trace the origins of law in the West and in ancient China, it is evident that the notion and scope of 'law' diverge vastly in the Chinese and Western

---

[8] William Alford, 'On the Limits of "Grand Theory" in Comparative Law' (1986) 61 *Washington Law Review* 945, 945–56.
[9] ibid.

contexts.[10] In Western society, the term 'law' can be translated into *jus* and *lex*. The meanings of *jus* and its equivalent translations ('*droit*', '*Recht*', '*diritto*', or '*derecho*') are complex, abstract, and rich with philosophical significance, and incorporate concepts of law, rights, fairness and justice. *Lex* ('*loi*', '*Gesetz*, '*lege*', or '*ley*'), on the other hand, takes a relatively simple meaning, which refers to specific rules or statues. This features the Western linguistic phenomenon of combining 'law' and 'rights' into one, and reflects the basic premise of Western law – law is considered the guarantor of rights and the measure of freedom.[11]

The Chinese notion of 'law', a translation of the character *fǎ* ('法'), had a different root. The origin of the Chinese character *fa* ('灋' in traditional Chinese) was interpreted by Shen Xu of the East Han dynasty (circa 58–147 AD) in the famous book on the explanation of Chinese characters[12] as follows: the ancient form of *fa* was *fá* ('罰'), meaning punishment. The left hand of the character *fa* refers to 'water', evoking the idea of a criminal suspect in the water drifting away with the current; the right hand of the character *fa* symbolises '*zhi*', referring to a one-horned imaginary animal, who can distinguish right from wrong – the one who was touched by the animal was considered to be responsible or guilty.[13] The ancient pronunciation for the Chinese character *fǎ* closely resembled that for the Chinese character 'to punish', namely *fá* ('罰'). In ancient Chinese texts, there are two very important characters that can serve as an explanation of the word *fa*. One is *xing* ('刑'), the other is *lü* ('律'). *Fa, xing* and *lü* were often used interchangeably.[14] In this sense, the Chinese character of *fa* had a much narrower scope than in the Western language of law, which was purely functional, without any connotations of 'right' or 'fairness'. On the other hand, the Chinese looked at human society beyond the order of laws, in the broader context of the universe. They believed that the optimal order in society was the harmony between the rule of nature and the rule of human society, the so-called *tian ren he yi*. These notions were expressed in Chinese as *li* ('理') or *dao* ('道'), meaning natural rules; and *li* ('礼') or *lijiao* ('礼教'), meaning the standard of human behaviour or rituals. In this sense, the Chinese took a more universal and holistic vision of society.

---

[10] The difference in the meaning of 'law' in China and in the West has been elaborated delicately by Zhiping Liang in Zhiping Liang, 'Explicating "Law": A Comparative Perspective of Chinese and Western Legal Culture' in Tahirih Lee (ed), *Basic Concepts of Chinese Law* (New York, Garland Publishing, 1997) 121–57.

[11] Roscoe Pound, 'The Foundation of Law' (1961) 10 *American University Law Review* 124, 129. Olga Tellegen-Couperus, *A Short History of Roman Law* (London, Routledge, 1993) 174.

[12] *The Explanation of Chinese Characters* (《说文解字》), preface dated 100 AD, was purportedly written by Shen Xu, and was the first real dictionary of the Chinese language.

[13] '灋, 刑也。平之如水。从水, 廌所以触不直者去之, 从去, 会意。' 许慎:《说文解字》(Shen Xu, *The Explanation of Chinese characters*: 'Law is punishment, leveled as even as water. Thus it comes from the character water. Fa is also '*zhi*', in that it strikes those who are not upright and removes them, which refers to the meaning "to remove"').

[14] From a chronological perspective, what we refer to today as ancient law was referred to as '*xing*' during the Three Dynasties (Xia, Shang and West Zhou Dynasties), as '*fa*' during the Spring and Autumn Period and the Warring States Period; and as '*lü*' during the Qin, Han and later dynasties.

Given the differences in values and concepts, the Western definition of law and the Western idea of the rule of law cannot help us to understand Chinese legal culture fully. If we dip a Western spoon into the river of Chinese history, we have already prejudged the shape of the water. In order to get a more objective and sensible portrait, we should attempt to use some more universal utensils or models, in order to understand, to the extent that we can, that tradition on its own terms. In this regard, the author borrows a model developed by Professor Yu Xingzhong – 'civil order' – a basic framework to harmonise the relationships between man and man, man and himself, man and society, as well as man and nature.[15] Using this model, Chinese traditional society can be characterised as a 'moral civil order', contrasted to the 'legal civil order' of the West, or the 'religious civil order' in Islamic countries.[16] Taking this universal historical perspective, we will not judge the Chinese tradition with the concepts familiar to the Western society of a legal civil order such as 'rule of law', 'rights', 'obligations', 'due process', 'property', and 'contract'. Instead, we shall try to understand that tradition with the original languages used in imperial Chinese society of a moral civil order, such as *'tian ren he yi'* (harmony between the rule of nature and the rule of human society), *'li'* (rituals), *'he wei gui'* (emphasis on harmony), *'zhongyong'* (the doctrine of middle way), and *'rang'* (concession).

Using this model, traditional Chinese society can be characterised in the following ways: in terms of 'authority', it emphasised on rituals instead of texts or institutions (section 8.1); in terms of 'institutions', it was based on the relational network to which an individual belonged, not the individual itself (section 8.2); in terms of 'popular consciousness', the populace considered litigation as disgraceful conduct (section 8.3). To trace the root of commercial arbitration, we will also examine commercial history and dispute resolution in imperial China (section 8.4). Based on the above analysis, we will try to unfold the historical links to modern practice (section 8.5).

8.1 THE EMPHASIS ON RITUALS

One distinct feature of traditional Chinese legal culture can be characterised by the deeply-rooted emphasis on *li* (rituals).

Generally speaking, the Western tradition is law–man–law; every person must obey the law, and the enactment and amendment of law must follow legal procedures. In other words, the Western tradition emphasises legality. The law not only controls each individual, but also governs the entire society, and brings

---

[15] 於兴中,《法治与文明秩序》, (北京, 中国政法大学出版社, 2006), 第18–33, 52–62页(Xingzhong Yu, Rule of Law and Civil Order (Beijing, China Politics and Law University Press, 2006), 18–33, 52–62).

[16] ibid. (Yu argues that in societies under different civil orders, the concepts, institutions, authority, and popular consciousness of the order vary significantly.)

186 *Traditional Legal Culture*

all social life within an impersonalised framework.[17] This is the philosophical foundation of the modern Western theory of the rule of law.[18] Individualist ideals in the West promoted the establishment of legal institutions as private guardians. Formal law was perceived to have supremacy and power.

In China, however, law was never perceived as a means of preserving rights, freedom, or justice. According to Professor Liang Zhiping:

> Law was punishment . . . According to traditional ideas, law was above all a tool of suppression. It was one of countless methods of governing, which could be used and constituted at will by the ruler . . . [T]here were rulers, but there were no laws of governing . . . This fact was the source of what the ancient Chinese political system considered the 'rule of man'.[19]

The Chinese model is thus man–law–man. The feudal rulers had absolute control over the entire country. This centralised power structure constitutes a closed pyramidal system of dominance by man, which excludes any possibility of joint rule or rule by any other source. In addition, the law was interwoven with ethical rules. The emphasis of law is on the protection of government powers and social interests rather than on the protection of individual rights and private interests. The patriarchal system and the totalitarian regime do not allow or even tolerate the existence of individual rights or interests that may foster rebellion against the regime. The feudal rulers, in the name of the ultimate head of the entire patriarchal system and the paramount leader of the totalitarian regime, assume their interests to be the legitimate public interests and substitute them for individual interests. As a result of this assertion, state, community and family, which constitute the different levels of the fabric of feudal society, are the primary concerns of the law.[20]

8.1.1 *Li v Fa*

To understand the values and norms of traditional Chinese culture, one must bear in mind the concept of 'li' advocated by Confucianism, the concept of 'fa'

---

[17] Liang, 'Explicating "Law": A Comparative Perspective of Chinese and Western Legal Culture', 154.

[18] For literature on the rule of law, see Gottfried Dietze, *Two Concepts of the Rule of Law* (Indianapolis, Liberty Fund, 1973); Ronald Dworkin, *Law's Empire* (Cambridge, Mass, Harvard University Press, 1986); John Finnis, *Natural Law and Natural Rights* (Oxford, Clarendon Press, 1980); Herbert Lionel Adolphus Hart, *The Concept of Law* (Oxford, Clarendon Press, 1961); Friedrich Hayek, *The Rule of Law* (Menlo Park, California, Institute for Humane Studies, 1975); Franz Leopold Neumann, *The Rule of Law: Political Theory and the Legal System in Modern Society* (New Hampshire, Berg Publishers Ltd, 1986); John Rawls, *A Theory of Justice* (Cambridge, Mass, The Belknap Press of Harvard University Press, 1971); Yu, *Rule of Law and Civil Order*; 李步云,《论法治》, (北京, 社会科学文献出版社, 2008) (Buyun Li, *On The Rule of Law*, (Beijing, Social Sciences Literature Press, 2008)).

[19] Liang, 'Explicating "Law": A Comparative Perspective of Chinese and Western Legal Culture', 155.

[20] Chengguang Wang and Xianchu Zhang (ed), *Introduction to Chinese Law* (Hong Kong, Sweet & Maxwell Asia, 1997) 6–7.

advocated by Legalism and the relationship between the two.[21] This leads us back to the 'Era of Philosophy', which began to flourish in the sixth century BC. In the Spring and Autumn Period (770–476 BC), the succession system from the West Zhou Period, according to which imperial power was passed to the first-born son, began to lapse. The nobles initiated various campaigns against the emperors to fight for power.[22] Political chaos, however, led to an unprecedented era of cultural prosperity in Chinese history: different philosophies developed, and most of the great classical works were written during the time, on which Chinese practices were to be based for the next two and a half millennia. The great thinkers during the time include Confucius, Mencius, Lao Zi, Xun Zi, and Han Feizi. This period is thus often referred to as the period of the 'Hundred Schools of Thought Contending' (*bai jia zheng ming*).[23]

The school of thought that had the most enduring effect on subsequent Chinese life was Confucianism. The written legacy of Confucianism is embodied in the Confucian Five Classics,[24] which were to become the basis for the order of traditional society. Confucius's ideas and teachings were compiled by his students in the 'Analects of Confucius' (*lunyu*). Underlying the Confucian position is a positive view of human nature, the basic virtues of which can be refined by moral persuasion, or *li*. *Li* is profoundly relational, and fulfillment in personal life is akin to the fulfillment of roles, whether familial, professional or political. Since *li* is not sovereign command, it may be flexibly interpreted in a consensual manner, such that harmony in society is preserved through mutual reinforcement of norms rather than dispute over their content.[25] Mencius, or Meng Zi, was a Confucian disciple who made major contributions to the humanism of Confucian thought. Mencius declared that man was good by nature. He proposed the idea that a ruler could not govern without the people's tacit consent and that the penalty for unpopular, despotic rule was the loss of the 'mandate of heaven'.[26] The effect of the combined work of Confucius, the

---

[21] For discussions of the concepts of '*li*' and '*fa*' and their relationship, see Goh Bee Chen, *Law Without Lawyers, Justice Without Courts: On Traditional Chinese Mediation* (Surrey, Ashgate Publishing, 2002) 29–36; Yongping Liu, *Origins of Chinese Law: Penal and Administrative Law in its Early Development* (Oxford, Oxford University Press, 1998) 87–105;马汉宝,《法律与中国社会之变迁》, (台北, 韩芦图书出版有限公司, 1999), 第3–6页 (Hanbao Ma, *The Law and the Changes of the Chinese Society*, (Taipei, Hanlu Press, 1999), 3–6);瞿同祖,《中国法律与中国社会》(北京, 商务印书馆, 1981), 第6章 (Tongzu Qu, *Chinese Law and Chinese Society* (Beijing, Commercial Publishing House, 1981), ch 6).

[22] Ma, *The Law and the Changes of the Chinese Society*, 177.

[23] For a discussion of the Hundred Schools of Thought, see 郭建,《中国法文化漫笔》(北京,东方出版中心, 1999), 第204–10页, (Jian Guo, *Discussions of Chinese Legal Culture* (Beijing, Oriental Publishing Center, 1999), 204–10).

[24] 《易经》(Book of Change), 《诗经》(Book of Poetry),《诗经》(Book of Documents),《周礼》(Classic of Rites), 《春秋》(Spring and Autumn Annals).

[25] Roger T Ames, *Rites and Rights: The Confucian Alternative* (Notre Dame, University of Notre Dame Press, 1988) 201; Derek Bodde and Clarence Morris, *Law in Imperial China* (Cambridge, Massachusetts, Harvard University Press, 1967) 21; Patrick Glenn, *Legal Traditions of the World*, 4th edn (Oxford, Oxford University Press, 2010) 289.

[26] See 《孟子》, translated by Irene Bloom. Irene Bloom, *Mencius*, (Columbia, Columbia University Press, 2009) 14–19.

codifier and interpreter of a system of relationships based on ethical behavior, and Mencius, the synthesiser and developer of applied Confucian thought, was to provide traditional Chinese society with a comprehensive framework on which to order virtually every aspect of life. Diametrically opposed to Mencius, was the interpretation of Xun Zi, another Confucian follower. Xun Zi preached that man is innately selfish and evil and that goodness is attainable only through education and conduct befitting one's status. He advocated the use of both *li* and *fa* in regulating human affairs.[27]

Xun Zi's unsentimental and authoritarian inclinations were developed into the doctrine embodied in the school of law (*fa*), or legalism. The doctrine was formulated by Han Feizi, who maintained that human nature was selfish and therefore the only way to preserve the social order was to 'impose discipline from above' and to enforce laws strictly. The law by which people were governed, the legalists insisted, should be the authoritative principle for the people and the basis of government. Contrary to the Confucian idea of moral persuasion, legalists argued that moral considerations should be rigorously excluded in the conduct of government. Legalists advocated that the ruler must rely on penal law and the imposition of heavy punishments as the main instruments to govern his people. A principle frequently invoked is that, were the smallest offence to be met with severe punishment, in the end the people would cease to offend the rules and recourse to punishment itself would become unnecessary, according to the principle of 'avoiding criminal offences by heavy penalties' (*yi xing qu xing*).[28] A hallmark of legalist thinking was that there should be equality before the law. All, except for the ruler himself, should be subject to regular punishments if they committed offences. While advocating the impartial application of publicly codified laws, legalism was hardly the 'rule of law', which imposed limits on ruling elites, but rather, the 'rule by law'. Law was simply a pragmatic tool for obtaining and maintaining political control and social order. The ruler retained the authority to promulgate and change laws, and remained above and beyond the law.

The legalist theory was implemented in the Qin dynasty, when the first centralised imperial state was established. In order to secure its central power, the Qin emperor imposed severe penal codes and punishments, and destroyed all the Confucianists' writings. The Legalists' ascent to power during the Qin dynasty was short lived and when that dynasty was replaced by the Han dynasty, Confucianism once again became the national orthodoxy.

The heated debates between Confucianism and Legalism cooled down after the Han dynasty, when the most practical and useful aspects of Confucianism

---

[27] See *Hsun Tzu, Basic Writings* (Columbia, Columbia University Press, 1996) ch 8, The Regulation of the King.

[28] See 《商君书•勒令篇》:' 行刑重其轻者, 轻其重者, 轻者不至, 重者不来, 此谓以刑去刑, 刑去事成' (The Book of Lord Shang, ch 13 Making Orders Strict, 'In applying punishments, light offences should be punished heavily; if light offences do not appear, heavy offences will not come. This is said to be abolishing penalties by means of penalties, and if penalties are abolished, affairs will succeed'.

and Legalism were synthesised.[29] A hybrid system of governance – the Confucian *li* with the Legalist *fa* – came into existence, and was used by Chinese emperors to regulate, control and harmonise society until the late nineteenth century. Many Confucian ethical norms and values were incorporated into law.[30] In fact, most of the codes after the Han dynasty were promulgated by Confucian officials.[31] As a result, Confucian ethical rules were taken into account when written codes were drafted. This phenomenon is referred to by some scholars as 'Confucianisation of law',[32] or 'legalisation of Confucianism'.[33] With the Confucianisation of law, the Confucian concept of *li* was integrated into *fa*. *Li* became an important component of traditional Chinese law.

8.1.2 Codification Centered on Criminal Offences and Rigidity of Written Law

The codification of laws in China is said to have appeared even earlier than the Roman Twelve Tables Law, promulgated in 451 BC. As early as 536 BC during the Spring and Autumn Period, a government official in Zheng State,[34] named Zi Chan, decided to inscribe the code of criminal law onto the surface of a bronze tripod vessel, and make the bronze vessel available to the general public, so that people could learn the provisions of the law. This event in history has been described as the 'publication of the law' (*zhu xing shu*).[35] Since then, written laws were significantly developed in ancient China in volume and in sophistication[36]. The systematic codification of laws is said to have started during the Warring States Period, when the Book of Laws (*fa jing*) edited by Li Kui was published (around 406 BC).[37] However, while the Roman tradition had led to the development of an advanced civil law and the system of the rule of law in Western society, the large body of codified law did not promote the development of a similar system in China.

In traditional Chinese society, the distinction between civil and criminal cases was vague. Many disputes, which are civil by modern standards, were classified as criminal. Formal law and legal process in traditional Chinese society were principally concerned with penal law and punishment. From the Book of Laws in the

---

[29] Qu, Chinese Law and Chinese Society, 334–51.
[30] ibid.
[31] ibid. 杨鸿烈, 《中国法律思想史》(台北, 台湾商务印书馆, 1964), 第75 页 (Honglie Yang, *The History of Chinese Legal Thoughts* (Taipei, Taiwan Commercial Publishing House, 1964), 75).
[32] 瞿同祖, 《瞿同祖法学论著集》, (北京, 中国政法大学出版社, 1998), 第361–81页 (Tongzu Qu, Selected Works of Qu Tongzu, (Beijing, China Politics and Law University Press, 1998), 361–81).
[33] John Wu, 'The Status of the Individual in the Political and Legal Traditions of Old and New China' in Charles Moore (ed), *The Status of the Individual in East and West* (Hawaii, University of Hawaii Press, 1968) 394.
[34] During the time, China was divided into a number of small states; Zheng State was one of them.
[35] See 《左传•昭公六年》 (Zuo's Commentary, the Sixth Year of Duke Zhao).
[36] Legal historians have argued that the publication of law may be traced back to the West Zhou dynasty or even earlier.
[37] 李悝, 《法经》 (Kui Li, *The Book of Laws*).

Warring States period to the Qin Code, the Han Code, all the way through to the Tang, Ming and Qing Codes, the tradition of criminal-centered codification was reinforced dynasty after dynasty.[38] These written laws, using contemporary legal classification, are all essentially penal codes, although they also cover provisions about civil and administrative matters as well as litigation. Most provisions of these codes provide for punishment as the legal consequences of wrongdoing. Throughout the history of imperial China, there has not been a single civil code in the modern sense.

Furthermore, written laws in imperial China were often too strict and did not correspond with the realities of daily life. As a result, large bodies of codes were only 'paper laws', and were not implemented in practice. On the one hand, with the process of the Confucianisation of law, a number of moral standards were adopted into written codes, which essentially served an educational purpose guiding people to act according to Confucian norms. For instance, in the Tang Code, disrespect of parents is considered a serious crime. If the parents passed away, the children had to hold a 'funeral service' (*fu sang*) for a period of 27 months, during which the daughter-in-law was not allowed to become pregnant, a rule violation of which would lead to one year in prison.[39] The legislator realised that this was too harsh a punishment and commented in the Tang Code that the punishment could be waived if the daughter-in-law 'confessed' her pregnancy. Consequently, this law was rarely implemented in practice. However, this rigid provision was maintained in order to guide the general public to follow the social norm of filial piety. On the other hand, throughout imperial history, the emperor primarily relied on military force to govern the state, while *fa* was used only as a secondary source to support the emperor's control. Thus, the emperors implemented *fa* as a political strategy without considering its practicability and enforceability. For instance, the Ming and Qing Codes prohibited cursing, a rule the violation of which would result in a caning punishment of ten blows. This provision was drafted into the law to show the government's policy guidance. However, in reality, it was almost impossible to implement. This led to the phenomenon of 'law is law, life is life' in traditional Chinese society. Law was disregarded by the general public. People's social lives were predominately governed by rituals and moral standards, instead of rigid law.

8.1.3 Implementation of Law: *Qing* Mixed with *Fa*

In the traditional legal system, a single local official, called the magistrate (*fumu guan*) was vested with a range of investigatory, prosecutorial, adjudicatory and other responsibilities. Charged with these many and varied tasks, the magistrate

---

[38] For a list of the legal codes in Chinese history, see Huang, *Legal Transplant and Recent Chinese Law*, 10–11.
[39] 长孙无忌,《唐律疏议》。(Zhang Sun Wu Ji, *Annotated Commentaries on Laws of Tang Dynasty*).

was not a professional, legally trained judge, but a man who had demonstrated a mastery of the Confucian classics.[40] When deciding a case, magistrates rely on the law, but are not restricted to the rigid provisions of written legal texts. They enjoyed the discretion to supplement the rigidity and gaps of written statutes with human sentiments (*ren qing*). This phenomenon can be illustrated by the board in ancient local courts hung facing the local magistrates, which read as '*tianli, guofa, renqing*' – natural rules, national laws, and human sentiments. The board served to remind the officials to implement the law following the rule of nature, pursuant to the state laws, and taking into account human sentiments.

Renqing refers to the flexibility to take into account actual circumstances and to the tolerance of minor mistakes; it corresponds to the notion of tolerance (*shu*), as Confucius put it: 'if you do not want it for yourself, do not impose it on others'.[41] According to Confucian doctrine, law is too rigid and cruel, and must be adjusted by flexibility and tolerance. Similar to *renqing*, another term that frequently appeared in ancient legal materials is '*qingli*' – the sentiment of reasonableness. *Renqing* and *qingli* are often referred to together as '*qing*', featured by the notion of human sentiments, reasonableness, and flexibility.

Compared to the complexity of real life, legal provisions appeared to be overly simplified. As 'no two cases are alike', the Chinese were sceptical about attempts to characterise all possible circumstances under generalised legal categories. As a result, magistrates viewed (within their scope of discretion) the legal code as providing certain guidelines, but relied heavily on the unique features of the cases in their judgment. Historical records of 'good judgments' often praised the magistrates' ability to understand the legal spirit and appreciate human sentiments in rendering a decision. For instance, the *Exemplary Court Decisions* recorded numerous cases when the magistrate made the judgment according to *qing*, when the strict application of written texts appeared to lead to an unfair result.[42] A study on case law in the Qing dynasty also notes the frequent reference to *qing* and *li* by officials in rendering their judgments; very few decisions were concluded by referring to the express provisions of written law.[43] As Benjamin Schwartz stated, 'it is the judgment and not the law which makes justice'.[44] The gaps in the law were filled by human sentiments and social norms, and the operation of the law was supplemented by human sentiments and social norms. In this sense, *qing* was also mixed with *fa*.

---

[40] Alford, 'On the Limits of "Grand Theory' in Comparative Law', 952.

[41] 《论语•颜渊篇》: "己所不欲,勿施于人。" (*Analects: Chapter of Yan Yuan*: 'Do not do to others what you don't want to be done to you'.)

[42] 郑克,《折狱龟鉴》(Ke Zheng, *Exemplary Court Decisions*). For a discussion and further examples, see梁治平,《法意与人情》,(北京,法制出版社, 2003, 第233–39页 (Zhiping Liang, *The Legal Spirit and Human Sentiments* (Beijing, Legal Press, 2003)), 233–39.

[43] See 滋贺秀三[日]:《明清时期的民事审判与民间契约》王亚新、范愉、陈少峰译, 法律出版社1998年版(しが・しゅうぞう (*The Civil Trial and Social Contract During the Ming and Qing Period*, (Beijing, Legal Press 1998), translated by Yaxin Wang, Yu Fan and Shaofeng Chen.)

[44] Benjamin Schwartz, 'On Attitudes Toward Law in China' in Tahirih Lee (ed), *Basic Concepts of Chinese Law* (New York, Garland Publishing, 1997) 166.

8.2 THE EMPHASIS ON RELATIONAL NETWORK

Another important difference between traditional Chinese legal culture and that of the West is the role of the individual in the society.

The idea of natural law can be traced back to the ancient Greek and Roman period. Socrates and his philosophic followers Plato and Aristotle argued for the existence of natural justice or natural rights, which existed beyond the laws implemented by the states or governments and should apply to all human beings.[45] In the seventeenth and eighteenth century, the concept of individual 'natural rights' emerged. The most representative advocates for natural rights are Thomas Hobbes, John Locke and Jean-Jacques Rousseau. They believed that each individual lives in a 'state of nature', and enjoys natural rights that are indispensable for living well.[46] The idea of natural right has since become one of the basic principles in Western legislation. For instance, the Code of Frederick the Great of Prussia, the 1804 French Civil Code, the 1896 German Civil Code, and the 1907 Swiss Civil Code all contained the idea of protecting individual rights and individual freedom, equality and security.[47] Since the nineteenth century, although the idea of natural law was challenged by the legal positivists, the importance of individual freedom and rights was never denied. The idea of individual protection can be found in almost all modern Western legislations. In short, the protection of individual rights has been the core of Western legal culture and also an indispensable part of the political democracy.

Western concepts of 'individual rights', 'natural rights', and 'freedom' did not exist in traditional Chinese society. Confucius defines the social structure of society as a network of relations of persons enacting certain 'social roles'. Social roles do not merely place individuals in certain social locations but also bear within themselves normative prescriptions of how people ought to act within

---

[45] On natural law, see Heinrich Albert Rommen and Thomas R Hanley, *The Natural Law, a Study in Legal and Social History and Philosophy* (St Louis, B Herder Book Co, 1947); Tony Burns, *Aristotle and Natural Law* (London; New York, Continuum, 2011); Patrick Farrell, Sources of St Thomas' Concept of Natural Law (1957) (Part of thesis, Pontificio Istituto 'Angelicum', Rome); John Finnis, *Natural Law and Natural Rights* (Oxford, Clarendon Press, 1980); Otto Friedrich von Gierke and Ernst Troeltsch, *Natural Law and the Theory of Society, 1500 to 1800* (Cambridge, England, Cambridge University Press, 1958); Jacques Maritain and Doris C Anson, *The Rights of Man and Natural Law* (New York, Gordian Press, 1971); Mark C Murphy, *Natural Law in Jurisprudence and Politics* (Cambridge, England,Cambridge University Press, 2006); EJ Simcox, *Natural Law. An Essay in Ethics* (Boston, Osgood & Company, 1877); Yves René Marie Simon and Vukan Kuic, *The Tradition of Natural Law; A Philosopher's Reflections* (New York, Fordham University Press, 1965); Lloyd L Weinreb, *Natural Law and Justice* (Cambridge, Mass, Harvard University Press, 1987); John Daniel Wild, *Plato's Modern Enemies and the Theory of Natural Law* (Chicago, University of Chicago Press, 1953); Robert N Wilkin and Arthur Leon Harding, *Origins of the Natural Law Tradition* (Port Washington, NY, Kennikat Press, 1971).

[46] See Thomas Hobbes, *Leviathan, or the Matter, Forme, & Power of a Common-Wealth Ecclesiasticall and Civil* (1651); John Locke, *Two Treatises of Government* (1689); Jean-Jacques Rousseau, *Du contrat social aux Principes du droit politique* (1762).

[47] See Edger Bodenheimer, *Jurisprudence – The Philosophy and Method of the Law* (Cambridge, Mass, Harvard University Press, 1974) 58–59.

these roles. Confucianism categorises society into five relationships ('Five Ethical Codes'), which are presumed to embrace all fundamental relationships – relations between the ruler and the ministers, father and child, husband and wife, elder and younger siblings, friend and friend.[48] The most important relations are the ones between the ruler and the ministers, father and child, and husband and wife – referred to by the Han Confucianists as the 'Three Bonds'.[49] In Confucian ideology, these ethical rules should be achieved by rules of *li*, which guide people's behaviour.[50] The essential rituals include benevolence (*ren*), loyalty (*yi*), ritualism (*li*), wisdom (*zhi*), and sincerity (*xin*).

To understand traditional legal culture in China, it is important to bear in mind that the basic unit in imperial Chinese society was not the individual, but the social group.[51] The most basic of these groups was the family, where rules of customary behaviour emphasised the authority of the elder generations over the younger ones. Families themselves were organised into clans, which instructed members on Confucian morality and settled disputes among members. Yet another collective grouping was the guild, which was an organisation of merchants or artisans in the same trade or craft. The guilds controlled prices, competition, training and admission to practise the trade or craft. These social groups dominated the individual. Implicit in the Confucian concept is the notion of hierarchy between individuals and certain obligations inherent in these hierarchical structures.[52] In such society, most civil relations were regulated by the customs of *li*, or the rules within each social group. Under the Confucian principle of *li*, individual rights can be sacrificed for the interests of the whole group, in order to achieve social harmony.

Moreover, law in imperial China was essentially used by the rulers to control, not to protect, the individual. While Western civilisation was born as a result of social compromise between pluralistic groups, law was used to preserve the rights of the various segments of society and to balance the power of the ruler; Chinese civilisation was created in the form of a single clan to exercise its legitimatised control – a system of strict upper class control to preserve stability within the system. As a consequence, individual rights were not a prominent feature of the political landscape of traditional China. Rather, the rulers were more interested in securing their ultimate power so as to maintain stability in society.

---

[48] 《中庸》：'君臣也，父子也，夫妇也，昆弟也，朋友之交也，五者天下之达道也。' (Doctrine of Middle Way: 'Ruler and ministers, father and son, husband and wife, brothers, and friends – these are the five great ways').

[49] See 《白虎通德伦》(Records of White Tiger Temple Seminar) 79 AD.

[50] 《孝经．广要道章》："安上治民莫善于礼。(*Classic of Filial Piety*, ch 12: 'In serving the supreme and governing the populace nothing is more appropriate than rituals').

[51] See Jerome Cohen, 'Chinese Mediation on the Eve of Modernization' (1966) 54 *California Law Review* 3, 1924; Lubman, 'Mao and Mediation: Politics and Dispute Resolution in Communist China' 1216–222; Hui-chen Wang Liu, *The Traditional Chinese Clan Rules* (Locust Valley, NY, Augustin, 1959); DJ MacGowan, 'Chinese Guilds or Chambers of Commerce and Trade Unions' (1888–1889) XXI *Journal of the North China Branch of the Royal Asiatic Society*.

[52] Cohen, 'Chinese Mediation on the Eve of Modernization'; Lubman, 'Mao and Mediation: Politics and Dispute Resolution in Communist China', 1216–22.

8.3 THE EMPHASIS ON HARMONY AND CONFLICT AVOIDANCE

Randle Edwards has characterised five themes of legal values underlying both ancient and contemporary Chinese law and legal institutions, one of which is the non-adversarial method of dispute resolution.[53] The reasons for this aversion towards litigation in traditional Chinese society can be explained by the philosophical influence of the pursuit of harmony (section 8.4.1), and by the traditional legal practice of suppressing litigation (section 8.4.2).

8.3.1 Philosophical Influence

The development of mediation has deeply embedded philosophical basis in traditional Chinese culture. Confucianists are the strongest advocates for avoiding litigation in order to maintain social harmony. Confucius believed that the optimal resolution of most disputes was to be achieved not by the exercise of legal power but by moral persuasion:

> Lead them by political maneuvers, restrain them with punishments: the people will become cunning and shameless. Lead them by virtue, restrain them with ritual: they will develop a sense of shame and a sense of participation.[54]

Confucius maintained that to rely solely or even predominantly on law to achieve social order was not ideal. Laws backed by punishments may induce compliance in the external behaviour of individuals, but they are powerless to transform the inner character of members of society. Confucius's goal was not simply a stable political order in which everyone coexists in relative harmony and isolation from each other, with each afraid to interfere with the other for fear of legal punishment. Rather, Confucius set his sights considerably higher. He sought to achieve a harmonious social order in which each person was able to realise his or her full potential as a human being through mutually beneficial relations with others. At the heart of Confucian teaching are the concepts of harmony (*he wei gui*), moderation in all things – the doctrine of middle way (*zhongyong*), concession or yielding (*rang*), and avoidance of litigation (*xisu*). This provides the philosophical basis for the development of mediation (*tiaojie*) in China.

From the perspectives of Confucianism, the preservation of harmony between humanity and nature, and the spheres of man and nature were thought of as forming a single continuum (*tian ren gan tong*).[55] Therefore, social disharmony

---

[53] Randle Edwards, Louis Henkin and Andrew Nathan (ed), *Human Rights in Contemporary China* (New York, Columbia University Press, 1986) 43–47.

[54] 《论语 • 为政第二》, translated by Simon Leys. Simon Leys, *The Analects of Confucius*, (New York, WW Norton and Company, 1997).

[55] Bodde and Morris, *Law in Imperial China*, 43; Huang, Legal Transplant and Recent Chinese Law, 7–9.

would lead to a violation of the whole cosmic order.[56] In the Confucian view, law is applied only to those who have fallen beyond the bounds of civilised behaviour. Civilised people are expected to observe proper rituals. Only social outcasts must have their actions controlled by the law. According to Confucianists, 'the legal process was not one of the highest achievements of Chinese civilisation but was, rather, a regrettable necessity'.[57] Involvement in a lawsuit symbolises disruption to social harmony and thus should be avoided at all costs. When a dispute occurred, Confucianism believes that the key to the successful resolution of the dispute is not to find whose rights have been infringed or to award damages to the innocent party. Rather, it is to educate the disputants about the moral precepts. Such moral precepts include the doctrine of middle way and concession. The doctrine of middle way advocates that the right course of action was always some middle point between two extremes, excess (too much) and deficiency (too little). The goal of mediation is the settlement of disputes through compromise, and finding the 'middle way' is an intrinsic part of mediation. Litigation is more about entrenched positions often offering extremes, which runs counter to basic Chinese instincts.[58]

Another important moral value that Confucius sought to teach was concession and self-criticism. Professor Goh Bee Chen made the following statements:

> In traditional view, when the Confucian gentleman was unreasonably treated by another, he ought to regard it as a result of some personal failings on his part and to seek the source and solution of the problem. He would then be seen to be engaged in self-criticism, a first step towards the cultivation of moral virtue. Thus, by this process of self-improvement, a positive response might come about from the other party and the problem which could lead to a dispute would thereby be terminated even before it started. The emphasis here is dispute dissipation, which bears a preventative quality, rather than dispute resolution, which may be regarded as a more remedial.[59]

In a society of a moral civil order, the domain of *li* is greater than the domain of *fa*. Conflicts can easily be resolved: to insist on one's rights will run counter to the spirit of *li*; thus both sides will be ready to make concessions.[60] A lawsuit implies some falling from virtue on one's own part through obstinacy or lack of moderation, or the failure to elicit an appropriate concession from another as a matter of respect for one's own 'face'. Thus, mediation took precedence over direct confrontation. The virtue of concession (*rang*) was strongly encouraged to ward off disharmony. In connection with *rang*, it was better to meet an opponent half-way than to stand on principle.

---

[56] Bodde and Morris, *Law in Imperial China*, 43–44; Phillip Chen, *Law and Justice: The Legal System in China 2400 BC to 1960 AD* (New Jersey, Dunellen Publishing Company, 1973) 14–15; Sybille van der Sprenkel, *Legal Institutions in Manchu China: A Sociological Analysis* (London, The Athlone Press, 1962) 29.
[57] Cohen, 'Chinese Mediation on the Eve of Modernization', 1206.
[58] Niall Lawless, 'Cultural Perspectives on China Resolving Disputes Through Mediation' (2008) 5 *Transnational Dispute Management* 4.
[59] Chen, *Law Without Lawyers, Justice Without Courts: On Traditional Chinese Mediation*, 68.
[60] Schwartz, 'On Attitudes Toward Law in China', 163–64.

Confucianism was not alone in advocating the pursuit of harmony. Legalists also took the prevention of disputes seriously, for the purpose of strengthening the state.[61] They believed that disputes among people would weaken the state. In order to win the case, disputants needed to spend time and resources. If there were too many disputes among the people, the state's productive capacity would decrease. For Taoism, being in harmony with nature and maintaining harmonic relationships with others are the happiest of achievements. Taoists take self-restraint as the essential element to form a harmonic society. The utopia Lao Zi depicted is a world without disputes. The way of heaven prefers the state of being natural. One who has no disputes with others acts in accordance with the Way of Heaven. The idea is expressed as the 'inactiveness of Heaven'.[62] Despite the ideological differences, all major schools of traditional Chinese philosophies shared one common theme – the pursuit of harmony, which is considered to be paramount to maintaining social stability.[63] Different schools of philosophy propose divergent ways to eliminate disputes: Confucianism by way of moral persuasion through li, Legalists deterred people from having disputes by punishments; and Taoism by self-restraints and inactiveness. This common belief in pursuit of harmony created a culture in traditional Chinese society in which litigation was considered the last resort because it signified the breakdown of social harmony. This culture has greatly influenced the development of dispute resolution in China.

8.3.2 Practice to Suppress Litigation

Apart from philosophical influences, the magistrate's suppression of litigation (section 8.3.2.A) and the limitation on an individual's right to sue within local groups (section 8.3.2.B) also contributed to the Chinese traditional culture of aversion towards litigation.

A. *Suppression of Litigation by Local Magistrates*

On opening any Chinese historical books, one will find anecdotes of local magistrates being praised for their 'achievement' in minimising lawsuits by successfully persuading the general public to make concessions and avoid conflicts. Litigation was condemned as a moral wrongdoing to society and the other party. Too many lawsuits filed by the general public were considered to impose too heavy a burden on the government's workload and should be avoided. A good judge was thus supposed to promote a settlement by 'good persuasion'. Furthermore, state resources were limited. The magistrate received a budget to

---

[61] For the conceptual differences between Confucianism and Legalism, *see* s 8.1.1.
[62] See, Bobby Wong, 'Chinese law: Traditional Chinese Philosophy and Dispute Resolution' (2000) 30 *Hong Kong Law Journal* 313–15.
[63] See *ibid*, 304.

cover all expenses, including the costs of administering justice. The funds fell far short of the amount required to meet all of the costs of government. By relying heavily on informal mechanisms to resolve disputes, magistrates were able to put the available funds to other, arguably more productive, uses.

In the Ming dynasty, the officials at Song Jiang area followed such a practice: when a lawsuit was filed, the magistrate would persuade the parties to return home and rethink their differences carefully. If a compromise could not be found, the parties could come back the next day to initiate the litigation formally.[64] Officials considered that the majority of lawsuits could be avoided by skillful persuasion with *li* or moral standards/social norms, and thus harmony could be achieved. They stressed the virtue of yielding (*rang*) and the superiority of non-contentiousness. The mediation technique that they often used was self-criticism, making the disputant ask himself, 'what did I do to cause this?' This spirit of self-criticism is consistent with Confucian ideology – the model Confucian gentleman did not insist on his 'rights' or on the correctness of his position, but settled a dispute through mutual concessions that permitted each to save face and maintain the relationship. Thus, the moment when the parties realise that their actions have contributed to the dispute is often a turning point for settlement.

On the whole, extra-judicial dispute settlement by mediation offered considerable advantages to litigants and government. First, mediation afforded the parties 'a method of terminating disputes that was socially acceptable in the light of Confucian ethic and group mores'.[65] Because prevailing social values stressed the importance of saving face and reaching a compromise satisfactory to both parties, disputants were better able to bargain with each other during mediation than in more formal proceedings. Mediation emphasised the necessity of avoiding conflict, observing proper rules of behaviour, and relying on the social group to resolve differences, it provided auxiliary support for the dissemination of Confucian standards and values. Second, the perils of litigation restrained many people from bringing suit at the magistrate's *yamen* and left them with few alternatives to the non-adversarial means of settling disputes.[66] A number of the ancient Chinese proverbs reflect the attitude of the Chinese people towards litigation and the general lack of confidence in the formal judicial process. For instance, 'to enter a court of law is to enter a tiger's mouth', 'of ten reasons by which a magistrate may decide a case, nine are unknown to the public', 'avoid litigation; for once you resort to law there is nothing but trouble', 'the yamen (the court) gate is wide open, with rights but

---

[64] This practice is said to have been initiated by an official named Zhao Yu. A popular local saying, 'come back tomorrow for your lawsuit at Song Jiang Prefecture' (松江太守明日来) describes this practice at Song Jiang area. See Guo, Discussions of Chinese Legal Culture, 207.

[65] Cohen, 'Chinese Mediation on the Eve of Modernization'.

[66] See, for instance, Lubman, *Bird in a Cage: Legal Reform in China After Mao*, 24; Wang, 'The Unification of the Dispute Resolution System in China: Cultural, Economic and Legal Contributions', 9.

no money, don't go in'. Finally, extra-judicial mediation eased the government workload and helped avoid friction between magistrates and persons and groups in their jurisdiction.[67]

To be sure, we cannot assume that the Chinese court system had always been mediatory rather than adjudicatory. The discovery and opening up of archival collections in Taiwan and the PRC in recent decades have revealed for the first time details of the way in which Qing magistrates handled civil disputes. Studies based on these archives tend to emphasise the important of law and legal institutions in the resolution of civil disputes in Qing dynasty. For instance, Professor Melissa Macauley revisited the dynamic relationship between state and society in her social history of China's litigation masters. Her narrative portrays that the Chinese society in Qing dynasty was much more litigious than one previously thought.[68] Professor Philip Huang, by analysing 628 Qing court cases pertaining to land, debt, marriage, and inheritance, the four major types of civil cases from three provinces, presented a rather sophisticated civil justice system in Qing dynasty. In the great majority of the 221 cases that persisted into a formal court session (most of others being settled through societal mediation), the courts ruled according to the Qing code.[69] These studies present a far more complicated picture of the judicial system in China than the 'traditional' view.[70]

Nevertheless, it should be noted that the archives these recent studies relied on were mainly from Qing dynasty, and cannot be said to reflect the tradition throughout the Chinese history. Further, the studies only relied on a portion of

---

[67] Lubman, *Bird in a Cage: Legal Reform in China After Mao*, 26, Utter, Justice Robert F, 'Dispute Resolution in China' (1987) 62 *Washington Law Review* 383.

[68] Melissa Macauley, *Social Power and Legal Culture: Litigation Masters in Late Imperial China* (Stanford, Stanford University Press, 1999).

[69] Philip Huang, 'Between Informal Mediation and Formal Adjudication: The Third Realm of Qing Civil Justice' (1993) 19 *Modern China* 3, Tables E1, E2, E2. Philip Huang, *Civil justice in China : Representation and Practice in the Qing* (Stanford, Stanford University Press, 1996), Table 3. (In 170 of the cases (76.9%) the courts found out-right for one or the other party, in 22 other cases (10%), they adjudged that there was no clear-cut violation of the law by either party; and in another 10 cases (5%), they ordered further investigation. Only a small minority of court rulings for one or the other party (a total of 6.4%) were accompanied by compromises in the interest of maintaining kin or community harmony. In no case did the court engage in compromise-working through persuasion and moral education to obtain the supposedly voluntary agreement of the litigants.)

[70] See also, (日)夫马进,《明清时期的诉师与诉讼制度》, 载滋贺秀三[日],《明清时期的民事审判与民间契约》(Fu Majin (Japan), 'The Litigation Masters and Litigation System in Ming and Qing Dynasties', in しが・しゅうぞう, *The Civil Trial and Social Contract During the Ming and Qing Period*); 侯欣一,《清代江南地区民间的健讼问题 — 以地方志为中心的考察》,《法学研究》第4辑, 2006年, (Xinyi Hou, 'The Litigation Propensity in the South of Yangtze River Area in Qing Dynasty – An Investigation Focused on Local Gazetteers', 2006 (4) *Legal Studies*); 刘馨珺,《明镜高悬：南宋县衙的狱讼》(北京, 北京大学出版社, 2007), (Xinjun Liu, *A Just Trial by an Honest Official: Litigation at the Yamen in South Song Dynasty* (Beijing, Beijing University Press, 2007)); 陈俊,《清代简约型司法体制下的健讼问题研究 — 从财政制约的角度切入》,《法商研究》第2辑, 2012年 (Chenjun You, 'The Problem of Litigation Propensity under the Simple Legal System of Qing Dynasty – From the Perspective of the Financial Restraints', 2012(2), *Legal and Commercial Studies*); 邓建鹏,《讼师秘本与清代诉状的风格 — 以"黄岩诉讼档案"为考察中心》,《浙江社会科学》第4辑, 2005年 (Jianpeng Deng, 'The Secret of Litigation Masters and the Style of Qing Litigation Complaint – An Investigation Focused on the Huangyan Litigation Archive', 2005(4) *Zhejiang Social Science*).

selected cases, which may not necessarily be representative. Even in Qing dynasty, Huang himself acknowledged that 'despite the reality of adjudicatory actions by the courts, the Qing held on tightly to the ideal of settling disputes among the people by societal mediation'.[71]

B. Limitation on Individual's Right to Sue within Local Groups

Furthermore, the existing social institutions (ie, the family, clan, village and guild) played a significant role in dispute resolution in traditional Chinese society, frequently outweighing the role of the formal courts of law.[72] The local groups generally attempted to avoid the participation of government officials in settling quarrels of their members. Recourse to a magistrate without prior attempts to settle disputes within groups was actively discouraged and sometimes prohibited by the group's internal regulations.[73]

Within the small family itself, the head of the family – father or grandfather (*jia zhang*) – controlled and supervised general family matters. Conflicts within the family were frequently decided by the head of the family, whose authority was absolute. Yet it is often believed that the head of the family also sought to reconcile the disputes.[74] As the Chinese saying goes 'family scandals cannot be exposed to outsiders', most disputes among the family members were resolved internally within the family.

The clan (*zu*) can be considered as extended family. The clan rules generally put the promotion of cooperation and harmony between clan members as one of their principal objectives. The primary duty of the clan heads was to preserve social harmony within the clan itself.[75] For instance, the rules of the Hsu clan in Kiangsu required the head of the clan to settle matters to avoid lawsuits:

> If there should occur in the zu any attempts at oppression of the young by relying on one's age, at bullying the weak by relying on one's strength, or, worse, should quarrels and fights take place, these cases should be brought before the head of the zu. He is to convene the whole zu to discuss the matter publicly and to settle the matter so that the injuries between 'bond and flesh' (near relatives) or lawsuits that ruin the family may be avoided.[76]

---

[71] Philip Huang, 'Court Mediation in China, Past and Present' (2006) 32 *Modern China* 3.
[72] See for instance, Cohen, 'Chinese Mediation on the Eve of Modernization'; Lubman, 'Mao and Mediation: Politics and Dispute Resolution in Communist China'; Chen, *Law Without Lawyers, Justice Without Courts: On Traditional Chinese Mediation*; Sprenkel, *Legal Institutions in Manchu China*. See, above s 8.2.
[73] Lubman, 'Mao and Mediation: Politics and Dispute Resolution in Communist China', 1297. Cohen, 'Chinese Mediation on the Eve of Modernization', 1223.
[74] See Cohen, 'Chinese Mediation on the Eve of Modernization', 1216–17.
[75] ibid; Lubman, 'Mao and Mediation: Politics and Dispute Resolution in Communist China'; Sprenkel, *Legal Institutions in Manchu China: A Sociological Analysis*.
[76] Hsien Chin Hu, *The Common Descent Group in China and its Fuctions* (New York, The Viking Fund, 1948) 133.

200 *Traditional Legal Culture*

In villages,[77] disputes were resolved by the village heads or other informal leaders who were respected because of their age, knowledge, or reputation. These village officials were

> usually eager to settle disputes outside the magistrate's yamen, because the magistrate held them responsible for lack of harmony within the village and they knew that he did not want to be bothered with a large volume of petty litigation.[78]

In guilds – collective merchant associations,[79] the members were constrained from resolving disputes through litigation. Resolving disputes through internal channels was preferred. To prevent litigation, the guilds provided an internal mechanism for dispute resolution:

> Among members of our compatriots who come here there are those who engage in business transactions and have current accounts, as well as those who enter into joint speculations. It is impossible to say that disputes may not arise among them. If anything of the sort occurs, the guild may settle the difficulty in the manner most advantageous to all. Justice shall be observed, and the facts of the case brought to light. That justice may be manifested, there must be no concealment.[80]

To summarise, local groups generally actively encouraged – or in the case of clans and guilds, *required* – the parties to exhaust their remedies within the group before looking to the magistrate for relief. These groups held 'informal sway' in the ordinary person's life and 'helped to smooth the inevitable frictions in the Chinese society by inculcating moral precepts upon their members, mediating disputes, or, if need arose, imposing disciplinary sanctions and penalties'.[81] The magistrate,

> overburdened with the duties of administering the country and of disposing of homicide, theft and other cases in which the government had a vital interest, often cooperated in enforcing this requirement by sending back to the village, clan or guild minor disputes that had not been proceeded by it.[82]

8.4 COMMERCIAL HISTORY AND DISPUTE RESOLUTION

A legal system is based on and shaped by a certain economic structure. Economic conditions also influence the development of a legal system. To

---

[77] A village can consist of only one family with the same surname, ie, from the same clan. Therefore, the village leadership and lineage structure appeared to be connected. See Sprenkel, *Legal Institutions in Manchu China*, 19.

[78] Cohen, 'Chinese Mediation on the Eve of Modernization', 1219.

[79] For a more detailed discussion of the practices of the guilds in ancient China, see, ss 8.3.2-B and 8.4.2-B below.

[80] Jernigan, *China in Law and Commerce*, 210.

[81] Bodde and Morris, *Law in Imperial China*, 5–6; Sprenkel, *Legal Institutions in Manchu China: A Sociological Analysis*. (In her study of Qing legal institutions, she also emphasised the great extent to which conflicts were resolved through informal, non-judicial mediation in the family clan, craft or merchant guild.)

[82] Cohen, 'Chinese Mediation on the Eve of Modernization', 1223.

understand commercial regulations in imperial China, it is therefore useful to take a look at commercial history.

8.4.1 Agrarian Economy and Lack of Commercial Laws

Historically, the Chinese economy was predominately a small-scale peasant economy, in which people were self-sufficient and self-employed (*zi ji zi zu*) on their own land. Throughout dynastic China, it was agriculture that was the driving force of the economy. Commerce and trade were not essential.[83]

There were, nevertheless, records of the existence of trade and commerce in dynastic China. According to the historians, from the Shang dynasty to the end of the Spring and Autumn Periods, the size of the merchant community remained small by reason of a relative lack of demand for merchant services.[84] During the Warring States Period, a small number of wealthy merchants reached social prominence through the purchase of land and offices for the first time.[85] Commercial activities continued to increase in the Han dynasty. Comparing the contemporaneous Han dynasty and the Roman legal system, Professor Hugh Scogin noted that 'markets, commercial transactions and contracts . . . were present in China earlier, and to a greater extent, than they were in the West'. Both the Han dynasty and Roman legal systems ratified contracts through writings and witnesses. The physical format and the use of documents were 'remarkably consistent'.[86] In the meantime, the central Asian sections of the trade routes, such as the Silk Road, were expanded around 114 BC by the Han dynasty, largely through the missions of the Han diplomat Zhang Qian (? – 114 BC),[87] although earlier trade routes across the continents already existed. The Silk Road served as an extensive network of trading routes connecting China with the Middle East, Western Asia (eg, India) and the Mediterranean world, North and North East Africa, as well as Europe. Extending over 4,000 miles, these routes enabled the Chinese to trade with other countries, by exporting goods such as silk, satin and other fine fabrics, musk, perfumes, spices, medicines, jewels, glassware outside China and importing plants, furs, spices, medicines, and jewellery into China. In the Tang and Song Dynasties, China experienced the first 'commercial revolution'.[88] According to Shi Chenxia,

---

[83] Conrad Schirokauer, *A Brief History of Chinese Civilization* (New York, City University of New York, 1991).

[84] Wellington Chan, *Merchants, Mandarins and Modern Enterprise in Late Ch'ing China* (Cambridge, Mass, Havard University Press, 1977) 15.

[85] Chenxia Shi, 'Commercial Development and Regulation in Late Imperial China: An Historical Review' (2005) 35 *Hong Kong Law Journal* 483.

[86] Hugh Scogin, 'Between Heaven and Man: Contract and State in Han Dynasty China' (1990) 62 *South California Law Review* 1325, 1372–75.

[87] Luce Boulnois, *Silk Road: Monks, Warriors & Merchants* (Hong Kong, Odyssey Publications, 2005) 66.

[88] Mark Elvin, *The Pattern of the Chinese Past* (London, Eyre Methuen, 1973).

beginning with the Song dynasty, credit facilities, trade, and the handicraft industry had developed into a complex network of inter-regional activities by merchants and officials that operated under the cover of correct ideology. Around 1000 AD Chinese society experienced a massive increase of domestic markets and inter-regional trade.[89]

In the Ming and Qing Dynasties, trade and large-scale commercialisation in the economy were tremendously developed.

As far as the general economic conditions in the country were concerned, agriculture, not trade, still occupied the dominant position.[90] Self-sufficient natural economy was the main form of production. Farming was the major industry and land was the main source of wealth as markets for commodities were small for a lengthy period of time in Chinese history. The scope of commercial activities was limited.

> Despite some rapid commercial and industrial development in the late Qing period and the emergence of a capitalist economy in the early nineteenth century, the economy remained overwhelmingly agrarian, with 95% of the population still living in villages and market towns.[91]

The policy of 'emphasizing agriculture and repressing commerce' (*zhong nong yi shang*) dominated Chinese society for thousands of years, which hindered the development of commerce and trade in dynastic China. The state traditionally regarded agrarian societies as the proper social base for the empire. In an ideal agrarian order, 'the overwhelming majority of the people would live off the land, producing their own food and clothing and providing the state with revenue and military recruits'.[92] As a result, the merchants enjoyed a very low social status and no particular legal protection was provided for them. People were generally classified into four classes in ancient China: ranked at the top of the society was the warrior-administrator, followed by the farmers who, in turn, were followed by the artists and artisans, with merchants at the bottom of the ladder. Indeed, the merchants were subjected to overwhelming state control and exploitation. Their rights and social status were restricted by law in terms of social mobility and lifestyle. The merchants paid heavy taxes and could not wear silk or own land. Even their descendants were barred from becoming officials which was traditionally a source of many rights and privileges in China.[93]

Under such an economic and political structure, commercial laws in imperial China did not develop as they did in the West. For instance, out of 436 statutes

---

[89] Shi, 'Commercial Development and Regulation in Late Imperial China: An Historical Review', 484.

[90] Fang Xing, *Chinese Feudal Economic Structure and Capitalist Germination, Historical Research*, vol 4, 1981.

[91] Shi, 'Commercial Development and Regulation in Late Imperial China: An Historical Review', 485–86.

[92] ibid.

[93] Chan, *Merchants, Mandarins and Modern Enterprise in Late Ch'ing China*, 18.

in the Qing Code, only eight dealt with commercial trade.[94] The Tang Code was one of the few compilations where the law dealt with commercial trade. A provision of the Tang Code stated that disputes between foreigners of the same nationality should be determined by referring to the foreigners' customs and laws; disputes between foreigners of different nationalities should be resolved under the Code.[95] Unfortunately, no subsequent body of commercial law was developed after the Tang dynasty. In fact, commercial law became rather useless once the Ming dynasty banned foreign trade, as the emperor considered that trade meant movement and change, which would threaten imperial China's status quo.[96] As there was little formal code to regulate commercial practices, commercial activities were mainly regulated through the tax system under the economic principle that 'no one could claim the right to do business without paying the tax'.[97] The supplementary tax collection system was used by the government to grant merchants the right to make profits from the commercial activities they monopolised and therefore ensure the state's income from the supplementary tax.[98]

8.4.2 Resolution of Commercial Disputes

A. *Government-organised Marketplaces*

While in Europe foreign trade led to the settlement of commercial disputes through the private courts of Law Merchant and the staple fairs, no similar mechanism came into being in China. Different from the Law Merchant fairs, the Chinese conducted trade in government-organised marketplaces. Merchants operating in those marketplaces were registered and had to pay certain commercial taxes.[99] The best documented example is the market of the Eastern Han capital, Lo-yang. An administrative force of 36 supervised the registration process, periodically set basic prices, and supervised sales contracts.[100] This regulation applied only to merchants in these urban marketplaces, who were generally persons of low status. On the market sites, there were officials called *zhi ren*, whose role was to harmonise sales and sale prices in the market place and to draft contracts for parties to sales agreements.[101]

---

[94] Rosser Brockman, 'Commercial Contract Law in Late Nineteenth-Century Taiwan' in Jerome Cohen, Randle Edwards and Fu-Mei Chang Chen (eds), *Essays on China's Legal Tradition* (Princeton, Princeton University Press, 1980) 85–87.
[95] 长孙无忌:《唐律疏议》(Zhang Sun Wuji, *Annotated Commentaries on the Laws of Tang Dynasty*).
[96] Gemmell, *Western and Chinese Arbitration: The Arbitral Chain*, 123.
[97] Eiichi Motono, *Conflict and Cooperation in Sino-British Business, 1860–1911: The Impact of the Pro-British Commercial Network in Shanghai* (London, Macmillan, 2000) 5.
[98] Shi, 'Commercial Development and Regulation in Late Imperial China: An Historical Review', 485.
[99] Scogin, 'Between Heaven and Man: Contract and State in Han Dynasty China', 1400.
[100] ibid, citing Hans Bielenstein, 'Lo-yang in Later Han Times' (1976) 48 *Bulletin of Museum Far East Antiquities* 1, 58–59.
[101] ibid.

B. *Guilds* (hanghui) *and* Landsmannschaften (huiguan)

As the government failed to address the merchants' growing needs and to protect their legal status, the merchants united to protect themselves by organising collective merchant associations (*hanghui*),[102] often translated generically as 'guilds' – associations of people for mutual aid or the pursuit of a common goal.[103] When these trade associations first appeared, they were identified as *huiguan*, meaning literally 'club-houses', formed by merchants whose native place was different and usually far away from the city in which they were residing. In this respect, the term *huiguan* resembled more of the concept *Landsmannschaf* in medieval Europe – commercial associations based on a common geographical location.[104] Broadly speaking, three types of guilds existed in traditional China: (i) craft guilds – associations organised by craftsmen in the same industry; (ii) trade guilds – associations organised by merchants in the same industry, such as fish guilds, fruit guilds, meat guilds; and (iii) professional guilds – other associations, which were neither purely commercial, nor based on craft skills.[105] In earlier times, the craft and trade guilds were similar in many ways, and both began in the Sui dynasty.[106]

It is important to note that the guilds in imperial China were of a form and nature different from the merchant guilds in medieval Europe: In medieval Europe, merchant guilds arose to provide protection to foreign merchants away from their homes, but also protection for local merchants against fly-by-night foreign merchants. As merchants began to transact beyond the political, cultural and geographical barriers, they transported local trade practices to foreign markets. The bonds of localised systems were broken to develop an international system of commercial law – *lex mercatoria* or Law Merchant.[107] By the end of the eleventh century, *lex mercatoria* came to govern most commercial transactions in Europe, providing a uniform set of standards across large numbers of locations. In imperial China, however, rules of the merchant guilds had

---

[102] For a discussion on the guilds in ancient China, see Greif, Milgrom and Weingast, 'Coordination, Commitment, and Enforcement: The Case of the Merchant Guild'; Kwang-Ching Liu, 'Chinese Merchant Guilds: An Historical Inquiry' (1988) 57 *Pacific Historical Review* 1; DJ MacGowan, 'Chinese Guilds or Chambers of Commerce and Trade Unions' (1888–1889) XXI *Journal of the North China Branch of the Royal Asiatic Society*; 全汉升, 《中国行会制度史》(天津, 百花文艺出版社, 2007), (Hansheng Quan, *History of the Guild System in China*) (Tianjin, Baihua Wenyi Press, 2007); 史景星, 《行业协会概论》(上海, 复旦大学出版社, 1989), (Jingxing Shi, *The Overview of the Chinese Guilds* (Shanghai, Fudan University Press, 1989)); 彭泽益 (编), 《中国工商行会史料集》(香港, 中华书局, 1995), (Zeyi Peng (ed), *A Collection of Historical Materials on Chinese Industrial and Commercial Guilds* (Hong Kong, China Books, 1995)).
[103] Concise Oxford English Dictionary, 11th edn (Oxford University Press, 2009).
[104] The term '*Landsmannschaft*' was first used to describe Chinese guilds by MacGowan, 'Chinese Guilds or Chambers of Commerce and Trade Unions', 133–92, esp 144. See also Liu, 'Chinese Merchant Guilds: An Historical Inquiry', n 20.
[105] See, Quan, *History of the Guild System in China*, 50–53.
[106] See ibid.
[107] Milgrom, North and Weingast, 'The Role of Institutions in the Revival of Trade: The Law Merchant, Private Judges, and the Champagne Fairs', 4.

never reached such a level of consistency and transparency. Different from *lex mercatoria*, the merchant manuals created within the Chinese guilds also dealt with human relations in the business world, in particular from the perspective of Confucian tradition. The merchant manuals addressed the spiritual and ethical needs of people pursuing commercial professions, apart from providing advice on commercial success and social respectability. They advocated moral values, such as sincerity, seriousness, trustworthiness, seriousness, reciprocity and an enlightened self-interest, in line with Confucianism. [108]

Furthermore, the Chinese guilds were organised on a personal level, not a systemic organisational level. They had to rely on social networks and government support. Chinese businesses have traditionally been part of social networks based on family and geographical affiliation.[109] Social networks and connections can bring about private business agreements underpinned by interpersonal customs, not by economic transaction cost-based contracts.[110] In this sense, 'the institutional entrenchment that can arise from such a structure may cause managers to subscribe to moralities that keep the networks in harmony, but which might not be helpful to achieve economic efficiency'.[111]

There is no similar tradition of *lex mercatoria* – that 'modern international commercial arbitration has purported to ground itself in expeditious, low cost, informal and speedy mercantile justice'[112] – in Chinese history. In medieval Europe, disputes over transactions at merchant fairs required a resolution mechanism that suited the needs of the merchant class, which paved the way for the development of arbitration. Disputes were resolved by arbitrators out of the merchant class itself. Arbitration, like *lex mercatoria*, was outside the judicial system of any nation, and amounted to self-regulation by the merchant class.[113] In ancient China, however, merchant guilds have not pushed for the development of a similar dispute resolution mechanism. The purpose of the guilds was to enhance the friendly relations between the members, not to litigate or adjudicate the cases.[114] If disputes between members could not be settled by friends, witnesses of a transaction, or middlemen, they were sometimes heard in the guild hall by a group of guild officers. On occasions like these, parties and witnesses would give testimony, and then a decision would be reached. The rules of the guilds have provided for the settlement of disputes among their members such as in the following:

---

[108] Richard John Lufrano, *Honorable Merchants: Commerce and Self-Cultivation in Late Imperial China* (Honolulu, University of Hawaii Press, 1997).
[109] Shi, 'Commercial Development and Regulation in Late Imperial China: An Historical Review', 489.
[110] Masahiko Aoki, Bo Gustafsson and Oliver E. Williamson, *The Firm as a Nexus of Treaties* (London, Sage, 1990).
[111] Shi, 'Commercial Development and Regulation in Late Imperial China: An Historical Review', 489–90.
[112] Trackman, 'Legal Traditions and International Commercial Arbitration'.
[113] Burdick, 'What is the Law Merchant', 472–75.
[114] See s 8.3.2-B above.

It is agreed that members having disputes about money matters with each other shall submit their cases to arbitration at a meeting of the guild, where the utmost will be done to arrive at a satisfactory settlement of the dispute. If it is proven impossible to arrive at an understanding, appeal may be made to the authorities, but if the complainant has recourse to the official direct, without first referring to the guild, he shall be subjected to a public reprimand.[115]

Despite the use of the term 'arbitration', the notion of such internal resolution mechanism cannot be said to be equivalent to that of the fair arbitration in medieval Europe. The prevailing notions of dispute settlement emphasised that guild leaders should try to make the parties compromise to arrive at a 'satisfactory' settlement. Furthermore, remedies within the guild had to be exhausted before the parties could bring the matter to a formal tribunal.

It should be noted that the function of the dispute resolver in traditional Chinese society was neither equivalent to that of a mediator nor that of an arbitrator defined in the Western context. Sometimes their role resembled that of an arbitrator, who heard the arguments of the parties and then handed down a decision. Although not directly enforceable as a judgment, such decision was often respected by the disputing parties. In the closely-knit context of social life, social pressure largely supplanted legal coercion as a method of settling disputes. Having said that, it is likely that on numerous occasions the dispute resolver performed a conciliatory role in suggesting ways in which the disputants could come to a compromise or in suggesting possible solutions satisfactory to both disputing parties. In that sense, their role may be comparable to that of a mediator, who assists the parties to arrive at a satisfactory settlement. However, they did not merely act as a channel of communication between the disputants, but played a far greater role. They were seen as 'authoritative, instructive, educative' people who bore a 'social responsibility for maintaining peace, unity, order and stability'.[116] The notion of settlement facilitation and decision making was historically blurred in Chinese minds. [117]

As the Chinese saying goes, 'we may sleep in the same bed but dream different dreams'. Even when the same term is used, the connotations, the perceptions, conceptions and management of these proceedings may vary significantly, due to the divergent cultural background and legal traditions in different societies. Commercial arbitration, as an external resolution mechanism,[118] which was essentially based on private law such as *jus civile* in ancient Roman law and *lex mercatoria* in medieval Europe lacked roots in Chinese soil. Even though there

---

[115] Jernigan, *China in Law and Commerce*, 209.

[116] Michael Palmer, 'The Revival of Mediation in the People's Republic of China: (1) Extra-Judicial Mediation' in WE Butler (ed), *Yearbook on Socialist Legal Systems* (Ardsley, New York, Transnational Publishers, 1987) 224, 244.

[117] For a discussion of the different notions of mediation and arbitration in Chinese and Western legal traditions, see Kun Fan, 'Glocalisation of Arbitration: Transnational Standards Struggling with Local Norms' (2013) *Harvard Negotiation Law Review*.

[118] On the two paradigms of dispute resolution, namely, internal resolution and external resolution, see Donald Clarke, 'Dispute Resolution in China' (1991) 5 *Journal of Chinese Law*, 245.

was reference to the term 'arbitration' in the literature, it was, in fact, a method of internal resolution within the social institutions, rather than a semi-formal neutral institution which resolved disputes on the principles of free will and the concept of 'private justice'. Professor Gemmell concluded in his study that no 'arbitral chain' could be found in Chinese history.[119] It is true at least to the extent that no similar historical link and substantial degree of continuity from Roman arbitration to modern day arbitration could be found in Chinese history.

C. Transplantation of Arbitration in China

The establishment of chambers of commerce in the last Qing dynasty paved the way for the emergence of commercial arbitration in China. It is generally understood that the system of commercial arbitration was transplanted from the West in the late-Qing and early-Republican period.

In 1904, the first chamber of commerce – a modern merchant's association – came into being. The chambers of commerce were granted the right and duty to mediate and arbitrate the commercial disputes between Chinese merchants, as well as commercial disputes between Chinese and foreign merchants.[120] Shortly after the establishment of the chambers of commerce, there were discussions about setting up specialised commercial arbitration institutions. The Western model of commercial arbitration was introduced in the Official Journal of Commerce in 1906.[121] However, when the Western notion of 'arbitration' was imported to China, there was much discussion on the use of terminology.

The chambers of commerce proposed adopting the term 'adjudication' (*caipan*). In 1907, the first institution established by the Chengdu Chamber of Commerce was called a 'commercial adjudicatory institute' (*shangshi caipansuo*).[122]

Subsequently, such proposal was rejected by the Ministry of Justice, as they were suspicious about the establishment of an independent body which could exercise an adjudicatory function outside the state courts. The government suggested, or indeed imposed, the adoption of the term 'arbitration' (*gongduan*), in order to distinguish the power of these institutions from judicial courts. An important limitation was imposed on their scope of authority, in that their decisions would not be binding unless both parties accepted them. In 1909, the institutions established under the Chongqing and Baoding Chambers of Commerce adopted the name 'commercial arbitral body' (*shangshi gongduanchu*). Since then, other newly established bodies under the chambers of commerce consistently used the term 'commercial arbitral body'.

[119] Gemmell, *Western and Chinese Arbitration: The Arbitral Chain*.
[120] 《奏定商会简明章程二十六条》(Twenty Six Rules of Simplified Arts of Association for the Chambers of Commerce).
[121] 杨志洵,《商业机关释》,《商务官报》第25期, 光绪三十二年十一月初五日, 第6页。Zhizun Yang, *Explanation of Commercial Bodies*, 25 *Official Journal of Commerce* (1906) 6).
[122] 《四川成都商会商事裁判所规则》,《华商联合报》第17期, "海内外公牍", 第1页。(*Rules of the Commercial Adjudicatory Institute of Sichuan Chengdu Chamber of Commerce, 17 United Journal of Chinese Merchants*, 1).

In 1912, the Ministry of Justice defined the scope of authority of the newly established commercial arbitral bodies in a reply to the Ministry of Industry and Commerce as follows:

> The commercial arbitral bodies are to 'arbitrate', and their functions should be distinguished from the national courts. Those commercial bodies are empowered to mediate commercial disputes between the merchants. When they exercise the power to arbitrate, the decision must be accepted by both parties to be binding, and there should not be a compulsory element (emphasis added). If one party does not agree with the result of arbitration, he may bring the matter to the courts.[123]

The authority of commercial arbitral bodies was further clarified in their Articles of Association in 1913, which provided that 'the result of arbitration must be accepted by both parties to be binding; if one party is not satisfied with the result, he may appeal'.[124]

When the Western model of arbitration was first imported into China, there was a reluctance to recognise an important feature of arbitration – the adjudicatory function and the finality of the result. The transplanted institutions (so-called 'commercial arbitral bodies') were given local traits, in that they did not have the adjudicatory function and their decisions were not binding unless both parties accepted them. After a complex process of selection, resistance, reform and integration, the binding effect of an arbitral decision was finally recognised in 1923 in the draft Arbitration Act.[125] This process demonstrates the complex interplay among the state actors (eg, Ministry of Finance, Ministry of Industry and Commerce) and non-state actors (eg, chambers of commerce) and the active role they play in conceptualising the borrowed institution.[126]

8.5 ANALYSIS OF HISTORICAL LINKS TO MODERN PRACTICE

This journey into China's past may help to resolve some of our questions. Chinese arbitration practice, with the emphasis on amicable resolution, the role of *guanxi* and *renqing* in arbitral practice, and Chinese flexibility to get around the rigidity of law, can be traced back to China's legal traditions. It is now time to summarise our findings on history in order to see how these traditions can explain today's legal practice.

---

[123] 《司法部咨工商部商事公断处准援案设立如有一造不服仍应受法庭审判之》,《政府公报》, 1912年7月10日, 第71号 "公文", 引自虞和平,《清末民初商会的商事仲裁制度建设》,《学术月刊》 2004年第4辑, 第90页. (A Reply from the Ministry of Justice Concerning the Jurisdiction of the Court if One Party Disagrees with the Arbitration Result, 10 July 1912, Official Gazette No 71, cited in Heping Yu, 'The Construction of a Commercial Arbitration System in Late-Qing and Early-Republican China' (2004) 4 *Academic Monthly* 90.

[124] 《商事公断处章程》 (Articles of Association of the Commercial Arbitral Bodies).

[125] 《公断法草案》 (Draft Arbitration Act).

[126] For a discussion of the transplantation of arbitration in China, see Fan, 'Glocalisation of Arbitration: Transnational Standards Struggling with Local Norms'.

8.5.1 Flexibility in Implementation of the Law and the Emphasis on Equity – The Historical Emphasis on Rituals

First of all, in traditional Chinese legal culture, the law was disregarded by the general public, due to the conceptual limitation of the meaning of law, the influence of Confucian philosophy emphasising *li*, the codification centered on criminal offences, the rigidity of written law, and the frequent reference to *qing* in the implementation of the law. The rule of law was not developed, despite the comprehensive codification of written laws. In that sense, traditional Chinese society was characterised by the rule of *li* as opposed to the rule of *fa*. How is this tradition reflected in modern practice?

The review of current arbitration practice in China demonstrates that there is a wide gap between the laws written on paper and their implementation in actual practice. To deal with the uncertainty in the outcome, a notion of 'finding flexible ways around laws' (*biantong*) seems to make the normative force of law somewhat weaker in China than elsewhere. This is evidenced by the inconsistent court decisions illustrated in the case studies above.[127]

Apart from the deficiencies in the legislation, one may find a linkage or continuation from the sentiment of *qing* in traditional Chinese society to the notion of *biantong*. Like the ancient officials (judges) who relied heavily on the unique features of the special circumstance and on reasonableness to determine each individual case, today's arbitrators in China also rely heavily on equitable principles. Law is only one of the factors to be considered to determine the rights of the parties, together with equity and reasonableness. In the Chinese saying, 'a just decision must be in conformity with law and reasonableness' (*he li he fa*).

The Arbitration Law expressly states that 'in arbitration, disputes shall be resolved on the basis of facts, in compliance with law and *in a fair and reasonable manner* (emphasis added)'.[128] In practice, a review of arbitral awards shows that, in the early years, the CIETAC's predecessors placed more emphasis on the principle of fairness than on the law in rendering their decisions. They were keen on resolving disputes in a way that would result in each disputing party making a compromise, and thus some pertinent legal issues may not have been adequately treated.[129] According to a series of interviews conducted by the author and Professor Kaufmann-Kohler in March–April 2007, most of the Chinese arbitrators consider that the fairness consideration is still quite relevant in their decision making, particularly for issues on which the law is vague.[130] This is different from the principle of '*ex equo et bono*' or '*amiable compositeur*' in the West, which

---

[127] See, ch2, s2.1.2 and s.2.2.2 C; ch 4, s4.2.3.
[128] Art 7 of the Arbitration Law.
[129] Wang, 'The Unification of the Dispute Resolution System in China: Cultural Economic and Legal Contributions', 30–31.
[130] Introduction, fn 18.

allows the arbitrators to render a decision solely based on equitable principles, only if the parties grant them such power by consent. The Chinese arbitrators, on the other hand, are granted the statutory power to apply equitable principles, not dependent on the parties' consent.

8.5.2 The Conceptual Differences in Arbitration – The Historical Emphasis on Relational Network

Furthermore, while individual rights and freedoms have been at the core of Western civilisation, traditional Chinese society was based on the individual's social role in the group, and his or her obligations in accordance with the norms of *li*. On the whole, the starting point of the law in traditional China is the protection of governmental powers and social interests rather than the protection of individual rights and private interests.

This element of legal culture is still present in contemporary society and influences the practice of arbitration in today's China. Although the Arbitration Law adopted the generally accepted principle of 'party autonomy', this principle is not fully implemented in arbitration practice. The notion of control can be found throughout arbitration proceedings; this restricts party autonomy and arbitral autonomy, the core of modern arbitration.

Despite the recognition of private rights in the process of legal modernisation in China, the notion remains that the rights are not inherent, but granted. This Chinese characteristic of 'public control' taking over 'private autonomy' may find its roots in the historical emphasis on group interest instead of individual rights. Furthermore, the role of individuals in traditional Chinese culture is also reflected in the current mentality of collectivism and the Chinese preference towards institutions over individuals. This may help us to understand the reluctance of the Chinese legislation to recognise ad hoc arbitration in China, as it does not come under government supervision.

8.5.3 The Emphasis on Amicable Resolution – The Historical Legal Culture of Avoidance of Litigation

Lastly, Chinese philosophy seeking harmony and avoiding conflicts, together with the ancient practice of suppressing litigation, have created a legal culture characterised by its aversion towards litigation with the result that disputants often resorted to informal means of dispute settlement. While trade and contract with foreigners took place, commercial law was not developed in China. Commercial disputes were resolved predominately internally within social groups. The policy of 'emphasizing agriculture and repressing commerce' (*zhong nong yi shang*), the low social status of merchants, and the preference for resolving disputes within the guilds formed a structural obstacle for the development of commercial arbitration in imperial China.

In the process of transplanting arbitration into China, we can see that the borrowed concept was severely challenged by the native legal culture. The extra judicial nature of arbitration – a semi-formal institution with an adjudicatory function which produces a binding result – was incompatible with the 'local soil condition', which provided a foundation for the informal process of resolving disputes to restore harmony. The existing local institutions that resolve disputes outside state courts were part of the internal resolution mechanism. The decisions by the dispute resolver, even though they were often respected by the disputants voluntarily as a result of social pressure, were not legally enforceable before the state courts. The adjudicatory function was reserved to the national courts. The notion of party autonomy was historically foreign to the Chinese mind and was challenged by the native culture emphasising group interests and social harmony.

Furthermore, local culture does not clearly draw the line between the role of a mediator and that of an arbitrator. The family heads, clan heads, village leaders, guild officials or other dispute resolvers often attempted to facilitate the parties to settle their disputes with a result satisfactory to both. If a settlement was not reached, the same person would play a more authoritative role and render a decision. In the constant struggling between the borrowed institution and deeply embedded local tradition, the concept of arbitration was translated into its native language, which differed from its original meaning. As a result of this 'cultural translation', the native tradition of mediation was integrated into the Western notion of arbitration. A new form of institution or process gradually came into being – the integration of mediation into arbitration. This practice remains one of the main features of the contemporary arbitration regime in today's China.[131] According to an online survey conducted in November 2011 and April 2012 with Chinese arbitrators on the combination of mediation and arbitration in China,[132] 88.9 per cent of the respondents consider that it is appropriate for the arbitrators to facilitate settlement. In actual practice, a majority of the arbitrators have made attempted mediation during the arbitration proceedings. Fifty per cent of the respondents have proposed mediation to the parties in over 90 per cent of the cases when they act as arbitrators. The mean response is 66.24 per cent and the median response is 87.5 per cent. The survey also shows that the Chinese arbitrators consider that the

---

[131] See ch 6, § 6.3 above.
[132] Between November 2011 and April 2012, the questionnaires were distributed to more than 100 arbitrators, with the kind assistance of the CIETAC and the BAC and by the author's direct distribution to arbitrators by email. A total of 38 responses have been received. After filtering out two incomplete responses, the analysis is based on 36 complete responses. See Kun Fan, 'Can You Leave Your Hat On? An Empirical Study on Arbitrators Facilitating Settlement in China', paper presented at the *Journal of Empirical Legal Studies Conference on Asian Empirical Scholarship* held at the Hawaii University on 4 June 2012.

combination of mediation and arbitration reflects traditional values, among which 'the pursuit of harmony', 'avoiding litigation' and the 'moderation in all things' were viewed the most relevant. This may be a sign of the continuity of the traditional Chinese legal culture and its impact on the contemporary dispute resolution pattern.

9

The Modernisation of Law and Cultural Influences on Arbitration Practice

'It doesn't matter if a cat is black or white, if it catches mice, it's a good cat'.

Deng Xiaoping

WE HAVE SO far identified the historical links between the deeply rooted legal culture in China's imperial history and contemporary practice. In dispute settlement, widely held cultural values discouraged people from resorting to the authority of formal legal rules or to agencies tasked with formally enforcing and applying such rules. Commercial law was not advanced in this society due to the low legal status of merchants and the policy of 'emphasizing agriculture and repressing commerce'. Values related to social harmony, the integration of *li* into *fa*, and the emphasis on group interests over individual rights featured in Chinese traditional legal culture.

Legal culture is not static and must be understood in the context of changes in society. The introduction of Western civilisation into China during the eighteenth and nineteenth centuries resulted in significant changes of the political, economic and cultural structures in Chinese society. The pre-existing social order was destroyed by several major political upheavals, and the legal tradition that was part of that social order was greatly challenged by the new values, ideologies, and norms imported from the West. How do these legal thoughts and the related legal system influence social life? How do the changes of social life affect legal thinking and the related legal system?

Since the Opium War in 1840, Western powers had opened the door of Imperial China with force, and brought an end to the traditional Chinese legal system, which had lasted in a closed society for over 2000 years. A series of legal reforms was introduced, which marked the 'modernisation' process of the Chinese legal system. The reforms were driven by internal and external pressures in the late Qing dynasty. The internal pressures included the strong desire of all Chinese people to wipe out the humiliation suffered by the nation, the awareness of the crisis and the necessity to reform, as well as the desire to import advanced Western military, commercial and technological advances. The external pressures included the force of guns and powder, the threat of signing unequal treaties with Western powers, and the temptations open to Qing officials if they accepted legal reception from the West. External pressure from Western powers was the determinative force for the modernisation of the Chinese legal system, the so-called 'external-driven legal modernisation'.[1] As a result, the traditional Chinese legal system was almost entirely abandoned within 10 years during the late Qing legal reforms. In its place, a Western legal system and laws were introduced. Nevertheless, the traditional values were so deeply rooted in Chinese legal culture, which had dominated China for thousands of years, that the reforms of the legal system could not change the legal culture and people's attitudes towards the law in a short period of time. Due to the constant struggle between the norms imported from the West and the deeply rooted local culture, the process of reform is naturally a zigzagging one. We can divide the modernisation process of the Chinese legal system into four stages:[2]

First, there was the process of '[e]mploying things Western to serve Chinese needs' (*zhong ti xi yong*),[3] which started in the Opium War in 1840 and lasted until 1919. This was the period when Western laws were introduced to supplement Chinese law, while traditional values and norms were maintained.

Second was the process of 'Westernisation', starting from the 'New Culture Movement' in 1919 to the establishment of the People's Republic of China in 1949. During this period, the ruling Nationalists abrogated traditional Chinese law, and enacted a new body of laws based largely on European style civil law.

Third came the process of 'learning from the Soviets' from 1949 to the end of the Cultural Revolution in 1976. Soon after 1949, the government of the PRC abolished the old Nationalist laws pursuant to the 'instructions' issued by the Chinese Communist Party (the CCP) in February 1949,[4] and began to build a socialist legal system. The new government rejected Nationalist legal theory,

---

[1] See范忠信,《中国法制近代化的历史法学反省》,"中国传统法律文化新论"学术研讨会,香港中文大学,2010年5月14–16日(Zhongxin Fan, 'Reflections on the Modernisation of the Chinese Legal System', paper presented at *Symposium on the New Discussions on the Traditional Chinese Legal Culture*, held 吕世伦、姚建宗,《略论法制现代化的概念、模式和类型》,《法制现代化研究》第1辑, 1995年(Shilun Lu and Jianzong Yao, 'Research on the Modernization of Legal System', (1995 (1) Legal Modernisation Studies); 王伯琦,《近代法律思潮与中国固有文化》(台北, 司法行政部印行, 1956), 第18页(Boqi Wang, *Legal Thoughts in Modern History and Traditional Chinese Culture* (Taipei, Legal and Administrative Burea, 1956), 18); Huang, *Legal Transplant and Modern Chinese Law*, 18–20.

[2] Fan, 'Reflections on the Modernisation of the Chinese Legal System'.

[3] See 张之洞,《劝学篇》(Zhidong Zhang, *On Learning*).

[4] Instructions of the Chinese Communist Party Central Committee Relating to Abolishing the Complete Six Laws of the Guomingdang and Establishing Judicial Principles for the Liberated Areas, 1949, reprinted in《法学理论学习参考资料》, 1953 (Reference Materials for the Study of Jurisprudence and Legal Theory). The instructions stated: 'The judicial organs should educate and transform the judicial cadres with a spirit that holds in contempt and criticizes the Six Laws of the Nationalists and all reactionary laws and regulations, and holds in contempt and criticizes all the anti-people laws and regulations of bourgeois countries in Europe, America and Japan. To accomplish this aim, they should study and master the concepts of state and law of Marxism-Leninism and Mao Zedong Thought, and new democratic policies, programmatic principles, laws, orders, regulations and decisions'.

along with its laws, and sought to develop a new 'socialist legality' to serve the needs of a socialist country. This process entailed a campaign of criticism against Western legal theory and large-scale borrowings from the Soviet model. The subsequent evolution has been marked by successive political, economic and cultural movements. The most significant movements include the 'Three-Anti Campaign' against corruption, delay and bureaucracy in 1952; the 'Five-Anti Campaign' against bribery, tax evasion, theft of state assets, and theft of state economic secrets also in 1952; the 'Hundred Flowers Movement', an attempt to regain the support of intellectuals in 1956; the ideological 'Anti-Rightist Movement' in the 1950s and early 1960s, consisting of a series of campaigns to purge alleged 'rightists' within the CCP and abroad; the 'Great Leap Forward' from 1958 to 1961, which aimed at rapidly transforming China from a primarily agrarian economy into a modern communist society through the process of agriculturalisation and industrialisation; and the 'Cultural Revolution', a period of widespread social and political upheaval in the PRC between 1966 and 1976.[5]

Fourth and last, there was the process of modern legal reform, taking into account both Chinese and Western ideas, started in 1978, along with economic reform and opening up. With the intention of generating sufficient surplus value to finance the modernisation of the mainland Chinese economy, economic reform has been carried out in China since 1978. In this economic renewal, many of the capitalist legal structures and concepts were re-introduced which the early reformers had sought to eradicate.[6] The modern legal reform has led to drastic changes to the Chinese legal regime.

As a result, the new legal system in China is shaped by often divergent models drawn from China's historical experience on the one hand, and models based on the experience of Western countries and the newly industrialised nations of Asia on the other hand. In this modernisation process, what are the continuities and discontinuities from China's traditions? How are these changes reflected in arbitration law and practice in modern China? This chapter will focus on the process of modern legal reform in China which has accompanied robust economic reform since the 1970s. The effects of modernisation of the Chinese legal system will be examined under the following headings, namely, the role of law in modern China (section 9.1), the role of individuals in modern China (section 9.2), cultural aversion to formal dispute resolution (section 9.3), and the development of commercial law in the economic transition (section 9.4). On this basis, we will attempt to explain the features of Chinese arbitration from cultural and historical perspectives, taking into account the recent developments of China's modern legal reforms (section 9.5).

---

[5] See generally Doak Barnett, *Cadres, Bureaucracy, and Political Power in Communist China* (New York, Columbia University Press, 1967); Franz Schurmann, *Ideology and Organization in Communist China* (Berkeley, CA, University of California Press, 1968).

[6] Xingzhong Yu, 'Legal Pragmatism in the People's Republic of China' in Tahirih Lee (ed), *Basic Concepts of Chinese Law* (New York, Garland Publishing, 1997) 316, (1989) 3 *Journal of Chinese Law* 29.

9.1 THE ROLE OF LAW IN MODERN CHINA

The examination of China's ancient past reveals no signs of a rule of law. Since Western ideas of law and individual rights were imported, China has made significant changes in developing a legal system that reflects, and in some respects is consistent with, Western legal norms. Nevertheless, the Confucian legacy of the past, as well as persistent political interference, raise questions as to whether a true rule of law exists or will exist in China. Two well-known scholars on Chinese law have made in-depth studies on this subject and have reached different conclusions.

Professor Lubman portrays the systemic and ideological limitations of Communist Party rule as a cage confining the bird of Chinese legal reform. While he credits China with significant achievements in legislation and institution building, Professor Lubman concludes that the CCP's dominance constrains the role of law to such an extent that China cannot be said to have a legal system. He argues that the absence of a unifying concept of law and the considerable fragmentation of legal and political authority, which are both compounded by problems of ideology and corruption, work to inhibit the emergence of a rule of law system that can impose on state and society alike predictable and enforceable standards for socioeconomic and political behaviour.[7]

Professor Peerenboom discusses the rule of law from the perspective of philosophical pragmatism that balances thick and thin theories on the rule of law. Recognising that concepts of law are unavoidably contentious and embedded in their local cultural context, he suggests that, despite the many problems and contradictions inherent in the development of law in China, this process can indeed be described as 'in transition' towards the rule of law. Direct and indirect evidence of the transition includes the constitutional recognition of the objective of building a 'socialist rule of law state', the vigorous promulgation of laws, the institutional build up to implementing the laws, the rise of legal consciousness and the increasing importance of law in everyday life. Professor Peerenboom views the development of China's legal system as a historical process of socioeconomic change that makes unavoidable the gradual progression toward a system which, while not necessarily matching the models of Europe or North America, nonetheless qualifies as a rule of law system.[8]

Despite the different conclusions, both approaches suggest that the economic reform process has created opportunities for *increased reliance on law* in the management of economy and society. We shall use this as a starting point to examine the role of law in modern China.

---

[7] Lubman, *Bird in a Cage: Legal Reform in China After Mao*.
[8] Randall Peerenboom, *China's Long March Toward Rule of Law* (Cambridge, Cambridge University Press, 2002).

9.1.1 The Instrumental Notion of Law

Law must be envisaged in the context of the underlying social norms and practices. In China's imperial past, law was viewed as the will of the rulers and an instrument of suppression; its primary manifestation was dominance by punishment, not the protection of individual rights. The introduction of Western civilisation and norms began to challenge the traditional values of law in China. The Chinese are asking fundamental questions which the Americans have also asked themselves: is law really an instrument of control that is opposed to democracy, or is law really a protector of democratic rights?[9] This debate is very active today.

Despite the influence of Western values, the instrumental facet of law remains a prominent component in today's China. Instrumentalists see law as an instrument for shaping society. Since the establishment of the PRC, the instrumental view has gone through two major stages. First, immediately after the founding of the PRC, law was regarded as an instrument for class domination, an instrument that would allow the proletariat to dominate and thereby eventually extinguish the bourgeois class and all other reactionaries. Second, in 1978, the CCP decided to shift priority from class struggle to economic development. Since then, it has pursued a series of new economic policies designed to invigorate the internal economy and open China to the outside world.[10] As a result, the primary role of law as an instrument is now to serve economic development.[11] Law's instrumental role in the service of economic development is illustrated by the CCP's policy that all government leaders and economic units must use legal means, supplemented by other means, to maintain economic order.[12]

Traditional Chinese notions do not consider law as divinely endowed and nor do they relate law to the abstract values of 'fairness' and 'justice'. Even in today's China, law is still not understood in the context of rights and freedom as it is in many Western countries. Law is considered as 'actuality' (*shiji*) as determined by the CCP.[13] In the early years of its rule, the CCP deemed that the 'actuality' of class struggle was paramount.[14] Since 1978, the CCP perceives general economic construction as the guiding 'actuality'.[15] The change of China's

---

[9] Jerome Cohen, 'Is There Law in China?' in Tahirih Lee (ed), *Basic Concepts of Chinese Law* (New York, Garland Publishing, 1997) 8, originally published in *International Trade Law Journal, Work Shop Proceedings* 74.

[10] See 《中国共产党第十一届中央委员会第三次全体会议公报》 (Communique of the Third Plenary Session of the 11th Central Committee of Communist Party of China), passed on 22 December 1978.

[11] Yu, 'Legal Pragmatism in the People's Republic of China', 327.

[12] ibid.

[13] ibid.

[14] See 毛泽东《关于农村社会主义教育运动中一些具体问题政策的规定》 (Mao Zedong, *Regulations Concerning Some Specific Policies in the Movement of Socialist Education in Rural China*) 1964, in which the policy of 'the focusing on class struggle' was raised by Mao Zedong.

[15] See the Communique of the Third Plenary Session of the 11th Central Committee of Communist Party of China, in which 'taking the economic construction as the central task' is drafted into the CCP's political plans.

'actuality' has produced law that adapts to the objective needs of development. On the positive side, the 'actuality' of the need for economic development necessitates more laws to encourage investment, protect investors, and induces various market mechanisms into the economy. On the negative side, because only the CCP can make an 'objective' determination of the 'actuality' that is the source of policy, law is inextricably linked with CCP policy. As Professor Yu noted, '[t]he CCP first determines 'actuality', then through the medium of policy, promulgates appropriate laws and regulations'.[16]

9.1.2 The Remarkable Burst of Legislative Efforts and the Lack of an Integrated Legal System

Decimated by the Cultural Revolution, the Chinese legal system had to be rebuilt virtually from scratch. One of the first tasks was to start passing laws. Since the reform and opening up in 1978, China has aggressively enacted laws, rules and regulations, especially in areas of property, corporations, trade and investment, most of which are imported from the West. As a result, China now has a growing body of commercial law. There are now in place at the national level the General Principles of Civil Law, detailed domestic and foreign-related contract laws, a fairly comprehensive collection of laws and regulations for authorising and attracting various forms of foreign direct investment, a number of regulations relating to loans, guarantees, foreign exchange controls and other financial matters, a company law, central and commercial banking legislation, detailed regulations for the securities industry, a negotiable instruments law, a law on security interests, a trial bankruptcy law, a series of laws concerning income taxation of enterprises and individuals as well as other taxes, several laws on labour protection and trade unions, elaborate laws for the protection of intellectual property rights and for the prohibition of unfair competition, a real estate law, and a considerable body of environmental and consumer protection legislation, to name just a few. International legislation has also been a major part of this effort. The PRC now is a signatory to most of the principal multilateral treaties for economic cooperation, such as the Vienna Convention on Contracts for the International Sale of Goods, the Paris Convention for the Protection of Industrial Property Rights, the New York Convention, and the Hague Convention on Service Abroad of Documents in Civil and Commercial Matters. China has, in addition, erected an impressive network of bilateral agreements to promote trade and investment with many countries, including numerous tax treaties, BITs and judicial assistance agreements.

In line with the development of commercial law and the creation of private rights, the dispute resolution regime has also evolved to resolve increasing disputes and to protect the parties' lawful rights under Chinese laws and regula-

---

[16] Yu, 'Legal Pragmatism in the People's Republic of China', 333.

tions. The first Civil Procedure Law of China (for Trial Implementation) was promulgated in March 1982, and came into force on 1 October 1982. During nine years of implementation and experimentation lessons were learned and experiences accumulated. The Civil Procedure Law was promulgated and came into force on 9 April 1991, and was amended in 28 October 2007 and then on 31 August 2012.[17] The Arbitration Law was promulgated on 31 August 1994; this legitimised arbitration in China.[18] In line with the CCP's policy of encouraging mediation and maintaining social stability, the first mediation law – the People's Mediation Law – was promulgated in August 2010 and came into force on 1 January 2011.[19] With these efforts, a comprehensive legal framework for the resolution of disputes is emerging.

Nevertheless, to date, the building of an integrated legal system is far from complete. Although the SPC publishes in its Gazette opinions on typical cases selected for 'guidance' of lower courts and general prospective interpretations of laws, it contains only a fraction of the rulings and interpretations of national legislation. Systematically assembled collections of cases and administrative interpretations of existing normative rules are not available to the public. Further, these judicial decisions are often summaries with little analysis of the reasoning that underlies the result.

Within the court, the judge's decision may be overridden by higher authorities within the court, such as the adjudication committee. This creates a phenomenon within the Chinese judicial system – 'those who try the case do not decide it, and those who decide the case do not try it' (*shenzhe bu pan, panzhe bu shen*). The courts, as a whole, are also subject to numerous outside pressures and are particularly vulnerable to local government influence, as local government appoints the judges and continues to supervise their activities. The courts also often lack sufficient bureaucratic clout to enforce their judgments against administrative units. The court presidents generally have a lower bureaucratic rank than the chief executives of the government at the same level. Thus, a low-status judge does not have the prerogative to disobey, much less to command, a higher-status official.[20] As Professor Cohen has noted:

> It is relatively easy to adopt legislative frameworks and regulatory regimes – often imported from abroad – to govern broad fields of activity. It is much more difficult and time consuming to put those laws into practice, to adapt them to local conditions, to fill in the gaps and to develop a body of interpretation and precedent that can make the rules meaningful in specific cases. Most difficult and time consuming of all – as evidenced by the continued weakness of the Chinese judiciary – is the task of building

---

[17] Ch 1, s 1.2.1-A, fn 17.
[18] Ch 1, s 1.2.1-A, fn 15.
[19] Adopted on 28 August 2010 at the 16th Session of the Standing Committee of the 11th NPC, and came into force as of 1 January 2011.
[20] See Donald Clarke, 'Dispute Resolution in China' in Tahirih Lee (ed), *Contract, Guanxi, and Dispute Resolution in China* (New York, Garland Publishing, 1997) 390–91, (1991) 3 *Journal of Chinese Law* 245.

institutions that can effectively, consistently and fairly enforce those laws across a country as vast as China.[21]

9.1.3 The Implementation of Law: *heqing, heli, hefa*

Ancient Chinese officials were guided by the principle of '*tianli, guofa, renqing*' – natural rules, human feelings/social norms and state laws. In today's China, when implementing the law, Chinese judges refer to the principles of '*heqing, heli, hefa*' – human feelings, the principles of reasonableness and national laws. This reflects China's historical emphasis on substantive over procedural justice. In the clash between morals and law, morals have often won out. Professor Tay observes that '[w]hereas Western legal procedure tends to depersonalise all claims in order to bring out more sharply the question at issue, Chinese tradition personalises all claims, seeing them in the context of human relations'.[22] According to a study by Professor Cheng and Professor Rosett, Chinese judges consider that contract enforcement is not best accomplished by too rigid an insistence on the letter of the law and the precise terms of the contract. They feel much freer to soften the precise terms of the contract by deference to the relationship between the parties and the moral demands of accommodation.[23]

9.2 THE ROLE OF THE INDIVIDUAL IN MODERN CHINA

We have seen earlier that in traditional Chinese society, the basic unit was not the individual, but the group to which he or she belonged – family, clan, village, or guild. Individual rights were not paramount in the traditional legal system. Rather, individual interests needed to be sacrificed when they were in conflict with group interests, so as to maintain social harmony.

The tendency to define individual identity in group and relational terms persists in contemporary Chinese societies. After the victory in 1949, the Chinese Communists mounted extensive programmes of economic reconstruction and social change. They have reorganised Chinese society by weakening or totally abolishing the family, clan, village, and guild.[24] Yet new social groups were created as the basic unit of modern society. A monumental task for the newly established regime was the registration of individuals as members of a house-

---

[21] Jerome Cohen and John Lange, 'The Chinese Legal System: A Primer for Investors' (1997) 17 *New York Law School Journal of International and Comparative Law* 345, 348–49.
[22] Alice Erh-Soon Tay, 'The Struggle for Law in China' (1987) 21 *University of British Columbia Law Review* 561, 562.
[23] Lucie Cheng and Arthur Rosett, 'Contract With a Chinese Face: Socially Embedded Factors in the Transformation From Hierarchy to Market 1978–1989' in Tahirih Lee (ed), *Contract, Guanxi, and Dispute Resolution in China* (New York, Garland Publishing, 1997) 202, (1991) 5 *Journal of Chinese Law* 143.
[24] See generally Lubman, 'Mao and Mediation: Politics and Dispute Resolution in Communist China', 1284–359.

hold and as part of a work unit (*danwei*). The common interests of all members of society were emphasised and they were seen as 'eating from one big communal pot' (*daguofan*) – a metaphor for the system of egalitarianism, within which everyone gets equal pay regardless of the work done.[25] Thus, an idealised and undifferentiated vision of the community was created. Individual identity was connected to membership of a large collectivity. Commercial activity was located within this largely undifferentiated collectivity.

The reforms since 1978 have been, in part, a reaction to the excesses of this collectivist perspective. New and smaller units were created. The absorption of foreign capital and technology introduced diversified ownership, such as joint ownership of entities, and private ownership, which were not in existence prior to 1978. Nevertheless, laws remain to be imposed on society from the top down, not from below. In Chinese minds, a right is not inherent or inalienable, but rather granted by the state from above. Further, rights are not absolute, but relative, and must be accompanied by duties. There is no right that does not call for a duty, nor is there any duty that does not lead to a right. Law is understood, therefore, not as having the function of protecting individual rights. Instead, it is used both to grant and to restrict rights.

9.3 THE CULTURAL AVERSION TO FORMAL DISPUTE RESOLUTION

9.3.1 The Impact of Communist Ideology

Since 1949, Communist ideology, Mao's views of society, social control, and social conflict have decisively influenced dispute resolution in contemporary China. The new government readily adopted this non-adversarial system of dispute resolution in its effort to reorder Chinese society and mobilise mass support. A report on judicial work in the T'ai Hsing district of Shanxi Province issued in 1946 stressed the ideological superiority of mediation, which was regarded as an efficient instrument for 'protecting the democratic interests of the great masses of people'.[26]

Like Confucianism, Communism is hostile to litigation and places a great emphasis upon transforming the thought of individuals.[27] The impact of Communism on Chinese dispute resolution tendencies is traceable from the early period when the Maoist strategy for mobilising the masses was developed in the late 1930s and the 1940s:

> The technique embodying the Maoist approach to mobilization of the people is the celebrated 'mass line', under which the Communist Party maintains constant and

---

[25] See generally Pat Howard, *Breaking the Iron Rice Bowl: Prospects for Socialism in China's Countryside* (Armonk, ME Sharpe, Inc, 1988) 77–143.
[26] Lubman, 'Mao and Mediation: Politics and Dispute Resolution in Communist China', 1286, 1306–07, citing the Report on the General Situation in Judicial Work in T'ai-Hsing District (1946).
[27] See ibid.

222 *Modernisation of Law*

close contact with the general populace, engaging in propaganda, discussion, persuasion, and exhortation to gauge mass reactions to policy and to lead mass action.[28]

This general approach follows the admonition of Mao Zedong that 'disputes among the people (as distinguished from those involving enemies of the people) ought to be resolved, whenever possible, by democratic methods, methods of discussion, of criticism, of persuasion and education, not by coercive, oppressive methods'.[29] As Professor Cohen pointed out, even though there are vast differences between Confucianism and the thoughts of Mao Zedong, 'each of these dominant ideologies is plainly hostile to litigation and places great emphasis upon "criticism-education", "self-criticism" and "voluntarism"'.[30] Influenced by Maoist ideology, most civil disputes between individuals are settled by extra-judicial mediation.

9.3.2 The Relational Mode of Association

Professor Fei Xiaotong describes Chinese society, traditional as well as present, as a 'differential mode of association' (*chaxu geju*) as contrasted to the Western organisational mode of association:[31]

> The Chinese pattern of social organization is like the circles that appear on the surface of a lake when a rock is thrown into it. Everyone stands at the center of the circles produced by his or her own social influence. Everyone's circles are interrelated. One touches different circles at different times and places.[32]

The concentric circles thus formed are hierarchical in relation to the individual, with the innermost circle being the closest. As a result, Professor Fei further explains:

> Our social relationships spread out gradually, individual by individual, resulting in an accumulation of personal connections. These social relations for a network composed of each individual's personal connections. Therefore our social morality makes sense only in terms of these personal connections.[33]

Within such a relational structure, one's web of *guanxi* is important not only for social but economic reasons. Through the media of *guanxi*, families collaborated with other families, individuals unrelated by blood collaborated with each other, and commercial relationships heavily relied on networks facilitated

---

[28] ibid.
[29] See Mao Zedong, 毛泽东, 《关于如何处理当前处理人民内部矛盾》(*How to Deal With the Disputes Among the Peoples*) 27 February 1957.
[30] Cohen, 'Chinese Mediation on the Eve of Modernization', 1223.
[31] Gary Hamilton and Zheng Wang, 'From the Soil: The Foundations of Chinese Society' (a translation of Fei Xiaotong's Xiangtu Zhongguo) (Berkeley, CA, University of California Press, 1992) 25–36.
[32] ibid.
[33] ibid.

by go-betweens. People often rely on business partners they are related to, or with whom they are connected by a common friend. The two parties to a commercial transaction are likely to be introduced directly or indirectly by the common friend. In a commercial relationship built on *guanxi* and trust, confronting the party who has caused the problem is to be avoided.

It is true that with the drastic development of international trade and commerce driven by economic reforms, Chinese people are now increasingly involved in doing business with strangers and distant partners; and commercial relationships are becoming less interpersonal. Nevertheless, informal business networks continue to play a major role in the growth of China's economy. For instance, a contract is often not signed at the negotiation table in a formal setting. The Chinese prefer to do business with people they are familiar with. After sitting together at a round table at a Chinese dinner, after a few toasts (*gan bei*), and sometimes even after a karaoke session, a contractual relationship is built in a much less formal atmosphere. Contracts do not only structure economic relations in China; they can also 'transform an economic relationship into a social one, and thus turn outsiders into insiders'.[34] Sometimes, after doing business for a few years with the same person, the business partners will be considered to be insiders (*zijiren*). In this sense, Chinese society is still a relationship based society.

9.4 THE DEVELOPMENT OF COMMERCIAL LAW IN THE ECONOMIC TRANSITION

9.4.1 Centralised Planned Economy and Internal Resolution

From 1949 to the late 1970s, China adopted a strict, planned economic system under which the government directly or indirectly controlled all the significant aspects of the economy. Under the highly-centralised planned economy, enterprises were either owned by the people as a whole (*quan min suo you zhi*) or by collectives (*ji ti suo you zhi*). The means of production were allocated and distributed according to the economic plan. The administrative system was hierarchical meaning that the higher-level authorities could crucially shape or thwart the plans of lower-level counterparts, and the superiors of enterprises maintained close supervision over the enterprises in order to deal with problems that might arise between them.

The traditional model of the planned economy views the state as essentially one giant vertically-integrated productive firm, 'China, Inc'. Various ministries are divisions within the firm, and enterprises are factories. When a dispute arises, the parties complain to government administrators, and the dispute may

---

[34] Cheng and Rosett, 'Contract With a Chinese Face: Socially Embedded Factors in the Transformation From Hierarchy to Market 1978–1989', 196.

eventually rise to the first administrator with authority over both factories.[35] Professor Clarke suggests that in the planned economy, disputes between enterprises in the state-owned and collective sectors must be analysed under the paradigm of 'internal resolution'. By internal resolution, he refers to the situation when the dispute resolver has authority not because of his or her specialised function as dispute resolver, but because of some other distinct relationship with the parties. Moreover, the well-being of the parties bears directly on the well-being of the dispute resolver. The structure of the planned economy makes various government organs keenly interested in the maximising values such as the collective well-being of the whole dispute triangle – the two parties and the resolver – than in deciding who should win.[36]

9.4.2 Development of Commercial Law in the Transition to the Market Economy

A. *Legislative Efforts to Establish Recognition and Authorisation of 'Private Rights' Legally*

China's law reform programme began in late 1978 when the third Plenum of the 11th Central Committee of the CCP was convened. The Plenum reflected a tentative policy consensus about the need to reform the state-planned economy and build a legal system that would support economic growth. The economic reform has changed the role of the state in important ways, with the essential thrust being toward greater devolution of economic responsibility, greater autonomy for enterprises and greater differentiation between the role of the state as sovereign and its role as an economic actor. Fewer and fewer enterprises are entirely state-owned, and an increasing number of those that are entirely state-owned are being transformed into stock companies with limited liability and, in many cases, share ownership distributed among a number of governmental entities and state-owned enterprises.[37]

Significant changes have taken place in the nature and incidence of disputes, conflicts and social disturbances, and the mechanisms for addressing them. Economic reform has meant a reduction in the scope of internal dispute resolution. Consistent with the basic principles of the reform programme, the Chinese government is less likely to stand behind the debts of a Chinese business enterprise simply because that enterprise is owned, directly or indirectly, by the state.[38]

As with economic and governance reforms, the government has adopted a pragmatic and problem-solving approach in order to meet the broad and some-

---

[35] Clarke, 'Dispute Resolution in China', 372–76.
[36] ibid.
[37] Jerome A Cohen and John E Lange, 'The Chinese Legal System: A Primer for Investors' (1997) 17 *New York Law School Journal of International and Comparative Law*, 349.
[38] ibid.

times conflicting goals of justice and efficiency while maintaining socio-political stability and rapid economic growth. Private ownership was reintroduced as a result of economic reforms. Diversified ownership, such as joint ownership of entities was introduced to attract foreign capital and technology. A great number of commercial laws were introduced to provide a favourable legal environment to attract foreign investors. These efforts correspond to the state's need to establish recognition and authorisation of 'private rights' legally for promoting the market-orientated economy. As a result, China has a growing body of commercial laws and formal legal institutions that have begun to interpret and apply these laws with some regularity.

B. Continued State Control and the Struggle for Authority among Central, Provincial and Local Government

Nevertheless, the embedded ideologies of the 'centralised plan' and 'socialist public' persist, which make institutions remain subject to state control. The state is still uncomfortable with the idea of letting individuals make their own deals, whether in dispute resolution or in the marketplace. Some institutions are reluctant to share their previous monopolies with the private sector. The key challenge ahead is thus not to decide what laws are missing and to put them in place, but 'to enable the establishment of a set of institutions by state or non-state actors', which will be able to respond with flexibility to the needs of the market economy. Many of these institutions almost by definition cannot be created by the state; they should be 'empowered', but not 'forced' into existence.[39] The system as a whole should allow for the flexible creation, adaptation, and elimination of institutions according to social and economic needs as determined through a bottom-up, not a top-down approach.

Furthermore, the vastness of China and the existence of entrenched local power bases often make it difficult for central government to enforce laws that it adopts for the protection of foreign investors throughout China. To carry out the policy of reform and opening up, central government has devolved control to local provinces and officials. This transfer of power, originally intended to promote economic activity, has resulted in the increased independence of lower-level government, and thus conflict between central and local government. In their desire to promote local economic development, local government regularly ignores central laws and policies, issues regulations that are inconsistent with national level laws, or engages in local protectionism. The reform process in China is thus taking place against the backdrop of a vigorous struggle for authority among central, provincial and local levels of government. The result of this for foreign investors is further uncertainty and confusion concerning governmental policies, applicable laws and regulations, and required approvals.

---

[39] Donald Clarke, 'China: Creating a Legal System for a Market Economy' (2007) *Asian Development Bank*, GWU Legal Studies Research Paper No 396; GWU Law School Public Law Research Paper No 396, at SSRN: ssrn.com/abstract=1097587.

226 *Modernisation of Law*

Often, 'investors are caught in the middle, between the more investor-friendly local authorities and the more macro-oriented central authorities, each offering their own-often sharply divergent visions of the applicable regulatory framework and the proper way to proceed'.[40]

9.5 EXPLANATION OF CONTEMPORARY ARBITRAL PRACTICE FROM CULTURAL AND HISTORICAL PERSPECTIVES

Recent Chinese history shows the transition towards a modern legal system compatible with an industrialised and modernised society. To date, this transition is far from being completed. In the transition, a new legal system is formed in the tensions between a globalised system of liberal legal norms and deeply embedded system of local values; the tensions between the central, provincial and local levels of government struggling for authority; and the tensions between formal modes of operation and the pervasive informal arrangements within the Chinese web of *guanxi*. In the clash of cultures and legal traditions, we see elements of continuity from China's historical past, as well as discontinuity, with new ingredients transplanted from foreign sources. In this process of legal transplantation, a 'Chinese face' is put on the transplanted system of arbitration. To what extent are those Chinese characteristics influenced by its traditional legal culture? These new elements from China's recent history can help us to reveal the complete picture of the puzzle now.

In describing the continuity of legal culture in China, we will use the model of 'culture dimensions' developed by Professor Geert Hofstede. Based on data generated through questionnaires in 56 countries and regions around the world, Hofstede crystallises the concept of culture by measuring it with five dimensions, namely Power Distance Index (PDI), Individualism (IDV), Masculinity (MAS), Uncertainty Avoidance Index (UAI) and Long-Term Orientation (LTO).[41] For the purpose of this book, three dimensions will be discussed. First, UAI, which deals with a society's tolerance for uncertainty and ambiguity. It indicates to what extent a culture programmes its members to feel either uncomfortable or comfortable in unstructured situations. Second, we look at IDV, which is contrasted to collectivism – the degree to which individuals are integrated into groups. Third, we examine LTO, which is contrasted to short-term orientation. Long-term societies value perseverance and thrift. Hofstede's study calculated scores for different cultures under each dimension. Chart 8 below demonstrates the difference between the cultural dimensions of China and

---

[40] Cohen and Lange, 'The Chinese Legal System: A Primer for Investors', 349.
[41] Geert Hofstede's Value Survey Module is designed for measuring culture-determined differences between matched samples of respondents from different countries and regions. It consists of 20 content questions and six demographic questions. See Geert Hofstede, *Culture's Consequences. Comparing Values, Behaviors, Institutions, and Organizations Across Nations* (Thousand Oaks, CA, Sage Publications, 2001).

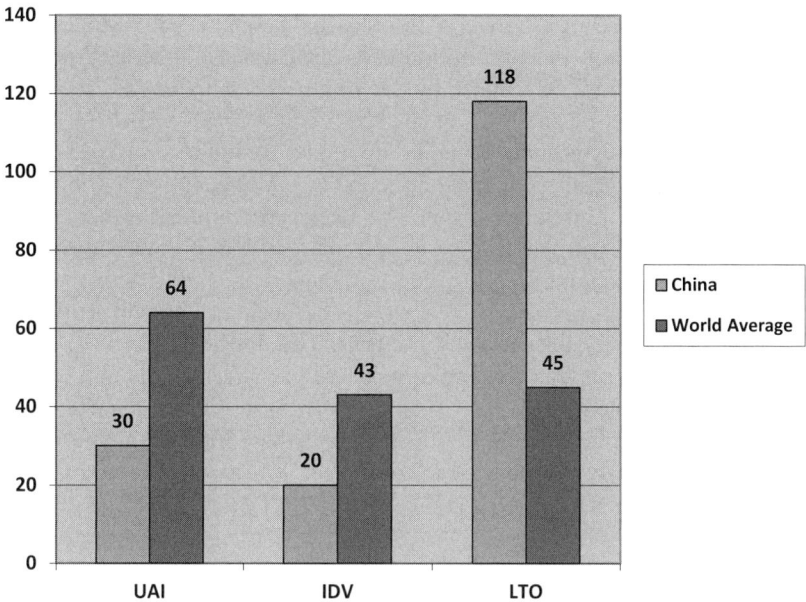

Chart 8: Comparison of Cultural Dimensions Between China and World Average[42]

[Bar chart showing China vs World Average: UAI China 30, World 64; IDV China 20, World 43; LTO China 118, World 45]

those of the world average. Using the model of cultural dimensions, current Chinese society is featured by low UAI – tolerance for uncertainty (a), low IDV – collectivist society (b), and extremely high LTO – relational mode of society (c). We shall now further illustrate these cultural characteristics, their continuities from the tradition, and their impact on the dispute resolution mechanism.

9.5.1 Tolerance of Uncertainty and the Notion of *Biantong* – The Sustained Tolerance of Uncertainty

The low UAI ranking of China indicates that the society has a high tolerance for uncertainty. In this culture, 'people are more tolerant of opinions different from what they are used to; they try to have as few rules as possible'.[43] In these societies, people tend to be more contemplative and tend not to express emotions openly. 'Tolerant v rigid' might be another name for this dimension.

This tolerance for uncertainty is deeply rooted in Chinese traditional legal culture. Law enforcers often referred to *qing* to supplement the rigidity of *fa*. Facing uncertainty in a lawsuit, the general public had a tendency to seek informal means to resolve their disputes. Chinese legal culture emphasises the unique

---

[42] Data collected from www.geert-hofstede.com/hofstede_dimensions.php.
[43] See ibid.

circumstances of each individual case, and is thus naturally more tolerant of uncertainty.

In its recent history, although China has made significant progress towards building a system of rule of law, the Chinese legal system is still a work in progress. Signs of the instrumental notion of law remain: Chinese legal pragmatism regards 'actuality', determined by the 'objective' evaluation of the CCP, as the standard for making and revising law; the broad majority of people who are not in a position to determine 'actuality' do not have confidence in the law.[44]

As a paradox to the instrumental notion in law making, a notion of biantong can be found in legal implementation. The historical sentiment of *qing* – flexibility/tolerance and reasonableness – is still influential in the way disputes are resolved today. When implementing the law, today's judges and arbitrators often refer to the principles of '*heqing, heli, hefa*' – according to human sentiments, the principle of reasonableness, and the laws. The notion of *biantong* is even more present in the popular legal culture. There are 'uncertainties and tensions as to the permissible parameters for guanxi behavior and the parameters for formal institutional behavior – in other words, where legal requirements and processes end and where informal relations may legitimately be permitted to have influence'.[45]

9.5.2 The Lack of Party Autonomy and Administrative Features of Arbitration – The Collectivist Society

The Chinese score for IDV is less than half of the world's average. It ranks lower than any other Asian country in the IDV ranking, at 20 compared to an average of 24.[46] This indicates a high level of collectivism, as compared to individualism. According to Professor Hofstede:

> The low IDV ranking is manifest in a close and committed member 'group', be that a family, extended family, or extended relationships. Loyalty in a collectivist culture is paramount. The society fosters strong relationships where everyone takes responsibility for fellow members of their group.[47]

This is contrasted with an individualist society, in which the ties between individuals are loose. Everyone is expected to look after him/herself and his/her immediate family.

The collectivist culture is deeply rooted in the emphasis on relational network and group interests in traditional Chinese society. This collectivism continued in the system of planned economy between 1949 and 1978, in which all economic

---

[44] Yu, 'Legal Pragmatism in the People's Republic of China', 315–37.
[45] Pitman Potter, *The Chinese Legal System: Globalization and Local Legal Culture* (London, Routledge, 2001), 31.
[46] n 42 above.
[47] ibid.

activities were carried out in accordance with a centralised plan, and administrative control played leading functions. An arbitration system born in such a background may not be free from administrative interference.

The economic reconstruction and social change in the past two decades has greatly challenged the collectivist mentality of the Chinese, as evidenced by the 'one-child' policy and the so-called 'strangers' society'. Assertions of 'private rights' and individual economic interests have been recognised in Chinese law, in order to promote the market-orientated economy. Rights consciousness is far beyond what we have seen in the past. Nevertheless, the notion of 'public control' and 'collective interest' rooted in the planned economy remains to be seen in many aspects of Chinese society. In arbitration, although the generally accepted principle of party autonomy is recognised in the Arbitration Law, it is not fully integrated in the arbitration practice. The notion of control can be found throughout the arbitration proceedings, from the determination on the arbitral jurisdiction to the appointment of arbitrators, from the conduct of arbitration proceeding to the recognition and enforcement of arbitral awards. One can find numerous examples when administrative powers interference with the key players of the arbitration proceedings – the parties and the arbitral tribunal.[48] The persistent collectivism approach from top-down explains the authority's difficulty in treating arbitration institutions as independent and autonomous institutions free of administrative interference and reluctance in allowing ad hoc arbitration. This leads us back to our metaphor – 'bird in a cage'.[49] If the economic reform has liberated the economic bird from its cage – the economic plan, further legal reforms are needed to liberate the legal bird from its cage.

9.5.3 The Wide Use of Mediation – The Cultural Preference for Amicable Resolution

China has the highest-ranking factor for LTO, which constitutes a salient feature of Chinese culture. It indicates the Chinese attitude of perseverance. They persist in achieving long term objectives, and are willing to invest for the future instead of for short term profits.[50] Maintaining a relationship in the long run is considered more important than asserting one's right in a particular matter. This is reflected in the cultural preference for amicable resolution of all disputes.

In traditional China, mediation was the primary mode of dispute resolution. The Confucian philosophy of conflict avoidance, the limitation on individuals' right to sue, the weakness of the formal dispute resolution system, and uncertainties in the outcome left the disputants with few choices but to seek informal means to settle their disputes. Over the past thousands of years, while dynasties

---

[48] See Ch 2, s 2.2.2; Ch 3, s 3.1.2 and s 3.2.2; Ch 4, s 4.2.1; Ch 5, s 5.2 and s 5.3.
[49] Ch 7, s 7.3, fn 5.
[50] n 41 above.

changed, governments changed, laws changed, and the legal system changed, the aversion to litigation and preference for mediation remained. The brief years of the Republic from 1911 to 1949 did not appreciably reduce the preference for mediation.[51] This tradition even survived the revolution in the 1940s which brought fundamental ideological changes to the country. In the early days after the establishment of the PRC, the mediation system was enhanced by the Communists' effort to reorder Chinese society and mobilise mass support, although the political function of mediation was more prominent than its social function. Since the economic reforms and opening up in 1978, Chinese society has undertaken dramatic changes: the formal dispute resolution system has significantly developed, the concept of 'rights' and legal awareness have been increasing as a result of widespread public legal education, and the economic development has surged since the reforms towards a market economy. Rigorous civil justice reforms were carried out in the 1980s and 1990s, which emphasised law, litigation and courts as institutions for resolving civil grievances. Such reforms are accompanied by a decline in mediation in the 1990s. Since 2003, mediation has regained its momentum, when the Party and courts began to shift their priority from adjudicatory back to mediatory justice.[52] The recent revival of mediation can be seen as a result of the party-state commitment to a 'socialist harmonious society',[53] and the top-down authoritarian response motivated by social stability concerns.[54]

Apart from the political reasons, the importance of mediation in contemporary China can also be explained by the cultural feature of LTO. Even though with the dramatic changes of social and economic structures, Chinese businessmen are now more used to dealing with strangers, informal business networks remain important in their social and economic relationships. The traditional *guanxi* system retains its importance, but 'must operate alongside an increasingly formal set of largely imported rules and processes made necessary by the increased complexity of social, economic and political relations'[55]. In *guanxi*-based commercial relations, aggressive assertion of rights may be considered less important than maintaining an ongoing relationship. As a result, Chinese people are more likely to seek amicable means to settle disputes, in the interest of maintaining long term relations. Even when a formal proceeding is initiated,

---

[51] Lubman, 'Mao and Mediation: Politics and Dispute Resolution in Communist China', 1294.

[52] See Hualing Fu, 'Access to Justice in China: Potentials, Limits and Alternatives' (2009), available at SSRN ssrn.com/abstract=1474073; Carl Minzner, 'China's Turn Against Law' (2011) 59 *American Journal of Comparative Law* 4.

[53] Michael Palmer, 'Compromising Courts and Harmonizing Ideologies: Mediation in the Administrative Chambers of the People's Courts in the People's Republic of China', in Andrew Harding and Penelope Nicholson (eds) *New Courts in Asia* (London, Routledge, 2009).

[54] Carl Minzner, 'China's Turn Against Law'; Haitian Lu, 'State Channeling of Social Grievances: Theory and Evidence from China' (2011) 41 *Hong Kong Law Journal* 2; Hualing Fu and Richard Cullen, 'From Mediatory to Adjudicatory Justice: The Limits of Civil Justice Reform in China', in Margaret Woo and Mary Gallagher (eds), Chinese Justice: Civil Dispute Resolution in Contemporary China (Cambridge, Cambridge University Press, 2011).

[55] Pitman Potter, *The Chinese Legal System: Globalization and Local Legal Culture*, 13.

the judges/arbitrators tend to play an active role in facilitating settlement, and the parties are more ready to accept such an attempt. Although the spirit of mediation today is significantly different from that of ancient times, the art of persuasion adopted by ancient officials and the relationship-orientated and forward-looking approaches are continued in today's mediation practice.

To summarise, history shows us that the change of any legal culture is a process requiring simultaneous changes of the legal system, legal norms, legal theory and legal consciousness in a given society. The reform and construction of a legal system always involves balancing different interests between various social groups. Therefore, the reform and improvement of a legal system must be accompanied by reforms of political, economic, social and culture elements, and particularly changes of traditional concepts. As Judge Ma Hanbao pointed out, 'to change law is difficult, but to change the conception of law is far more difficult'.[56] Without changes of ideology and concepts, new laws can hardly exist; even if new laws are created, they will be difficult to implement. Therefore, the reception of law cannot be the literal transplant of the 'bones' of the legal provisions, but must integrate the 'meat' of the legal concepts into actual social life so as to make the law alive.

---

[56] Ma, *The Law and the Changes of the Chinese Society*, 56.

10

Conclusion

'It has been said that arguing against globalisation is like arguing against the laws of gravity'.

Kofi Annan

'ubi societas ibi jus, ubi jus ibi societas'

SO FAR, WE have examined the contemporary law and practice of arbitration in China thoroughly and highlighted its unique features measured by transnational standards (chapters one to seven). Additionally, we have examined China's past in order to trace the historical links that can explain contemporary practice from cultural, economic, political and sociological perspectives (chapters eight and nine). From the above analysis, we can see that local tradition and culture still play a significant role in accepting and reshaping a borrowed legal institution, despite the general trend that the globalisation of law is inevitable. In this process, various state and non-state actors played an active role in conceptualising transnational standards with local norms. In the constant struggle between borrowed norms and local traditions, arbitration, as a transplanted institution, was put on a Chinese face. This process can be described as 'localised globalism' – global norms are localised when domestic actors translate and conceptualise the borrowed concepts by referring to local notions.

A natural question to follow is whether understanding the influence of legal tradition on contemporary practice may have any implications for future trends of development. Will those local norms be projected on to the global arena? With the harmonisation of law and practice of arbitration worldwide, is China showing signs of adapting to transnational standards or will Chinese legal culture influence the evolution of transnational arbitration?

The process of legal evolution can also be explained by the theory of Darwinism, according to which all legal systems develop through the natural selection of small, inherited variations that increase the system's ability to compete, survive, and reproduce. Those aspects of legal culture that are more adapted to the social needs of society are likely to survive and may spread to other systems; those aspects that fail to meet the needs of society will evolve and adapt, or gradually be abandoned. Therefore, to understand future development, we need to evaluate whether the continuities of the tradition exert a positive or negative influence on the current system.

In a comparative study, one cannot judge whether one culture is better or worse than another culture in and of itself; there are only differences in concepts. Thus, we cannot make a judgemental evaluation as to whether Chinese tradition based on the rule of *li* is good or bad, compared to Western tradition which features the rule of law. Then how can we judge whether the influence of that tradition on modern practice is positive or negative? There is no black or white answer either. It depends on which criteria we use to make our judgement. If we take the perspective of the legal modernisation process in China, we can perhaps attempt to evaluate the influence of Chinese tradition on contemporary practice based on the following aspects.

First, the continuity from the heavy reliance on *li* in traditional culture to the tolerance of uncertainty in contemporary society is like a double-edged sword. On the positive side, the Chinese vision of the law can be said to be at a higher level, as it assumes absolute legal certainty cannot be achieved and offers some degree of flexibility to fit societal needs more effectively. On the negative side, too much uncertainty may undermine the authority of law and lead to public distrust of the system. This will hinder the modernisation process of law in China.

Second, the continuity of the limited role of the individual in society appears to exert a negative influence on the modernisation process, which is reflected in the form of top-down state control and restrictions on party autonomy in the arbitration system. This constitutes an obstacle to the development of arbitration as a private mode of dispute resolution, which is based on parties having the choice of resolving their disputes outside national courts.

Lastly, the influence of the Confucian philosophy of harmony and the cultural preference towards amicable resolution on the current practice of integrating mediation in arbitration proceedings can be said to be a positive one. This combined practice has its merits in enhancing the efficiency of the process, improving the administration of justice, and maintaining the relationship between the parties. With this understanding, we may be able to predict where we are going from here. On the one hand, we can see Chinese law and practice adapting to transnational standards (section 10.1); on the other hand, Chinese legal culture is also showing signs of having an influence on the practice of arbitration elsewhere (section 10.2).

10.1 ADAPTATIONS OF CHINESE LAW AND PRACTICE TOWARDS TRANSNATIONAL STANDARDS

The transition toward a market-based economy may support the expansion of improved legal institutions and processes in China, particularly the development of dispute resolution. As Professor Pitman Potter describes:

Economic opportunity challenges the indeterminism of informal governance, driving economic actors to seek more predictability through reliance on formalised processes for managing transactions, and also to seek more formal limits on state power. Economic change also challenges the inflexibility of the formal, since market forces are often not as predictable as the former state planners would prefer, and the commercial interests of market actors are unlikely to be satisfied by bureaucratic reliance on regulatory litanies that are unresponsive to the practical realities of economic behavior.[1]

In the interplay of imported and local norms, the interplay of formal and predictable with informal and flexible regulation, a dynamic of 'selective adaptations'[2] is taking place in China. In this process, non-local institutional practices and organisational forms are mediated by local norms. The shift of China's actuality from political transformation to economic growth, decreasing state involvement in market regulation, increasing reliance on law and legal institutions, and changing approaches to mediation, arbitration, and litigation, all reflect the signs of adaptations. With respect to arbitration, in particular, adaptations have taken place both at the legislative level (section 10.1.1) and the institutional level (section 10.1.2) to bring Chinese practice in line with transnational standards.

10.1.1 Legislative Reforms

Although not constitutionally empowered with legislative power, the SPC has played an active role in filling the gaps in the law and addressing lingering issues in legislation that are at odds with transnational standards. Since the adoption of the Arbitration Law, the SPC has issued a number of judicial interpretations concerning the application of the Arbitration Law, with respect to such issues as jurisdiction over interim measures, the handling of jurisdictional challenges, and the setting aside and enforcement of awards. The SPC Interpretation 2006 represents China's latest effort to bring both the law and practice of arbitration more closely in line with commonly accepted transnational standards. Furthermore, some HPCs, such as the Shanghai HPC and the Beijing HPC, have issued opinions and provisions on matters that the SPC has not interpreted. In some instances, the 'opinions' from higher courts are subsequently ratified by the SPC in its judicial interpretations. These judicial interpretations often take a more liberal approach towards arbitration and react more quickly to the changes of commercial needs than the legislative body. They may indeed drive further reforms of the arbitration legislation in China.

---

[1] Pitman Potter, 'Legal Reform in China: Institutions, Culture, and Selective Adaptation' (2004) 29 *Law and Social Inquiry* 465, 481–82.

[2] For a discussion of selective adaptation in China's legal reforms, see Pitman Potter, 'Globalization and Economic Regulation in China: Selective Adaptation of Globalized Norms and Practices' (2003) 2 *Washington University Global Study Law Review* 119, 119–51; Potter, 'Legal Reform in China: Institutions, Culture, and Selective Adaptation', 465–96.

10.1.2 Institutional Reforms

Arbitration institutions also play an essential role in improving arbitration practice in China. As the leading arbitration institution in China, the CIETAC's efforts serve as a driving force for institutional reform. To bring its rules in line with modern international practice, the CIETAC is constantly reviewing and revising its arbitration rules. The most recent revision of its arbitration rules shows many positive adaptations, including the less prescriptive panel list, the ability of arbitral tribunals to decide on their own jurisdiction upon the CIETAC's delegation, the list system for selecting the presiding arbitrator, the freedom of the parties to choose the seat of the arbitration and the place of the hearing, and the arbitral tribunal's discretion to take an inquisitorial or an adversarial approach. The liberal approach taken by the CIETAC has served to promote the practice of arbitration in China, and to facilitate legislative reforms. At the municipal level, some local arbitration institutions have achieved great success in their institutional reforms, such as the BAC and the WAC, which have gained an increasing reputation nationwide and abroad. Experience could be drawn from this so as to push for further reforms of various arbitration institutions all over China.

A. Reforms of the Financial System

To achieve institutional independence, financial reform is the first step. Arbitration institutions should be designated as not-for-profit bodies which provide arbitration services to the public. The assets of arbitration institutions mainly consist of (i) financial contributions by the founders; and (ii) the surplus value created by the arbitrators and the institutional personnel. The financial contributions by the founders have become the assets owned by the institutions, which will be used to improve its arbitration service to the public. The surplus value created by the arbitrators and institutional personnel after its initiation are by nature 'service fees' and will, without doubt, be owned by the arbitration institutions. The arbitration institutions should have full discretion to dispose of their assets to pay for the remuneration of arbitrators, the salaries of their personnel, the daily expenses for the management of the institutions, the training of arbitrators, the marketing of the institutions, etc. Even though certain arbitration institutions may still need governmental financial support for their establishment and sustainability, this does not justify the government's financial control and intervention into the operations of these institutions. Given the private nature of arbitration, the government's financial support could be understood as the government's purchase of arbitration institutions' legal services, or indirect financial support through tax reduction. Leaders of arbitration institutions should take the initiative to achieve financial independence from government funding, and reform their financial system to meet the demands of a market economy.

One successful example is the BAC. Benefitting from the lack of interference of local government and the openness of the institution's leaders, the BAC was able to become financially self-supporting without any dependence on the government three years after its establishment. Initially, officials from relevant departments of the Beijing Government had stated that 'the best governmental support to arbitration is non-interference'.[3] The BAC purchased its office building and facilities through successful bidding in an auction and gained a price 40 per cent lower than the market rate. The BAC's success shows that by participating in the market economy, arbitration institutions will survive and continue their development.[4]

Wuhan, Guangzhou, Shenzhen, Qingdao, Shanghai, Changsha followed suit with financial reforms. Arbitration institutions in those cities have achieved complete financial independence from local government funding. The WAC, for instance, maintains independent financial expenditure, although its expenses are still under the supervision of local government.[5]

B. Reforms of the Management System

In reforming the management system, Chinese arbitration institutions must reorganise various elements of talent, capital, and property assets to better adjust themselves to market needs. In this regard, experience can be drawn from the audacious reforms taken by the BAC in terms of its management system:

a. Management of Arbitrators

In order to improve the quality of its arbitration services, the BAC considered one of its most important tasks was to ensure the high calibre, professionalism and independence of its arbitrators.

(i) Hiring of Arbitrators

In terms of hiring arbitrators, the BAC published its standards for arbitrators through the Administrative Measures for the Employment of Arbitrators, which emphasise professional background and practical capabilities. Through its computer searching system, parties can examine an arbitrator's basic information, educational background, professional expertise and experience and the number of cases the arbitrator has dealt with and is still handling, etc.

---

[3] Speech by the Head of the Justice Bureau of Beijing Municipality, news report *in Shanghai Justice Daily*, 12 December 2004.

[4] Interview with Hongsong Wang, Secretary General of BAC, in Beijing, on 10 April 2007.

[5] Interview with Shizhong Xiong, who was the Vice Chairman of WAC at the time of the interview, in Wuhan, on 2 April 2007.

(ii) Independence of Arbitrators

In order to ensure the independence of arbitrators from institutional influence, the BAC has eliminated 'internal arbitrators'. Learning from the ICC Court's experience, the BAC now expressly prohibits its own personnel from serving as arbitrators for cases before the BAC.[6] To avoid conflicts of interest of the arbitrators, the BAC enhanced the disclosure system and made clear that the disclosure duty remains throughout the arbitral proceedings. A further reform of the BAC requires all those who serve as its arbitrators to cease serving as advocates in other cases before the BAC, including on applications to set aside, or applications for non-enforcement of, an arbitral award rendered by the BAC in court.[7] The BAC believes that, even if foreign institutions find it unnecessary, given the nature of Chinese society and the small arbitration community, such a reform is warranted at present in order to prevent a 'you scratch my back, I will scratch your back' ethos from damaging the impartiality of arbitrators.[8]

(iii) Training and Assessment of Arbitrators

To ensure the quality of arbitration services, the BAC requires arbitrators to attend practical arbitration training,[9] and introduced an assessment system for arbitrators. In the Decision to Enhance the Training and Assessment System of Arbitrators, the BAC stated that it would give priority to arbitrators who had gone through the training process and passed the examinations.

(iv) Arbitrators' Remuneration

Since 2003, the BAC has promulgated the Methods for Remuneration of Arbitrators, which made the standards and principles of arbitrators' remuneration transparent. The latest Methods for Remuneration of Arbitrators were revised on 26 August 2008; these significantly increased arbitrators' remuneration.

b. Management of its Personnel

The BAC has introduced a new hiring and management system for its staff to meet market demand: (i) to appoint committee members from experts in the field of law, economics, and trade, instead of governmental officials; (ii) to hire

---

[6] BAC's amended Articles of Association provide that 'the Chairman and staff of BAC shall not be appointed as arbitrators for BAC cases; vice chairman and committee members shall not accept the appointment by one party to serve as an arbitrator for cases before the BAC, the BAC will not appoint them as its arbitrators, except that both parties so appoint'.
[7] Art 9 of the BAC Ethical Standards for Arbitrators.
[8] Cohen, 'Time to Fix China's Arbitration'.
[9] Art 8 of the Administrative Measures for the Employment of Arbitrators provides that those who have not attended the necessary trainings shall not be appointed to handle cases before the BAC.

case managers openly on the market (who are mostly highly qualified law graduates) with no consideration of any *guanxi* or connections; and (iii) to implement a transparent hiring and assessment system for its personnel, so as to attract capable and talented staff and inspire them to produce their best work.

c. Information Network Management System

To increase the efficiency of its services, the BAC has adopted a comprehensive case management software system, which can be used to monitor arbitral proceedings, as well as being used for the purpose of statistics, time management of the case, search of arbitrators' information, financial management, and personnel assessment. According to Mrs Wang Hongsong, Secretary General of the BAC, 'with the assistance of the e-management of cases, the average time to close a case is only 63 days from the date of the composition of the tribunal'.[10]

C. Innovations in Arbitration Service

In participating in the market economy, arbitration institutions should also build up their unique characteristics. The WAC's innovation in its arbitration services offers a good example. The innovative services that the WAC provides include the following.

a. Partial Settlement

As we have seen in chapter six, mediation is widely used in arbitration proceedings all over China, which has been praised as the 'oriental experience' to improve the efficiency of dispute resolution. Even if the parties have not reached a settlement after the mediation attempt, the mediation process may have served to narrow down the issues remaining in dispute. The WAC thus initiated the practice of 'partial settlement', allowing the mediator to record the parties' consent with respect to certain issues, leaving only the remaining disputed issues to be determined in the following proceedings.[11]

b. Confirmation Arbitration

Apart from the traditional arbitration service by which arbitrators determine the existing dispute between the parties, the WAC created a new service of confirmation arbitration, which allows arbitrators to make an award to determine inherent or potential disputes. This service of confirmation arbitration is expressly provided for in Article 55 of the WAC Arbitration Rules 2007, which allows the arbitral tribunal to render an award to (i) confirm the validity of the

---

[10] Interview with Hongsong Wang, n 4.
[11] Interview with Shizhong Xiong, n 5.

contract, or (ii) to record the settlement agreement or mediation statement in the form of a consent award. While most institutional rules allow the arbitral tribunal to render a consent award, the rendering of an award to confirm the validity of the contract is a new service provided under the WAC rules.

According to Mr Xiong Shizhong, former Vice Chairman of the WAC, confirmation arbitration is typically used in cases with large amounts in dispute, a long performance period, and complicated legal relationships, such as relationships which occurred in the reforms of economic status from collective ownership to state ownership, compensation for inter-bank loans, reforms of state-owned farms, and reforms of state-owned enterprises. Confirmation arbitration in these cases allows the parties to clarify their legal relationship before disputes arise.[12] A question may arise as to whether the decision by the arbitrators is by nature an arbitral award, as it does not resolve a 'dispute'. The confirmation on the validity of the contract before any dispute arises may resemble an expert opinion, and may not be enforceable as an arbitral award under the New York Convention. As far as the author is aware, there are no decisions of confirmation arbitration that have been submitted to the court for enforcement yet. The parties may use the confirmation arbitration as part of their risk management of the contract, to avoid uncertainties left in economic restructuring and reforms of state-owned enterprises. After all, it is the parties' arbitration. If both parties agree to give the arbitrators power to render a decision on potential disputes, it should not be a particular concern for arbitration institutions to render such a service. According to the statistics of the WAC, approximately 30 per cent of arbitration cases accepted by the WAC relate to confirmation arbitration.[13]

10.1.3 Chinese Adaptations to Arb-Med

Another example of Chinese adaptations is the re-examination and evolution of the arb-med system in China towards better safeguards for fairness in the process, taking into consideration the Western concern of due process and impartiality when the same person acts as a mediator and an arbitrator.

For instance, in light of the concerns of impartiality of the mediator-turned-arbitrator, the BAC's latest Arbitration Rules allow the parties to request the *replacement* of an arbitrator on the ground that the results of the award may be affected by his or her involvement in the mediation phase of the proceedings.[14] This is in line with the provision of the IBA Guidelines on Conflicts of Interests in International Arbitration, which requires the arbitrator to resign if he considers himself to lack objectivity as a result of a failed mediation attempt. To deal with the same concern, the CIETAC has also revised its Arbitration Rules, which allow the CIETAC (instead of the arbitral tribunal) to assist parties to

---
[12] Ibid.
[13] The statistics of the WAC, unpublished internal document of the WAC, on file with the author.
[14] Art 58(2) of the BAC Rules 2008.

mediate disputes in a manner and procedure it considers appropriate, with the consent of both parties.[15] It is not yet clear how this provision will operate in practice, however, as the new Rules do not provide who will be responsible for the mediation (ie, whether this is to be conducted by the administrative staff of the CIETAC or whether professional mediators will be engaged by the CIETAC on the parties' behalf).

A further development that deserves attention is the BAC's launch of its separate Mediation Rules, which are derived from advanced mediation systems while maintaining unique features. Parties who are concerned with the incompatibility of the two roles can now choose the stand-alone Mediation Rules to conduct a separate mediation. The principles of the BAC Mediation Rules include: separating the mediation procedure from the arbitration procedure; allowing parties to choose mediators by agreement and not limiting them to the Panel of Mediators set up by the BAC; simplifying the mediation procedure to make it more flexible and convenient; and paying the majority of the mediation fees to the mediators directly to reduce the costs to the parties. The Secretary General of the BAC emphasised that the intention of the Mediation Rules was to fulfill the needs of the parties to resolve disputes through a multitude of ways.[16] Since the implementation of the BAC Mediation Rules on 1 April 2008, the BAC has accepted three stand-alone mediation cases (one international, two domestic), with a total amount in dispute of 138,000,000 yuan (ie, USD 20,909,700). Two of the mediation cases were successfully settled, and the parties reached a settlement. The BAC is planning to reduce its mediation fees in order to encourage parties to select the mediation process.[17]

These encouraging developments show that with the change in the people's mindset to respect the private nature of arbitration, the path seems to be open for the modernisation of international arbitration in China, making China a more attractive international arbitration forum for foreign investors. Indeed, the CIETAC has become one of the busiest arbitration centres of the world. The leading arbitration institutions are also beginning to see the growth of Chinese users. In light of the directives from the top in light of China's focus on economic development, and the changing attitude from below driven in part by economic growth and in part by increased exposure to international ideas, it is foreseeable that this trend of adaptations will continue, so as to bring China's arbitration practice in line with transnational standards.

---

[15] Art 45(8) of the CIETAC Rules 2012.
[16] 王红松,《替代性争端解决机制中律师的作用研讨会上的讲话》, 2007年8月27日 (Hongsong Wang, speech at the Symposium on the Role of Lawyers in the Alternative Dispute Resolution, Beijing, 29th August 2007).
[17] 王红松,《2009 年新春茶话会的讲话》(Hongsong Wang, 'Speech at the 2009 Chinese New Year's Tea Seminar', held in Beijing in 2009).

10.2 THE INFLUENCE OF CHINESE LEGAL CULTURE ON THE PRACTICE OF ARBITRATION WORLDWIDE

Will adaptations in the other direction take place? Will Chinese legal culture and practice influence the development of international arbitration elsewhere? There is no doubt that China is becoming an emerging economic power in the international arena. One can hardly pick up a newspaper today without finding a reference to the importance of China in the world economy. Corresponding to the growth of China's economy and improvements towards a more stable legal environment, the number of foreign investments in the Chinese market has increased drastically. Before entering the Chinese market, foreign investors are obliged to educate themselves about Chinese culture and customs. Almost all major foreign law firms have opened offices in China to assist foreign investors seeking to do business in China and be educated in Chinese law and culture. The effect of such education may make foreign businesses and individuals more aware of, and even adapted to, Chinese culture, traditions, and dispute resolution procedures, in order to play according to the rules of the Chinese game. As a result, they might be more likely to internalise those procedural norms articulated by Chinese legal culture and traditions.

One aspect of potential Chinese influence is its deeply rooted mediation culture. The Chinese consensual spirit in the pursuit of social harmony which seeks to resolve disputes in amicable ways may be of great value for the rest of the world. This is true particularly in the context of the ADR movements in the West in response to the overburdened judiciary. The Chinese practice of integrating mediation into arbitral and judicial proceedings may offer some experience to the West in order to meet the need of improving efficiency in the administration of justice.

Indeed, it already appears that objections to such a combined approach are less strong now, and that opponents are beginning to see the merits of the combination, in terms of saving cost and time. With the growth of international arbitration cases in China, it may be expected that Western arbitrators, whilst sitting on the same arbitral tribunals, will learn from their Chinese colleagues about the advantages of the combined approach. As Professor Tang Houzhi concluded at the ICCA conference in Seoul in 1996:

> Yes, there is an expanding culture that favors combining arbitration with mediation in the world. This culture has been existing in the East for a long time and is now expanding to the West and other parts of the world in one way or another.[18]

Some case examples may illustrate this trend.

---

[18] Tang, 'Is there an Expending Culture that Favors Combining Arbitration with Conciliation or other ADR Procedures?', 101.

Case 1:

An English arbitrator reported his arb-med experience when he acted as the presiding arbitrator in an HKIAC arbitration involving a dispute between a Chinese party and a foreign party. At the hearing, both parties asked him to mediate. They subsequently agreed to a 'standstill' period in the arbitration pending the outcome of the mediation, that the mediator could meet with the parties separately or together, that everything said or done for the purpose of mediation could not be referred to in the arbitration, and that the mediator would continue to act as the chairman if mediation failed. After spending some hours meeting with the parties separately trying to draw their attention to the wider commercial interests that made a settlement desirable, a settlement was eventually reached. Through the successful use of arb-med, a hearing scheduled to last three weeks and an estimated arbitrators' fee of some HK$1.5 million were saved. The arbitrator further stated he did not think that anything said or seen during his discussions with the parties would have inhibited him from continuing with the arbitration if it had gone ahead.[19]

Case 2:

The author has also personally observed a successful arb-med in an ICC arbitration conducted by a tribunal consisting of an American chairman, with Chinese and German co-arbitrators, relating to a disputes between a Chinese and a German party. Before the first hearing, the parties agreed that the tribunal would conduct mediation on the first day, and that if no settlement was reached the arbitrators would resume their role and the arbitration hearing would start on the second day. During the mediation day, the tribunal first explained to the parties the procedure and reconfirmed the parties' consent, then verified the participants' authority to settle. When meeting the parties separately, the tribunal tried to convey to each of them the strengths and weaknesses of their case. At the end of the mediation day, no settlement was reached, as the claimant's final offer did not reach the maximum at which the respondent was authorised to settle. However, the differences were substantially narrowed.

The next day, the arbitration hearing started, and the tribunal members emphasised that they were 'shifting their hat back as arbitrators' and repeated that what had been heard during the mediation proceeding the day before could not be used in the arbitration proceedings. The hearing lasted one whole day, and then the parties were invited to exchange further submissions. Interestingly enough, during the dinner after the hearing (all of the parties and the arbitral tribunal stayed in the hotel where the hearing was held), the parties were voluntarily sitting at the same table and presumably some negotiation discussions continued during dinner. A few months later, a settlement was eventually reached between the parties themselves and the arbitration claims were withdrawn.

[19] Hwang, 'The Role of Arbitrators as Settlement Facilitators: Commentary', 579–90, annex I.

These practices and the general movement towards less formal dispute resolution mechanisms are exerting further influence on legal systems that do not traditionally accept that an arbitrator may act as a settlement facilitator. A good example can be seen in the Commission on Settlement in International Arbitration (CEDR Commission) in London to study settlement facilitation in arbitration with a view to drafting a set of best practices. England strictly distinguishes between the role of the adjudicator who renders a binding decision and that of the conciliator or mediator who lacks such power. Having considered the different approaches currently adopted for the promotion of settlement by international arbitrators, including Chinese practice, the CEDR Commission has published a number of recommendations and the CEDR Rules for the Facilitation of Settlement in International Arbitration in its Final Report in November 2009. The CEDR Commission also proposed a number of safeguards for arbitrators who use private meetings with each party as a means of facilitating settlement.[20] If proper precautions are taken, an effective combination of mediation and arbitration can be achieved without breaching the principle of due process and natural justice.

The Chinese tradition of seeking informal and amicable resolution may well converge with the West in the episodic alteration between values of 'formalism' and 'informalism':[21] arbitration was developed in reaction to the excessive formalism of the courts. As a result of parties' constant demand for new procedural rights, arbitration is now criticised as having become too expensive, too slow, too proceduralised and judicialised, and more similar to court procedures (in their classical formal form).[22] This excessive formalisation of arbitration will inevitably lead to the development of new forms of dispute resolution (which may include combinations of different methods), featured by informalism, de-proceduralisation and flexibility, focusing more on the parties' interest and re-establishing peace between the parties rather than sending them home with a winner and a loser.[23] The Chinese approach of combining mediation with arbitration is people-orientated, relationship-focused, and tempered with flexibility (*biantong*). It appears to be in line with the trend of general legal evolution, and may indeed be a point of convergence where the East meets the West.

To conclude our findings, there are signs of adaptations on both sides. On the one hand, China has made rigorous legal reforms to bring its arbitration law and practice in line with transnational standards; on the other hand, Chinese culture and practice has demonstrated some potential influences on the practice of arbitration in the rest of the world. This finding comes as no surprise. Commercial arbitration

---

[20] The Final Report of the CEDR Commission on Settlement in International Arbitration, November 2009, available at www.cedr.com/about_us/arbitration_commission/Arbitration_Commission_Doc_Final.pdf.

[21] Simon Roberts and Michael Palmer, *Dispute Processes: ADR and the Primary Forms of Decision-Making*, 2nd edn (Cambridge University Press, 2005) 9.

[22] See Clay, *L'arbitre*, 169–70; Oppetit, 'Arbitrage, médiation et conciliation', 27–34.

[23] Kaufmann-Kohler, 'When Arbitrators Facilitate Settlement: Towards a Transnational Standard', 205.

was born from the wisdom of businessmen in order to maximise efficiency and minimise costs and risks. As in any dispute resolution mechanism, international commercial arbitration is influenced by various factors, including tangible, intangible, historical, social, economic, political, religious, and ideological ones. However, certain factors are discernible as affecting it more than others. Commercial arbitration handles disputes among businessmen, or business corporations, who are practice-orientated and more concerned with efficiency than theory. As a result, priority will be given to efficiency and cost performance. Less attention will be paid to the national development of law, which would dominantly affect the national court system.[24] The common intention of businessmen may ultimately drive the process towards the convergence and harmonisation of an international commercial arbitration culture. In the age of accelerated economic convergence, Eastern and Western traditions are bound to interact with each other more frequently and will therefore influence each other more directly. We may thus predict the future of international arbitration as a global convergence.

The example of arbitration in China and its reactions to the movement of transnational arbitration may also broaden our understanding about the globalisation of law, local culture, and traditions. Where there is society, there is law. Where there is law, there is society (*ubi societas ibi jus, ubi jus ibi societas*). No legal systems exist independently of a particular social and cultural context. The globalisation of law can be seen as an entanglement process, with the combinatory operations of legal, social, cultural, economic and political elements in different societies. There is a necessary interaction between local traditions and global norms. On the one hand, globalisation is localised when domestic actors translate and conceptualise the borrowed concepts by referring to local notions – 'localised globalism' or 'micro-globalisation'; on the other hand, local norms may be globalised when they are expanded beyond territorially-constrained statehood and projected on to the global arena – 'globalised localism' or 'macro-localisation'.[25] The trend of harmonisation in the law and practice of arbitration will not lead to the 'universality of arbitration', erasing all the differences. Rather, the development of transnational arbitration will continue as a process of 'glocalisation',[26] which reflects combined impacts of globalisation of law and local culture and traditions.[27]

Walking along the Chang'an Avenue, in the heart of Beijing, one looks straight at the Forbidden City, the remembrance of China's imperial history and the dynastic rules that gripped China for over four thousand years. Just in front

---

[24] See eg Yasuhei Taniguchi, 'Is There a Growing International Arbitration Culture? – An Observation from Asia' in Albert Jan van den Berg (ed), *ICCA Congress series no 8* 1996) 31–40.

[25] See Boaventura de Sousa Santos, *Towards a New Common Sense: Law, Sciences and Politics in the Paradigmatic Transition* (New York, Routledge, 1995) 65.

[26] Roland Robertson is one of the pioneers in the study of globalisation. See for instance, Roland Robertson, 'Glocalization: Time-space and Homogeneity – Heterogeneity' in Michael Featherstone et al (ed), *Global Modernities* (London, Sage, 1995).

[27] For an argument on glocalisation of arbitration, see Fan, 'Glocalisation of Arbitration: Transnational Standards Struggling with Local Norms'.

of the Forbidden City is Tiananmen Square, a symbol of China's recent history. On the left, one can see the Great Hall of the People, where legislators pass today's laws. Looking further west, there is a building full of modernity perfectly integrating with China's historical and symbolic monuments – the Grand National Theatre, designed by a French architect. This might echo the prospects of international arbitration, the coexistence of the historical and the contemporary, and the coexistence of China and the West, all in harmony.

Bibliography

Books

Ali, Shahla, *Resolving Disputes in the Asia-Pacific Region: International Arbitration and Mediation in the East Asia and the West* (London, Routledge, 2011).
Aoki, Masahiko, Gustafsson, Bo and Williamson, Oliver, *The Firm as a Nexus of Treaties* (London, Sage, 1990).
Ames, Roger T, *Rites and Rights: The Confucian Alternative* (Notre Dame, University of Notre Dame Press, 1988).
Atias, Christian, *Épistémologie juridique* (Paris, Dalloz, 2002).
Barnett, Doak, *Cadres, Bureaucracy, and Political Power in Communist China* (New York, Columbia University Press, 1967).
Bodde, Derk and Morris, Clarence, *Law in Imperial China* (Cambridge, MA, Harvard University Press, 1967).
Bodenheimer, Edger, *Jurisprudence – The Philosophy and Method of the Law* (Cambridge, MA, Harvard University Press, 1974).
Boulnois, Luce, *Silk Road: Monks, Warriors & Merchants* (Hong Kong, Odyssey Publications, 2005).
Buhring-Uhle, Christian, *Arbitration and Mediation in International Business* (The Hague, Kluwer Law International, 1996).
Buhring-Uhle, Christian, Kirchhoff, Lars and Scherer, Gabriele, *Arbitration and Mediation in International Business*, 2nd edn (The Hague, Kluwer Law International, 2006).
Bush, Robert and Folger, Joseph, *The Promise of Mediation: The Transformative Approach to Conflict* (San Francisco, Jossey-Bass, 2005).
Chan, Wellington, *Merchants, Mandarins and Modern Enterprise in Late Ch'ing China* (Cambridge, MA, Harvard University Press, 1977).
Cheng, Dejun, Moser, Michael and Wang, Shengchang, *International Arbitration in the People's Republic of China: Commentary, Cases and Materials* (Singapore, Butterworths Asia, 1995).
Choong, John and Weeramantry, Romesh (eds), *The Hong Kong Arbitration Ordinance, Commentary and Annotations* (Hong Kong, Sweet & Maxwell, 2011).
Clay, Thomas, *L'arbitre* (Paris, Dalloz, 2001).
Demogue, René, *L'unification Internationale du Droit Privé: Leçons faites à la Faculté de droit de l'Université de Buenos Ayres* (Paris, Rousseau & Co, 1927).
Dezalay, Yves and Garth, Bryant, *Dealing in Virtue: International Commercial Arbitration and the Construction of a Transnational Legal Order* (Chicago, University of Chicago Press, 1996).
Drahozal, Christopher and Naimark, Richard, *Towards a Science of International Arbitration: Collected Empirical Research* (The Hague, Kluwer Law International, 2005).

Bibliography

Dworkin, Ronald, *Law's Empire* (Cambridge, Mass, Harvard University Press, 1986).
Edwards, Randle, Henkin, Louis and Nathan, Andrew (eds), *Human Rights in Contemporary China* (New York, Columbia University Press, 1986).
Folberg, Jay and Taylor, Alison, *Mediation: A Comprehensive Guide to Resolving Conflicts Without Litigation* (San Francisco, Jossey-Bass Publishers, 1984).
Freedman, Maurice, *Lineage Organization in Southeastern China* (London, The Athlone Press, University of London, 1958).
Friedman, Lawrence M, *The Legal System: A Social Science Perspective* (New York, Russell Sage Foundation, 1975).
Fung, Daniel R and Wang, Shengchang (eds), *Arbitration in China: A Practical Guide*, vol 1 (Hong Kong, Sweet & Maxwell Asia, 2004).
Gaillard, Emmanuel, *Aspects philosophiques du droit de l'arbitrage international* (Leiden, Martinus Nihoff Publishers, 2008).
Gaillard, Emmanuel and Savage, John (eds), *Fouchard Gaillard Goldman on International Commercial Arbitration* (The Hague, Kluwer Law International, 1999).
Gaillard, Emmanuel and Pietro, Domenico di, *Enforcement of Arbitration Agreements and International Arbitral Awards: The New York Convention in Practice* (London, Cameron May, 2008).
Gallagher, Norah and Shan, Wenhua, *Chinese Investment Treaties: Policies and Practice* (Oxford, Oxford University Press, 2009).
Gelfand, Michele and Brett, Jeanne, *The Handbook of Negotiation and Culture* (Stanford, California, Stanford University Press, 2004).
Gemmell, Arthur, *Western and Chinese Arbitration: The Arbitral Chain* (Lanham, University Press of America, 2008).
Genn, Hazel, *Judging Civil Justice* (London, Cambridge University Press, 2009).
Gharavi, Hamid, *The International Effectiveness of the Annulment of an Arbitral Award* (The Hague, Kluwer Law International, 2002).
Glenn, Patrick, *Legal Traditions of the World*, 4th edn (Oxford, Oxford University Press, 2010).
Goh, Bee Chen, *Law Without Lawyers, Justice Without Courts: On Traditional Chinese Mediation* (Surrey, Ashgate Publishing, 2002).
Greenberg, Simon, Kee, Christopher and Weeramantry, Romesh, *International Commercial Arbitration: An Asia-Pacific Perspective* (Cambridge, Cambridge University Press, 2011).
Greif, Avner, *Institutions and the Path to the Modern Economy: Lessons from Medieval Trade* (Cambridge, Cambridge University Press, 2006).
Gu, Weixia, *Arbitration in China: Regulation of Arbitration Agreements and Practical Issues* (Hong Kong, Sweet & Maxwell, 2012).
Halpin, Andrew and Roeben, Volker, *Theorising the Global Legal Order* (Oxford, Hart Publishing, 2009).
Hamilton, Gary and Wang, Zheng, *From the Soil: The Foundations of Chinese Society* (a translation of Fei Xiaotong's Xiangtu Zhongguo) (Berkeley, CA, University of California Press, 1992).
Hart, Herbert Lionel Adolphus, *The Concept of Law* (Oxford, Clarendon Press, 1961).
Hayek, Friedrich, *The Rule of Law* (Menlo Park, CA, Institute for Humane Studies, 1975).
He, Ming, *Civil Judicia Mediation and Case Analysis* (Beijing, People's Court Press, 2005).

Hofstede, Geert, *Culture's Consequences: Comparing Values, Behaviors, Institutions, and Organizations Across Nations* (New York, Sage Publications, 2001).
Howard, Pat, *Breaking the Iron Rice Bowl: Prospects for Socialism in China's Countryside* (Armonk, ME Sharpe, Inc, 1988).
Hsiao, Kung-Chuan, *Rural China: Imperial Control in the Nineteenth Century* (Seattle, University of Washington Press, 1967).
—— *Compromise in Imperial China* (Seattle, University of Washington Press, 1979).
Hu, Hsien Chin, *The Common Descent Group in China and its Functions* (New York, The Viking Fund, 1948).
Huang, Philip, *Civil Justice in China: Representation and Practice in the Qing* (Stanford, Stanford University Press, 1996).
Hunter, Martin et al, *Redfern and Hunter on International Arbitration* (Oxford, Oxford University Press, 2009).
ICCA, *ICCA's Guide to the Interpretation of the 1958 New York Convention: A Handbook for Judges* (The Hague, International Council for Commercial Arbitration, 2011).
Jackson, Vicki, *Constitutional Engagement in a Transnational Era* (Oxford, Oxford University Press, 2010).
Jarrosson, Charles, *La notion d'arbitrage* (Paris, LGDJ, 1987).
Jernigan, Thomas, *China in Law and Commerce* (New York, The Macmillan Company, 1905).
Kronke, Herbert et al, *Recognition and Enforcement of Foreign Arbitral Awards: A Global Commentary on the New York Convention* (The Hague, Kluwer Law International, 2010).
Lew, Julian, Mistelis, Loukas and Kröll, Stefan, *Comparative International Commercial Arbitration* (The Hague, Kluwer Law International, 2003).
Liu, Hui-chen Wang, *The Traditional Chinese Clan Rules* (Locust Valley, NY, Augustin, 1959).
Lowenfeld, Andreas F, *International Economic Law* (Oxford, Oxford University Press, 2003).
Lubman, Stanley, *Bird in a Cage: Legal Reform in China After Mao* (Palo Alto, Stanford University Press, 1999).
Lufrano, Richard John, *Honorable Merchants: Commerce and Self-Cultivation in Late Imperial China* (Honolulu, University of Hawaii Press, 1997).
Lynch, Katherine, *The Forces of Economic Globalization—Challenges to the Regime of International Commercial Arbitration* (The Hague, Kluwer Law International, 2003).
Macauley, Melissa, *Social Power and Legal Culture: Litigation Masters in Late Imperial China* (Stanford, Stanford University Press, 1999).
MacDowell, Douglas, *The Law in Classical Athens* (Ithaca, Cornell University Press, 1978).
Moffitt, Michael and Bordone, Robert, *The Handbook of Dispute Resolution* (San Francisco, Jossey-Bass Publishers, 2005).
Moore, Christopher, *The Mediation Process: Practical Strategies for Resolving Conflict*, 3rd edn (San Francisco, Jossey-Bass Publishers, 2003).
Moser, Michael, *Law and Social Change in a Chinese Community: A Case Study From Rural Taiwan* (London, Oceana Publications, 1982).
—— (ed) *Managing Business Disputes in Today's China – Duelling with Dragons* (The Hague, Kluwer Law International, 2007).

Bibliography

Moser, Michael, *Investor-State Arbitration: Lessons for Asia* (Huntington, Juris Publishing, 2008).
Moser, Michael and Cheng, Teresa, *Hong Kong Arbitration: A User's Guide* (The Hague, Kluwer Law International, 2004).
Motono, Eiichi, *Conflict and Cooperation in Sino-British Business, 1860–1911: The Impact of the Pro-British Commercial Network in Shanghai* (London, Macmillan, 2000).
Motulsky, Henri, *Ecrits, Etudes et notes sur l'arbitrage*, vol II (Paris, Dalloz, 1974).
Mousarakis, George, *The Historical and Institutional Context of Roman Law* (Surrey, Ashgate Publishing, 2003).
Mustill, Michael and Boyd, Stewart, *Mustill & Boyd: Commercial Arbitration*, 2nd edn (London, Butterworths, 1989).
Nelken, David and Feest, Johannes (eds), *Adapting Legal Cultures* (Oxford, Hart Publishing, 2001).
Newman, Lawrence and Hill, Richard (eds), *Leading Arbitrators' Guide to International Arbitration*, 2nd edn (Huntington, Juris Publishing, 2008).
Neumann, Franz Leopold, *The Rule of Law: Political Theory and the Legal System in Modern Society* (New Hampshire, Berg Publishers Ltd, 1986).
Olson, Walter, *The Litigation Explosion: What Happened When America Unleashed the Lawsuit* (New York, Dutton, 1991).
Pasternak, Burton, *Kinship and Community in Two Chinese Villages* (Stanford, Stanford University Press, 1972).
Peerenboom, Randall, *China's Long March Toward Rule of Law* (Cambridge, Cambridge University Press, 2002).
Potter, Pitman, *The Economic Contract Law of China* (Seattle, University of Washington Press, 1992).
—— *The Chinese Legal System: Globalization and Local Legal Culture* (London, Routledge, 2001).
Rawls, John, *A Theory of Justice* (Cambridge, MA, Harvard University Press, 1971).
Roberts, Simon and Palmer, Michael, *Dispute Processes: ADR and the Primary Forms of Decision-Making*, 2nd edn (Cambridge University Press, 2005).
Roebuck, Dereck, *Ancient Greek Arbitration* (Oxford, Holo Books, 2001).
—— *The Charitable Arbitrator: How to Mediate and Arbitrate in Louis XIV's France* (Oxford, Holo Books, 2002).
—— *Early English Arbitration* (Oxford, Holo Books, 2008).
—— *Disputes and Differences: Comparisons in Law, Language and History* (Oxford, Holo Books, 2010).
Roebuck, Dereck and Fumichon, Bruno de Loynes de, *Roman Arbitration* (Oxford, Holo Books, 2004).
Santos, Boaventura de Sousa, *Towards a New Common Sense: Law, Science and Politics in the Paradigmatic Transition* (New York, Routledge, 1995).
Schirokauer, Conrad, *A Brief History of Chinese Civilization* (New York, City University of New York, 1991).
Schurmann, Franz, *Ideology and Organization in Communist China* (Berkeley, CA, University of California Press, 1968).
Shan, Wenhua and Gallager, Nora, *Chinese Investment Treaties, Policies and Practice* (Oxford, Oxford University Press, 2009).
Shapiro, Martin, *Courts: A Comparative and Political Analysis* (Chicago, University of Chicago Press, 1981).

Sprenkel, Sybille van der, *Legal Institutions in Manchu China: A Sociological Analysis* (London, The Athlone Press, 1962).
Stein, Peter, *Roman Law in European History* (Cambridge, Cambridge University Press, 2002).
Tao, Jingzhou, *Arbitration Law and Practice in China*, 2nd edn (The Hague, Kluwer Law International, 2008).
Telford, ME, *Med-Arb: A Viable Dispute Resolution Alternative* (Kingston, Ontario, IRC Press Queen's University, 2000).
Tellegen-Couperus, Olga, *A Short History of Roman Law* (London, Routledge, 1993).
Teubner, Gunther (ed), *Global Law without a State* (Aldershot, Ashgate, 1997).
Touraine, Alain, *Pourrons-nous vivre ensemble? égaux et différents* (Paris, Fayard, 1997).
Twining, William, *Globalisation and Legal Theory* (London, Butterworths, 2000).
—— *General Jurisprudence: Understanding Law From a Global Perspective* (Cambridge, Cambridge University Press, 2009).
Wang, Chengguang and Zhang, Xianchu (eds), *Introduction to Chinese Law* (Hong Kong, Sweet & Maxwell Asia, 1997).
Watson, Alan, *Legal Transplants* (Edinburgh, Scottish Academic Press, 1974).
Watt, John R, *The District Magistrate in Late Imperial China* (New York, Columbia University Press, 1972).
von Wunschheim, Clarisse, *Enforcement of Commercial Arbitral Awards in China*, 2nd edn (New York, Thomson Reuters Business, 2012).
Yang, Lien-Sheng, *Studies in Chinese Institutional History* (Cambridge, MA, Harvard University Press, 1961).
Yang, Martin, *A Chinese Village: Taitou, Shantung Province* (New York, Columbia University Press, 1945).
Zeng, Xianyi, Zheng, Ding and Zhao, Xiaogeng (eds), *A History of Chinese Law* (Beijing, People's University Press, 2004).
郭建,《中国法文化漫笔》(北京, 东方出版中心, 1999), (Guo, Jian, *Discussions of Chinese Legal Culture* (Beijing, Oriental Publishing Center, 1999)).
梁治平,《法意与人情》(北京,法制出版社, 2003),(Liang, Zhiping, *The Legal Spirit and Human Sentiments* (Beijing, Legal Press, 2003)).
刘馨珺,《明镜高悬：南宋县衙的狱讼》(北京, 北京大学出版社, 2007), (Liu, Xinjun, *A Just Trial by an Honest Official: Litigation at the Yamen in South Song Dynasty* (Beijing, Beijing University Press, 2007)). 黄源盛,《法律继受与近代中国法》(台北, 元照出版有限公司, 2007), (Huang, Yuansheng, *Legal Transplant and Recent Chinese Law* (Taipei, Yuanzhao Press, 2007)).
强世功 (编),(《调解、法制与现代性：中国调解制度研究》). (北京, 中国法制出版社, 2001), (Jiang, Shigong, *Mediation, Law and Modernization: A Study on Chinese Mediation* (Beijing, China Legal Publishing House, 2001)).
康明,《商事仲裁服务研究》(北京, 法律出版社, 2005), (Kang, Ming, *Research on Commercial Arbitration Service* (Beijing, Legal Press, 2005)).
李步云,《论法治》(北京, 社会科学文献出版社, 2008), (Li, Buyun, *On The Rule of Law* (Beijing, Beijing Social Science Literature Press, 2008)).
马汉宝,《法律与中国社会之变迁》,(台北, 韩芦图书出版有限公司, 1999), (Ma, Hanbao, *The Law and the Changes of the Chinese Society*, (Taipei, Hanlu Press, 1999)).
彭泽益 (编),《中国工商行会史料集》(香港,中华书局, 1995), (Peng, Zeyi (ed), *A Collection of Historical Materials on Chinese Industrial and Commercial Guilds* (Hong Kong, China Books, 1995)).

乔欣，《仲裁权研究–仲裁程序公正与权利保障》(北京，法律出版社，2001)，(Qiao, Xin, *The Research on Power of Arbitration – the Due Process of Arbitration and the Right Protection* (Beijing, Legal Press, 2001)).

瞿同祖，《中国法律与中国社会》(北京，商务印书馆，1981)，(Qu, Tongzu, *Chinese Law and Chinese Society* (Beijing, Commercial Publishing House, 1981)).

瞿同祖，《瞿同祖法学论著集》(北京，中国政法大学出版社，1998)，(Qu, Tongzu, *Selected Works of Qu Tongzu* (Beijing, China Politics and Law University Press, 1998)).

全汉升，《中国行会制度史》(天津,百花文艺出版社，2007)，(Quan, Hansheng, *History of the Guild System in China*) (Tianjin, Baihua Wenyi Press, 2007).

史景星，《行业协会概论》(上海，复旦大学出版社，1989)，(Shi, Jingxing, *The Overview of the Chinese Guilds* (Shanghai, Fudan University Press, 1989)).

宋连斌，《国际商事仲裁管辖权研究》(北京，法律出版社，2000)，(Song, Lianbin, *Research on the Jurisdiction of International Commercial Arbitration* (Beijing, Legal Press, 2000)).

谭兵，《中国仲裁制度研究》(北京，法律出版社，1995)，(Tan, Bing, *Research on the Arbitration System in China* (Beijing, Legal Press, 1995)).

王伯琦，《近代法律思潮与中国固有文化》(台北，司法行政部印行，1956)，(Wang, Boqi, *Legal Thoughts in Modern History and Traditional Chinese Culture* (Taipei, Legal and Administrative Burea, 1956)).

王生长，《仲裁与调解相结合的理论与实务》(北京，法律出版社，2001)，(Wang, Shengchang, *The Combination of Arbitration and Mediation: Theory and Practice,* (Beijing, Legal Press, 2001)). 杨良宜，《国际商务仲裁》(北京，中国政法大学出版社，1998)，(Yang, Liangyi, *International Commercial Arbitration* (Beijing, China Politics and Law University Press, 1998)).

杨鸿烈，《中国法律思想史》(台北，台湾商务印书馆，1964)，(Yang, Honglie, *The History of Chinese Legal Thoughts* (Taipei, Taiwan Commercial Publishing House, 1964)).

於兴中，《法治与文明秩序》(北京,中国政法大学出版社，2006)，(Yu, Xingzhong, *Rule of Law and Civil Order* (Beijing, China Politics and Law University Press, 1998)).

滋贺秀三[日]，《明清时期的民事审判与民间契约》(北京，法律出版社，1998)，王亚新、范愉、陈少峰 译，(しが・しゅうぞう, *The Civil Trial and Social Contract During the Ming and Qing Period* (Beijing, Legal Press 1998), translated by Yaxin Wang, Yu Fan and Shaofeng Chen)).

张希坡、韩延龙 (编)，《中国革命法制史》(北京，中国社会科学出版社，2007)，(Zhang, Xipo and Han, Yanlong, *The History of Chinese Revolution and Law* (Beijing, China Social Science Press, 2007)).

中国孔子基金会，《中国儒学百科》，(北京，中国大百科全书出版社，1997)，(China Confucian Institute, *Encyclopedia of Chinese Confucian Philosophy* (Beijing, China Encyclopedia Press, 1997)).

Theses

Clay, Thomas, *L'arbitre*, Préface de Philippe Fouchard (Paris, Dalloz, 2001).

De Menthon, François, *Le rôle de l'arbitrage dans l'évolution judiciaire* (Thèse Paris, 1926).

Gu, Weixia, *The Regulation of Arbitration Agreements in China: Practical Constraints and Prospective Reforms for Chinese Arbitration*, thesis for the degree of SJD at the University of Hong Kong, 2008.

Jarrosson, Charles, *La notion d'arbitrage*, préface de Bruno Oppetit, LGDJ, Bibliothèque de droit privé, Tome CXCVIII, 1987.

Wang, Wenying, *Arbitral Power in the People's Republic of China: Reality and Reform*, thesis for the degree of SJD at the University of Hong Kong, 2004.

Yang, Caixia, *La validité de la convention d'arbitrage dans le commerce international* (Etude comparative), thèse Université Panthéon-Assas (Paris II), sous la direction de Marie Goré, 2008.

Articles

Abdulla, Zina, 'The Arbitration Agreement' in Gabrielle Kaufmann-Kohler and Blaise Stucki (eds), *International Arbitration in Switzerland: A Handbook for Practitioners* (The Hague, Kluwer Law International, 2004).

Abramson, Harold, 'Protocols For International Arbitrators Who Dare to Settle Cases' (1999) 10 *American Review of International Arbitration* 1.

Alford, William, 'Of Arsenic and Old Laws: Looking Anew at Criminal Justice in Late Imperial China' (1984) 72 *California Law Review* 1180.

—— 'On the Limits of "Grand Theory" in Comparative Law' (1986) 61 *Washington Law Review* 945.

Ali, Shahla, 'The Morality of Conciliation: An Empirical Examination of Arbitrator "Role Moralities" in East Asia and the West' (2011) 16 *Harvard Negotiation Law Review* 1.

Atias, Christian, 'Présence de la tradition juridique' (1997) *Revue de recherche juridique*.

Ball, Markham, 'The Essential Judge: The Role of the Courts in a System of National and International Commercial Arbitration' (2006) 22 *Arbitration International*.

Berg, Albert Jan van den, 'New York Convention of 1958: Refusals of Enforcement' (2008) 18 *ICC Bulletin* 2.

Berger, Klaus-Peter, 'Integration of Mediation Elements into Arbitration: Hybrid Procedures and "Intuitive" Mediation by International Arbitrators' (2003) 19 *Arbitration International* 3.

Berkowitz, Daniel, Pistor, Katharina and Richard, Jean-Francois, 'The Transplant Effect' (2003) 51 *American Journal of Comparative Law* 163.

Bermann, George, '"Domesticating" the New York Convention: The Impact of the Federal Arbitration Act' (2011) 2 *Journal of International Dispute Settlement* 2.

Bersani, Matthew D, 'Enforcement of Arbitration Awards in China: Foreigners Find the System Solely Lacking' (1992) 19 *China Business Review* 5.

Blessing, Marc, 'The New International Arbitration Law in Switzerland – A Significant Step Towards Liberalism' (1988) 5 *Journal of International Arbitration* 2.

—— 'Globalization (and Harmonization?) of Arbitration' (1992) 9 *Journal of International Arbitration* 1.

Bockstiegel, Karl-Heinz, 'Presenting, Taking and Evaluating Evidence in International Arbitration' in Thomas Carbonneau (ed), *Handbook on International Arbitration & ADR* (New York, JurisNet, 2006).

Briner, Robert, 'Switzerland' in Jan Paulsson (ed), *International Handbook on Commercial Arbitration* (The Hague, Kluwer Law International, 1998).

—— 'Arbitration in China Seen from the Viewpoint of the International Court of Arbitration of the International Chamber of Commerce' in Albert Jan van den Berg (ed), *ICCA Congress Series no 12* (The Hague, Kluwer Law International, 2005).

Brockman, Rosser, 'Commercial Contract Law in Late Nineteenth-Century Taiwan' in Jerome Cohen, Randle Edwards and Fu-Mei Chang Chen (eds), *Essays on China's Legal Tradition* (Princeton, Princeton University Press, 1980).

Brower, Charles, II, Charles Brower and Sharpe, Jeremy K, 'The Coming Crisis in the Global Adjudication System' (2003) 19 *Arbitration International* 4.

Buchanan, Mark A, Public Policy and International Commercial Arbitration' (1988) 26 *American Business Law Journal* 511.

Buhring-Uhle, Christian, Kirchhoff, Lars and Scherer, Gabriele, 'The Arbitrator as Mediator: Some Recent Empirical Insights' (2003) 20 *Journal of International Arbitration* 2.

Burdick, Francis, 'What is the Law Merchant?' (1902) 2 *Columbia Law Review* 470.

Cai, Hongda, 'Discussion on Issues Related to Re-conduct of Arbitration' (2000) 2 *Arbitration and Law*.

Campbell, Andrew M, 'Annotation, Refusal to Enforce Foreign Arbitration Awards on Public Policy Grounds' (1998) 144 *American Law Report Federal* 481.

Cao, Lijun, 'Combining Conciliation and Arbitration in China: Overview and Latest Development' (2006) 9 *International Arbitration Law Review* 3.

Carter, James, 'Issues Arising From Integrated Dispute Resolution Clauses' in Albert Jan van den Berg (ed), *ICCA Congress series no 12* (The Hague, Kluwer Law International, 2005).

—— 'Issues Arising From Integrated Dispute Resolution Clauses' in *New Horizons in International Commercial Arbitration and Beyond* (The Hague, Kluwer Law International, 2005).

—— 'Issues Involving Confidentiality' in Albert Jan van den Berg (ed), *ICCA Congress series no 12* (The Hague, Kluwer Law International, 2005).

Cassese, Sabino, 'The Globalization of Law' (2005) 37 *New York University Journal of International Law and Politics* 973.

Chan, EHW and Tse, R, 'Cultural Considerations in International Construction Contracts' (2003) 129 *Journal of Construction Engineering and Management ASCE* 4.

Cheng, Lucie and Rosett, Arthur, 'Contract With a Chinese Face: Socially Embedded Factors in the Transformation From Hierarchy to Market 1978–1989' in Tahirih Lee (ed), *Contract, Guanxi, and Dispute Resolution in China* (New York, Garland Publishing, 1997) originally published in (1991) 5 *Journal of Chinese Law* 143.

Chew-Lafitte, 'The Resolution of Transnational Commercial Disputes in the People's Republic of China: A Guide for Legal Practitioners' (1982) 8 *Yale Journal of World Public Order* 236.

Chia, Ho-Beng, Lee-Patridge, Joo Eng and Chong, Chee-Leong, 'Traditional Mediation Practices: Are We Throwing the Baby Out with the Bath Water?' (2004) 24 *Conflict Resolution Quarterly* 4.

Choong, John and Yuen, Peter, 'The Supreme People's Court's Draft Interpretation to Several Issues Regarding Application of PRC Arbitration Law' (2006) 7 *Mealey's International Arbitration Quarterly Law Review* 3.

Chow, Deborah, 'Development of China's Legal System Will Strength its Mediation Programs' (2001) 3 *Cardozo Journal of Conflict Resolution*.

Chow, Daniel CK, 'Culture Matters' (2003) 18 *Ohio State Journal on Dispute Resolution* 89.

Clark, Kevin, 'The Philosophical Underpinning and General Workings of Chinese Mediation Systems: What Lessons Can American Mediators Learn?' (2002) 2 *Pepperdine Dispute Resolution Law Journal* 117.

Clarke, Donald, 'Dispute Resolution in China' in Tahirih Lee (ed), *Contract, Guanxi, and Dispute Resolution in China* (New York, Garland Publishing, 1997), originally published in (1991) 3 *Journal of Chinese Law* 245.
—— 'China: Creating a Legal System for a Market Economy' (2007) GWU Law School Public Law Research Paper No 396.
Coe, Jack, 'From Anecdote to Data: Reflections on the Global Center's Barcelona Meeting' (2003) 20 *Journal of International Arbitration* 1.
Cohen, Jerome, 'Chinese Mediation on the Eve of Modernization' (1966) 54 *California Law Review* 3.
—— 'Drafting People's Mediation Rules' in John Wilson Lewis (ed), *The City in Communist China* (Stanford, Stanford University Press, 1971).
—— 'Is There Law in China?' in Tahirih Lee (ed), *Basic Concepts of Chinese Law* (New York, Garland Publishing, 1997), originally published in *International Trade Law Journal, Work Shop Proceedings* 74.
—— 'Reforming China's Civil Procedure: Judging the Courts' (1997) 45 *American Journal of Comparative Law*.
—— 'Time to Fix China's Arbitration' (2005) 168 *Far Eastern Economic Review* 31.
Cohen, Jerome and Lange, John, 'The Chinese Legal System: A Primer for Investors' (1997) 17 *New York Law School Journal of International and Comparative Law* 345.
Colatrella, Michael, '"Court-Performed" Mediation in the People's Republic of China: A Proposed Model to Improve the United States Federal District Courts' Mediation Programs' (1999–2000) 15 *Ohio State Journal on Dispute Resolution* 391.
Cole, Sarah Rudolph and Blankley, Kristen, 'Arbitration' in Michael Moffitt and Robert Bordone (eds), *The Handbook of Dispute Resolution* (San Francisco, Jossey-Bass, 2005).
Collins, Michael, 'Do International Arbitral Tribunals Have Any Obligations to Encourage Settlement of the Disputes Before Them?' (2003) 19 *Arbitration International* 3.
Commission, The Beijing Arbitration & Resolution, The Straus Institute for Dispute Resolution, 'East Meets West: An International Dialogue on Mediation and Med-Arb in the United States and China' (2009) 9 *Pepperdine Dispute Resolution Law Journal* 379.
Conbere, John, 'Is ADR Ready to be Globalized: Reflections on Intercultural Approaches' (2006) 27 *Hamline Journal of Public Law and Policy* 263.
Cook, Judith and Fonow, Mary Margaret, 'Knowledge and Women's Interests' in Joyce McCarl Neilson (ed), *Feminist Research Methods: Exemplary Readings in the Social Sciences* (Boulder, Westview Press, 1990).
Coons, John, 'Approaches to Court Imposed Compromises – The Uses of Doubt and Reason' (1964) 58 *Northwestern University Law Review* 750.
Crampton, Alexandra, 'Addressing Questions of Culture and Power in the Globalization of ADR' (2006) 27 *Hamline Journal of Public Law and Policy* 229.
Crawford, Alastair, 'Plotting your Dispute Resolution Strategy: From Negotiating the Dispute Resolution Clause to Enforcement against Assets' in Chris Hunter (ed), *Dispute Resolution in the PRC: A Practical Guide to Litigation and Arbitration in China* (Asia Law & Practice, 1995).
Cremades, Bernardo M, 'Overcoming the Clash of Legal Cultures: The Role of Interactive Arbitration' (1998) 14 *Arbitration International* 2.
Curtin, Kenneth-Michael, 'Redefining Public Policy in International Arbitration of Mandatory National Laws' (1997) 64 *Defence Counsel Journal* 271.

256 Bibliography

Darwazeh, Nadia and Yeoh, Friven, 'Recognition and Enforcement of Awards under the New York Convention – China and Hong Kong Perspectives' (2008) 25 *Journal of International Arbitration* 6.

David, René, 'Arbitrage et droit comparé' (1959) 1 *Revue internationale de droit comparé*.

Dendorfer, Renate and Lack, Jeremy, 'The Interaction Between Arbitration and Mediation: Vision v Reality' (2007) 1 *Dispute Resolution International* 1.

Derains, Yves and Goodman-Everard, Rosabel, 'French National Report' in Jan Paulsson (ed), *International Handbook on Commercial Arbitration* (The Hague, Kluwer Law International, 1998).

Diamant, Neil J, 'Conflict and Conflict Resolution in China: Beyond Mediation-Centered Approaches' (2000) 44 *Journal of Conflict Resolution* 4.

Donahey, M Schott, 'Seeking Harmony: Is the Asian Concept of the Conciliator/Arbitrator Applicable in the West?' (1995) 50 *Dispute Resolution International* 2.

Drahozal, Christopher R, 'Of Rabbits and Rhinoceri: A Survey of Empirical Research on International Commercial Arbitration' (2003) 20 *Journal of International Arbitration* 1.

Dulac, Elodie, 'The Emerging Third Generation of Chinese Investment Treaties' (2010) 7 *Transnational Dispute Management* 4.

Eliasson, Nils, 'Investor-State Arbitration and Chinese Investors. Recent Developments in Light of the Decision on Jurisdiction in the Case Mr Tza Yap Shun *v* The Republic of Peru' (2009) 2 *Contemporary Asia Arbitration Journal* 2.

Epstein, Lee and King, Gary, 'The Rules of Inference' (2002) 69 *University of Chicago Law Review* 1.

Fadlallah, Ibrahim, 'Arbitration Facing Conflicts of Culture' (2009) 25 *Arbitration International* 3.

Fan, Kun, 'Arbitration in China: Practice, Legal Obstacles and Reforms' (2008) 19 *ICC Bulletin* 2.

—— 'Mediation and Civil Justice Reform in Hong Kong' (2011) 27 *International Litigation Quarterly* 2.

—— 'Prospects of Foreign Arbitration Institutions Administering Arbitration in China' (2011) 28 *Journal of International Arbitration* 4.

—— 'The Risks of Apparent Bias When An Arbitrator Acts As a Mediator: Remarks on Hong Kong Court's Decision in Gao Haiyan' (2011) 13 *Yearbook of Private International Law* 93.

—— 'Glocalisation of Arbitration: Transnational Standards Struggling with Local Norms' (2013) *Harvard Negotiation Law Review*.

Fazzi, Cindy, 'How to Avoid Cultural Collision' (2004) 59 *Dispute Resolution Journal* 105.

Fei, Lanfang, 'Implementation of the New York Convention in China: A Case Study' (2008) 4 *Asian International Arbitration Journal* 2.

—— 'Enforcement of Arbitral Awards between Hong Kong and Mainland China: A Successful Model?' (2009) 8 *Chinese Journal of International Law* 3.

—— 'Setting Aside Foreign-related Arbitral Awards under Chinese Law: A Study in Perspective of Judicial Practice' (2009) 26 *Journal of International Arbitration* 2.

—— 'Public Policy as a Bar to Enforcement of International Arbitral Awards: A Review of the Chinese Approach' (2010) 26 *Arbitration International* 2.

Feinerman, James, 'The History and Development of China's Dispute Resolution System' in Chris Hunter (ed), *Dispute Resolution in the PRC: A Practical Guide to Litigation and Arbitration in China* (Asia Law & Practice, 1995).

Friedman, Lawrence M, 'Legal Rules and the Process of Social Change' (1967) 19 *Stanford Law Review* 4.
—— 'Legal Culture and Social Development' (1969) 4 *Law and Society Review* 1.
—— 'The Law and Society Movement' (1986) 38 *Stanford Law Review* 3.
—— 'Total Justice: Law, Culture, and Society' (1986) 40 *Bulletin of the American Academy of Arts and Sciences* 3.
—— 'Litigation and Society' (1989) 15 *Annual Review of Sociology* 17.
—— 'The Concept of Legal Culture: A Reply' in David Nelken (ed), *Comparing Legal Cultures* (Aldershot, Dartmouth, 1997).
Friedman, Ray et al, 'Causal Attribution for Inter-Firm Contract Violation: A Comparative Study of Chinese and American Commercial Arbitrators' (2007) 92 *Journal of Applied Psychology* 3.
Fu, Hualing, 'Understanding People's Mediation in Post-Mao China' (1992) 6 *Journal of Chinese Law* 211.
—— 'The Politics of Mediation in a Chinese Country: The Case of Luo Lianxi' (2003) 5 *The Australian Journal of Asian Law* 107.
—— 'Access to Justice in China: Potentials, Limits and Alternatives' (2009).
Fu, Hualing and Cullen, Richard, 'From Mediatory to Adjudicatory Justice: The Limits of Civil Justice Reform in China' in Margaret Woo and Mary Gallagher (ed), *Chinese Justice: Civil Dispute Resolution in Contemporary China* (Cambridge, CUP, 2011).
Gaillard, Emmanuel, 'Arbitrage commercial international, Convention d'arbitrage, Effets, Droit commun et conventionnel' (1994) *Juris-Classeur Droit international, fasc.*
—— 'L'interférence des juridictions du siège dans le déroulement de l'arbitrage' in *Liber Amicorum Claude Reymond. Autour de l'arbitrage* (Paris, Litec, 2004).
Gaillard, Emmanuel and Banifatemi, Yas, 'Negative Effect of Competence-Competence: The Rule of Priority in Favor of the Arbitrators' in Emmanuel Gaillard and Domenico Di Pietro (eds), *Enforcement of Arbitration Agreements and International Arbitral Awards: The New York Convention in Practice* (London, Cameron May, 2009).
Galanter, Marc, 'The Vanishing Trial: An Examination of Trials and Related Matters in Federal and State Courts' (2004) 1 *Journal of Empirical Legal Studies*.
Gélinas, Fabien, 'Peeking Through the Form of Uniform Law: International Arbitration Practice and Legal Harmonization' (2010) 27 *Journal of International Arbitration* 3.
Gillespie, John, 'Developing a Framework for Understanding the Localisation of Global Scripts in East Asia' in Andrew Halpin and Volker Roeben (eds), *Theorising the Global Legal Order* (Oxford, Hart Publishing, 2009).
Gingjiang, Kong, 'Bilateral Investment Treaties: The Chinese Approach and Practice' (2003) 8 *Asian Yearbook of International Law* 105.
Ginsburg, Tom, 'The Culture of Arbitration' (2003) 36 *Vanderbilt Journal of Transnational Law*, 1335.
Glassman, Eric, 'The Function of Mediation in China: Examining the Impact of Regulations Governing the People's Mediation Committees' (1992) 10 *UCLA Pacific Basin Law Journal*.
Glenn, Patrick, 'Legal Tradition and Legal Traditions' (2007) 2 *Journal of Comparative Law* 69.
—— 'Cosmopolitan Legal Orders' in Andrew Halpin and Volker Roeben (eds), *Theorising the Global Legal Order* (Oxford, Hart Publishing, 2009).
Golann, Dwight, 'Is Legal Mediation a Process of Repair – or Separation? An Empirical Study, and Its Implications' (2001) 7 *Harvard Negotiation Law Review* 301.

Gold, Julia Ann, 'ADR Through a Cultural Lens: How Cultural Values Shape our Disputing Processes' (2005) *Journal of Dispute Resolution* 289.

Goode, Roy, 'The Adaptation of English Law to International Commercial Arbitration' (1992) 8 *Arbitration International* 1.

—— 'The Role of the Lex Loci Arbitri in International Commercial Arbitration' (2001) 19 *Arbitration International*.

Greenblatt, Jonathan L and Griffin, Peter, 'Towards the Harmonization of International Arbitration Rules: Comparative Analysis of the Rules of the ICC, AAA, LCIA and CIETAC' (2001) 17 *Arbitration International* 1.

Greif, Avner, Milgrom, Paul and Weingast, Barry, 'Coordination, Commitment, and Enforcement: The Case of the Merchant Guild' (1994) 102 *Journal of Political Economy* 4.

Grenner, William B, 'The Evolution of Foreign Trade Arbitration in the People's Republic of China' (1988–1989) 21 *New York University Journal of International Law and Politics* 293.

Gu, Weixia and Zhang, Xianchu, 'The China-Style Commission-Oriented Competence on Arbitral Jurisdiction: Analysis of Chinese Adaptation into Globalization' (2006) 9 *International Arbitration Law Review* 6.

Halegua, Aaron, 'Reforming the People's Mediation System in Urban China' (2005) 35 *Hong Kong Law Journal*.

Halpin, Andrew and Roeben, Volker, 'Introduction' in Andrew Halpin and Volker Roeben (eds), *Theorising the Global Legal Order* (Oxford, Hart Publishing, 2009).

Han, Bo, 'Empirical Study and Theoretical Reflection of Judicial Mediation. A Survey on the Implementation of SPC Provisions on Court's Civil Mediation Work' (2007) 4 *Legal Application* 75.

Harten, Gus Van and Loughlin, Martin, 'Investment Treaty Arbitration as a Species of Global Administrative Law' (1006) 17 *European Journal of International Law* 121.

Hasegawa, Ko, 'Hou no Kureouru no Gainen ni tsuite no Kisoteki Kousatsu' (2007) 58 *Kokkaido Law Review* 3 (Ko Hasegawa, Fundamental Considerations on the Concept of the Creole of Law).

—— 'Incorporating Foreign Legal Ideas through Translation' in Andrew Halpin and Volker Roeben (eds), *Theorising the Global Legal Order* (Oxford, Hart Publishing, 2009).

Hausman, Daniel M, 'Fairness and Social Norms' (2008) 75 *Philosophy of Science* 5.

Heymann, Monika CE, 'International Law and the Settlement of Investment Disputes Relating To China' (2008) 11 *Journal of International Economic Law* 507.

Himma, Kenneth Einar, 'The Instantiation Thesis and Raz's Critique of Inclusive Positivism' (2001) 20 *Law and Philosophy* 1.

Hinman, George Burke, 'China, Modernization, and Sino-United States Trade: Will China Submit to Arbitration' (1980) 10 *California Western International Law Journal* 1.

Hober, Kaj and Eliasoon, Nils, 'Investor-State Arbitration and China – An Overview' in Michael Moser (ed), *Business Disputes in China* (Huntington, Juris Publishing, 2009).

Hoellering, Michael, 'Comments on the Growing Inter-Action of Arbitration and Mediation' in Albert Jan van den Berg (ed), *ICCA Congress series no 8* (The Hague, Kluwer Law International, 1998).

Hok, Gotz-sebastian, 'Chinese Arbitration Requirements – A Trap For FIDIC–ICC Arbitration?' (2008) 25 *The International Construction Law Review* 190.

Holtzmann, Howard M and Donovan, Donald Francis, 'National Report for the United States of America' in Jan Paulsson (ed), *International Handbook on Commercial Arbitration (Supp No 44)* (The Hague, Kluwer Law International, 2005).

Hong, Xue, 'Online Dispute Resolution for E-Commerce in China: Present Practices and Future Developments' (2004) 34 *Hong Kong Law Journal* 377.

Hong-lin, Yu, 'Total Separation of International Commercial Arbitration and National Court Regime' (1998) 15 *Journal of International Arbitration* 2.

Houtte, Hans van, 'Conduct of Arbitral Proceedings' in Šarčević Petar (ed), *Essays on International Commercial Arbitration* (London, Graham & Trotman, 1989).

—— 'Conduct of Arbitral Proceedings' (1989) *Essays on International Commercial Arbitration*.

Howson, Nicola and West, Mark, 'Laws, Norms, and Legal Change: Global and Local in China and Japan' (2006) 27 *Michigan Journal of International Law* 687.

Hualing, Fu, 'Understanding People's Mediation in Post-Mao China' (1992) 6 *Journal of Chinese Law*.

Huang, Jin and Du, Huanfang, 'Chinese Judicial Practice in Private International Law: 2003' (2008) 7 *Chinese Journal of International Law* 1.

Huang, Philip, 'Between Informal Mediation and Formal Adjudication: The Third Realm of Qing Civil Justice' (1993) 19 *Modern China* 3.

—— 'Divorce Law Practices and the Origins, Myths, and Realities of Judicial "Mediation" in China' (2005) 31 *Modern China* 2.

—— 'Civil Adjudication in China, Past and Present' (2006) 32 *Modern China* 2.

—— 'Court Mediation in China, Past and Present' (2006) 32 *Modern China* 3.

—— 'Whither Chinese Law?' (2007) 33 *Modern China* 2.

Huang, Yanming, 'Mediation in the Settlement of Business Disputes: Two Typical Examples of Cases Settled by Mediation at the CIETAC's Shenzhen Commission' (1991) 8 *Journal of International Arbitration* 4.

Hunter, Martin, 'Commentary on Integrated Dispute Resolution Clauses' in Albert Jan van den Berg (ed), *ICCA Congress series no 12* (The Hague, Kluwer Law International, 2005).

Hwang, Michael, 'The Role of Arbitrators as Settlement Facilitators. Commentary' in Albert Jan van den Berg (ed), *ICCA Congress series no 12* (The Hague, Kluwer Law International, 2005).

Jackson, Vicki, 'Transnational Constitutional Values and Democratic Challenges' (2010) 8 *International Journal of Constitutional Law* 517.

Jarrosson, Charles, ' L'instance arbitrale : Le rôle respectif de l'institution, de l'arbitre et des parties dans l'instance arbitrale' *Revue de l'arbitrage* (1990), 381.Johnston, Graeme, 'Bridging the Gap Between Western and Chinese Arbitration Systems: A Practical Introduction for American Business' (2007) *Business Disputes in China*.

Jones, Doug, 'Various Non-binding (ADR) Processes' in Albert Jan van den Berg (ed), *ICCA Congress series no 12* (The Hague, Kluwer Law International, 2005).

Kahn-Freund, Otto, 'On Uses and Misuses of Comparative Law' (1974) 37 *Modern Law Review* 1.

Kaufmann-Kohler, Gabrielle, 'Identifying and Applying the Law Governing the Arbitral Procedure – the Role of the Place of Arbitration' in Albert Jan van den Berg (ed), *ICCA Congress Series no 9* (The Hague, Kluwer Law International, 1999).

—— 'Globalization of Arbitral Procedures' (2003) 36 *Vanderbilt Journal of Transnational Law* 1313.

Kaufmann-Kohler, Gabrielle, 'Global Implications of the US Federal Arbitration Act: The Role of Legislation in International Arbitration' (2005) 20 *ICSID Review* 2.

—— 'When Arbitrators Facilitate Settlement: Towards a Transnational Standard' (2009) 25 *Arbitration International* 2.

Kaufmann-Kohler, Gabrielle and Bonnin, Victor, 'Arbitrators as Conciliators: A Statistical Study of the Relation between an Arbitrator's Role and Legal Background' (2007) 18 *ICC Bulletin* 2.

Kaufmann-Kohler, Gabrielle and Fan, Kun, 'Integrating Mediation into Arbitration: Why It Works In China?' (2008) 25 *Journal of International Arbitration* 4.

Kerr, Michael, 'Reflections on 50 Years' Involvement in Dispute Resolution' (1998) 64 *Arbitration*.

Kirby, Jennifer, 'The ICC Court: A Behind-the-Scenes Look' (2005) 16 *ICC Bulletin* 2.

Koa, Christopher M, 'International Bank for Reconstruction and Development and Dispute Resolution: Conciliating and Arbitrating with China through the International Centre for Settlement of Investment Disputes' (1991–1992) 4 *New York University Journal of International Law and Politics* 439.

Kong, Yuan, 'Recent Cases Relating to Arbitration in China, (2006) 2 *Asian International Arbitration Journal* 2.

Kovach, Kimberlee, 'Mediation' in Michael Moffitt and Robert Bordone (eds), *The Handbook of Dispute Resolution* (San Francisco, Jossey-Bass, 2005).

Kronstein, Heinrich, 'Business Arbitration—Instrument of Private Government' (1944) 54 *Yale Law Journal* 36.

—— 'Arbitration is Power' (1963) 38 *New York University Law Review* 661.

Lalive, Pierre, 'Arbitration – The Civilized Solution?' (1998) 16 *ASA Bulletin* 483.

—— 'The Role of Arbitrators as Settlement Facilitators: A Swiss View' in Albert Jan van den Berg (ed), *ICCA Congress series no 12* (The Hague, Kluwer Law International, 2005).

Lalive, Pierre and Gaillard, Emmanuel, 'Le nouveau droit de l'arbitrage international en Suisse' (1989) 116 *JDI* 905.

Langbein, John, 'The German Advantage in Civil Procedure' (1985) 52 *University of Chicago Law Review* 4.

Lawless, Niall, 'Cultural Perspectives on China Resolving Disputes Through Mediation' (2008) 5 *Transnational Dispute Management* 4.

Lazareff, Serge, 'Terms of Reference' (2006) 17 *ICC Bulletin* 1.

Lee, Tahirih V, 'Risky Business: Courts, Culture, and the Marketplace' (1993) 47 *University of Miami Law Review* 1335.

Lefebvre-Teillard, Anne, 'L'arbitrage en droit canonique' *Revue de l'arbitrage* 1 (2006).

Legrand, Pierre, 'Comparative Legal Studies and Commitment to Theory' (1995) 58 *Modern Law Review* 262.

Lemley, Kevin, 'I'll Make Him an Offer He Can't Refuse: A Proposed Model for Alternative Dispute Resolution in IP Disputes' (2004) 37 *Arkon Law Review* 293.

Levine, Judith, 'Amendments to ICSID Arbitration Rules and Regulations' (2006) *Transnational Dispute Management* 5.

Lew, Julian, 'Multi-Institutionals Conciliation and the Reconciliation of Different Legal Cultures' in Albert Jan van den Berg (ed), *ICCA Congress series no 12* (The Hague, Kluwer Law International, 2005).

—— 'Achieving the Dream: Autonomous Arbitration?' in Julian Lew and Loukas Mistelis (eds), *Arbitration Insights: Twenty Years of the Annual Lecture of the School of International Arbitration* (The Hague, Kluwer Law International, 2007).

Leyda, José Alejandro Carballo, 'A Uniform, Internationally Oriented Legal Framework for the Recognition and Enforcement of Foreign Arbitral Awards in Mainland China, Hong Kong and Taiwan?' (2007) 6 *Chinese Journal of International Law* 345.

Li, Hu, 'Enforcement of Foreign Arbitral Awards and Court Intervention in the People's Republic of China' (2004) 20 *Arbitration International* 167–78.

Li, Jie, 'What Does Settlement Rate Tell Us? An Analysis of the Assumption that the Settlement Rate Positively Correlates with Harmony' (2008) 10 *Journal of Legal Application* 49.

Li, Mengyuan, 'Amiable Composition' in Jian Han (ed), *Judicial Review of the Foreign-related Arbitration* (Beijing Legal Press, 2006).

Li, Qiangui, Xu, Keke and Lin, Qiao, 'The Legal Thoughts of *Ad Hoc* Arbitration in China' in Jian Han (ed), *Judicial Review of the Foreign-related Arbitration* (Beijing, Legal Press, 2006).

Li, Xianbo and Wang, Huan, 'The Application and Development of the Linkage and Interaction System of Three Mediations in Hunan Province' (2009) 17 *Asia Pacific Law Review* Special Issue on Mediation.

Liang, Zhiping, 'Explicating "Law": A Comparative Perspective of Chinese and Western Legal Culture' in Tahirih Lee (ed), *Basic Concepts of Chinese Law* (New York, Garland Publishing, 1997).

Lin, Mark and Wong, Terence, *China: SPC Issues New Interpretation of Issues Relating to the Applicability of the PRC Arbitration Law*, Lovells newsletter 2006.

Liu, Hui-Chen Wang, 'An Analysis of Chinese Clan Rules: Confucian Theories in Action' in DS Divison and AF Wright (eds), *Confucianism in Action* (Stanford, Stanford University Press, 1959).

Liu, Kwang-Ching, 'Chinese Merchant Guilds: An Historical Inquiry' (1988) 57 *Pacific Historical Review* 1.

Liu, Yuwu, 'Arbitration Agreement: The Chinese Practice and Future Trends' (2001) 16 *Mealey's International Arbitration Report* 8.

Lloyd, Humphrey, et al, 'Drafting Awards in ICC Arbitrations' (2005) 16 *ICC Bulletin* 2.

Lockett, James K, 'Dispute Settlement in the People's Republic of China: The Developing Role of Arbitration in Foreign Trade and Maritime Disputes' (1981–1982) 16 *George Washington Journal of International Law and Economy* 239.

Love, Lela, 'Preface to the Justice in the Mediation Symposium' (2004) 5 *Cardozo Journal of Conflict Resolution* 2.

Lowenfeld, Andreas, 'Public Policy and Private Arbitrators: Who Elected Us and What Are We Supposed to Do?' (2006) *Transnational Dispute Management* 5.

Lu, Haitian, 'State Channeling of Social Grievances: Theory and Evidence from China' (2011) 41 *Hong Kong Law Journal* 2.

Lu, Song, 'National Report for China' in Jan Paulsson (ed), *International Handbook on Commercial Arbitration* (The Hague, Kluwer Law International, 2009).

Lubman, Stanley, 'Mao and Mediation: Politics and Dispute Resolution in Communist China' (1967) 55 *California Law Review* 5.

—— 'Dispute Resolution in China after Deng Xiaoping: Mao and Mediation Revisited' (1999) 11 *Columbia Journal of Asian Law* 2.

Lubman, Stanley and Wajnowski, Gregory, 'International Commercial Dispute Resolution in China: A Practical Assessment' (1993) 4 *American Review of International Arbitration* 2.

Macauley, Melissa, 'Social Power and Legal Culture: Litigation Masters in Late Imperial China' (1999).
MacCormack, Geoffrey, 'Assistance in Conflict Resolution: Imperial China' in Transactions of the Jean Bodin Society for Comparative Institutional History (ed), *Assistance in Conflict Resolution* (Bruxelles, De Boeck University, 1996).
MacGowan, DJ, 'Chinese Guilds or Chambers of Commerce and Trade Unions' (1888–1889) XXI *Journal of the North China Branch of the Royal Asiatic Society*.
Macneil, Roderick, 'Contract in China: Law, Practice and Dispute Resolution' (1986) 38 *Stanford Law Review* 393.
Main, Thomas, 'ADR: The New Equity' (2005–2006) 74 *University of Cincinnati Law Review*.
Malanczuk, Peter, 'Domestic and Foreign-related Arbitration in Mainland China' (2005) *ICC China International Commercial Arbitration Yearbook*.
Marriott, Arthur, 'Arbitrators and Settlement' in Albert Jan van den Berg (ed), *ICCA Congress series no 12* (The Hague, Kluwer Law International, 2005).
—— 'Arbitrators and Settlement' (2005) *ICCA Congress series no 12*.
Mayer, Pierre, 'Le principe de bonne foi devant les arbitres du commerce international' in *Etudes de droit international en l'honneur de Pierre Lalive* (Basel, Helbing & Lichtenhahn, 1993).
—— 'The Limits of Severability of the Arbitration Clause' in Albert Jan van den Berg (ed), *ICCA Congress Series no 9* (The Hague, Kluwer Law International, 1999).
McCobb, John B, 'Foreign Trade Arbitration in the People's Republic of China' (1972) 5 *New York University Journal of International Law and Politics* 205.
McConnaughay, Philip J, 'The Risks and Virtues of Lawlessness: A "Second Look" at International Commercial Arbitration' (1999) 93 *NorthWest University Law Review* 453.
Mehren, Arthur von, 'Concluding Remarks' (1995) Special Supplement, The Status of the Arbitrator *ICC Bulletin* 126.
Mehren, Robert B von, 'Enforcement of Foreign Arbitral Awards in the United States' (1998) 1 *International Arbitration Law Review* 6.
Melnitzer, Julius, *Reforms Make Arbitration in China a Safer Bet, Regs Still Not Up to US Standards*, InsideCounsel, Global Views (2005).
Mentschikoff, Soia, 'Commercial Arbitration' (1961) 846 *Columbia Law Review*.
Milgrom, Paul, North, Douglass and Weingast, Barry R, 'The Role of Institutions in the Revival of Trade: The Law Merchant, Private Judges, and the Champagne Fairs' (1990) 2 *Economics and Politics* 1.
Mills, Karen, 'Cultural Differences & Ethnic Bias in International Dispute Resolution. An Arbitrator/Mediator's Perspective' (2006) *Transnational Dispute Management* 5.
Ming, Wu, 'The Strange Case of Wang Shengchang' (2007) 24 *Journal of International Arbitration* 2.
Minzner, Carl, 'China's Turn Against Law' (2011) 59 *American Journal of Comparative Law* 4.
More, Alberto, 'The Revpower Dispute: China's Breach of the New York Convention?' in Chris Hunter (ed), *Dispute Resolution in the PRC: A Practical Guide to Litigation and Arbitration in China* (Hong Kong, Asia Law and Practice Ltd, 1995).
Moser, Michael, 'China and the Enforcement of Arbitral Awards' (1995) 2 *Arbitration*.
Moser, Michael and Yu, Jianlong, 'CIETAC and its Work – An Interview with Vice Chairman Yu Jianlong' (2007) 24 *Journal of International Arbitration* 6.

Moser, Michael and Yuen, Peter, 'The New CIETAC Arbitration Rules' (2005) 21 *Arbitration International*.

Moser, Michael J, 'Commentary on Arbitration and Conciliation Concerning China' in *New Horizons in International Commercial Arbitration and Beyond* (The Hague, Kluwer Law International, 2005).

Moser, Michael J and Yeoh, Friven, 'Commentary: New Supreme People's Court Interpretation On Mainland China's Arbitration Law' (2006) 21 *Mealey's International Arbitration Quarterly Law Review* 9.

Mustill, Michael, 'Arbitration: History and Background' (1989) 6 *Journal of International Arbitration* 2.

—— 'The History of International Commercial Arbitration' in Lawrence Newman and Richard Hill (eds), *Leading Arbitrators' Guide to International Arbitration* (Huntington, Juris Publishing, 2008).

Myron, L Cohen, 'Lineage Organization in North China' (1990) 49 *The Journal of Asian Studies* 3.

Nariman, Fali, 'East Meets West: Tradition, Globalization and the Future of Arbitration' (2004) 20 *Arbitration International* 2.

Nelken, David, 'Towards a Sociology of Legal Adaptation' in David Nelken and Johannes Feest (eds), *Adapting Legal Cultures* (Oxford, Hart Publishing, 2001).

Netto, Carlos Nehring, 'Is There an Expanded Culture that Favors Combining Arbitration with Conciliation or Other ADR Procedures?' in Albert Jan van den Berg (ed), *ICCA Congress series no 8* (The Hague, Kluwer Law International, 1998).

—— 'The Brazilian Approach to Arbitrators as Settlement Faciliators' in Albert Jan van den Berg (ed), *ICCA Congress series no 12* (The Hague, Kluwer Law International, 2005).

Onyema, Emilia, 'The Use of Med-Arb in International Commercial Dispute Resolution' (2001) 12 *American Review of International Arbitration* 3–4.

Oppetit, Bruno, 'Arbitrage, médiation et conciliation' *Revue de l'arbitrage* (1984) 308.

Oyekunle, Tinuade, 'Is There an Expanded Culture that Favors Combining Arbitration with Conciliation or Other ADR Procedures?' in Albert Jan van den Berg (ed), *ICCA Congress series no 8* (The Hague, Kluwer Law International, 1998).

Pair, Lara, 'Cross-cultural Arbitration: Do the Differences Between Cultures Still Influence Commercial Arbitration Despite Harmonization?' (2002–2003) 9 *ILSA Journal of International & Comparative Law*.

Palay, Marc, 'Legal Aspects of China's Foreign Trade Practices and Procedures' (1977–1978) 12 *Journal of International Economic Law* 105.

Palmer, Michael, 'The Revival of Mediation in the People's Republic of China: (1) Extra-Judicial Mediation' in William Elliott Butler (ed), *Yearbook on Socialist Legal Systems* (New York, Transnational Juris Publishing, 1987).

—— 'The Revival of Mediation in the People's Republic of China: (2) Judicial Mediation' in William Elliott Butler (ed), *Yearbook on Socialist Legal Systems* (New York, Transnational Juris Publications, 1989).

—— 'Compromising Courts and Harmonizing Ideologies: Mediation in the Administrative Chambers of the People's Courts in the People's Republic of China' in Andrew Harding and Penelope Nicholson (eds), *New Courts in Asia* (London & New York, Routledge, 2009).

Paulsson, Jan, 'The Extent of Independence of International Arbitration from the Law of the Situs' in Julian Lew (ed), *Contemporary Problems in International Arbitration*

(London, Queen Mary College, University of London: Centre for Commercial Studies, 1986).

Paulsson, Jan, 'Towards Minimum Standards of Enforcement: Feasibility of a Model Law' in Albert Jan van den Berg (ed), *ICCA Congress Series no 9* (The Hague, Kluwer Law International, 1999).

—— 'Interference by National Courts' in Lawrence Newman and Richard Hill (eds), *The Leading Arbitrators' Guide to international Arbitration* (Huntington, Juris Publishing, 2008).

Peck, Sarah Catherine, 'Playing by a New Set of Rules. Will China's New Arbitration Laws and Recent Membership in the ICC Improve Trade with China?' (2004) 12 *Journal of International Arbitration* 4.

Peerenboom, Randall, 'Seek Truth From Facts: An Empirical Study of Enforcement of Arbitral Awards in the PRC' (2001) 49 *American Journal of Comparative Law* 249.

Perkovich, Robert, 'A Comparative Analysis of Community Mediation in the United States and the People's Republic of China' (1996) 10 *Temple International and Comparative Law Journal*.

Peter, James T, 'Med-Arb In International Arbitration ' (2005) *Doutrina International*.

Petsche, Alexander and Platte, Martin, 'The Arbitrator – The Arbitrator as Dispute Settlement Facilitator' in Peter Klein, Christian Klausegger et al (eds), *Austrian Arbitration Yearbook* (Vienna, CH Beck, Stämpfli & Manz, 2007).

Plant, David, 'The Arbitrator as Settlement Facilitator' (2000) 17 *Journal of International Arbitration* 1.

—— 'ADR and Arbitration' in Lawrence Newman and Richard Hill (eds), *The Leading Arbitrators' Guide to International Arbitration* (New York, JurisNet, LLC, 2008).

Polkinghorne, Michael, 'Practical Issues in Arbitration Practice Involving the People's Republic of China' (2006) 21 *Mealey's International Arbitration Quarterly Law Review* 9.

Potter, Jack, 'Land and Lineage in Traditional China' in Maurice Freedman (ed), *Family and Kinship in Chinese Society* (Stanford, Stanford University Press, 1970).

Potter, Pitman, 'Globalization and Economic Regulation in China: Selective Adaptation of Globalized Norms and Practices' (2003) 2 *Washington University Global Study Law Review* 119.

—— 'Legal Reform in China: Institutions, Culture, and Selective Adaptation' (2004) 29 *Law and Social Inquiry* 465.

Pound, Roscoe, 'The Causes of Popular Dissatisfaction with the Administration of Justice' (1906) 29 *Annual Report of the American Bar Association*.

—— 'The Foundation of Law' (1961) 10 *The American University Law Review*.

Pryles, Michael, 'Commentary on Issues Involving Confidentiality' in Albert Jan van den Berg (ed), *ICCA Congress series no 12* (The Hague, Kluwer Law International, 2005).

Radi, Yannick, 'The Application of the Most-Favoured-Nation Clause to the Dispute Settlement Provisions of Bilateral Investment Treaties: Domesticating the "Trojan Horse"' (2007) 18 *European Journal of International Law* 757.

Raeschke-Kessler, Hilmar, 'The Arbitrator as Settlement Facilitator' (2005) 21 *Arbitration International*.

Reed, Lucy and Freda, James, 'Narrow Exceptions: A Review of Recent US Precedent Regarding the Due Process and Public Policy Defenses of the New York Convention' (2008) 25 *Journal of International Arbitration* 6.

Reinstein, Ellen S, 'Finding a Happy Ending for Foreign Investors: The Enforcement of Arbitration Awards in the People's Republic of China' (2005).
Robertson, Roland, 'Glocalization: Time-space and Homogeneity-heterogeneity' in Michael Featherstone et al (eds), *Global Modernities* (London, Sage, 1995).
Roebuck, Derek, 'Best to Reconcile: Mediation and Arbitration in the Ancient Greek World' (2000) 6 *Arbitration* 4.
Roebuck, Derek and Wong, K, 'Rapid Change and Traditional Morality – Enforcement of Foreign Arbitral Awards in the People's Republic of China' (1995) 5 *Australian Journal of Corporate Law*.
Rooney, Kim M, 'ICSID and BIT Arbitrations and China' (2007) 24 *Journal of International Arbitration* 6.
Sabahi, Borzu, 'Recent Developments in Awarding Damages in Investor-State Arbitrations' (2007) 4 *Transnational Dispute Management* 4.
Sanders, Pieter, 'The 1996 Alexander Lecture, Cross-Border Arbitration – A View on the Future' (1996) 62 *Arbitration* 3.
Sattar, Sameer, 'National Courts and International Arbiration: A Doubled-edged Sword?' (2010) 27 *Journal of International Arbitration* 1.
Sawada, Toshio, 'Hybrid Arb-Med: Will West and East Never Meet?' (2003) 14 *ICC Bulletin* 2.
Schill, Stephan W, 'Tearing Down the Great Wall: The New Generation Investment Treaties of the People's Republic of China' (2007) *Cardozo Journal of International and Comparative Law*.
Schneider, Michael, 'Combining Arbitration with Conciliation' in Albert Jan van den Berg (ed), *ICCA Congress series no 8* (The Hague, Kluwer Law International, 1996).
—— 'Combining Arbitration with Conciliation' (1996) *International Dispute Resolution: Towards an International Arbitration Culture* 1.
Schwartz, Benjamin, 'On Attitudes Toward Law in China' in Tahirih Lee (ed), *Basic Concepts of Chinese Law* (New York, Garland Publishing, 1997).
Schwartz, Eric, 'Do International Arbitrators Have a Duty to Obey the Orders of the Courts at the Place of the Arbitration? Reflections on the Role of the Lex Loci Arbitri in the Light of a Recent ICC Award' in *Global Reflections on International Law, Commerce and Dispute Resolution. Liber Amicorum in honour of Robert Briner* (Paris, ICC Publishing, 2005).
Schwebel, Stephen, 'A Celebration of the United Nation's New York Convention' (1996) 12 *Arbitration International* 1.
Scogin, Hugh, 'Between Heaven and Man: Contract and State in Han Dynasty China' (1990) 62 *South California Law Review* 1325.
Shi, Chenxia, 'Commercial Development and Regulation in Late Imperial China: An Historical Review' (2005) 35 *Hong Kong Law Journal*.
Silberman, Linda, 'International Arbitration: Comments from a Critic' (2002) 13 *American Review of International Arbitration* 9.
Silveira, Mercédeh Azeredo da and Lévy, Laurent, 'Transgression of the Arbitrators' Authority: Article V(a)(c) of the New York Convention' in Emmanuel Gaillard and Domenico di Pietro (eds), *Enforcement of Arbitration Agreements and International Arbitral Awards: The New York Convention in Practice* (London, Cameron May, 2008).
Slate, William K, 'The Impact of Culture on International Commercial Arbitration' in Albert Jan van den Berg (ed), *ICCA Congress series no 12* (The Hague, Kluwer Law International, 2005).

Smith, Robert, 'An Inside View of the ICC Court' (1994) 10 *Arbitration International* 1.

Song, Lianbin, Zhao, Jian and Li, Hong, 'Approaches to the Revision of the 1994 Arbitration Act of the People's Republic of China' (2003) 20 *Journal of International Arbitration* 2.

Stallard, Amanda, 'Joining the Culture Club: Examining Cultural Context When Implementing International Dispute Resolution' (2002) 17 *Ohio State Journal on Dispute Resolution* 463.

Sternberg, Cole, 'Chinese Courts: More of a Gamble than Arbitration?' (2004) 31 *International Business Law Review*.

Steyn, Johan, 'Towards a New English Arbitration Act' (1991) 7 *Arbitrational International* 17.

Street, Laurence, 'The Language of Alternative Dispute Resolution' (1992) 66 *Australia Law Journal*.

Tang, Houzhi, 'Is There an Expending Culture that Favors Combining Arbitration with Conciliation or Other ADR Procedures?' in Albert Jan van den Berg (ed), *ICCA Congress Series no 8* (The Hague, Kluwer Law International, 1996).

—— 'The Arbitration Road – In Commemoration of the 50th Anniversary of the Founding of CCPIT' in CIETAC and CMAC (eds), *China International Commercial Arbitration Yearbook* 2000–2001).

—— 'Combination of Arbitration with Conciliation – Arb/Med' in Albert Jan van den Berg (ed), *ICCA Congress Series no 12* (The Hague, Kluwer Law International, 2005).

Tang, Houzhi and Wang, Shengchang, 'PR China' in Jan Paulsson (ed), *International Handbook on Commercial Arbitration* (The Hague, Kluwer Law International, 1998).

Taniguchi, Yasuhei, 'Is There a Growing International Arbitration Culture? – An Observation from Asia' in Albert Jan van den Berg (ed), *ICCA Congress series no 8* 1996).

—— 'Is There a Growing International Arbitration Culture? An Observation from Asia' (Kluwer Law International, 1998).

Tao, Jingzhou, 'Several Practical Issues of International Commercial Arbitration in China' (2005) *ICC China International Commercial Arbitration Yearbook*.

—— 'One Award – Two Obstacles. Trouble When Enforcing Arbitral Awards in China' (2008) 4 *Asian International Arbitration Journal* 1.

Tao, Jingzhou and Wunschheim, Clarisse von, 'Articles 16 and 18 of the PRC Arbitration Law: The Great Wall of China for Foreign Arbitration Institutions' (2007) 23 *Arbitration International* 2.

Tay, Alice Erh-Soon, 'The Struggle for Law in China' (1987) 21 *University of British Columbia Law Review* 561.

Tercier, Pierre, 'ICC Rules of Arbitration: A Decade of Use' (2008) 19 *ICC Bulletin* 1.

Thomas, Breckenridge, 'International Arbitration: A Historical Perspective and Practical Guide Connecting Four Emerging World Cultures: China, Mexico, Nigeria and Saudi Arabia' (2006) 17 *American Review of International Arbitration* 2.

Trackman, Leon, 'Legal Traditions and International Commercial Arbitration' (2006) 17 *American Review of International Arbitration* 1.

Turner, Peter J, 'Investor-State Arbitration' in Michael Moser (ed), *Managing Business Disputes in Today's China – Duelling with Dragons* (The Hague, Kluwer Law International, 2007).

Twining, William, 'Diffusion of Law: A Global Perspective' (2006) 1 *Journal of Comparative Law* 237.

—— 'Implications of "Globalisation" for Law as a Discipline' in Andrew Halpin and Volker Roeben (eds), *Theorising the Global Legal Order* (Oxford, Hart Publishing, 2009).
Twinning, William, 'Globalization and Legal Theory: Some Local Implications' (1996) 49 *Current Legal Problems* 1.
Utter, Robert F, 'Dispute Resolution in China' (1987) 62 *Washington Law Review* 383.
Veeder, VV, 'English National Report' in Jan Paulsson (ed), *International Handbook on Commercial Arbitration* (The Hague, Kluwer Law International, 1997).
Venus, Paul, 'Advantages in Mandatory Mediation' (2003) 41 *Law Society Journal* 10.
—— 'Court Directed Compulsory Mediation – Attendance or Participation?' (2004) 15 *Australian Dispute Resolution Journal* 1.
Vera, Carlos De, 'Arbitrating Harmony: "Med-arb" and the Confluence of Culture and Rule of Law in the Resolution of International Commercial Disputes in China' (2004) 18 *Columbia Journal of Asian Law* 149.
Voser, Nathalie and Gola, Pascale, 'The Arbitral Tribunal' in Gabrielle Kaufmann-Kohler and Blaise Stucki (eds), *International Arbitration in Switzerland: A Handbook for Practitioners* (The Hague, Kluwer Law International, 2004).
Vries, Henry P de, 'International Commercial Arbitration: A Transnational View' (1984) 1 *Journal of International Arbitration* 1.
Wagoner, David, 'A Breath of Fresh Air in Chinese Dispute Resolution' (2006) 24 *ASA Bulletin* 1.
Wakeman, Frederic, 'The Civil Society and Public Sphere Debate' (1993) 19 *Modern China* 2.
Wang, Guiguo, 'The Unification of the Dispute Resolution System in China: Cultural Economic and Legal Contributions' (1996) 13 *Journal of International Arbitration* 2.
—— 'One Country, Two Arbitration Systems. Recognition and Enforcement of Arbitral Awards in Hong Kong and China' (1997) 14 *Journal of International Arbitration* 1.
Wang, Liming, 'Characteristics of China's Judicial Mediation System' (2009) 17 *Asia Pacific Law Review* Special Issue on Mediation.
Wang, Marcus, 'Dancing with the Dragon: What US Parties Should Know About Chinese Law When Drafting a Contractual Dispute Resolution Clause' (2009) 29 *Northwestern Journal of International Law and Business* 309.
Wang, Shengchang, 'The Practical Application of Multilateral Conventions Experience with Bilateral Treaties Enforcement of Foreign Arbitral Awards in the People's Republic of China' in Albert Jan van den Berg (ed), *ICCA Congress series no 9* (The Hague, Kluwer Law International, 1999).
—— 'Combination of Arbitration with Conciliation and Remittance of Awards – With Special Reference to the Asian-Oceania Region' (2002) 19 *Journal of International Arbitration* 1.
—— 'CIETAC's Perspective on Arbitration and Conciliation Concerning China' in Albert Jan van den Berg (ed), *ICCA Congress series no 12* (The Hague, Kluwer Law International, 2005).
—— 'Arbitration Under the New CIETAC Rules' (2006) *ICC China International Commercial Arbitration Yearbook*.
Wang, Wenying, 'The Role of Conciliation in Resolving Disputes: A PRC Perspective' (2005) 20 *Ohio State Journal on Dispute Resolution* 2.
—— 'Distinct Features of Arbitration in China – An Historical Perspective' (2006) 23 *Journal of International Arbitration*.

Warner, Hugo and Sheppard, Audley, 'Appeals and Challenges to Investment Treaty Awards: Is it Time for an International Appellate System?' (2005) 2 *Transnational Dispute Management* 2.

Watkins, Robert, 'An Analysis of Chinese Contractual Policy and Practice' (1980–1981) 27 *Wayne Law Review* 1229.

Watson, Alan, 'Comparative Law and Legal Change' (1978) 37 *Cambridge Law Journal* 313.

——'Legal Change: Sources of Law and Legal Culture' (1983) 131 *University of Pennsylvania Law Review* 5.

——'The Evolution of Law' (1987) 5 *Law and History Review* 2.

——'From Legal Transplants to Legal Formants' (1995) 43 *The American Journal of Comparative Law* 3.

——'Aspects of Reception of Law' (1996) 44 *The American Journal of Comparative Law* 2.

Wells, Louis, 'Double Dipping in Arbitration Awards? An Economist Questions Damages Awarded Karaha Bodas Company in Indonesia' (2003) 19 *Arbitration International* 4.

Wenger, Werner, 'The Role of the Arbitrator in Bringing about a Settlement' (2006) *Best Practices in International Arbitration, ASA Special Series*.

Whitesell, Anne Marie, 'Independence in ICC Arbitration: ICC Court Practice Concerning the Appointment, Confirmation, Challenge and Replacement of Arbitrators' (2007) *ICC Bulletin* Independence of Arbitrators – Special Supplement.

Wolff, Arthur, *Is There Scope for ICC Arbitration in China?* Denton Wilde Sapte, Arbitration newsflash, September 2002.

Wolski, Bobette, 'Culture, Society and Mediation in China and the West' (1996–1997) 3 *Commercial Dispute Resolution Journal* 97.

Wong, Bobby, 'Chinese Law: Traditional Chinese Philosophy and Dispute Resolution' (2000) 30 *Hong Kong Law Journal* 304.

Woychuk, Denis, 'Commercial Dispute Settlement in China-United States Trade: Conciliation in Perspective' (1982) 6 *Fordham International Law Journal* 1.

Wu, John, 'The Status of the Individual in the Political and Legal Traditions of Old and New China' in Charles Moore (ed), *The Status of the Individual in East and West* (Hawaii, University of Hawaii Press, 1968).

Wunschheim, Clarisse von and Fan, Kun, 'Arbitrating in China: The Rules of the Game – Practical Recommendations Concerning Arbitration in China' (2008) 26 *ASA Bulletin* 1.

Xiaowen, Guo, 'The Validity and Performance of Arbitration Agreements in China' (1994) 11 *Journal of International Arbitration* 1.

Ye, Ariel, 'Commentary on Integrated Dispute Resolution Systems in the PRC' in Albert Jan van den Berg (ed), *ICCA Congress series no 12* (The Hague, Kluwer Law International, 2005).

Yeoh, Friven and Yu, Fu, 'The People's Courts and Arbitration – A Snapshot of Recent Judicial Attitudes on Arbitrability and Enforcement' (2007) 24 *Journal of International Arbitration* 6.

Yu, Jianlong, 'The Arbitrators' Mandate: Private Judge, Service-Provider or Both?' (2007) 3 *Stockholm International Arbitration Review*.

Yu, Xingzhong, 'Legal Pragmatism in the People's Republic of China' in Tahirih Lee (ed), *Basic Concepts of Chinese Law* (New York, Garland Publishing, 1997), originally published in (1989) 3 *Journal of Chinese Law* 29.

Yuan, Kong, 'Recent Cases Relating to Arbitration in China' (2006) 2 *Asian International Arbitration Journal* 2.

Zeng, Xianyi, 'Mediation in China – Past and Present' (2009) 17 *Asia Pacific Law Review*, Special Issue on Mediation.

Zhan, Mo, 'International Civil Litigation in China: A Practical Analysis of the Chinese Judicial System' (2002) 25 *Boston College International and Comparative Law Review* 59.

Zhang, Xianchu, 'The Agreement between Mainland China and the Hong Kong SAR on Mutual Enforcement of Arbitral Awards: Problems and Prospects' (1999) 29 *Hong Kong Law Journal* 463.

Zhao, Xiuwen and Kloppenberg, A Lisa, 'Reforming Chinese Arbitration Law and Practices in the Global Economy' (2006) 31 *University of Dayton Law Review* 3.

Zhou, Jian, 'Arbitration Agreements in China: Battles on Designation of Arbitral Institution and *Ad hoc* Arbitration' (2006) 23 *Journal of International Arbitration*.

Zhu, Jianli, 'Alternative Dispute Resolution in the Context of Chinese Commercial Law' (1999) *International Arbitration Law Review*.

Zhu, Mingxing, 'Main Features of Chinese Court Arbitration and Maritime Litigation in China' (1989) 11 *Loyola of Los Angeles International and Comparative Law Journal* 311.

Zurndorfer, Harriet T, 'Learning, Lineages, and Locality in Late Imperial China. A Comparative Study of Education in Huichow (Anhwei) and Foochow (Fukien) 1600–1800 Part 1' (1992) 35 *Journal of the Economic and Social History of the Orient* 2.

—— 'China and "Modernity": The Uses of the Study of Chinese History in the Past and the Present' (1997) 40 *Journal of the Economic and Social History of the Orient* 4.

* * *

陈福勇,《直面仲裁机构现状的复杂性 — 关于问卷调查的几点补充说明与思考》,《北京仲裁》第63辑, 2007年 (Chen, Fuyong, 'Facing the Complexity of the Current Status of Arbitration Institutions – Several Supplements and Thoughts on the Questionnaire', (2007) 63 *Beijing Arbitration*).

邓建鹏,《讼师秘本与清代诉状的风格 – 以"黄岩诉讼档案"为考察中心》,《浙江社会科学》第4辑, 2005年 (Deng, Jianpeng, 'The Secret of Litigation Masters and the Style of Qing Litigation Complaint – An Investigation Focused on the Huangyan Litigation Archive', 2005(4) *Zhejiang Social Science*).

费宗祎,《费宗祎先生谈仲裁法的修改》,《北京仲裁》第62期, 2007年 (Fei, Zongyi, 'Comments on the Reforms of the Arbitration Law by Mr Fei Zongyi', (2007) 62 *Beijing Arbitration*).

(日) 夫马进,《明清时期的讼师与诉讼制度》,载滋贺秀三[日],《明清时期的民事审判与民间契约》(Fu Majin (Japan), 'The Litigation Masters and Litigation System in Ming and Qing Dynasties', in しが・しゅうぞう, *The Civil Trial and Social Contract During the Ming and Qing Period*).

侯欣一,《清代江南地区民间的健讼问题 – 以地方志为中心的考察》,《法学研究》第4辑, 2006年, (Hou, Xinyi, 'The Litigation Propensity in the South of Yangtze River Area in Qing Dynasty – An Investigation Focused on Local Gazetteers', 2006 (4) *Legal Studies*).

吕世伦、姚建宗,《略论法制现代化的概念、模式和类型》,《法制现代化研究》第1辑, 1995年(Lu, Shilun and Yao, Jianzong, 'Research on the Modernization of Legal System', (1995) (1) *Legal Modernisation Studies*).

麦宜生,《纠纷与法律需求: 以北京的调查为例》,《江苏社会科学》第1辑, 2003年, 第 72–80页 (Ethan Michelson, 'Dispute and Legal Demands: Taking the Beijing Survey as an Example', (2003) 1, Jiangsu Social Science, 72–80).

王红松,《中国仲裁面临的机遇和挑战》,《北京仲裁》第64辑, 2008年(Wang, Hongsong, 'The Opportunities and Challenges of Chinese Arbitration', (2008) 62 *Beijing Arbitration*).

王红松,《贯彻党的十七大精神, 加快推进仲裁机构体制改革》,《北京仲裁》第65辑, 2008年 (Wang, Hongsong, 'Implementing the Spirits of the Communist Party's Seventeenth Conference and Promoting the Structural Reform of Arbitration Institutions' (2008) 65 *Beijing Arbitration*).

王红松,《仲裁行政化的危害及应对之策》,《北京仲裁》第62辑, 2007年 (Wang, Hongsong, The Detriments of and Measures Against the Administrative Influence on Arbitration, (2007) 62 Beijing Arbitration).

王亚新,《关于仲裁机构问卷调查的统计分析》,《北京仲裁》第63辑, 2007年, 第6-11页 (Wang, Yaxin, 'The Statistical Analysis on the Questionnaires to Arbitration Institutions', (2007) 63 *Beijing Arbitration*, 6–11).

肖峋,《在仲裁机构民间化建设座谈会上的发言》,《北京仲裁》第63辑, 2007年(Xiao, Xun, 'The Speech at the Symposium of Establishing Arbitration Institutions of a Private Nature', (2007) 63 *Beijing Arbitration*).

尤陈俊,《清代简约型司法体制下的健讼问题研究 – 从财政制约的角度切入》,《法商研究》第2辑, 2012年 (You, Chenjun, 'The Problem of Litigation Propensity under the Simple Legal System of Qing Dynasty – From the Perspective of the Financial Restraints', 2012(2), *Legal and Commercial Studies*).

虞和平,《清末民初商会的商事仲裁制度建设》,《学术月刊》2004年第4辑 (Yu, Heping, 'The Construction of a Commercial Arbitration System in Late-Qing and Early-Republican China' (2004) 4 Academic Monthly)

仲裁研究所,《中国国际经济贸易仲裁委员会五十年回顾和展望》,《仲裁与法律》第92辑, 2004年, 第 73–90页 (Arbitration Research Center,《仲裁与法律》第92nnaires to Arbitration dministrative Influence on, (2004) 92 *Arbitration and Law*).

Conference Papers

范忠信,《中国法制近代化的历史法学反省》, "中国传统法律文化新论" 学术研讨会, 香港中文大学, 2010年5月14–16日 (Fan, Zhongxin, 'Reflections on the Modernisation of the Chinese Legal System', paper presented at *Symposium on the New Discussions on the Traditional Chinese Legal Culture*, held at Chinese University of Hong Kong on 14–16 May 2010).

Fan, Kun, 'Can You Leave Your Hat On? An Empirical Study on Arbitrators Facilitating Settlement in China', paper presented at the *Journal of Empirical Legal Studies Conference on Asian Empirical Scholarship* held at Hawaii University on 4 June 2012.

刘贵祥、沈红雨,《我国承认和执行外国仲裁裁决的司法实践述评》, 2011年 "国际私法全球论坛", 2011年10月22–23日, 北京. (Guixiang Liu and Hongyu Shen, 'Recognition and Enforcement of Foreign Arbitral Awards in China: A Reflection on the Court Practices', report presented at *Private International Law Global Forum*, held in Beijing on 22–23 October 2011).

王红松, 替代性争端解决机制中律师的作用研讨会上的讲话》, 2007年8月27日 (Hongsong Wang, 'Speech at the Symposium on the Role of Lawyers in the Alternative Dispute Resolution', held in Beijing on 29 August 2007).

王红松,《2009 年新春茶话会的讲话》(Hongsong Wang, 'Speech at the 2009 Chinese New Year's Tea Seminar', held in Beijing in 2009).Tang, Houzhi, 'The Use of Conciliation in Arbitration' (1996).

Tang, Houzhi, 'Conciliation in China (updated)' (2000).

Official and Historical Documents

《商君书•勒令篇》(The Book of Lord Shang).

《论语》,translated by Simon Leys. Simon Leys, The Analects of Confucius, (New York, WW Norton and Company, 1997.

《孟子》, translated by Irene Bloom. Irene Bloom, *Mencius*, (Columbia, Columbia University Press, 2009).

《左传•昭公六年》(Zuo's Commentary, The Sixth Year of Duke Zhao).

李悝,《法经》(Kui Li, The Book of Laws).

《汉书•董仲舒传》(History of Han Dynasty: Biography of Dong,Zhongshu).

《晋书•刑法志》(History of Jin Dynasty, Section on Criminal Law).

长孙无忌,《唐律疏议》。(Zhang Sun Wu Ji, Annotated Commentaries on Laws of Tang Dynasty).

郑克,《折狱龟鉴》(Zheng, Ke, Exemplary Court Decisions).

《大明律集解附例•刑律•杂犯》(The Great Ming Code: Criminal Code: Miscellaneous Crimes).

《太祖实录》(The Veritable Records of Ming Emperor).

张卤(编)《皇明制书》卷9《教民榜文》。(Zhang, Lu (ed), Veritable Records of the Emperors, vol 9, Announcement for Educating the General Public.)

顾炎武,《日知录•卷八•政事•乡亭之职》。(Gu, Yanwu, Record of Daily Study, vol 8, Political Affairs, The Function of Elders.)

《奏定商会简明章程二十六条》(Twenty Six Rules of Simplified Arts of Association for the Chambers of Commerce).

杨志洵,《商业机关释》,《商务官报》第25期,光绪三十二年十一月初五日,第6页。(Zhizun Yang, Explanation of Commercial Bodies, 25 Official Journal of Commerce (1906) 6).

《四川成都商会商事裁判所规则》,《华商联合报》第17期,"海内外公牍", 第1页。(Rules of the Commercial Adjudicatory Institute of Sichuan Chengdu Chamber of Commerce, 17 United Journal of Chinese Merchants, 1).

司法部咨工商部商事公断处援案设立如有－造不服仍应受法庭审判之》,《政府公报》,1912年7月10日, 第71号 "公文" "A Reply from the Ministry of Justice Concerning the Jurisdiction of the Court if One Party Disagrees with the Arbitration Result, 10 July 1912, Official Gazette No 71).

《商事公断处章程》(Articles of Association of the Commercial Arbitral Bodies).

《公断法草案》(Draft Arbitration Act).

毛泽东,《关于如何处理当前处理人民内部矛盾》,1957年2月27日 (Mao, Zedong, '*How to Deal With the Disputes Among the Peoples*', 27 February 1957).

《人民法院案例选, 1991–2011》(Selected Cases of the SPC, 1992–2011).

《法学理论学习参考资料》1953 年版 (*Reference Materials for the Study of Jurisprudence and Legal Theory*, 1953).

《中国共产党第十一届中央委员会第三次全体会议公报》(Communique of the Third Plenary Session of the 11th Central Committee of Communist Party of China), passed on 22 December 1978.

Legislative Affairs Commission of the Standing Committee of the National People's Congress of the People's Republic of China (ed), *Arbitration Laws of China* (Sweet & Maxwell Asia, 1997).

万鄂湘(主编),《中国涉外商事海事审判指导与研究》,人民法院出版社,总1–6辑 (Wan, Exiang (ed), *Guide and Study on China's Foreign-related Commercial and Maritime Trials*, vols 1–6).

万鄂湘(主编),《涉外商事海事审判指导》人民法院出版社, 总7–18辑 (Wan, Exiang (ed), *Guide on Foreign-related Commercial and Maritime Trials*, vols 7–18).

北京仲裁委员 (会编),《仲裁员手册》(一)至(六) (Beijing Arbitration Commission (ed), *Arbitrators Manual*, vols 1–6).

Consultation Document for CEDR Commission on Settlement in International Arbitration. (2009).

Appendix 1: Arbitration Law of the People's Republic of China (1995)

Adopted by the Ninth Meeting of the Standing Committee of the Eighth National People's Congress on 31 August 1994 and promulgated by Decree No 31 of the President of the People's Republic of China on 31 August 1994 effective from 1 September 1995.

Chapter 1. General Provisions

Article 1

This Law is formulated in order to ensure the impartial and prompt arbitration of economic disputes, to protect the legitimate rights and interests of the parties and to safeguard the sound development of the socialist market economy.

Article 2

Contractual disputes and other disputes over rights and interests in property between citizens, legal persons and other organisations that are equal subjects may be arbitrated.

Article 3

The following disputes may not be arbitrated:
(1) marital, adoption, guardianship, support and succession disputes;
(2) administrative disputes that laws require to be handled by administrative authorities.

Article 4

The parties' submission to arbitration to resolve their dispute shall be on the basis of both parties' free will and an arbitration agreement reached between them. If a party applies for arbitration in the absence of an arbitration agreement, the arbitration commission shall not accept the case.

Article 5

If the parties have concluded an arbitration agreement and one party institutes an action in a People's Court, the People's Court shall not accept the case, unless the arbitration agreement is void.

Article 6

The arbitration commission shall be selected by the parties by agreement.

In arbitration, there shall be no jurisdiction by level and no territorial jurisdiction.

Article 7

In arbitration, disputes shall be resolved on the basis of facts, in compliance with law and in an equitable and reasonable manner.

Article 8

Arbitration shall be carried out independently according to law and shall not be subject to interference from administrative authorities, social organisations or individuals.

Article 9

A system of a single and final award shall be implemented for arbitration. If a party applies for arbitration or institutes proceedings in a People's Court regarding the same dispute after an arbitral award has been made, the arbitration commission or People's Court shall not accept the case.

If an arbitration award is set aside or its enforcement is refused by the People's Court in accordance with law, a party may apply for arbitration on the basis of a new arbitration agreement reached between the parties, or institute court proceedings in the People's Court, regarding the same dispute.

Chapter 2. Arbitration Commissions and the Arbitration Association

Article 10

Arbitration commissions may be established in municipalities directly under the central government and in municipalities that are the seats of the People's Governments of provinces and autonomous regions. They may also be established in other municipalities with districts, according to need. Arbitration commissions shall not be established at each level of the administrative divisions.

To establish an arbitration commission, the People's Governments of the municipalities referred to in the preceding paragraph shall arrange for the relevant departments and chambers of commerce to organize such commissions in a unified manner.

The establishment of an arbitration commission shall be registered with the administrative department of justice of the relevant province, autonomous region or municipality directly under the central government.

Article 11

An arbitration commission shall meet the conditions set forth below:

(1) to have its own name, domicile and charter;
(2) to have the necessary property;
(3) to have the personnel that are to form the commission; and
(4) to have appointed arbitrators.

The charter of an arbitration commission shall be formulated in accordance with this Law.

Article 12

An arbitration commission shall be composed of one chairman, two to four vice chairmen and seven to eleven members.

The offices of chairman, vice chairman and member of an arbitration commission shall be held by experts in the field of law, economy and trade and by persons with practical working experience. At least two-thirds of the persons forming an arbitration commission shall be experts in the field of law, economy and trade.

Article 13

Arbitration commissions shall appoint their arbitrators from among righteous, upright persons.

An arbitrator shall meet one of the conditions set forth below:

(1) has been engaged in arbitration work for eight years;
(2) has worked as a lawyer for eight years;
(3) has served as a judge for eight years;
(4) has been engaged in legal research work or legal education work and has a senior title; or
(5) has acquired the knowledge of the law, engaged in the professional work of economy and trade, etc and possessed a senior title or attained an equivalent professional level.

Arbitration commissions shall draw up lists of arbitrators according to different professions.

Article 14

Arbitration commissions shall be independent from administrative authorities and there shall be no subordinate relationships between arbitration commissions and administrative authorities. There shall also be no subordinate relationship between arbitration commissions.

Article 15

The China Arbitration Association shall be a social organisation with the status of a legal person. Arbitration commissions shall be members of the China Arbitration Association. The charter of the China Arbitration Association shall be formulated by the National Congress of Members.

The China Arbitration Association shall be a self-regulating organisation of arbitration commissions. It shall supervise arbitration commissions and their members and arbitrators as to whether or not they breach discipline, in accordance with its charter.

The China Arbitration Association shall formulate rules of arbitration in accordance with this Law and the relevant provisions of the Civil Procedure Law.

Chapter 3. Arbitration Agreement

Article 16

An arbitration agreement includes an arbitration clause included in the contract, and an agreement on submission to arbitration that is concluded in other written forms before or after the dispute arises.

An arbitration agreement shall contain the following particulars:

(1) an expression of the intention to apply for arbitration;
(2) matters for arbitration; and
(3) a designated arbitration commission.

Article 17

An arbitration agreement shall be void if one of the following facts exists:

(1) the agreed matters for arbitration exceed the scope of arbitrable matters as specified by law;
(2) one party that concluded the arbitration agreement has no capacity for civil acts or has limited capacity for civil acts; or
(3) one party coerced the other party into concluding the arbitration agreement.

Article 18

If an arbitration agreement contains no or unclear provisions concerning the matters for arbitration or the arbitration commission, the parties may reach a supplementary agreement. If no such supplementary agreement can be reached, the arbitration agreement shall be void.

Article 19

An arbitration agreement shall exist independently. The amendment, rescission, termination or invalidity of a contract shall not affect the validity of the arbitration agreement.

The arbitration tribunal has the right to affirm the validity of a contract.

Article 20

If a party challenges the validity of the arbitration agreement, he may request the arbitration commission to make a decision or the People's Court to give a ruling. If one party requests the arbitration commission to make a decision and the other party requests the People's Court for a ruling, the People's Court shall rule.

A party's challenge of the validity of an arbitration agreement shall be raised prior to the arbitration tribunal's first hearing.

Chapter 4. Arbitration Proceedings

Section 1. Application and Acceptance

Article 21

A party's application for arbitration shall meet the following requirements:

(1) there is an arbitration agreement;
(2) there is a specific arbitration claim and there are facts and reasons; and
(3) the application is within the scope of the arbitration commission's acceptability.

Article 22

To apply for arbitration, a party shall submit to the arbitration commission the written arbitration agreement and a written application for arbitration, together with copies thereof.

Article 23

A written application for arbitration shall specify the following particulars:

(1) the parties' names, sexes, ages, occupations, work units and domiciles, and in the case of legal persons or other organisations, their names and domiciles and the names and positions of their legal representatives or principal officers;
(2) the arbitration claim and the facts and reasons on which the claim is based; and
(3) the evidence, the source of the evidence and the name and domicile of the witness.

Article 24

If, when an arbitration commission receives a written application for arbitration, it considers that the application complies with the conditions for acceptance, it shall accept the application and notify the party within five days from the date of receipt. If the arbitration commission considers that the application does not comply with the conditions for acceptance, it shall inform the party in writing of its rejection of the application and explain its reasons for rejection within five days from the date of receipt.

Article 25

After an arbitration commission accepts an application for arbitration, it shall, within the time limit specified in the rules of arbitration, deliver a copy of the rules of arbitration and a list of arbitrators to the claimant, and serve one copy of the application together with the rules of arbitration and a list of arbitrators on the respondent.

After receiving the copy of the application, the respondent shall submit a written defense to the arbitration commission within the time limit specified in the rules of arbitration. After receiving the written defense, the arbitration commission shall serve a copy thereof on the claimant within the time limit specified in the rules of arbitration. Failure on the part of the respondent to submit a written defense shall not affect the progress of the arbitration proceedings.

Article 26

If the parties have concluded an arbitration agreement and one party institutes an action in a People's Court without declaring the existence of the agreement and, after the People's Court accepts the case, the other party submits the arbitration agreement prior to the first hearing, the People's Court shall dismiss the case unless the arbitration agreement is void. If the other party does not, prior to the first hearing, raise an objection to the People's Court's acceptance of the case, he shall be deemed to have renounced the arbitration agreement and the People's Court shall continue to try the case.

Article 27

The claimant may renounce or amend its arbitration claim. The respondent may accept or refute an arbitration claim and shall have the right to make a counterclaim.

Article 28

A party may apply for interim measures of protection of property if it may become impossible or difficult to implement the award due to an act of the other party or other causes.

If a party applies for interim measures of protection of property, the arbitration commission shall submit the party's application to a People's Court in accordance with the relevant provisions of the Civil Procedure Law.

If the application is wrongful, the applicant shall compensate for the losses suffered by the party against whom the interim measures have been taken.

Article 29

A party or statutory agent may appoint a lawyer or other agent to carry out the arbitration activities. To appoint a lawyer or other agent to carry out the arbitration activities, a power of attorney shall be submitted to the arbitration commission.

Section 2. Formation of Arbitration Tribunal

Article 30

An arbitration tribunal may be composed of either three arbitrators or one arbitrator. An arbitration tribunal composed of three arbitrators shall have a presiding arbitrator.

Article 31

If the parties agree that the arbitration tribunal shall be composed of three arbitrators, they shall each appoint, or entrust the chairman of the arbitration commission to appoint one arbitrator. The parties shall jointly select or jointly entrust the chairman of the arbitration commission to appoint the third arbitrator who shall be the presiding arbitrator.

If the parties agree that the arbitration tribunal shall be composed of one arbitrator, they shall jointly appoint or jointly entrust the chairman of the arbitration commission to appoint such arbitrator.

Article 32

If the parties fail to agree on the method of formation of the arbitration tribunal or to select the arbitrators within the time limit specified in the rules of arbitration, the arbitrators shall be appointed by the chairman of the arbitration commission.

Article 33

After the arbitration tribunal has been formed, the arbitration commission shall notify the parties in writing of the tribunal's formation.

Article 34

In one of the following circumstances, the arbitrator must withdraw, and the parties shall also have the right to challenge the arbitrator for a withdrawal:

(1) the arbitrator is a party in the case or a close relative of a party or of an agent in the case;
(2) the arbitrator has a personal interest in the case;
(3) the arbitrator has another relationship with a party or his agent in the case which may affect the impartiality of the arbitration; or
(4) the arbitrator has privately met with a party or agent or accepted an invitation to entertainment or a gift from a party or agent.

Article 35

If a party challenges an arbitrator, he shall submit his challenge, with a statement of the reasons therefor, prior to the first hearing. If the matter which gives rise to the challenge becomes known after the first hearing, the challenge may be made before the conclusion of the final hearing of the case.

Article 36

The decision as to whether or not the arbitrator should withdraw shall be made by the chairman of the arbitration commission. If the chairman of the arbitration commission serves as an arbitrator, the decision shall be made collectively by the arbitration commission.

Article 37

If an arbitrator cannot perform his duties due to his withdrawal or for other reasons, a new arbitrator shall be selected or designated in accordance with this Law.

After a substitute arbitrator has been selected or appointed due to an arbitrator's withdrawal, a party may request that the arbitration proceedings already carried out shall be carried out anew. The decision as to whether or not to permit such proceedings to be carried out anew shall be made by the arbitration tribunal. The arbitration tribunal may also make a decision of its own motion as to whether or not the arbitration proceedings already carried out should be carried out anew.

Article 38

If the circumstances described in item (4) of Article 34 hereof apply to an arbitrator and such circumstances are serious, or if the circumstances described in item (6) of Article 58 hereof apply to an arbitrator, such arbitrator shall assume legal liability according to law and the arbitration commission shall remove his name from the list of arbitrators.

Section 3. Hearing and Award

Article 39

Arbitration shall be conducted by means of hearings. If the parties agree to arbitration without hearings, the arbitration tribunal may render an arbitration award on the basis of the written application, the written defense and other material.

Article 40

Arbitration shall be conducted in camera. If the parties agree to public arbitration, the arbitration may be public, unless state secrets are involved.

Article 41

The arbitration commission shall notify the parties of the date of hearing within the time limit specified in the rules of arbitration. A party may, within the time limit specified in the rules of arbitration, request a postponement of the hearing if he has justified reasons therefor. The arbitration tribunal shall decide whether or not to postpone the hearing.

Article 42

If the claimant fails to appear before the tribunal without justified reasons after having been notified in writing or leaves the hearing prior to its conclusion without the permission of the arbitration tribunal, he may be deemed to have withdrawn his application for arbitration.

If the respondent fails to appear before the tribunal without justified reasons after having being notified in writing or leaves the hearing prior to its conclusion without the permission of the arbitration tribunal, a default award may be made.

Article 43

Parties shall provide evidence in support of their own arguments.

The arbitration tribunal may of its own motion collect such evidence as it considers necessary.

Article 44

If the arbitration tribunal considers that a special issue requires appraisal, it may refer the issue for appraisal to an appraisal department agreed on by the parties; or to an appraisal department designated by the arbitration tribunal.

If requested by a party or required by the arbitration tribunal, the appraisal department shall send its appraisers to attend the hearing. Subject to the permission of the arbitration tribunal, the parties may question the appraiser.

Article 45

Evidence shall be presented during the hearings and may be examined by the parties.

Article 46

Under circumstances where evidence may be destroyed or lost or be difficult to obtain later, a party may apply for interim measures of protection of evidence. If a party applies for interim measures of protection of evidence, the arbitration commission shall submit his application to the basic-level People's Court in the place where the evidence is located.

Article 47

The parties shall have the right to carry on debate in the course of arbitration. At the end of the debate, the presiding arbitrator or sole arbitrator shall solicit final opinions from the parties.

Article 48

The arbitration tribunal shall make records of the hearings in writing. The parties and other participants in the arbitration shall have the right to apply for correction of the record of their own statements if they consider that such record contains omissions or errors. If no corrections are made, their application for correction shall be recorded.

The record shall be signed or sealed by the arbitrators, the recordist, the parties and the other participants in the arbitration.

Article 49

After an application for arbitration has been made, the parties may settle on their own. If the parties reach a settlement agreement, they may request the arbitration tribunal to make an arbitration award in accordance with the settlement agreement; alternatively, they may withdraw their application for arbitration.

Article 50

If a settlement agreement reached by the parties is repudiated after the application for arbitration is withdrawn, an application for arbitration may be filed again in accordance with the arbitration agreement.

Article 51

The arbitration tribunal may carry out conciliation prior to giving an award. The arbitration tribunal shall conduct conciliation if both parties voluntarily seek conciliation. If conciliation is unsuccessful, an arbitration award shall be made promptly.

If conciliation leads to a settlement agreement, the arbitration tribunal shall make a written conciliation statement or make an arbitration award in accordance with the settlement agreement. A written conciliation statement and a written arbitration award shall have equal legal validity and effect.

Article 52

The written conciliation statement shall specify the arbitration claim and the results of the settlement reached between the parties. The written conciliation statement shall be signed by the arbitrators and sealed by the arbitration commission. After the written conciliation statement has been so signed and sealed, it shall be served on both parties.

The written conciliation statement shall become legally effective immediately after both parties have signed for receipt thereof.

If the written conciliation statement is repudiated by a party before he signs for receipt thereof, the arbitration tribunal shall promptly make an arbitration award.

Article 53

The arbitration award shall be made in accordance with the opinion of the majority of the arbitrators. The opinion of the minority of the arbitrators may be entered in the record. If the arbitration tribunal is unable to form a majority opinion, the arbitration award shall be made in accordance with the opinion of the presiding arbitrator.

Article 54

The arbitration award shall specify the arbitration claim, the facts of the dispute, the reasons for the decision, the result of the award, the allocation of arbitration costs and the date of the award. If the parties agree that they do not wish the facts of the dispute and the reasons for the decision to be specified in the written arbitration award, the same may be omitted. The arbitration award shall be signed by the arbitrators and sealed by the arbitration commission. An arbitrator with dissenting opinions as to the arbitration award may either sign or not sign the award.

Article 55

In arbitration proceedings, if a part of the facts involved have already become clear, the arbitration tribunal may first make an award in respect of such part of the facts.

Article 56

If there are literal or calculation errors in the arbitration award, or if matters which have been decided by the arbitration tribunal are omitted in the arbitration award, the arbitration tribunal shall correct or supplement the award.

Within thirty days from the date of receipt of the award, the parties may request the arbitration tribunal to correct and/or supplement the award.

Article 57

The arbitration award shall be legally effective from the date on which it is made.
Chapter 5. Application for Setting Aside Arbitration Awards

Article 58

A party may apply for setting aside an arbitration award to the intermediate People's Court in the place where the arbitration institution is located if he can produce evidence which proves that the arbitration award involves one of the following circumstances:

(1) there is no arbitration agreement;
(2) the matters decided in the award exceed the scope of the arbitration agreement or are beyond the arbitral authority of the arbitration institution;
(3) the formation of the arbitration tribunal or the arbitration procedure was in violation of statutory procedure;
(4) the evidence on which the award is based was forged;
(5) the other party has withheld evidence sufficient to affect the impartiality of the arbitration;
(6) while arbitrating the case, the arbitrators committed embezzlement, accepted bribes, practiced graft or made an award that perverted the law.

The People's Court shall rule to set aside the arbitration award if a collegiate bench formed by the People's Court verifies upon examination that the award involves one of the circumstances set forth in the preceding paragraph.

If the People's Court determines that the arbitration award is contrary to the public interest, it shall rule to set aside the award.

Article 59

A party that wishes to apply for setting aside an arbitration award shall submit such application within six months from the date of receipt of the award.

Article 60
The People's Court that has accepted an application for the setting aside of an arbitration award shall rule to set aside the award or to reject the application within two months from the date of acceptance.

Article 61
If the People's Court that has accepted an application for setting aside an arbitration award considers that re-arbitration can be carried out by the arbitration tribunal, it shall notify the tribunal that it should re-arbitrate the dispute within a certain time limit and shall rule to stay the setting aside procedure. If the arbitration tribunal refuses to re-arbitrate the dispute, the People's Court shall rule to resume the setting aside procedure.

Chapter 6. Enforcement

Article 62
The parties shall perform the arbitration award. If a party fails to perform the arbitration award, the other party may apply to the People's Court for enforcement in accordance with the relevant provisions of the Civil Procedure Law. The People's Court that accepts such an application shall enforce the award.

Article 63
If the party against whom the enforcement is sought presents evidence which proves that the arbitration award involves one of the circumstances set forth in the second paragraph of Article 217 of the Civil Procedure Law (see Annex to the Law), the People's Court shall, after examination and verification by a collegiate bench formed by the People's Court, rule to refuse enforcement.

Article 64
If one party applies for enforcement of an arbitration award and the other party applies for setting aside the arbitration award, the People's Court shall rule to suspend the enforcement proceedings.

If the People's Court rules to set aside the arbitration award, it shall rule to terminate the procedure. If the ruling is made to reject the application for setting aside of the arbitration award, the People's Court shall rule to resume the enforcement procedure.

Chapter 7. Special Provisions for Foreign-related Arbitration

Article 65
This Chapter applies to the arbitration of disputes arising from economic, trade, transportation and maritime activities involving a foreign element. For matters not covered in this Chapter, the other provisions of this Law shall apply.

Article 66

Foreign-related arbitration institutions may be organized and established by the China Chamber of International Commerce.

A foreign-related arbitration institution shall be composed of one chairman, several vice chairmen and members.

The chairman, vice chairmen and members of foreign-related arbitration institutions may be appointed by the China Chamber of International Commerce.

Article 67

Foreign-related arbitration institutions may appoint their arbitrators from among foreigners with special knowledge in the fields of law, economy and trade, science and technology, etc.

Article 68

If a party to a foreign-related arbitration applies for taking interim measures of protection of evidence, the foreign-related arbitration institution shall submit his application to the intermediate People's Court in the place where the evidence is located.

Article 69

A foreign-related arbitration tribunal may enter the details of the hearing in a written record or make written minutes thereof. The written minutes may be signed or sealed by the parties and the other participants in the arbitration.

Article 70

If a party presents evidence which proves that a foreign-related arbitration award involves one of the circumstances set forth in the first paragraph of Article 260 of the Civil Procedure Law, the People's Court shall, after examination and verification by a collegiate bench formed by the People's Court, rule to set aside the award.

Article 71

If the party against whom the enforcement is sought presents evidence which proves that the arbitration award involves one of the circumstances set forth in the first paragraph of Article 260 of the Civil Procedure Law, the People's Court shall, after examination and verification by a collegiate bench formed by the People's Court, rule to refuse the enforcement of the award.

Article 72

If a party applies for enforcement of a legally effective arbitration award made by a foreign-related arbitration institution and the party against whom the application for enforcement is sought or such party's property is not within the territory of the People's Republic of China, the party shall directly apply to a competent foreign court for recognition and enforcement of the award.

Article 73

Foreign-related arbitration rules may be formulated by the China Chamber of International Commerce in accordance with this Law and the relevant provisions of the Civil Procedure Law.

Chapter 8. Supplementary Provisions

Article 74

If there is prescription for arbitration stipulated by law, such prescription shall apply. If there is no such prescription for arbitration stipulated by law, the prescription for litigation shall apply to arbitration.

Article 75

Until the China Arbitration Association formulates rules of arbitration, the arbitration institutions may formulate tentative rules of arbitration in accordance with this Law and the relevant provisions of the Civil Procedure Law.

Article 76

Parties shall pay arbitration fees according to regulations.

The methods for charging arbitration fees shall be submitted to the commodity-price administration authorities for examination and approval.

Article 77

Regulations concerning arbitration of labor disputes and agricultural contractors' contract disputes arising within the agricultural collective economic organisations shall be formulated separately.

Article 78

In the event of conflict between the provisions governing arbitration regulations formulated prior to the implementation of this Law and the provisions of this Law, this Law shall prevail.

Article 79

Arbitration institutions in the municipalities directly under the central government, in the municipalities that are the seats of the People's Governments of provinces and autonomous regions and in other municipalities with districts that were established prior to the implementation of this Law shall be reorganized in accordance with this Law. Those of such arbitration institutions that are not reorganized shall cease to exist one year from the date of implementation of this Law.

Other arbitration institutions established prior to the implementation of this Law that do not comply with the provisions of this Law shall cease to exist from the date of implementation of this Law.

Article 80

This Law shall be implemented from 1 September 1995.

Appendix 2: Interpretation of the SPC on Certain Issues Relating to Application of the Arbitration Law of the People's Republic of China (2006)

Promulgated at the 1375th Session of the Judicial Committee of the SPC on 26 December 2005 and effective from 8 September 2006. Interpretation No. 7 [2006] of the SPC

Pursuant to the provisions of the Arbitration Law of the People's Republic of China and the Civil Procedural Law of the People's Republic of China and other legal provisions, we hereby give our interpretations concerning certain issues relating to the application of law for the People's Court to try arbitration-related cases as follows:

Article 1
An arbitration agreement in 'other written form' described in Article 16 of the Arbitration Law includes any agreement requesting for arbitration in the form of a contract, letter and electronic text (including telegraph, telex, facsimile, electronic data exchange and electronic mail), etc.

Article 2
Where the parties agree that the matters to be arbitrated are contractual disputes in general, the disputes arising out of formation, effectiveness, modification, assignment, performance, liabilities for breach, interpretation, rescission, etc. of the contract may all be ascertained as matters to be arbitrated.

Article 3
Where the name of an arbitration institution as stipulated in the agreement for arbitration is inaccurate, but the specific arbitration institution can be determined, it shall be ascertained that the arbitration institution has been selected.

Article 4
Where an arbitration agreement only provides the applicable arbitration rules, it shall be deemed that no arbitration institution is stipulated, unless the parties reach a supplementary agreement, or an arbitration institution can be determined pursuant to the arbitration rules agreed by the parties.

Article 5
Where an arbitration agreement provides for two or more arbitration institutions, the parties may choose either arbitration institution upon

agreement when applying for arbitration; where the parties are unable to agree on the choice of an arbitration institution, the arbitration agreement shall be invalid.

Article 6

Where an arbitration agreement provides for arbitration to be submitted with an arbitration institution at a fixed locality and only one arbitration institution exists at that locality, that arbitration institution shall be deemed as the stipulated arbitration institution. Where there are two or more arbitration institutions at that locality, the parties may choose one of the arbitration institutions by; where the parties concerned are unable to agree on the choice of the arbitration institution , the arbitration agreement shall be invalid.

Article 7

Where the parties agree that they may resolve a dispute either by applying for arbitration with an arbitration institution or bringing a lawsuit with the People's Court , the arbitration agreement shall be invalid, unless one party has submitted an arbitration request to an arbitration institution but the other party failed to object within the time limit stipulated in Article 20(2) of the Arbitration Law.

Article 8

Where a party is merged or divided upon the conclusion of an arbitration agreement, the arbitration agreement shall be binding on the successors to the rights and obligations of that party.

Where a party dies after the conclusion of an arbitration agreement, the arbitration agreement shall be binding on the party's inheritor who inherits his rights and obligations in the matter to be arbitrated.

The circumstances prescribded in the preceding two paragraphs shall not apply where the parties have agreed otherwise in the arbitration agreement.

Article 9

An arbitration agreement shall bind a transferee of any creditor rights and debts transferred whether in whole or in part, unless the parties have agreed otherwise, or where the transferee explicitly objected or was unaware of the existence of a separate arbitration agreement at the time of the transfer.

Article 10

Where a concluded contract has not taken effect or has been revoked, the provisions in the first paragraph of Article 19 of the Arbitration Law shall apply in the determination of the arbitration agreement's validity.

Where the parties reach an arbitration agreement when concluding a contract, the validity of the arbitration agreement shall not be affected if the contract is not formed.

Article 11

Where the contract provides that a valid arbitration clause of another contract or document shall apply in the resolution of a dispute arising from the first-mentioned contract, the parties shall apply for arbitration pursuant to such an arbitration clause in the event of a contractual dispute.

Where a foreign-related contract is governed by the arbitration provision of a relevant international treaty, the parties shall apply for arbitration pursuant to the arbitration provision in the international treaty in the event of a contractual dispute.

Article 12

Where a party applies to the People's Court to determine the validity of an arbitration agreement, the case shall fall within the jurisdiction of the intermediate People's Court at the location of the arbitration institution stipulated in the arbitration agreement; where the arbitration institution in the arbitration agreement is not clearly stipulated, the case shall fall within the jurisdiction of the intermediate People's Court at the location where the arbitration agreement was concluded, or at the respondent's domicile.

Where a party applies for the determination of validity of a foreign related arbitration agreement, the case shall fall within the jurisdiction of the intermediate People's Court at the location of the arbitration institution stipulated in the arbitration agreement, or at the location where the arbitration agreement was concluded, or at the claimant's or the respondent's domicile.

Where a party applies for the determination of validity of an arbitration agreement involving maritime or maritime commerce disputes, the case shall fall within the jurisdiction of the maritime court at the location of the arbitration institution stipulated in the arbitration agreement, or the location where the arbitration agreement was concluded, or at the claimant's or the respondent's domicile; where no maritime court is established at the said locations, the case shall fall within the jurisdiction of the nearest maritime court.

Article 13

Pursuant to the provisions of Article 20(2) of the Arbitration Law, where a party has not objected to the validity of an arbitration agreement before the first hearings, but subsequently applies to the People's Court to confirm the arbitration agreement is invalid, the People's Court shall not hear such a case.

Where an arbitration institution has decided on the validity of an arbitration agreement and a party subsequently applies to the People's Court to determine the validity the arbitration agreement or to revoke the decision of the arbitration institution, the People's Court shall not hear such a case.

Article 14

The term 'first hearing' mentioned in Article 26 of the Arbitration Law shall refer to the first trial organised by the People's Court after the period for defence has expired, excluding all procedural activities prior to the trial.

Article 15

The People's Court shall, in the determination of validity of arbitration agreement hearings, form a collegiate bench to conduct case hearings and inquiry the parties concerned.

Article 16

The validity of a foreign-related arbitration agreement shall be determined the law as agreed between the parties; where the parties have agreed on the place of arbitration but not the governing law, the law of the place of arbitration shall apply; where the parties have neither agreed on the governing law nor the place of arbitration or where agreement on the place of arbitration is unclear, the law of the place where the court is located shall apply.

Article 17

Where a party applies to set aside an arbitral award on a ground not stipulated in Article 58 of the Arbitration Law or Article 258 of the Civil Procedural Law (2007)[1] the People's Court shall not support such application.

Article 18

The term 'no arbitration agreement' as stipulated in Article 58(1)(1) of the Arbitration Law shall refer to the situations where the parties did not enter into an arbitration agreement. An arbitration agreement that is deemed invalid or is being revoked shall also be deemed as a case of having 'no arbitration agreement'. If the arbitration agreement is ascertained as invalid or is revoked, it shall be deemed that there is no arbitration agreement.

Article 19

Where a party applies for an arbitral award to be set aside on the ground that the subject matter of the arbitral award is outside the scope of the arbitration agreement, and the application is found true upon examination, the People's Court shall set aside the part of the arbitral award that exceeds the scope of the arbitration agreement. Where, however, the part of the award that exceeds the scope of the arbitration agreement cannot be separated from other matters in the arbitral award, the People's Court shall set aside the arbitral award.

---

[1] Amended according to Decision of the Supreme People's Court on Adjusting the Sequential Number of the Articles of the Civil Procedure Law of the People's Republic of China Cited in Judicial Interpretations and Other Documents. Now the corresponding article should be Art 274 of the Civil Procedure Law 2012.

Article 20

The term 'in violation of statutory procedures' as stipulated in Article 58 of the Arbitration Law shall refer to circumstances where the arbitration procedures violate provisions in the Arbitration Law and the arbitration rules selected by parties, which may affect the correct ruling of a case.

Article 21

Under any of the circumstances where a party applies to revoke an arbitral award in China, the People's Court may, pursuant to the provisions of Article 61 of the Arbitration Law, notify the arbitral tribunal to re-arbitration within a time limit:

(1) the arbitral award is based on forged evidence; or
(2) the counterparty has concealed evidence which affects a fair ruling.

The People's Court shall state in the notice the specific reasons for a re-arbitration.

Article 22

Where an arbitral tribunal re-arbitrates pursuant to the period stipulated by the People's Court, the People's Court shall rule to suspend the setting aside procedure; where the arbitral tribunal has not started re-arbitration, the People's Court shall rule to resume the setting aside procedure.

Article 23

A party dissatisfied a re-arbitrated award may apply to the People's Court to set aside the award, within six months from the date of delivery of the re-arbitrated award pursuant to the provisions of Article 58 of the Arbitration Law.

Article 24

Where a party applies to set aside an arbitral award, the People's Court shall form a collegiate bench to conduct hearings and inquiry the parties concerned.

Article 25

Where the People's Court has accepted an application by one party to set aside an arbitral award, and the other party applies for the enforcement of the same arbitral award, the People's Court shall rule to suspend the enforcement after accepting the application.

Article 26

Where, after an application filed by one party to set aside aside an arbitral award is rejected by the People's Court, the said party files an application to resist enforcement of the award based on the same ground, the People's Court shall not support such application.

Article 27

Where a party concerned has not objected to the validity of an arbitration agreement during the arbitration proceeding, and subsequently files an application to set aside or resist enforcement of an arbitral award after the award is made, the People's Court shall not support such application.

Where a party concerned objects to the validity of an arbitration agreement, and subsequently files an application to set aside or resist enforcement of an arbitral award after the award is made, the People's Court shall support such application, provided the assertion is verified to comply with provisions of Article 58 of the Arbitration Law or Article 213 or 258 of the Civil Procedural Law (2007)[2].

Article 28

Where a party concerned files an application to resist enforcement of reconciliation settlement agreement or a consent award rendered on the basis of the settlement agreement between the parties, People's Court shall not support such application.

Article 29

The application by a party to enforce of an arbitral award shall fall within the jurisdiction of the intermediate People's Court at domicile of the party against whom the award is to be enforced or at the location of the property to be enforced.

Article 30

The People's Court may, pursuant to the actual requirements of the hearing for an application for the setting aside or enforcement of an arbitral award, require the arbitration institution to make an explanation or to consult arbitration files from the relevant arbitration institution.

A ruling rendered by the People's Court in the process of handling a case revolving arbitration may be served on the relevant arbitration institution.

Article 31

This Interpretation shall come into from from the date of promulgation.
Where there is any inconsistency between this Interpretation and previously promulgated judicial interpretations, this Interpretation shall prevail.

---

[2] Amended according to Decision of the Supreme People's Court on Adjusting the Sequential Number of the Articles of the Civil Procedure Law of the People's Republic of China Cited in Judicial Interpretations and Other Documents. Now the corresponding article should be Arts 237 or 274 of the Civil Procedure Law 2012.

Appendix 3: Relevant Provisions of the Civil Procedure Law (2012 Amendment)

Adopted on 9 April 1991 at the Fourth Session of the Seventh NPC. The first revision was made according to the Decision of the Standing Committee of the NPC on Amending the Civil Procedure Law of the PRC as adopted at the 30th Session of the Standing Committee of the 10th NPC on 28 October 2007. The second revision was made according to the Decision of the Standing Committee of the NPC on Amending the Civil Procedure Law of the PRC as adopted at the 28th Session of the Standing Committee of the 11th NPC on 31 August 2012, which will come into force on 1 January 2013.

Article 237

If the party against whom the enforcement is sought presents evidence which proves that the arbitration award involves one of the following circumstances, the People's Court shall, after examination and verification by a collegiate bench formed by the People's Court, refuse enforcement thereof:

(1) the parties have neither included an arbitration clause in their contract nor subsequently reached a written arbitration agreement;
(2) matters decided in the award exceed the scope of the arbitration agreement or are beyond the arbitral authority of the arbitration institution;
(3) the formation of the arbitration tribunal or the arbitration procedure was not in conformity with statutory procedure;
(4) the main evidence for ascertaining the facts was insufficient;
(5) application of law was truly incorrect; or
(6) in arbitration, arbitrators committed embezzlement, accepted bribes, practiced graft or made an award that perverted the law.

Chapter 26 Arbitration

Article 271

For disputes involving foreign economic, trade, transport, or maritime activities, if the parties have stipulated clauses on arbitration in their contracts or have subsequently reached written agreements on arbitration, they shall submit such disputes for arbitration to the foreign-affair arbitration institutions of the People's Republic of China and shall not bring lawsuits in a People's Court. If the parties have not stipulated clauses on arbitration in the contract or have not subsequently reached a written agreement on arbitration, they may file a lawsuit in a People's Court.

Article 272

If a party applies for the adoption of property preservation measure, the foreign-affair arbitration institution of the People's Republic of China shall submit the party's application to the intermediate People's Court located in the place where the person against whom the application for the property preservation is filed has his domicile or where the person's property is located.

Article 273

If one party fails to comply with the award made by a foreign-affair arbitration institution of the People's Republic of China, the other party may apply for the enforcement of the award to the intermediate People's Court located in the place where the person against whom the application for the enforcement is made has his domicile or where the property of the person is located.

Article 274

If a defendant provides evidence to prove that the arbitration award made by a foreign-affair arbitration institution of the People's Republic of China involves any of the following circumstances, the People's Court shall, after examination and verification by a collegial bench, rule to disallow the enforcement of the award:

(1) the parties have neither included an arbitration clause in their contract nor subsequently concluded a written arbitration agreement;
(2) the party against whom the enforcement is sought was not notified to appoint an arbitrator or to take part in the arbitration proceedings or the party against whom the enforcement is sought was unable to state his opinions due to reasons for which he is not responsible;
(3) the formation of the arbitral tribunal or the arbitration procedure was not in conformity with the rules of arbitration; or
(4) matters decided in the award exceed the scope of the arbitration agreement or are beyond the arbitral authority of the arbitration institution.

If a People's Court determines that the enforcement of an award will violate the social and public interest, the court shall make a ruling to disallow the enforcement of the arbitration award.

Article 275

If the enforcement of an arbitration award is disallowed, the parties may reach a written agreement on arbitration to re-submit their dispute for a new arbitration or file a lawsuit in a People's Court.

Index

ad hoc arbitration 40–4, 101, 103, 172, 174, 178, 229
administration 50–2, 125, 128–33, 156, 171–4, 228–9
administrative arbitration 115–16, 120, 133–4, 159–61, 179
adversarial approach, choice of 235
agrarian economy 200–3
agreements *see* arbitration agreements; contract
American Arbitration Association (AAA) 122
amicable resolution, cultural emphasis on
  biantong 180, 209
  Chinese characteristics 171, 180, 243
  clans 199, 211
  Communism 221–2, 230
  Confucianism 3, 197
  culture 3, 194–200, 210–12, 229–31
  family conflicts 199
  guanxi 180, 208, 222–3, 226, 230–1
  guilds 200, 210–11
  harmony 194–200, 233
  individual's right to sue within local groups, limitation on 199–200
  influence of Chinese culture 243
  local magistrates 196–9
  mediation 229–31, 233
  modernisation of law 3, 215, 229–31, 233
  relational mode of association 210–11, 222–3, 230–1
  suppression of litigation, practice of 196–200, 210–12
  traditional legal culture 3, 194–200, 210–12, 229–31
  villages 200
ancient Greece 2
ancient Rome *see* Roman law
analogy, arbitration by 145
appeals 10, 11, 18, 21, 76–8, 115, 208
appointment of arbitrators
  arbitration agreements, not in accordance with 75–6, 107–9
  Arbitration Law 64–6
  Beijing Arbitration Commission 66, 236
  Chinese practice 64–6
  CIETAC 66–9
  civil capacity to be appointed 64
  compulsory panel system, institutional control by 64, 65–6
  confirmation by court 62

constitution of tribunal 61, 62, 64–6
contract 176–7
freedom of choice 19, 61–4, 66, 120, 179
ICC Court 62
impartiality 62–4, 67–9
independence 62–4, 67–9
institutional arbitration 64–6
knowledge of appointment 106
management system, reform of 236
mechanisms 61, 62
moral qualifications 64–5
national committees 62
New York Convention 1958 74, 105–6
notice of appointment 74, 95, 105–6
panel lists 62–3, 66, 69
party-appointed arbitrators 62
party autonomy 65
qualifications 61, 64–6, 69
recognition and enforcement of arbitration awards 74–6, 97–8, 105–9
relevant law, not in accordance with 75–6, 107–9
sole arbitrators 62–3, 68
strict statutory qualifications 64–5
arbitrability 79, 95, 110
arbitral institutions *see* institutions
arbitral tribunals 54–70 *see also* particular tribunals (eg CIETAC)
arbitration agreements 29–52 *see also* validity of arbitration agreements
  appointment of arbitrators 75–6, 107–9
  autonomy of agreement with a limited scope, application of 29–33
  CIETAC 120
  consent 29
  constitution of tribunal 61
  foreign-related arbitration 19–20
  interpretation 95
  jurisdiction 29, 53–4
  New York Convention 1958 75–6
  recognition and enforcement of arbitration awards 74–6, 97–8, 107–8
  seat of arbitration 23, 25
  severability principle 29–34
  transnational standards 29
  UNCITRAL Model Law 6
arbitration awards *see* awards
Arbitration Law
  ad hoc arbitration 41
  administrative intervention 173

Arbitration Law (*cont.*):
  adoption 20
  appointment of arbitrators 64–5
  arbitrability 110
  arbitration agreements, need for valid 21
  arb-med 164, 165
  classification of arbitration 21–3
  conceptual differences 174–5
  culture 219
  deficiencies 173
  domestic awards 84–5
  finality of awards 21
  foreign arbitrations 44–7, 51–2
  foreign-related arbitration 21–2, 85
  'Great Wall' 44–5
  historical development 17–21
  ICC Court, designation of 46–7
  independence of arbitration 21
  institutions 21, 115–17
  interpretation 12, 37–9, 51, App 2
  jurisdiction 57–60
  local institutions 134
  local protectionism 113
  modernisation of law 219
  opening up policy 12
  party autonomy 20, 173, 179, 229
  principles 20–1
  private nature of arbitration 115
  protectionism 44–5
  reasonableness 209–10
  recognition and enforcement of arbitration awards 83–5, 87–90, 98–9, 113
  seat of arbitration 24, 50
  setting aside awards 83–4
  text App 1
  transnational standards 20–1, 234
  validity of arbitration agreements 37–8
arbitrators *see also* appointment of arbitrators
  arb-med 137–44, 152, 167, 168–9
  assessment 237
  availability 62–4, 67–70
  Beijing Arbitration Commission 237
  Chinese characteristics 172, 176–7
  CIETAC 120, 124, 127–33
  Code of Ethics 124
  consent, powers by 210
  contract 127, 176–7
  ICC Court 119, 123
  local institutions 135
  nationality 119, 123
  number of arbitrators 61
  qualifications 22, 61, 64–6, 69, 124, 127, 172, 179
  quality 53, 65–7, 69, 172, 236–7
  relationship with institutions 127–33
  replacement 239
  safety 44
  sole arbitrators 62, 69

  theoretical debates on role in settlement facilitation 138–44
  training 124–5, 237
arb-med 137–69
  administrative mediation 159, 160–1
  arbitral proceedings, mediation within 159, 163–9
  Arbitration Law 164, 165
  arbitrators
    impartiality 143–4
    role 137–44, 152, 167, 168–9
    theoretical debates on role in settlement facilitation 138–44
  BAC Rules 2008 148–9, 239–40
  binding decisions 142, 143
  cases 241–3
  caucusing (meeting parties separately) 140, 143, 154, 166–8, 243
  Chinese experience 155–64
  CIETAC 148, 163–6, 168, 239–40
  civil law jurisdictions 144–6, 154
  Civil Procedure Rules 146, 163
  codification 156–7
  combination, practice of 148–50
  common law jurisdictions 146–8, 151, 154
  confidentiality 143–4, 147–8
  Confucian values 155–6
  consent 147, 149–50, 163
  contemporary practice 159, 164–5
  corporate attitudes and practices 152–3
  costs, reduction in 146, 155
  culture 137, 140, 241–3
  customary international law 158
  delay 142, 153, 155, 163
  domestic arbitration 165–6
  due process 142, 143, 168, 239
  efficiency 139–40, 141–2
  empirical studies of arbitration practice 151–5
  encouragement/promotion of mediation 139, 143, 145–50, 162–3, 168–9
  enforcement 142, 143
  English law 146, 148
  ethics 139
  evaluative arbitration 166
  expenses 142
  facilitative arbitration 166
  fair hearings 143, 239
  flexibility 141
  free will and voluntariness of parties 140–1
  harmony 212
  historical development 155–8, 163–4
  ICC Court 159–50
  impartiality of arbitrators 143–4, 150, 167, 168, 239–40
  incentives to settle 155, 163
  independence 239
  institutional mediation 148–50, 159, 161–2

intervention 154–5
joint venture disputes 164
judicial costs, reduction in 146
judicialisation of arbitration proceedings 154
legality, principle of 162
litigation proceedings, mediation within 159, 162–3
mediator, role of 137, 211–12
national laws 144–8
natural justice 142, 143, 168
New York Convention 1958 142
ongoing process of arbitration, proposal for mediation during 166
opinion on the merits 167
opponents of arb-med 142–4
party autonomy 140, 162, 165
people's mediation committees 159–60
person, appearance of parties in 139
proposals for settlements 167
provisional views 140
psychological satisfaction 141
raising idea of mediation 165–6
rate of settlement 153–4
Romano-Germanic tradition 145–6
rules of institutions 148–50
settlement agreements 142, 150, 162–3
settlement, how arbitration facilitates 166–7
SPC Provisions on Court's Civil Mediation Work in 2004 163
supporters of arb-med 139–42
surveys 151–5, 164–5, 211–12
theoretical debates on role in settlement facilitation 138–44
timing of settlements 153
transnational standards 239–40
voluntariness of parties 140–1
when proposal for mediation is made 166
WIPO Arbitration Rules 149
zhong yong (compromise) 180
Aristotle 192
awards *see also* recognition and enforcement of arbitration awards; recognition and enforcement of foreign arbitral awards; setting aside awards
approval 131–2
binding nature 18, 76–7, 109, 142–3
CIETAC 120, 131–2
finality 2, 19, 21, 76, 87, 120, 207–8
ICC Court 127–8, 131–2
independence 132–3
notification 132
scrutiny 46, 127, 131–3
substance and form 131
suspension 76, 78, 90–1, 109

BAC *see* Beijing Arbitration Commission (BAC)

bai jia zheng ming (Hundred Schools of Thought Contending) 187
Baoding Chamber of Commerce 207
basic people's courts (BPC) 10–11
Beijing Arbitration Commission (BAC)
appointment of arbitrators 66, 236
Arbitrators Manual 5
CIETAC, competition with 16
court decisions, publication of 5
creation 16
fees for mediation 240
financial system, reform of 236
impartiality 239
independence 237
information network management systems 238
international recognition 171
Mediation Rules 240
reform 235
remuneration 237
replacement of arbitrators 239
research 5
rules 16, 148–9, 239–40
surveys 134–5
training and assessment of arbitrators 237
transnational standards 136
Beijing Mediation Center 161–2
biantong (flexibility) 141, 180, 190–1, 209–10, 226–8, 243
bias *see* impartiality
bilateral investment treaties (BITs) 15–16, 218
bilateral treaties on civil and commercial judicial assistance 85–6
binding force of awards 18, 76–7, 109, 142–3
bird in a cage metaphor 174, 229
Book of Laws *(fa jing)* 189–90
bottom up Western concept of arbitration 175–8, 180, 225
bureaucracy 44, 171, 215, 219

Canada 56, 147, 148
capacity 35, 64, 74, 101–4
case management 127–9
cases
arb-med 241–3
integrated system, lack of 219
New York Convention 1958 101–12
recognition and enforcement of arbitration awards 95–113
reports 72–3, 219
Selected Cases of the SPC 5
caucusing (meeting parties separately) 140, 143, 154, 166–8, 243
CEDR Commission 243
centralised economy *see* planned economy
chambers of commerce 117, 207–8

Index

Chengdu Chamber of Commerce 207
China Chamber of International Commerce, Arbitration Research Institute (ARI) of 92, 97
China Council for the Promotion of International Trade (CCPIT) 16, 119–20, 122, 161–2
China International Economic and Trade Arbitration Commission *see* CIETAC
China Maritime Arbitration Commission (CMAC) 17, 99, 115
Chinese characteristics in arbitration 9, 170–80, 208–9, 222–3, 226
Chinese practice
  adaptation of Chinese law and practice 233–40
  appointment of arbitrators 64–6
  arb-med 155–64
  arbitral tribunals 64–70
  constitution of tribunal 64–70
  dual supervision mechanism 87, 90–1
  foreign-related arbitration 85
  impartiality 67–70
  independence 67–70
  influence of Chinese culture 241–5
  jurisdiction 56–60
  man-law-man 186
  recognition and enforcement of arbitral awards 82–113
  rituals 184–91
  setting aside awards 83–4
Chongqing Chamber of Commerce 207
CIETAC
  1956–1966 121
  1967–1979 121
  1980–1988 121
  1989–1994 122
  1995–present 122
  acceleration period 122
  adjustment period 121
  administration
    fees 125, 130–1
    heavy administration 128–9, 132–3
  administrative arbitration, move from 120
  advance on costs 139
  adversarial approach, choice of 235
  appointment of arbitrators 66
  arbitration agreements 120
  arbitration research centre 124
  arbitrators
    appointment 66
    Code of Ethics 124
    contract 127
    freedom to choose 120
    qualifications 124
    relationship with institution 128–33
  arb-med 148, 163–5, 168, 239–40
  awards 120, 131–2
  case management 128–9
  caseload 121–2, 128–9, 171
  Chair and Vice-Chairs 124
  China Council for the Promotion of International Trade (CCPIT) 16, 119–20, 122
  Code of Ethics 124
  competition 16, 122
  contract 127
  costs 130
  development 119–22
  discretion 122, 235
  domain name 124
  domestic cases 21
  establishment 16, 119–22
  expansion period 122
  expenses 130
  expert consultation committees 132
  fairness 209–10
  fees 125–6, 130–1
  finality 120
  financial management 125–7
  foreign-related arbitration 17, 122
  Foreign Trade Arbitration Commission 16, 18–19, 120–1
  founding period 121
  freedom to choose arbitrators 120
  Government Administration Council 120, 122
  government, links with 122
  growth period 121
  ICC, comparison with 7, 115, 117–33
  impartiality 67–70
  independence 67–9, 126–7, 132–3
  inquisitorial approach, choice of 235
  jurisdiction 21, 57–9, 235
  language 124
  local institutions 16, 21, 134
  nature 119–22
  New York Convention 1958 103
  notice of proceedings 128
  number of cases 121
  oral hearings 98
  periods of development 120–2
  personnel management 124–5
  practice 115, 117–33
  principles 120
  procedural issues 128
  qualifications 124
  quality of staff 124–5
  recognition and enforcement of arbitral awards 92, 96–100, 120
  reforms 235
  remuneration 125, 130–1
  research 5, 118, 124
  retention of staff 124–5
  rules 21, 24–5, 132, 171
    adoption 120

appointment of arbitrators 67–70
arb-med 148, 163–4, 239–30
Beijing Arbitration Commission 16
jurisdiction 58–9
recognition and enforcement of arbitral awards 97, 98
review and revision 16, 122, 235
seat of arbitration 25
scrutiny of awards 132–3
seat of arbitration 25, 235
Secretariats 124, 128
severability principle 33–4
Soviet Union, relationship with 119
statistics 92
structure and personnel management 124–5
training 124–5
transnational standards 115, 120, 131, 136
United Nations 121
World Trade Organization 126
civil law 144–6, 154, 189–90, 218–19
Civil Procedure Law
amendments 219, App 3
classification of arbitration 21–3
culture 219
deficiencies 172–4, 208
entry into force 219
foreign arbitration 22–3, 50, 51–2
foreign-related arbitration 20, 22, 85, 94–101, 172
interpretation 172
modernisation of law 219
New York Convention 1958 106
opening up policy 12
party autonomy 172–3
recognition and enforcement of arbitral awards 83–5, 88–9, 92, 95–101, 173–4
rigidity of system 172–3, 208
setting aside awards 84
social and public interest 100–1
text App 3
Civil Procedure Rules (England) 146, 153
clans (*zu*) 199, 211
class struggle 217–18
classes of people 2, 202, 210, 217–18
classification of arbitration 21–3
codification 156–7, 189–90
collectivism 210, 221, 226–7, 228–9
commercial arbitration 206–8, 210–11
convergence 244
culture, influence of Chinese 243–4
harmonisation 244
local soil condition 211
Roman law 206–7
scope of authority 208
commercial law 200–8
agrarian economy and lack of commercial laws 200–3
central, provincial and local government, struggle for control among 225–6
chambers of commerce 207–8
commercial arbitration 206–8, 210–11, 243–4
development of law 215, 218, 223–6
economic conditions 200–3, 215, 218, 223–6
economic transition 215, 218, 223–6
government-organised marketplaces 203
guilds 204–7, 210–11
history 200–8
lex mercatoria 204–7
mediator, function of 206–7, 211
merchants, low status of 201–3, 210, 213
private rights, recognition and authorisation of 224–6
resolution of commercial disputes 203–8
state control, continuance of 225–6
trade associations/landsmannschaften (*huiguan*) 204–7
transplantation of arbitration in China 207–8
Commission of Legislative Affairs, Standing Committee of the National People's Congress (NPC) 5
communications and technology 3, 106
Communism
amicable resolution, cultural emphasis on 221–2, 230
class struggle 217–18
Confucianism 222
corruption 216
Cultural Revolution 218
individual, role of the 220–1
litigation proceedings, mediation within 159, 162–3
mediation 159, 162–3, 221–2, 229
systemic and ideological limits 216, 217–18
community leaders (*tiaoren*) 156–7
competence-competence, principle of 54–7, 59
competition 122, 136
compromise (*zhongyong*) 180, 185, 194–5
conceptual differences 171, 174–80
Arbitration Law 174–5
Chinese characteristics 171, 174–80
Chinese notion of arbitration (top-down) 179–80
contract 176–7
Western concept of consensual arbitration (bottom up) 175–8
confidentiality 143–4, 147–8
confirmation arbitration 238–9
conflict avoidance, culture of *see* amicable resolution, cultural emphasis on
conflict of laws 25
conflicts of interest 63, 67, 150, 237, 239
Confucianism
amicable resolution, culture of emphasis on 3, 197

Confucianism (*cont.*):
  arb-med 155–6
  Communism 222
  Confucianisation of law 189, 190
  culture 186–7
  fa versus li 186–9, 209
  guilds 205
  harmony 3, 194–6, 233
  hierarchy, notion of 193
  individual, role of the 192–3
  Legalism 186–9
  magistrates 191
  mediation 222, 229–30
  role of law in modern China 216
  social roles 192–3
  suppression of litigation, practice of 197
  Three Bonds 193
  tolerance 191
consent
  arbitration agreements 29, 34–6
  arbitrators, appointment of 176–7
  arb-med 147, 149–50, 163
  caucusing 166
  New York Convention 1958 74
  Western notion of consensual arbitration (bottom down) 176–7
constitution of arbitral tribunal 61–70 *see also* appointment of arbitrators
Constitution of the PRC 10, 12, 13, 159
contract 12, 17–20, 26, 38, 45–6, 127, 176–8, 201, 223 *see also* arbitration agreements
conventions *see* treaties and conventions
convergence 4, 244
corporal punishment 158
corruption 88–9, 91, 216
costs 128–9, 130, 139, 146, 155
criminal offences, codification based on 189–90
Cultural Revolution 214–15, 218
culture *see also* amicable resolution, cultural emphasis on; traditional legal culture and its influence
  administrative features of arbitration, lack of 228–9
  Arbitration Law 219
  arb-med 137, 140, 241–3
  central, provincial and local government, struggle for authority between 225–6
  Chinese characteristics 171
  civil law 218–19
  Civil Procedure Law 219
  collectivism 226–7, 228–9
  commercial arbitration 243–4
  commercial law, development of 215, 218, 223–6
  Confucianism 186–7
  contemporary practice from historical perspectives 213, 226–31

cultural dimensions model 226–9
definition of legal culture 181–5
economic transition 223–6
fa versus li 186–7
flexibility 243
foreign investors 241
formalism 243
globalisation 226, 244
guanxi 226, 228, 230
harmony 241
historical perspectives 213, 226–31
implementation of law 220
Individualism (IDV) 228-9
individuals 215, 220–1, 226, 228–9, 233
influence of Chinese culture worldwide 241–5
informalism 243
integrated system, lack of 219–20
legislative efforts 218–19
Long-Term Orientation (LTO) 226, 229–30
mediation 229–31, 241–2
modernisation of law 183, 213–31
party autonomy 228–9
planned economy 223–4
private rights 218–19, 224–5, 240
relational mode of association 222–3
social groups 193
state control 225–6
suppression of litigation, practice of 196–200, 211
traditional legal culture 226
transnational standards 233, 241–5
transplanted system of arbitration 226
treaties and conventions 218
uncertainty and notion of *biantong*, tolerance of 227–8
Uncertainty Avoidance Index (UAI) 226–8
customary international law 158
customs 205

dao (natural rules) 184
Darwinism 232–3
delay 60, 102–4, 113, 142, 153, 155, 163
Deng Xiaoping 120
disclosure, duty of 237
discretion 88, 105, 122, 191, 235
domain names 124
domestic arbitration
  administrative arbitration 115
  Arbitration Law 84–5
  arb-med 165–6
  binding force, awards without 18
  classification of arbitration 21–2
  consultation, dispute settlement through 17
  definition 22
  Economic Contract Law of the PRC 17–18
  foreign arbitrations 50
  foreign-related arbitration 99

historical development 17–18
ICC Court, designation of 50
independence, lack of 18
institutions, establishment of 21
local institutions 135–6
party autonomy, lack of 18
public policy 81
recognition and enforcement of arbitral awards 83–5, 87–9, 99
Regulations on Economic Contract Arbitration of the PRC 17–18
rules and regulations 17–18
setting aside awards 83–4, 87
specialised agencies 18
substantive review by courts 26–7
double exequatur problem 76
dual supervision mechanism 87, 90–1
dual system in current legal regime 25–8
due process
  arb-med 142, 143, 168, 239
  constitution of tribunal 61
  New York Convention 1958 74, 105–6
  recognition and enforcement of arbitral awards 74, 95–7, 105–6
duress 33

East Han Dynasty 184, 203
Economic Contract Law of the PRC 17–18
economic transition 171, 215–18, 223–6, 233–4
ethics 66, 122, 124, 139, 150, 195
enforcement *see* recognition and enforcement of arbitration awards; recognition and enforcement of foreign arbitral awards
English law
  Arbitration Act 1996 7, 31, 54, 61, 109
  arb-med 146, 148
  Civil Procedure Rules 146–7
  competence-competence, principle of 54
  constitution of tribunal 61
  encouragement of mediation 146
  harmonisation 7
  jurisdiction 54
  New York Convention 1958 109
  seat of arbitration 23
  severability principle 31
  Woolf reforms 146
equality before the law 188
evaluative arbitration 166
ex equo et bono, principle of 209–10
expenses 129–30, 142
experts
  ad hoc arbitration 42, 44
  Arbitration Law 115–16
  arbitrators, appointment of 65–6
  CIETAC 66, 124, 132
  expert opinion 161
  ICC Court 123

expropriation 14, 15
extra-territoriality 81

fa (law) 186–91, 195, 209–10, 227
fa jing (Book of Laws) 189–90
facilitative arbitration 166
fairness 74, 143, 209–10, 217, 239
family conflicts 199
fees
  ad valorem basis 130
  administration fees 125–6, 130–1
  allocation 129–31
  Beijing Arbitration Commission 240
  CIETAC 125–6, 130–1
  contract 176
  financial management 125–6
  ICC Court 125, 129–30
  schedules 130
  transnational standards 69
finality 2, 19, 21, 76, 87, 120, 207–8
financial management
  Beijing Arbitration Commission 236
  CIETAC 125–6
  fees 125–6
  founders, contributions from 235
  government support 235–6
  ICC Court 125
  income and distribution, separation of 125–6
  independence 126–7, 134, 235–6
  institutional arbitration 235–6
  local institutions 134
  reform 235–6
  Wuhan Arbitration Commission 236
Five Anti-Campaign 215
flexibility (*biantong*) 141, 180, 190–1, 209–10, 226–8, 243
foreign arbitral institutions
  Arbitration Law 44–7, 51–2
  Civil Procedure Law 50, 51–2
  definition 46–7
  designation of institutions 45–7
  domestic arbitration 50
  failure to designate an institution 44–7
  ICC Court, designation of 45–51
  inconsistent court decisions 47–50
  interpretation 44–6, 48, 51–2
  legal obstacles to administration of institution 50–2
  local institutions, competition with 51
  New York Convention 1958 49–51
  policy 51–2
  protectionism 44–5
  recognition and enforcement of foreign arbitral awards 50–1
  seat, lack of recognition of concept of a 50–1
  status, clarity of 44–52

foreign arbitration *see also* foreign arbitral institutions; foreign-related arbitration; recognition and enforcement of foreign arbitral awards
  Civil Procedure Law 22–3
  classification of arbitration 21–3
  definition 22–3
  Hong Kong 9, 22–3
  Macao 9
  remuneration 68–9
  setting aside awards 81–2
  Taiwan 9
foreign-related arbitration
  arbitration agreements 19–20
  Arbitration Law 21–2, 85
  arbitrators, freedom to choose 19
  authority of tribunal, exceeding the 99–100
  Chinese practice 85
  CIETAC 17, 115, 122
  Civil Procedure Law 20, 22, 85, 94–101, 172
  classification of arbitration 21–2
  China Maritime Arbitration Commission 115
  definition 22
  domestic arbitration 25–6, 99
  due process 96–7
  finality 19
  Foreign-Related Economic Contract Law 19–20
  Foreign Trade Arbitration Commission, establishment of 18–19
  harmonisation 19
  historical development 18–20
  institutions 21, 115
  joint ventures 19, 28
  judicial review 27
  local protectionism 27–8
  merits of the dispute 85
  number of arbitrations 122
  procedure, irregularities in 97–8
  Protocol for General Conditions of Delivery of Goods between China and the Soviet Union 18, 119
  public policy 85
  recognition and enforcement of arbitral awards 83, 85, 88–9, 94–101
  report systems 26, 27–8, 88–9
  scope of agreement, exceeding the 99–100
  setting aside awards 84
  social and public interest 85
  subsidiaries 28
  validity of arbitration agreements 95–6
Foreign Trade Arbitration Commission (FTAC) 16, 18–19, 120–1
formalism 186, 243
France
  arb-med 145–6, 239
  Civil Code 192
  Code of Civil Procedure 7, 54, 61, 145–6, 239
  competence-competence, principle of 54
  constitution of tribunal 61
  harmonisation 7
  ICC Court 120, 125
  individual rights 192
  jurisdiction 54
  New York Convention 1958 73, 77–8
  seat, popularity as 7
  setting aside awards 77–8
  severability principle 30
  transnational standards 7
Frederick the Great of Prussia, Code of 192
free will and voluntariness 2, 140–1
freedom of choice 19, 61–4, 66, 120, 179

Ge (orders from the emperor) 156
Germany
  analogy, arbitration by 145
  arb-med 144–5, 148, 152
  Civil Code 192
  Code of Civil Procedure 144–5
  German Institution of Arbitration (DIS) 148
  individual rights 192
  institutions 147
globalisation 3–4, 6, 226, 232, 244
good faith 2, 36–8
governing law 23
government
  central, provincial and local government, struggle for authority between 225–6
  CIETAC, links with 122
  commercial law in economic transition, development of 225–6
  financial system, reform of 235–6
  institutions, control of 134–6, 174
  local government 219–20, 225–6
  local institutions 134–6
  marketplaces organised by government 203
  provincial government 225–6
  restructuring of institutions 117
  state control 177–80, 225–6
Great Leap Forward 215
'Great Wall' 44–5
Greece 2
group interests *see* relational networks
guanxi (networks) 180, 208, 222–3, 226, 228, 230–1
guilds (*hanghui*) 200, 204–7, 210–11
guofa (national laws) 191, 220

Han Code 190
Han Dynasty 188–9, 190, 193, 201
Han Feizi 187–8
Hanfeizi, book of 156
hanghui (guilds) 200, 204–7, 210–11
harmonisation 3–4, 6–7, 19, 72, 244

harmony (*he wei gui*) 3, 184–5, 194–200, 212, 229–31, 233, 241
hefa (in accordance with national laws) 144–8, 220
heqing, heli, hefa (in accordance with human feelings, the principles of reasonableness and national laws) 171, 173, 209–10, 220
hierarchy, notion of 193
hierarchy of courts 173
High People's Court (HPC) 10–11, 27–8, 234
historical background
   agrarian economy 200–3
   arb-med 155–8, 163–4
   Chinese characteristics 171
   CIETAC 121–2, 163–4
   commercial law 200–8
   contemporary arbitral practice 213, 226–31
   cultural perspectives 213, 226–31
   legislation, development of 17–21
   modern practice, historical links to 208–12
   modernisation of law 213, 226–31
Hobbes, Thomas 192
Hong Kong 9, 22–3, 54, 56, 86–7, 147–8
huiguan (trade associations/ *landsmannschaften*) 204–7
Hundred Flowers Movement 215
Hundred Schools of Thought Contending (*bai jia zheng ming*) 187

ICC *see* International Chamber of Commerce (ICC) Court
ICSID Convention 14
impartiality
   arb-med 143–4, 150, 167, 168, 239–40
   Beijing Arbitration Commission 239
   caucusing 168
   Chinese characteristics 170–1
   CIETAC 168, 239–40
   constitution of tribunal 61, 62–4, 67–70
   International Bar Association 150, 239
   local institutions 135
   New York Convention 1958 107
   opinion on the merits 167
   replacement of arbitrators 239
implementation of law 171, 173, 209–10, 220
incentives to settle 155, 163
inconsistent decisions 47–50, 112–13
independence
   advocates, prohibition of 237
   appointment of arbitrators 62–4, 67–9
   arbitral tribunals 61–4, 67–70
   Arbitration Law 21
   arb-med 239
   awards, scrutiny of 131–3
   Beijing Arbitration Commission 237
   Chinese characteristics 170–1
   Chinese practice 67–70

   CIETAC 67–70, 132–3
   conflicts of interest 63, 67, 237
   disclosure duty 237
   domestic arbitration 18
   financial independence 126–7, 13–45, 235–6
   ICC Rules 62–3, 68
   institutions 21, 133–6, 174, 235–6
   internal arbitrators, exclusion of 237
   local institutions 133–6
   management system, reform of 236–7
   nationality 68–9
   panel lists 69
   party autonomy 69
   qualifications 62–3
   quality of arbitrators 67
   remuneration 68–9
   state-owned enterprises, involvement of 67
   transnational standards 68–9
individuals
   amicable resolution of disputes, culture of 199–200
   collectivism 221, 226, 228–9
   Confucianism 192–3
   Communism 220–1
   control of individuals 193
   culture 215, 220–1, 226, 228–9, 233
   group interests 220
   historical perspective 226, 228–9
   Individualism (IDV) 226, 228–9
   local groups, limitation on right to sue within 199–200
   modernisation of law 215, 220–1, 233
   party autonomy 233
   punishment 217
   relational network 192–3, 210, 220–1, 228–9
   rights and duties 221
   traditional legal culture 217, 220
informalism 1, 197, 200, 210–11, 223, 226–30, 234, 243
information network management system 238
innovations in arbitration service 238–9
inquisitorial approach, choice of 235
insiders (*zijiren*) 223
institutions 114–36
   ad hoc arbitration 40–1, 44, 174
   administration of arbitrations, legal obstacles to 50–2
   administrative arbitration 115–16
   administrative intervention 173–4
   appointment of arbitrators 64–6
   Arbitration Law 21, 44–7, 51–2, 115–17
   arbitrators
      appointment 64–6
      institution, relationship with 127–33, 176
   arb-med 148–50, 159, 161–2
   authority of institutions, matters in award exceeding the 99–100
   bureaucratic, as 44

304 Index

institutions (*cont.*):
　case management 127–9
　chambers of commerce 117
　Chinese characteristics 178
　Civil Procedure Law 50, 51–2
　compulsory panel system 64, 65–6
　control 64, 65–6
　courts versus institutions 59–60
　definition of arbitral institutions 115–16
　designate, failure to 44–7
　domestic arbitration 21
　establishment, nature and development 4–5, 21, 118–22
　fees, allocation of 129–31
　financial management 125–7, 235–6
　foreign arbitrations 44–51
　foreign-related arbitration 21, 115
　ICC Court, comparison with 117–33
　inconsistent court decisions 47–50
　independence and impartiality 21, 116, 170, 174, 235–6
　innovations in arbitration service 238–9
　interpretation 44–6, 48, 51–2
　jurisdiction 54, 57–9
　legislative background 114–17
　local institutions 16, 21, 51, 133–6
　management system, reform of 236–8
　nature of institutions 115
　New York Convention 1958 49–51
　number of institutions 114, 116
　organisation of arbitration between parties and institutions, contract for 176
　permanent mediation centres 159
　personnel 115, 123–5
　planned economy 115
　policy 51–2
　practice 6, 114–36
　private organisations, as 115–16
　protectionism 44–5
　recognition and enforcement of foreign arbitral awards 50–1
　reform 235–9
　regional centres 161
　restructuring of institutions 116–17
　status, clarity of 44–52
　structure 123–5, 175
　traditional legal culture and its influence 185
　transnational standards 6, 117, 235–9
　tribunals 57–9
　unilateral arbitration 184
instrumental notion of law 217–18
integrated system, lack of 219–20
intermediate people's courts (IPC) 10–11, 92
International Bar Association (IBA) 150, 239
International Centre for the Settlement of Investment Disputes (ICSID) 14
International Chamber of Commerce (ICC) Court

administration 125, 128
ADR Rules 150
advance on costs 129
appointment of arbitrators 61, 62
Arbitration Law 37–9, 46–7
arbitrators 61, 62, 119, 123
arb-med 149–50, 242
awards 128, 131–2
case management 127–8
Chair and Vice-Chairs 123
CIETAC 7, 115, 117–33
committee sessions 123
composition 123–4
consent 150
constitution of tribunal 61–4, 128
costs 128, 129
court members 123
designation of institutions 45–7
development 119–20
domestic arbitration 50
establishment 119–20
expenses 129–30
expertise 123
fees 125, 129–30
financial management 125
foreign arbitrations 45–51
French law, as being subject to 120, 125
impartiality 62–3, 68
independence 62–3, 68
languages 123
location 123
Model Clause 45–6
nationality 119, 123
nature 120
New York Convention 1958 22–3
notification of awards 132
peace, objective of 118–19
popularity 6, 118–19
provisional advance 129
research 118
Rules 46–7, 62–3, 68, 127–8, 149–50
scrutiny of awards 128, 131–3
seat of arbitration 50
Secretariat 123–4, 128
standard forms 45–6
structure and personnel management 123–4
substance and form of awards, scrutiny of 131
Terms of Reference 129
validity of arbitration agreements 46–7
workload 118–19, 123
international sources 14–16
interpretation
　arbitral institutions, designation of 38–9
　arbitration agreements 36–40, 95
　Arbitration Law 12, 37–9, 51, App 2
　binding awards 76–7
　Civil Procedure Law 172

dual supervision mechanism 91
effective interpretation, principle of 36–8
foreign arbitrations 44–6, 48, 51–2
good faith 36–8
high people's court 39–40
inconsistency 38–9, 112–13
judicial interpretation 234
national sources 12
New York Convention 1958 73, 76–7
public policy 110
recognition and enforcement of arbitral awards 95, 97, 112–13
Special People's Court 11–14, 39, App 2
standard clauses 38
strict interpretation of defective clauses 38–40
transnational standards 234
validity of arbitration agreements 36–40
intervention 85–6, 95–6, 154–5, 171, 173–4, 229
investment 14–16, 87–8, 218

Japan Commercial Arbitration Association Rules 149
joinder 95–6
joint ventures 19, 28, 96, 111–12, 164
judges
  bilateral treaties on civil and commercial judicial assistance 85–6
  judicial assistance, bilateral treaties on 85–6
  judicial nature of arbitration 177–8
  judicialisation of arbitration proceedings 154
  quality 89
judicial organisation 10–11
judicial review 26–7, 54–6, 72
jurisdiction
  arbitral institutions versus arbitral tribunals 57–9
  arbitral tribunals 54–60
  arbitration agreements 29, 53–4
  Arbitration Law 57–60
  Chinese practice 56–60
  CIETAC 21, 235, 57–9
  competence-competence, principle of 54–7, 59
  concurrent control 55
  court versus institutions 59–60
  delay 60
  English Arbitration Act 1996 54
  French Code of Civil Procedure 54
  institutional arbitration 54, 57–9
  institutions versus tribunals 57–9
  judicial organisation 11
  New York Convention 1958 55–6, 75, 108
  objections 58
  party autonomy 59, 179

recognition and enforcement of arbitral awards 90
resisting enforcement in another jurisdiction 90
review of decisions by courts 54–6
rigidity of system 172
setting aside awards 81
Special People's Court 11, 59–60
Swiss PIL 54
transnational standards 54–7, 60
UNCITRAL Model Law 54, 56
validity of arbitration agreements 21, 55–7, 60

Korea Commercial Arbitration Board (KCAB), Arbitration Rules of 149

landsmannschaften/trade associations (*huiguan*) 204–7
language 123–4
Lao Zi 187, 196
law (*fa*) 186–91, 195, 209–10, 227
law, definition of 183–5
'law is law, life is life' 190
law merchant 2, 204–7
legal framework 12–21 *see also* Arbitration Law; Civil Procedure Law
legal positivism 192
Legalism 186–9, 196
legality, principle of 81, 87, 162
lex mercatoria 2, 204–7
li (*rituals*) 184–91, 193, 195, 209–10, 213, 233
lijiao (standards of behaviour or rituals) 184
Lincoln, Abraham 169
Ling (administrative procedures) 156
litigation proceedings, mediation within 159, 162–3
local arbitral institutions 16, 21, 51, 133–6
local government 219–20, 225–6
local magistrates 196–9
local people's courts 10, 11
local protectionism 27–8, 88–9, 93, 95, 101, 113, 173, 225–6
local soil condition 211
Locke, John 192
London Court of International Arbitration (LCIA) 122, 148
Long-Term Orientation (LTO) 226, 229–30

Ma Xiwu Style Adjudication 162
Macao 9, 86–7
magistrates 190–1, 196–9
management system, reform of 236–8
man-law-man 186
Maoism 221–2
mediation *see also* arb-med
  ad hoc arbitration 42

mediation (*cont.*):
    amicable resolution, cultural preferences for 229–31
    BAC Mediation Rules 240
    commercial history 206–7, 211
    Communism 221–2, 229
    Confucianism 222, 229–30
    culture 229–31, 241–2
    harmony 194, 241
    historical perspective 229–31
    Long-Term Orientation (LTO) 229–31
    Maoism 221–2
    mediator, function of 206–7, 211
    modernisation of law 229
    partial settlement 239
    tiaojie, notion of 158, 194
    top-down Chinese notion of arbitration 230
    traditional culture 229–30
    wide use of mediation 229–31
    Wuhan Arbitration Commission 239
medieval Europe 2, 204–7
Mencius 187–8
merchant fairs 205–6
merchants, low status of 201–3, 210, 213
middle way, doctrine of the (*zhongyong*) 180, 185, 194–5
military force 190
military courts and other special people's courts 10
Ming Code 190
Ming Dynasty 157–8, 190, 197, 202–3
modernisation of law and cultural influences 183, 213–31
    1840–1919 214
    1919–1949 214, 223
    1949–1976 214, 223, 228–9
    1976 onwards 215, 217–18, 224, 228–9
    administrative features of arbitration 228–9
    amicable resolution, cultural emphasis on 3, 215, 229–31, 233
    Arbitration Law 219
    Biantong, notion of 227–8
    bilateral investment treaties 218
    central, provincial and local government, struggle for authority between 225–6
    centralised planned economy and internal resolution 223–4
    civil law 218–19
    Civil Procedure Law 219
    collectivist society 228–9
    commercial law in economic transition, development of 215, 218, 223–6
    continued state control 225–6
    cultural and historical perspectives, contemporary arbitral practice from 213, 226–31
    economic transition 223–6
    implementation of law 220
    individual in modern China, role of 215, 220–1, 233
    integrated system, lack of 219–20
    legislative efforts, burst of 218–19
    mediation, wide use of 229
    party autonomy, lack of 228–9
    People's Mediation Law 219
    four phases of modernisation 214–15
    political upheaval 213–15
    private rights 218–19, 224–5, 240
    relational mode of association 222–3
    role of law in modern China 215, 216–20
    Soviet Union, learning from the 214–15
    transnational standards 233
    treaties and conventions 218
    uncertainty and notion of *Biantong*, tolerance of 227–8
    Western tradition 213–15
morality 66, 122, 124, 139, 150, 195
most favourable regime principle 73, 77
multi-party arbitration 95–6

national committees 62
national laws 144–8, 220
National People's Congress 5, 12
national sources 12–13
nationalisation 14
nationality 23, 68–9, 119, 123
natural justice 82, 87, 142, 143, 168
natural law 192
natural rules (*dao*) 184
nature, state of 192
networks (*guanxi*) 180, 208, 222–3, 226, 228, 230–1 *see also* relational networks
New Culture Movement 214
New York Convention on the Recognition and Enforcement of Foreign Arbitral Awards 1958 3, 6, 72–82
    accession 14
    ad hoc arbitration 41, 43, 101, 103
    arbitrability 79, 110
    arbitration agreements 35–6, 75–6
    arbitrator, notice of appointment of 74, 105–6
    arb-med 142
    awards 73, 76–8
    binding awards 73, 76–7, 109
    capacity 74, 101–4
    case analysis 101–12
    CIETAC 103
    Civil Procedure Law 106
    commercial reservation 14
    composition of tribunal not in accordance with agreement 75–6, 107–9
    confirmation arbitration 239
    consent 74
    courts on their own motion, grounds which can be raised by 79–81

delay 102–4
discretion 88, 105
double exequatur problem 76
due process 74, 105–6
email, notification by 106
English Arbitration Act 1996 109
finality 76
ICC Court 22–3
impartiality 107
interpretation 73, 76–7
joint ventures 111–12
judicial assistance, bilateral treaties on 86
jurisdiction 55–6, 75, 108
local protectionism 113
merits, re-examination on the 73
minimum standards 73
mistake 74
most favourable regime principle 73, 77
notice of appointment, lack of proper 74, 105–6
notice of proceedings 74, 105–6
parties, grounds which must be raised by 74–8
procedural issues 73–4, 107–9
pro-enforcement bias 73
public policy 73, 80–1, 107, 110–12
reciprocity reservation 14
regularity, standard of 98
relevant law, composition of tribunal or procedure not in accordance with 75–6, 107–9
Report System 102
reporting cases 72–3
reservations 14
seat of arbitration 23
setting aside awards 73, 77–8, 81–2, 109
suspension of awards 76, 78, 109
ultra vires 74–5, 106
UNCITRAL Guide 72–3
uniformity 73
validity of arbitration agreements 35–6, 101–4
website 73
writing 35–6
notice of appointment of arbitrators 74, 95, 105–6
notice of proceedings 74, 95, 97, 105–6, 128

Official Journal of Commerce 207
Opium Wars 213–14
opening up policy 12, 121, 217–18
Organic Law of the People's Courts 10

'paper laws' 190
partial settlements 239
party autonomy
  ad hoc arbitration 44
  administration, interference from 173, 229

adversarial approach, choice of 235
appointment of arbitrators 65
Arbitration Law 20, 173, 229
arb-med 140, 162, 165
Chinese notion of arbitration 179–80
Civil Procedure Law 172–3
collectivism 229
culture 228–9
definition 20
domestic arbitration 18
historical perspective 228–9
impartiality 69
implementation of law, inconsistencies in 173
independence 69
individual, role of the 233
inquisitorial approach, choice of 235
jurisdiction 59
legislation 170
local institutions 136
modernisation of law 228–9
relational network 210, 211
rigidity of system 172–3, 208
validity of arbitration agreements 36
patriarchal system 186
penal law and punishment 189–90
people's mediation committees (PMCs) 159–60
People's Mediation Law 160, 219
permanent mediation centres 159
personalisation of claims 220
personnel management
  Beijing Arbitration Commission 237–8
  local institutions 135
  management system, reform of 237–8
  practice of institutions 123–5
  quality of staff 124–5
  retention of staff 124–5
  training 124–5
planned economy
  Chinese characteristics 171
  CIETAC 119
  collectivism 228–9
  commercial law, development of 223–4
  culture 223–4
  economic transition 171, 215–18, 223–6, 233–4
  local institutions 134, 136
  modernisation of law 223–4
Plato 192
policy 51–2 *see also* public and social policy
political upheaval 187, 213–15
private rights 1–3
  authorisation 218–19, 224–6
  Chinese notion of arbitration 179
  collectivism 229
  commercial law, development of 224–6
  culture 210, 218–19, 224–5, 240

private rights (cont.):
  local institutions 133–4
  modernisation of law 218–19, 224–5, 240
  recognition of private rights 210, 224–6
private sources 16
protectionism
  Arbitration Law 44–5
  foreign arbitrations 44–5
  local protectionism 27–8, 88–9, 93, 95, 101, 113, 173, 225–6
  public policy 113
Protocol for General Conditions of Delivery of Goods between China and the Soviet Union 18, 119
provincial government 225–6
public and social policy
  arbitrability 79
  Civil Procedure Law 100–1
  definition 80
  domestic policy 80–1
  foreign-related arbitration 85
  guidance 100
  international policy 80–1
  interpretation 110
  local institutions 135
  local protectionism 101
  mandatory provisions, breach of 110
  merits of dispute 85
  New York Convention 1958 73, 80–1, 107, 110–12
  protectionism 101, 113
  recognition and enforcement of arbitral awards 80–1, 85, 87, 100–1, 110–13
  setting aside awards 83, 84
  Swiss law 81
  transnational policy 80–1
  United States 81
public notices issued by local officials 156
public sources
  international sources 14–16
  national sources 12–14
publication of the law (*zhu xing shu*) 189

Qin Code 190
Qin Dynasty 188, 190, 198–9, 202–3, 207
Qing Code 190
Qing Dynasty 157–8, 182, 190–1, 213–14
qing (human sentiments, reasonableness and flexibility) 190–1, 209–10
qingli (reasonableness) 190–1, 209–10, 227–8
qualifications of arbitrators 22, 61, 64–6, 69, 124, 127, 172, 179
quality 53, 65–7, 69, 89, 124–5, 172, 236–7

rang (concessions) 185, 194–5, 197
reciprocity 14, 51, 85–6
recognition and enforcement of arbitration awards 71–113 *see also* New York Convention on the Recognition and Enforcement of Foreign Arbitral Awards 1958; recognition and enforcement of foreign arbitral awards
ad hoc arbitration 42–4
agreements
  composition of tribunal not in accordance with tribunal 75–6, 97–8, 107–8
  invalidity 42–4, 74, 95–6, 101–4
  procedure not in accordance with agreement 75–6, 97–8, 107–8
amount of awards 93–4
arbitrability 79, 95, 110
Arbitration Law 83–5, 87–90, 98–9, 113
arbitrators
  composition of tribunal 75–6, 97–8, 107–8
  notice of appointment 74, 95, 105–6
authority of institution, matters in award exceeding 99–100
binding, awards as not being 76–7, 109
capacity 74, 101–4
case analysis 95–113
challenges to awards 72
China Chamber of International Commerce, Arbitration Research Institute (ARUI) of 92, 97
Chinese practice 82–113
CIETAC 92, 96–100, 120
Civil Procedure Law 83–5, 88–9, 92, 95–100, 173–4
complications in enforcement 91–3
composition of tribunal not in accordance with agreement 75–6, 97–8, 107–8
corruption 88–9, 91
court on own motion, grounds which can be raised by 79–81
delays 113
discretion on enforcement, court has no 88
domestic awards 83–5, 87–9
dual supervision mechanism 87, 90–1
due process 74, 95–7, 105–6
finality of awards 87
foreign investment enterprises 87–8
foreign-related awards 83, 85, 88–9, 94–101
Hong Kong awards 43, 86–7
hostility of courts 91
inconsistent decisions 112–13
initiation of proceedings 72
integrated system, lack of 219–20
Intermediate People's Court and Maritime Courts, survey of 92
interpretation 95, 97, 112–13
intervention 95–6
joinder 95–6
joint ventures 96
jurisdiction, resisting enforcement in another 90

legal regime 83–91
legality, principle of 87
liberalisation 89
local protectionism 88–9, 93, 95, 101, 113
lower court corruption 88–9, 91
Macao awards 86–7
merits of dispute 85, 87–8
multi-party arbitration 95–6
nationality of awards 23
natural justice 87
notice of proceedings 74, 95, 97, 105–6
party, grounds which must be raised by 74–8
procedure not in accordance with agreement 75–6, 97–8, 107–9
protectionism 88–9, 93, 95, 101, 113
public interest 85, 100–1
public policy 80–1, 85, 87, 110–13
quality of judges 89
rate of enforcement 170
regularity, standard of 98
relevant law, composition of tribunal or procedure not in accordance with 75–6, 107–8
Report System 88–9, 94, 113
reporting system 89
research 5, 91–5
reviews 87–8
scope of agreement, exceeding the 99–100
seat of arbitration 25, 50, 72,
setting aside awards 76, 77–8, 81–4, 87–91, 94–8, 109
social interest 85, 100–1
statistical assessment of enforcement record 91–5
substantive review for domestic awards 87–8
supervision 90–1
suspension of awards 76, 78, 90–1, 109
Taiwan awards 87
time limits 95
transnational standards 72–82, 87, 99
transparency 89
ultra vires 74–5, 99–100, 105
UNCITRAL Model Law 6, 23–4
uniformity 72
unique features of legislation 87–91
valid agreement, lack of a 74, 95–6, 101–4
validity of agreements 74, 94–6, 101–4
recognition and enforcement of foreign arbitral awards 84–9, 95–7, 100–9
ad hoc awards 42–4
arbitration agreement, exceeding scope of 99–100
authority of institution, matters in award exceeding 99–100
bilateral treaties on civil and commercial judicial assistance 85–6
case analysis 95–113
Chinese practice 85–7, 95–6
Civil Procedure Law 95–101
corruption 88–9
due process 96–7
harmonisation 72
Hong Kong, Arrangement with 86
intervention 95–6
joinder 95–6
local protectionism 88–9, 101
Macao awards, Arrangement with 86–7
made in a foreign country, awards which are 85–6
multilateral treaties and conventions 86
reciprocity 85–6
refusal of enforcement 86
Report System 88–9
setting aside awards 84, 88–9, 95–6
social and public interest 100–1
surveys 94
Taiwan Judgments, SPC Regulation on 87
treaties and conventions 85–6
ultra vires 99–100
reform
CIETAC 235
financial system 235–6
innovations 238–9
institutions 235–9
management system 236–8
Special People's Court 234
World Trade Organization 9
Wuhan Arbitration Commission 235
regional mediation centres 161
regularity, standard of 98
relational networks
amicable resolution, cultural emphasis on 210–11, 222–3, 230–1
collectivism 210, 228–9
culture 210, 222–3
family groups 193
historical emphasis 210
individual, role of the 192–3, 210, 220–1
li 187, 193, 210
modernisation of law 222–3
natural law 192
party autonomy 210, 211
social roles 192–3
traditional legal culture and its influence 192–3, 210–11
relationship of parties, focus on 142, 153, 155, 164–7, 197, 229–31, 233, 243
remuneration 68–9, 131, 175
renqing (human sentiments) 191, 208
Report System 5, 27–8, 88–9, 94, 102, 112–13
Republican Period 207, 230
rigidity 172–3, 189–90, 208–9
Rites of Zhou 156
rituals (*li*) 184–91, 193, 195, 209–10, 213, 233

role of law in modern China 215, 216–20
  actuality of general economic reconstruction 217–18
  Communism, systemic and ideological limits of 216, 217–18
  Confucianism 216
  implementation 220
  increased reliance on law 216
  instrumental notion of law 217–18
  integrated system, lack of 219–20
  legislative efforts, burst of 218–19
  modernisation of law 215, 216–20
  opening up 217–18
  rule of law 216
  traditional legal culture and influence 216–18
  Western influence 216–17
Roman law 2, 145–6, 189, 201, 206–7
Roman Twelve Tables Law 189
Rousseau, Jean-Jacques 192
rule of law 185–6, 188, 216, 228, 233
rules
  appointment of arbitrators 67–70
  arb-med 148–50, 163–4, 239–40
  Beijing Arbitration Commission 16
  CIETAC 21, 24–5, 132, 171
    adoption 120
    appointment of arbitrators 67–70
    arb-med 148, 163–4, 239–30
    Beijing Arbitration Commission 16
    jurisdiction 58–9
    recognition and enforcement of arbitral awards 97, 98
    review and revision 16, 122, 235
    seat of arbitration 25
  German Institution of Arbitration 148
  ICC Court 46–7, 62–3, 68, 127–8, 149–50
  Japan Commercial Arbitration Association Rules 149
  jurisdiction 54, 58–9
  Korea Commercial Arbitration Board (KCAB), Arbitration Rules of 149
  London Court of International Arbitration 148
  publication 176
  seat of arbitration 25
  uniform rules 161
  Western concept of consensual arbitration 176
  WIPO Arbitration Rules 149
  Wuhan Arbitration Commission 238–9

scrutiny of awards 46, 127, 131–3
seat of arbitration
  arbitration agreements 23, 25, 50
  Arbitration Law 24, 50
  CIETAC 25, 235
  Civil Procedure Law 24–5

Conflict of Laws 2011 25
courts, supervisory and supportive powers of 23
definition 23–5
domestic arbitration 26
English law 23
France 7
governing law 23
ICC awards 50
lack of recognition of concept of legal seat 23–5, 50
legal consequences 23
location, change of 24
nationality of awards for enforcement 23
New York Convention 1958 23
outside China, domestic arbitration seat may not be 26
recognition and enforcement of arbitral awards 25, 50, 72
Switzerland 7, 23
territorial link 23
UNCITRAL Model Law 23–4
United Kingdom 7
validity of arbitration agreements 50
Selected Cases of the SPC 5
self-criticism 197, 222
self-regulation 2
self-restraint 196
setting aside awards
  Arbitration Law 83–4
  Chinese practice 83–4
  Civil Procedure Law 84
  domestic awards 83–4, 87
  extra-territoriality 81
  foreign awards 81–2
  foreign-related awards 84
  France 77–8
  grounds, list of 83, 84
  jurisdiction 81
  legality, principle of 82
  merits, review of 83–4
  natural justice 82
  New York Convention 1958 73, 77–8, 81–2, 109
  recognition and enforcement of arbitral awards 76, 77–8, 81–4, 87–91, 94–8, 109
  social and public interest, contrary to 83, 84
  Swiss PIL 82
  UNCITRAL Model Law 81–2
settlement agreements 142, 150, 162–3
severability principle 29–34, 179
Shan-Gan-Ning border region 162
Shang Dynasty 201
Shanxi Province 221
shenmingting (Pavilion for Extending Clarity) 157
Shi (guidance of implementation) 156
Shi lu (veritable records of emperors) 156

Shu pan (judges' decisions) 156
signatures 36
Silk Road 201
Singapore 147, 148, 151
social networks 205
social policy *see* public and social policy
Socrates 192
soft law 6
sole arbitrators 62–3, 68
Song Dynasty 201–2
sources of law 12–16
Soviet Union 18, 119, 214–15
Special Economic Zones (SEZs), establishment of 121
Special People's Court (SPC)
   foreign arbitration 22–3
   interpretation 11–14, 39, App 2
   jurisdiction 59–60
   organisation 10, 11
   Provisions on Court's Civil Mediation Work in 2004 163
   reform 234
   Report System 27–8
   Selected Cases of the SPC 5
   severability principle 32–3
   transnational standards 234
standard forms 38, 45–6
standards *see also* transnational standards
   standards of behaviour or rituals 184
   standards of treatment 15
state control 177–80, 225–6
state of nature 192
state-owned enterprises, involvement of 67
subject matter capable of settlement by court 35, 79
subsidiaries 28
Sui Dynasty 204
suppression of litigation, practice of (*xisu*) 196–200, 210–12
Supreme People's Court (SPC)
   appeals 11
   Guide and Study on Foreign-related Commercial and Maritime Trials 5
   Guide on Foreign-related Commercial and Maritime Trials 5
   interpretation 11–14
   interviews 5–6
   jurisdiction 11
   list of important interpretations 12–14
   Report System 5
   Selected Cases of the SPC 5
   supervision 11
surveys 94, 134–5, 151–5, 164–5, 211–12
suspension of awards 76, 78, 90–1, 109
Switzerland
   arb-med 145, 148
   Civil Code 192
   competence-competence, principle of 54, 56
   constitution of tribunal 61
   harmonisation 7
   individual rights 192
   jurisdiction 54
   liberalisation 7
   Private International Law 7, 20, 54, 61, 82
   Rules of International Arbitration 148
   seat of arbitration 7, 23
   setting aside awards 82
   severability principle 20
   transnational standards 7
   Zurich Code of Civil Procedure 145

Taiwan 9, 87
Taizu, Emperor 157
Tang Dynasty 201–2
Taoism 196
Tang Code 190, 203
Three-Anti Campaign 215
Three Bonds 193
tian ren gan tong 194–5
tian ren he yi (harmony) 184–5
tianli (natural rules) 191, 220
tiaoje, notion of 158, 194
tiaoren (village elders and community leaders) 156–7
timeline of Chinese history 182–3
tolerance 191, 226–8
top down Chinese notion of arbitration 179–80, 221, 229–30, 233
totalitarianism 186
trade associations/*landsmannschaften* (*huiguan*) 204–7
traditional legal culture and its influence 181–212
   abandonment of traditional culture 214
   agrarian economy and lack of commercial laws 200–3
   amicable resolution, cultural emphasis on 3, 194–200, 210–12, 229–31
   authority 185
   avoidance of litigation, historical legal culture of 210–11
   codification based on criminal offences 189–90
   commercial history 200–8, 210–11
   conceptual differences in arbitration 210
   conflict avoidance 194–200
   culture 181–5, 193, 232
   definition of law 183–5
   equity 209–10
   fa 186–91
   fairness 209–10, 217
   flexibility in implementation of law 209–10
   government-organised marketplaces 203
   guilds (*hanghui*) and *Landsmannschaften* (*huiguan*) 204–7
   harmony, emphasis on 3, 194–200

traditional legal culture and its influence (*cont.*):
 historical emphasis on relational network 210
 implementation of law 190–1, 209–10
 individual, role of the 217, 220
 institutions 185
 instrumental notion of law 217
 li 186–9, 209, 213, 233
 mediation 229–30
 modern practice, historical links to 208–12
 modernisation 183
 outside world, impact of law on behaviour of 181
 philosophical influence 194–6
 private rights, recognition of 210
 qing mixed with *fa* 190–1
 reasonableness 191, 209–10
 relational network, emphasis on 192–3, 210–11
 resolution of commercial disputes 203–8
 rigidity of written law 189–90, 209
 rituals, emphasis on 185–91, 209–10
 role of law in modern China 216–18
 rule of law 185, 216, 233
 social and legal forces 181
 structure and rules of law 181
 suppress litigation, practice to 196–200, 210–12
 timeline of Chinese history 182–3
 transplantation of arbitration in China 207–8
 Western legal norms 207–8, 216
 written law, rigidity of 189–90, 209
training 124–5, 237
transnational arbitration 4, 232
transnational standards *see also* New York Convention on the Recognition and Enforcement of Foreign Arbitral Awards 1958; UNCITRAL Model Law
 adaptation of Chinese law and practice 233–40
 arbitral tribunals 61–4
 arbitration agreements 29, 35–7
 Arbitration Law 20–1, 234
 arb-med, adaptation to 239–40
 Beijing Arbitration Commission 136
 Chinese characteristics 9
 CIETAC 115, 120, 131, 136
 constitution of tribunal 61–4
 culture 233, 243–4
 culture on arbitral practice worldwide, influence of Chinese 241–5
 fees 69
 globalisation 6
 harmonisation 6–7
 high people's courts 234
 impartiality 68–9
 independence 68–9
 institutional reforms 235–9
 judicial interpretations 234
 jurisdiction 54–7, 60
 legislative reforms 234
 local institutions 136
 market-based economy, transition to 233–4
 modernisation of law 233
 practice of institutions 6
 recognition and enforcement of arbitral awards 72–82, 87, 99
 selective adaptations 234
 severability principle 30–1
 soft law 6
 Special People's Court 234
 Switzerland 7
 UNCITRAL Model law 6
 validity of arbitration agreements 35–7
transparency 44, 89
transplantation of arbitration in China 207–8, 226
treaties and conventions
 bilateral investment treaties 15–16, 218
 judicial assistance, bilateral treaties on 85–6
 modernisation of law 218
 multilateral treaties and conventions 86
 recognition and enforcement of foreign arbitral awards 85–6
 source of law, as 14–16
tribunals *see* arbitral tribunals
types of arbitration 21–8
 classification of arbitration 21–3
 dual system in current legal regime 25–8
 seat, lack of recognition of legal 23–5

ultra vires 74–5, 99–100, 105–6
uncertainty, tolerance of 226–8
UNCITRAL Model Law
 ad hoc arbitration 41
 amendments 6, 31
 applicability 23
 arbitration agreements, enforcement of 6
 competence-competence, principle of 54
 constitution of tribunal 61
 dual supervision mechanism 90
 harmonisation 6
 jurisdiction 54, 56
 recognition and enforcement of arbitral awards 6, 23–4
 seat of arbitration 23–4
 setting aside awards 81–2
 severability principle 30–1
 transnational standards 6
 validity of arbitration agreements 35–6
 writing 35–6
uniformity 72–3, 161
United Kingdom *see also* English law
 seat, popularity as 7

transnational standards 7
United Nations (UN) 121
United States 77–8, 152–4

validity of arbitration agreements
  ad hoc arbitration 40–4
  arbitrability 79
  arbitration agreements 29
  Arbitration Law 21, 37–8
  capacity 35
  Civil Procedure Law 95–6
  composition of tribunal not in accordance with tribunal 75–6, 97–8, 107–8
  consent 34–6
  defined legal relationships, disputes in respect of 35
  delay 102
  effective interpretation, principle of 36–8
  enforcement of foreign ad hoc awards 42–4
  exclusion of ad hoc arbitration 40–2
  existing or future disputes, dealing with 35
  foreign-related arbitration 95–6
  good faith, interpretation in 36–8
  ICC Court 45–7
  inconsistent court decisions 47–50
  interpretation 36–40
  jurisdiction 21, 55–7, 60
  law and practice in China 37–52
  legal obstacles 50–2
  New York Convention 1958 35–6, 101–4
  party autonomy 36
  policy considerations 51–2
  practical difficulties 45–7
  procedure not in accordance with agreement 75–6, 97–8, 107–8
  recognition and enforcement of arbitral awards 74, 94–6, 99–104
  recognition of ad hoc arbitration, legal obstacles to the 44
  Report System 28
  scope of agreement, exceeding the 83, 88, 99–100
  seat, lack of recognition of concept of 50
  severability principle 29–34
  signatures 36
  status of foreign institutions, unclear status of 44–5
  strict interpretation of defective clauses 38–40
  subject matter capable of settlement 35, 79
  substantive requirements 34–52
  transnational standards 35–7
  ultra vires 74–5
  UNCITRAL Model Law 35–6
  writing 35–6
Veritable Records of the Emperor Taizu 157
village elders and community leaders (*tiaoren*) 156–7

villages 156–7, 200
voluntariness 2, 140–1

Warring States Period 189–90, 201
West *see also* individual countries
  ad hoc arbitration 175
  bottom up notion of arbitration 175–8
  Chinese characteristics 176–8
  consensual arbitration 176–8
  contract 175–8
  culture 207–8, 213–16
  Five Anti-Campaign 215
  globalisation 4
  Great Leap Forward 215
  Hundred Flowers Movement 215
  judicial nature of arbitration 177–8
  law-man-law 185–6
  modernisation of law 213–15
  New Culture Movement 214
  relational mode of association 222
  rituals 185–6
  role of law in modern China 216–17
  rule of law 216, 233
  state control, role of 177–8
  Three-Anti Campaign 215
  transplantation of arbitration in China 207–8, 226
Western Zhou dynasty 156, 187
WIPO Arbitration Rules 149
World Trade Organization (WTO) 9, 126
writing 35–6, 189–90, 201, 209
Wuhan Arbitration Commission (WAC)
  confirmation arbitration 238–9
  financial system, reform of 236
  innovations 238–9
  international recognition 171
  mediation 239
  reform 235
  research 5
  rules 238–9

Xia Dynasty 182
xiangting (mediators) 181
Xiao Yang 42–3
xisu (practice of suppression of litigation) 196–200, 210–12
Xun Zi 187–8

Yao and Shun period 156
Yuan Dynasty 157

zheng shu (official documents) 156
zhongyong (doctrine of middle way) 180, 185, 194–5
Zhou Enlai 120
zhu xing shu (publication of the law) 189
Zi Chan 189
zu (clans) 199, 211